W9-AVE-513

The Changing Earth

An Introductory Geology

The Changing Earth

An Introductory Geology

Brainerd Mears, Jr.
University of Wyoming

Van Nostrand Reinhold Company
New York   Cincinnati   Toronto   London   Melbourne

Van Nostrand Reinhold Company Regional Offices:
Cincinnati New York Chicago Millbrae Dallas

Van Nostrand Reinhold Company Foreign Offices:
London Toronto Melbourne

Copyright © 1970 by Litton Educational Publishing, Inc.

Library of Congress Catalog Card Number 69-17509

All rights reserved. No part of this work covered by the copyright hereon
may be reproduced or used in any form or by any means—graphic,
electronic, or mechanical, including photocopying, recording, taping, or
information storage and retrieval systems—without written permission of
the publisher. Manufactured in the United States of America.

Published by Van Nostrand Reinhold Company
450 West 33rd Street, New York, N. Y. 10001

Published simultaneously in Canada by
D. Van Nostrand Company (Canada), Ltd.

10 9 8 7 6 5 4 3 2 1

To my most constant critic, co-worker, and wife
Anne Carter Mears

Preface

The Changing Earth is intended for beginning students of geology who are enrolled in one-term courses in colleges, universities, and junior colleges. The book assumes no prior training in science, and I recognize that for many students the course for which this book is written is their sole exposure to formal instruction in a science at the college level. I have, therefore, introduced material on the nature of geology as human knowledge and science along with basic geologic facts and concepts.

After discussing the earth's broad planetary aspects, the text deals with the earth's materials, surface features related to erosional forces, internal structure, and dynamics. Earth history is then emphasized, beginning with methods and principles of historical reconstruction and moving to a discussion of fossil groups important in the geologic record, an account of evolving forms of life, and, finally, the changing scenes in the physical evolution of North America. The physical history of the earth is presented by regions, rather than as a period-by-period treatment, in order to facilitate the instructor's stressing of a continuous theme. The structure of the material is such that a well-integrated course may be based upon this book, for each section builds upon the preceding one.

For worthwhile criticism, I thank D. W. Boyd, R. W. Fairbridge, W. E. Frerichs, R. S. Houston, J. D. Love, P. O. McGrew, H. T. Ore, R. B. Parker, and H. D. Thomas. The influence of S. H. Knight on the diagrams will be recognized by many. V. J. Anderson, J. Berdan, E. A. Carter, C. MacClintock, T. Nichols, H. Pownall, J. Shelton, L. J. Prater, and many others helped greatly in the quest for photographs. Most of all, I am indebted to my wife not only for encouragement but also for many hours of work on illustrations, editing my prose, and assisting in proofreading.

Contents

CONTENTS

WEAR AND TEAR

THE STRUCTURE AND ARCHITECTURE OF THE EARTH

RECONSTRUCTING THE PAST

CONTENTS

one: The planet earth

In the immensity of space, the planet earth is hardly a speck of matter. It is one of the smallest of nine planets moving around the sun, which itself is an average star among billions of stars in a cluster called the Milky Way Galaxy. This galaxy is only one of many millions of such star groups that lie in every direction as far as the modern telescope can detect.

The astronomical speck called earth owes its importance to the fact that we live here. For those of us who are curious about this globe we live on, geology holds an intrinsic attraction and fascination.

THE SCIENCE OF THE EARTH

Geology is the study of the earth: its physical aspects and its history. It is the study of a volcano erupting in glowing gas, clouds of ash, and streams of molten rock. It is the reconstruction of prehistoric plants and animals on a landscape drained by rivers flowing into long gone seas—a scene that disappeared hundreds of millions of years ago. It is a concept of land rising from the sea to form lofty mountains that are later worn away to low rolling plains—all during an immensity of time. It is a mental picture of the earth's structure from the outer surface to the center 4000 miles inward, or of the neat arrangement of invisible particles which gives a crystal its outer form. In brief, geology is the study of the composition, structure, and history of the earth.

The great mass of detail that constitutes geology is classified under a number of subdivisions which, in turn, depend upon the fundamental sciences: physics, chemistry, and biology. In their study of rocks and minerals geologists apply chemical and physical concepts of atoms, molecules, and crystals. In determining the date when rocks were formed, geologists may use findings on radioactive isotopes from atomic physics. In paleontology, the science of "ancient life," geologists call upon key concepts of biology and on the details of anatomical findings to discover the past history of living things as recorded in the rocks.

Geology is a science. The facts and theories at its core are the deposit of a good three centuries of hard work and hard thinking. Someone once said that every volume of the old *Geological Survey Bulletin* represented a hundred pairs of worn-out shoes. Gathering facts, confirming them, suggesting theories, testing them, and organizing findings—this is all the work of science, and the methods of carrying it out are sometimes brought together and labeled *the scientific method.* The most telling test of the scientific method is in the detail of its application. The history of geology is full of plausible generalizations tested and discarded; on the other hand, seemingly half-baked fancies have proven, under close examination and repeated test, to be probable after all—for instance, the theory that the existing continents were once parts of larger masses that split and drifted apart.

The margin of every science as a "body of knowledge" is its most exciting part—an active zone of research where matters are not yet fixed and questions are not settled, and not every concept or theory that seems promising this year will prove out over the years to come. This problematical area is vital science. It is the growing edge. In geology this frontier, as in most of today's sciences, is so extensive and engages so many workers and thinkers that it is no longer possible to speak of a single science of the earth. New branches are continually demanded by the multiplication of knowledge.

While geology has as its central themes the materials and structure of the earth and the earth's history, it is overlapped by many other earth-oriented sciences. To name only a few, there are meteorology, for the study of the atmosphere; physical geography, for the external features of the globe; oceanography, for the earth's waters and their uneven depths; soil science, for its vital and special topic. Then there are the branches of geophysics and geochemistry, testifying to the sheer bulk of known and knowable matters that have required ever-growing specialization of scientists in our times.

Meanwhile in the midst of the earth sciences, geology exercises a many-sided attraction. It is as indispensable as engineering and mechanics are to the great practical mining and construction enterprises of our day. To the outdoorsman and the laboratory worker alike, it opens a world of detailed spectacle on every scale, from the vast mountain chain to the fascinating microscopic crystal. And for the contemplative spirit it lifts the curtain on an awesome cosmic drama of immense movements over immemorial time, dwarfing all but the astronomical scale with which it has so much in common. This link of earth science with astronomy is conspicuous as we begin the exploration of our planet earth by circling in upon it from the reaches of outer space.

THE EARTH IN SPACE

The picture of the galaxy described in the opening paragraph, now so widely accepted that most people take it for granted, goes against all common sense and even simple observation. Observation with the naked eye clearly indicates that the earth is the fixed and stable center of the universe, that the sun, moon, and visible planets

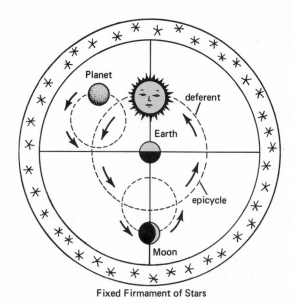

Fig. 1-1
Ptolemaic system of planetary and solar motion based on an earth-centered Universe. Adapted from a fifteenth-century German text.

are smaller bodies moving around us, and that the stars are points of light in a revolving sphere above us. Just such an earth-centered astronomy was fully developed by Ptolemy of Alexandria in the second century A.D. and, for many centuries, it was the accepted system (Fig. 1-1). Nicolaus

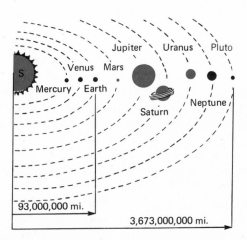

Fig. 1-2
Diagrammatic representation of the solar system by modern accounts (not to scale).

Copernicus (1473–1543) challenged this view, proposing a scheme for the solar system which has developed into the one we accept today.

Although educated people today can recite the "facts" of our present concept of a solar system, few have any idea as to why we think it holds true. In dealing only with the earth, evidences of shape and especially of motions are actually based on subtle observations and inspired reasoning. The now established view of the solar system, as shown in Fig. 1-2, was an early triumph of scientific thought over old common sense, and was a harbinger of many triumphs to come.

Rotation The earth rotates (spins) on an axis through its north and south poles (Fig. 1-3a). The time required for one rotation is about four minutes less than 24 hours. Thus a point on the earth's surface at the equator, where the circumference is 25,000 miles, is moving on a curve at a rate exceeding 1000 miles per hour. Exactly at the north and south poles the rate of speed is zero, and between the poles and the equator the rate varies with the circumference of the parallels. For example, the 60° parallel is a circumference half as great as the distance around the earth at the equator; hence a point at latitude 60° is rotating at about 500 miles per hour.

How do we know that the earth rotates? The apparent movement of the sun through the sky from east to west, which causes night and day, results from the earth's rotation. But it is not proof of rotation, because the same motion would occur if the earth were motionless and the sun moved around it.

In 1851 the French scientist Foucault performed his famous experiment, often cited as proof of the earth's rotation (Fig. 1-4). Inside a high building (the Pantheon in Paris) he suspended a heavy iron ball from a wire 200 feet long and carefully set it swinging. As the hours of the day passed, the path of this pendulum appeared to shift, to the right in Paris—and in later experiments in the Southern Hemisphere, to the left. There were two possible explanations. Either the pendulum's path was shifting and the earth was fixed, or the path was fixed in space and the earth actually shifted beneath it. Thus, at first glance, it might appear that we are no more sure which is which than we were when we watched the sun apparently move across the sky. But a pendulum can be manipulated and its motion studied, and it can be shown that the plane of a swinging pendulum is fixed in space. The Foucault pendulum swings, therefore, in a fixed plane, and its apparent shift is a result of the earth's moving beneath it.

The Germans during World War I encountered a more modern proof of the earth's rotation. Long-range artillery shells, shot some 75 miles south at a target in France, were unexpectedly missing their target by about 1500 feet to the right. As the shells did not deviate in their course from the gun muzzle, the deflection was judged to have resulted from the slightly different speed

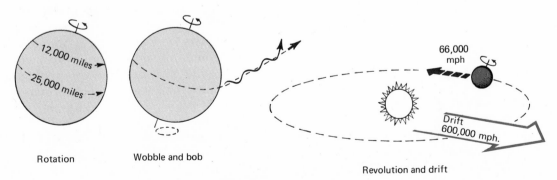

Rotation   Wobble and bob

Revolution and drift

Fig. 1-3
Movements of the earth.

Fig. 1-4
M. Foucault's famous experiment in Paris (1851) wherein he used a pendulum to demonstrate the earth's rotation.

of rotation of the earth's surface in the target area (Fig. 1-5). Although negligible for most shooting, at very long ranges the earth's rotation affects accuracy of aim.

Revolution   The earth revolves in an orbit around the sun. The average distance of the earth from the sun is about 93,000,000 miles, although this varies, since the orbit is slightly elliptical rather than a perfect circle. A trip around the orbit takes 365¼ days (one year). From this (assuming

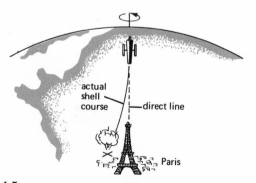

Fig. 1-5
Since the earth's surface was rotating more rapidly at Paris than where "Big Bertha" was fired, the cannon shell hit consistently to the right. It was a "moving" target and should have been sighted with a lead.

that the earth's orbit is circular to simplify things) we can calculate the earth's velocity in orbit as about 66,000 miles per hour.

Parallax of stars is one of several proofs now available for the earth's revolution. To demonstrate parallax, hold up a finger at arm's length, and closing your right eye, sight across the pointing finger to some distant object. Now open your right eye and close your left. Notice how the finger now points to the left of the distant object, as though it or the background had done some shifting. This effect is a parallactic shift. In Fig. 1-6 (much exaggerated) an observer on a revolving earth who sights a near star overhead at sunset, say in June, should see it shift against the background of remoter stars by December, and then shift back again by June—a kind of weaving back and forth as the earth reaches and leaves extreme positions in its orbit. We can put this expectation in the scientific form of the Copernican hypothesis to be tested, thus: *If the earth revolves around the sun*, then we predict that an observer will note a parallactic shifting back and forth of some fixed celestial objects against a background of other and more distant celestial objects. If no such effect is noted, then the earth is not revolving around the sun (or else all fixed celestial objects are at the same distance!).

The ancient Greeks were well aware of the simple logic of this hypothesis, and the fact that they could detect no parallactic shift among the stars over the seasons convinced them that the earth was motionless with respect to anything fixed in space. They did not realize that astronomical distances are so enormous that, with their limited means of observation, it was as if all fixed stars were at the same infinite distance. Only through refined modern instruments has it been possible to register the very slight displacement of nearer stars against farther stars over the course of the year and so confirm the hypothesis of Copernicus.

There are still other motions of the earth through space. The earth's axis of rotation is slowly moving around, making a circuit in about 26,000 years. This motion, called precession, is like the wobbling on its axis of a spinning top.

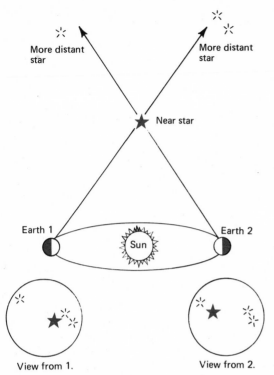

Fig. 1-6
Astronomers looked for parallax of stars a good many years before they found it because even the nearest stars—unlike the diagram—are tremendous distances away and any movement is very slight.

Besides this, the sun is moving at about 12 miles per second towards a point in the galaxy near where the star Vega is now. And as the sun moves, its planets, including the earth, drift with it (Fig. 1-3c). Thus, anything at rest on the surface of the earth (e.g., you reading in your chair) is moving rapidly through space in a motion that can be described with at least four components to say nothing of other less prominent ones.

THE EARTH AS A WHOLE

The sphere

Shape Magellan's sailors, who finished circling the globe in 1522, are generally held to have proved that the earth is a sphere. Their voyage

did indeed show that the earth is a solid of some sort and certainly not flat and that people would not fall off into space from an underside. But Magellan's crew could have sailed around a planet shaped like a banana (Fig. 1-7); so their voyage was not after all proof that the earth is a sphere.

A spherical earth had been proposed as early as the sixth century B.C. by the Greek, Pythagoras. In the fourth century B.C., Artistotle, the Greek philosopher and a great investigator of scientific questions, gave simple proofs based on observation. He noted that ships passing over the horizon at sea disappear hulls first, then decks, then masts (Fig. 1-8). If the manner, rate, and distance of disappearance are always the same in any direction and place on earth, the earth must be a sphere. He also noted that the shadow of the earth on the moon during a lunar eclipse is always an arc of a circle. This shadow is cast by different sides of the earth at different times, and the only possible shape that could do this is a sphere.

Size Once it is demonstrated that the earth is a sphere, the next question is how big it is. Today the circumference of the earth is known to be just under 25,000 miles. A good approximation of this was made in the third century B.C. by Eratosthenes.

His method of reasoning is as good today as it was then. Eratosthenes, living in Egypt, knew

Fig. 1-7
Circumnavigation did not prove the earth was a sphere.

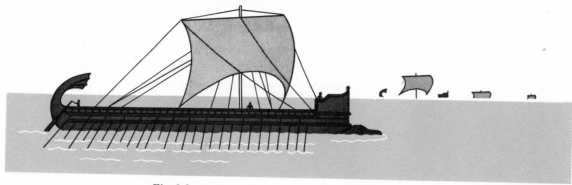

Fig. 1-8
Ancient Greek bireme seemingly dropping below the horizon.

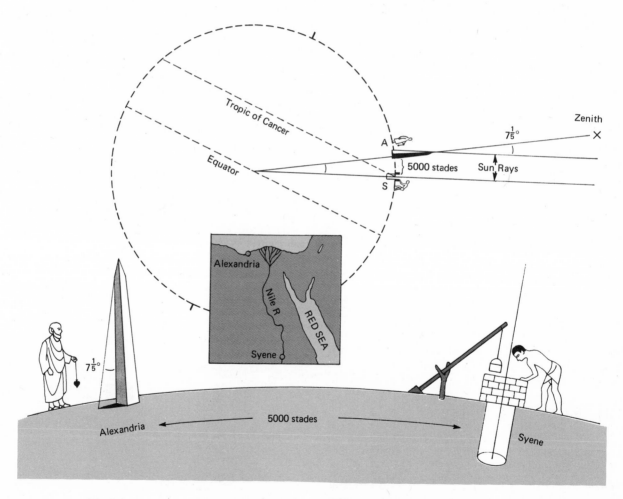

Fig. 1-9
Eratosthenes' method for determining the circumference of the earth.

that Alexandria was a distance of about 5000 Greek stades north of Syene (near modern Aswan); and that on noon of the longest day of the year, the June solstice, the sun was at its zenith (directly overhead) at Syene because its rays reached the bottom of a deep well there. At the same time at Alexandria, however, the sun was 7° south of the zenith as determined by observing the shadow cast by a vertical rod set in the ground (Fig. 1-9). The Greek astronomer took for granted that the earth is a sphere, that the sun's rays at Alexandria are parallel to the rays at Syene, and that a plumb bob points towards the center of the earth. He reasoned that when the plumb line extended to the sun at Syene, as it would when the bottom of the well was illuminated, it did not do so at Alexandria because of the curvature of the earth. As the angle between the plumb line and the sun's rays at Alexandria is equal to the angle between two straight lines drawn from Alexandria and Syene, respectively, to the center of the earth, it can be determined what part of a circle the ground distance between the two cities represents. Knowing this, Eratosthenes could calculate the circumference.

Eratosthenes' method was a good one and his result, a circumference of 250,000 stades is quite accurate if the stade he used was about 1/10 of a mile. Of this we are not sure, for three different stades were used in ancient times.

Oblateness The earth is not a perfect sphere. It is an oblate spheroid bulging slightly at the equator and slightly flattened at the poles. As a result the earth's polar diameter is about 27 miles shorter than its equatorial diameter—not much compared to the diameter of the earth of over 7900 miles, but enough to be a factor in precise mapping and surveys.

Deductive proof of the earth's oblateness was first given by Isaac Newton (1643–1727) from theoretical considerations of the law of gravity and the earth's rotation. In a general way it can be explained that because of gravity all points of the earth are attracted toward its center. This would make the earth a perfect sphere but for

one thing: the earth is not at rest with respect to itself. It rotates. Every particle on the surface of a rotating body tends to leave the curve in a straight line—a tangent—just as mud tends to fly off a rapidly spinning wheel. The inward force of gravity (centripetal force) greatly exceeds the momentum of any particle that tends to leave the earth at a tangent, but this momentum has an effect. Remember that the parts of the earth's surface move at different speeds. A particle on the equator is moving in a curve at more than 1000 miles an hour, while a particle near the North Pole may be moving in a curve at only 50 miles an hour. The momentum of the particles at the equator, tending to make them leave the curved surface on a tangent, is very much greater than the momentum of particles near the poles. Accordingly, since the earth is not completely rigid, the region of the equator bulges outward slightly and the polar regions are a little flatter than they would be if the earth were not rotating. As Newton predicted, the earth is found to be an oblate spheroid rather than a sphere (Fig. 1-10).

Observations indicating that the earth is oblate were completed some sixty years after Newton's

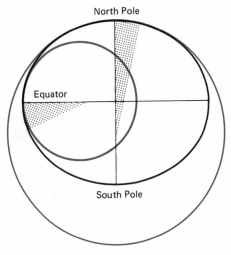

Fig. 1-10
Because of the earth's oblateness, a circle fitting the earth's circumference at the poles is larger than one fitting the circumference at the Equator.

work. In the first half of the eighteenth century, French scientists measured a number of arcs of the earth's surface, using the general method of Eratosthenes. They found that a degree of latitude nearer the equator represents a slightly shorter distance along the earth's surface than a degree nearer the poles. Today a degree of latitude is taken to be 69.407 miles around the poles and 68.704 miles near the equator; that is, the curvature of the earth's surface is more pronounced at the equator than at the poles. If the earth were a perfect sphere there should be no difference; so the earth must be an oblate spheroid.

There is now an ultramodern addition to our knowledge of the earth's general form. The orbits of artificial satellites are affected by variations in the earth's gravitational attraction, which in turn are related to the earth's general form. Observations in 1958 of the U.S. satellite Vanguard I suggest that the earth departs very slightly (about 50 feet) from the oblate spheroid figure. It is more broadly curved around the South Pole and less so around the North Pole resulting in a somewhat pear-shaped form. Overall then, the earth is almost a perfect sphere, slightly oblate, and very, very slightly pear-shaped.

Mass Ordinarily, weighing is no great trick; we just put an object on scales which record the earth's gravitational "pull," or force, on the ob-

ject's mass. Obviously we cannot weigh the earth itself; but mass, the amount of matter it contains, can be determined by Newton's law of gravity:

Every particle in the universe attracts every other particle with a force that is directly proportional to the product of their masses and inversely proportional to the square of the distance between them.

In mathematical form, the law is

$$F = G \frac{M_1 \times M_2}{d^2}$$

where F is the force of gravity, G is the gravitational constant (the gravitational force exerted on each other by given units of mass a given distance apart), M_1 is one mass, M_2 is another mass, and d is the distance between the centers of the two masses.

Before the earth's mass could be calculated, the value of G had to be determined. Any method requires very careful measurement, because the force of gravity is minute for objects small enough to be convenient in this determination.

In the Cavendish method for computing G (Fig. 1-11), two small silver spheres of known weight are put on opposite ends of a small rod which is then suspended at its center from a fine wire; two large lead spheres of known mass are then brought close to the silver ones. The gravitational attraction between the silver and lead

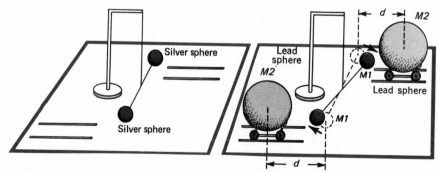

Fig. 1-11
Diagrammatic representation of how the gravitational constant was determined by the Cavendish method.

Table 1.1 Some of the Earth's Vital Statistics

Size	Approximate	More exact
Diameter	8,000 miles	7,927 miles, equatorial 7,900 miles, polar
Circumference	25,000 miles	24,902 miles, equatorial 24,860 miles, polar
Volume	259,600 million cubic miles	
"Weight"		
Mass	6×10^{21} tons (six followed by 21 zeros)	5.876×10^{21} tons
Average density	5.5	5.517
Surface		
Land area	29% 57,000,000 square miles	29.22% 57.5×10^6 square miles
Ocean area	71% 140,000,000 square miles	70.78% 139.4×10^6 square miles

spheres will cause a slight twisting (torsion) of the suspending wire. From the amount of torsion, the force of attraction can be calculated. Thus, in the original equation, it is possible to substitute, as known values, the masses of the spheres for M_1 and M_2, the measured distances between the centers of the silver and lead spheres for d, and the force of attraction as determined from the amount of torsion for F. The equation can then be solved for G, the only remaining unknown.

Once the value of G was known for small masses, it became possible to compute the mass of the earth. By Newton's equation, F for one of the small balls can be calculated, G is now known; M_1, the mass of the small ball, is known; and d is the radius of the earth. Hence, the equation can be solved for the one remaining unknown, M_2, which is the mass of the earth. The mass obtained is 6×10^{21} tons which, if you care to write it out, is 6 followed by 21 zeros.

The total mass of the earth is such a large number that it is difficult to grasp, so it is easier to deal with the earth's specific gravity. This is the ratio of the weight of a given volume of earth material, of average density, to the weight of the same volume of water. The specific gravity of the earth has been calculated as 5.5. In other words, a cubic foot of material, of average earth density, is about 5½ times as heavy as a cubic foot of water.

Surface features of the earth

Recent and subtle observations of the earth's shape bring forward very slight irregularities (e.g., "pear-shape"); but what is most impressive about this shape, rather, is its regularity and uniformity, especially as it might be seen from a distance in space. Only at close range does the detail of the earth's surface show up as far from uniform.

Land, Sea, and Air Even from some distance the contrasts of land, sea, and air would strike an observer. The *lithosphere*, i.e., the outer solid part of the earth, is visible on the surface as continents and islands. The *hydrosphere*, the liquid zone of water, shows up in the vast surfaces of the oceans and also in patches scattered over the land. The *atmosphere*, the gaseous envelope outside both lithosphere and hydrosphere, shows up chiefly in the bright moving patchworks of clouds—droplets of water suspended in the gaseous atmosphere and moving with currents of air (Fig. 1-12).

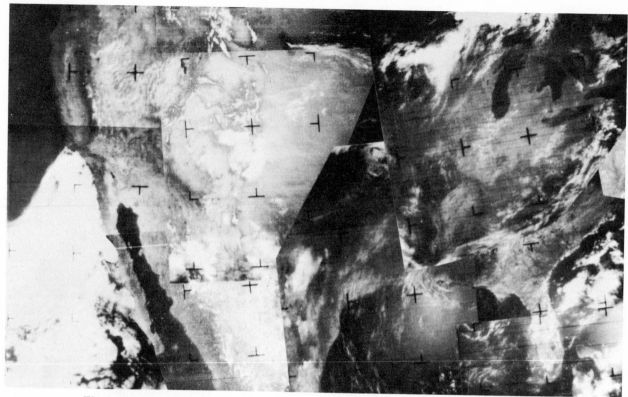

Fig. 1-12
In this photograph of the United States as seen from the Nimbus III meteorological satellite, the contrast of lithosphere, hydrosphere, and atmosphere is clearly visible.

The hydrosphere makes up the greatest part of the earth's visible surface, some 71 percent. Although the oceans have an average depth of two miles and a maximum of about seven, the hydrosphere is a mere surface film compared to the 4000-mile radius of the earth. The atmosphere, which thins rapidly outward from the earth's surface, has about 75 percent of its mass concentrated in the 10- or 12-mile zone directly above land and sea, and has no sharply defined outer limit. But if its extent is estimated at 400 miles, then its total thickness is a mere $\frac{1}{10}$ the earth's radius.

At the surface of the earth, the hydrosphere and atmosphere are extensive and important. Both have been in constant fluid motion, attacking and reworking materials of the more stable lithosphere through the enormous range of geo-

logic time. Atmospheric motion, in the form of mobile air masses and associated winds and currents, is generated by the sun's uneven heating of the earth and is complicated by the earth's rotation. The hydrosphere, in turn, is kept in motion mainly by the winds, which cause waves and currents, and by moving air masses, which carry moisture from the oceans to be dropped upon the lands by gravity and returned to the oceans as eroding streams. Over immense lengths of time, the hydrosphere has flooded and receded, leaving its mark on broad areas of the continental masses. The center of interest for many generations of geologists has been the lithosphere, its surface and depths. But in studying it they have given close attention to interactions among the land, the waters around it, and the winds above it. The sciences of oceanography

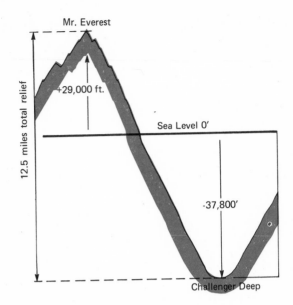

Fig. 1-13
Diagram representing the earth's total relief.

Relief The surface of the earth has obvious relief (an uneven surface). Local relief, the difference in elevation between valley bottoms and mountain tops is frequently impressive to the human observer, but greater than this is the total relief of the earth. This is the difference between the deepest known point on the ocean bottom (over 35,800 feet off the island of Guam in the Challenger Deep) and the highest mountain peak (Mount Everest, 29,000 feet above sea level). This difference is almost 65,000 feet—more than 12 miles (Fig. 1-13). However, it is small compared with the diameter of the earth. A billiard ball has, for its size, as rough a surface as the earth.

Yet the 12 miles of relief are critical. They provide the land we live on and give clues of forces working from within the earth. Relief features are broadly described as first-order (continents and ocean basins), second-order (the extensive mountain ranges, plateaus, and plains), and third-order (individual mountain peaks and other smaller forms, Fig. 1-14). Their origin and significance are of major interest to investigations in geology.

and meteorology now represent man's concern with hydrosphere and atmosphere and continue to grow in scope and detail.

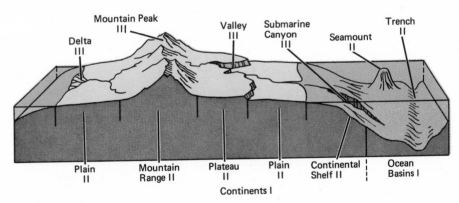

Fig. 1-14
Examples of the three orders of relief, or topographic, features of the earth's surface.

SUGGESTED READINGS

Albritton, C. C., editor, *The Fabric of Geology* (The Geological Society of America), Reading, Mass., Addison Wesley Publishing Co., 1963.

Beveridge, W. I. B., *The Art of Scientific Investigation*, New York, Random House, 1950 (paperback).

Bunbury, E. H., *A History of Ancient Geography*, New York, Dover Publications, Inc., 1959.

Conant, J. B., *Science and Common Sense*, New Haven, Conn., Yale University Press, 1956 (paperback).

Gilbert, G. K., *The Inculcation of the Scientific Method by Example*, American Journal of Science, 3rd Series, Vol. 31, pp. 284–299, 1886.

Spar, J., *Earth, Sea, and Air*, Reading, Mass., Addison Wesley Publishing Co., 1962.

Strahler, A. N., *Physical Geography*, 2nd Ed. New York, John Wiley & Sons, Inc., 1959.

Walker, M., *The Nature of Scientific Thought*, Englewood Cliffs, N.J., Prentice-Hall, Inc., 1963 (paperback).

Materials of the earth

In Chapter One we gained an idea of the character of the earth, its relationship to the rest of the universe and its size, shape, and weight. These fundamental things govern astronomy, meteorology, and oceanography and also govern geology. We begin our study of geology with an investigation of the minerals and rocks found in the earth's crust. These are the proper concern of geology.

two: Matter and minerals

Suppose you were to set out to make a list of all the materials on earth—all in the room where you are, in the scene outside, in the plants and animals there, in yourself, in the sea and the air. Long before you ran out of items to list you would run out of words, and in fact you could hardly bring the list to an end. What the ordinary observer cannot do has been largely achieved by physics and chemistry—not the least of their accomplishments—and an orderly arrangement of related substances has been disclosed underlying the hodgepodge of stuffs around us and inside us. The internal structure is often identical beneath different outward forms: for example, the pyrite crystals of Fig. 2-1a, despite their apparent diversity, all have a symmetrical internal arrangement of atoms (Fig. 2-1b).

Substances and mixtures

Matter is anything that has mass and takes up space. Chemically, matter can be sorted into two main groups: substances (including both elements and compounds) and mixtures.

Elements Chemists have discovered about 100 basic substances, of which 92 occur naturally in the earth. These are the elements which cannot be separated into simpler substances by ordinary chemical reactions because they consist entirely of the same kind of atoms. (Atoms are the infinitesimal building blocks of all substances.) Hydrogen, oxygen, copper, and gold are typical elements. They cannot be broken down into simpler things by mixing and cooking or passing an electric current through them.

Compounds The discovery of the chemical elements simplified the study of matter because it turned up a limited number of substances from which all others are derived. The great variety of substances comes about even though the elements are few, because they combine in a great variety of proportions to form multitudes of chemical compounds. Any compound contains two or more different kinds of atoms and can be separated into simpler substances by ordinary chemical reactions. For example, water is a compound which can be separated into hydrogen and oxygen by passing an electric current through it.

A given compound always contains the same proportion of elements. Ordinary water, H_2O, consists of two parts of hydrogen to one part of oxygen; never one to one, three to two, or any other combination. This is because the smallest particle of water that has the properties of water, the molecule, consists of two whole atoms of hydrogen bonded together with one whole atom of oxygen. Although there are vastly more molecules in a gallon of water than in a pint, the ratio of hydrogen to oxygen is the same in both because no matter how many molecules there are, each one has the same construction.

Compounds usually bear little resemblance to the elements which compose them. Table salt is a compound of two elements, chlorine and sodium. When uncombined, chlorine is a poisonous gas and sodium is a metal which catches fire on touching water. Separately, neither is recommended for seasoning food, but combined as salt they are harmless. The difference in appearance and properties between compounds and the elements which compose them gives a clue to our

Fig. 2-1a
Pyrite crystal from the Island of Elba, Italy. Courtesy of the Southwest Scientific Company, Scottsdale, Arizona.

Fig. 2-1b
Arrangement of atoms in pyrite. Large dark spots are iron atoms, smaller ones are sulfur atoms. Magnification, about 44 million diameters. Courtesy of M. J. Buerger, Massachusetts Institute of Technology.

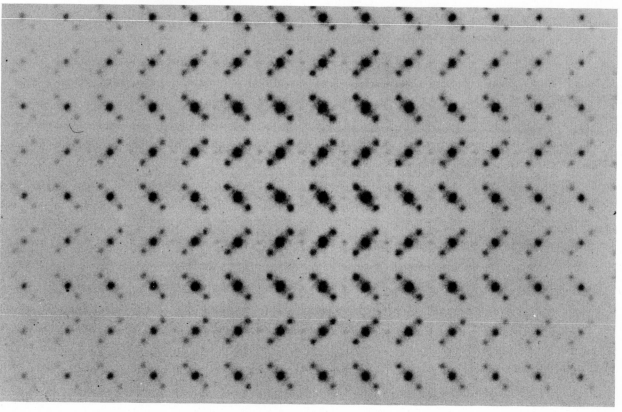

original problem, the confusing variety of materials around us. The possibilities of variety become clearer when we consider the number of combinations possible. Just as only 26 letters in different arrangements yield all the words in English and scores of other languages, then surely the 92 elements combined in various ways could form innumerable chemical compounds.

Mixtures Most things we see around us are not made up of a single element or even a single compound. They are mixtures, not pure substances. Mixtures are conglomerations of elements and compounds which retain their separate identity when blended. The molecules in a mixture do not react with each other to form new and different molecules. For example, salt and pepper thoroughly stirred together will form a mechanical mixture. The individual particles, each a mass of molecules, would be visible. Sugar dissolved in water forms a solution, another kind of mixture. Although the sugar disappears, it has merely divided into individual molecules. These are too small to see, but can still be tasted. The sugar is still sugar, the water is still water; they do not form a new compound. Also unlike a compound, a mixture may have components that vary in their proportions. Whether little or much sugar is dissolved in water, the two substances will mix in any ratio until you overdo the sugar.

The structure of matter

The atomic structure of matter—including the matter of the earth—was reasoned out long ago by Greek philosophers of the fifth century B.C. They pointed out that if a substance could be divided into smaller and smaller pieces, eventually a minute indivisible particle would be reached. Democritus named this particle the atom (that which cannot be cut). He also worked out a theory that the differences between substances corresponded to differences in combinations of only a few basic atomic forms. For centuries the idea was dormant. Then, in the early nineteenth century, John Dalton, an English

schoolmaster, conducted experiments clarifying the concept of the atom and demonstrating its value in explaining the nature and behavior of substances. That atoms are not ultimate, invisible, solid particles—as Dalton and the Greeks believed—emerged late in the nineteenth century. Ingenious laboratory investigations by Ernest Rutherford, J. J. Thomson, and other physicists demonstrated that atoms are mainly empty space containing still more fundamental particles.

Atoms Most of us have seen models of the atom as consisting of a nucleus of one or many positive charges and one or more orbiting electrons of negative charge. Such models are helpful for explanation and prediction, but the "particles in orbit" is very far from adequate as a picture of the true relations within the atom, and the shapes of orbits (orbitals) are by no means so simple as in the picture. The electron is conveniently pictured as a fast-moving particle with a negative electrical charge and a mass of next to nothing. The proton is thought of as a particle with a positive electrical charge and a mass 1837 times that of an electron. The charges of these two particles exactly balance each other. The neutron is a particle of about the same mass as the proton, but having no electrical charge. Neutrons and protons are concentrated at the center (nucleus) of the system of orbiting electrons.

For our purpose, atoms may be viewed as collections of protons and neutrons in a compact central nucleus, around which at great relative distances electrons are arrayed in a series of concentric orbits or shells. The innermost shell carries, at most, two electrons as in the atom of helium. The next shell beyond is filled when it contains eight electrons and succeeding shells may carry more electrons. Hydrogen, the simplest atom, has one proton in the nucleus and one orbital electron. Helium, the next slightly more complex atom, has two protons and two electrons; it also has two neutrons but these affect neither chemical nor electrical properties. The lithium atom has three protons (four neutrons) and three electrons (Fig. 2-2). In the same way, the atoms

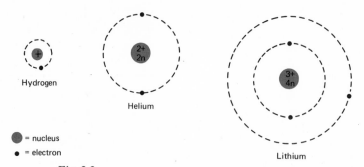

Fig. 2-2
Atomic structures of hydrogen, helium, and lithium.

of the other elements can be visualized as successively adding one more proton and one more electron to their structure. Uranium, the most complex natural atom, has 92 protons, 92 electrons, and 146 neutrons. (More complex atoms than uranium have been produced in the laboratory but are not known to occur naturally.)

Each ordinary atom is electrically neutral, since the number of protons in the nucleus equals the number of surrounding electrons. The chemical properties of atoms, their tendency to and method of combining with other atoms, are controlled by the number of electrons. But, since atoms may gain or lose electrons relatively easily (changing their chemical properties), the number of protons in their nuclei is considered the most fundamental property of atoms. Neutrons in the nucleus add to the weight of atoms, but are not reflected in the number of electrons.

Isotopes are different forms of the same element. They have the typical number of protons and electrons, hence the same chemical properties, but slightly different weights because of differing numbers of neutrons in the nucleus. For example, all forms of hydrogen have one proton and one electron. But hydrogen, which has no neutrons, has an isotope (deuterium) with one neutron in the nucleus, and another (tritium) having two neutrons.

Ions are electrically charged atoms. They result under certain conditions when an ordinary (uncharged) atom gains or loses electrons in its outer shell. Atoms tend to seek a stable configuration wherein they have full outer shells. Sodium, for example, may give up its single outermost electron, cutting back to a stable outer ring of eight electrons. With the original 11 protons remaining in the nucleus and only 10 peripheral

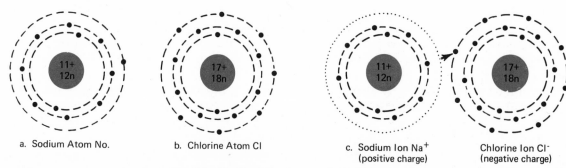

a. Sodium Atom No.   b. Chlorine Atom Cl   c. Sodium Ion Na$^+$ (positive charge)   Chlorine Ion Cl$^-$ (negative charge)

Fig. 2-3 *Bonding of sodium and chlorine ions.*

electrons, the ion has a positive charge. Chlorine achieves stability by acquiring an electron to bring its outer shell to eight. The added electron gives the chlorine ion a negative electrical charge (Fig. 2-3).

Bonding Their tendency to achieve a stable electron configuration is responsible for joining atoms into molecules and crystals, and the formation of chemical compounds. Most geological materials, minerals and rocks, contain elements joined by *ionic bonding*. Ions of sodium (Na^+) and chlorine (Cl^-), for example, have opposite electrical charges. Since unlike charges attract, sodium and chlorine ions will join, be bonded together, forming table salt (NaCl).

Atoms can also achieve a stable outer configuration through *covalent bonding*. In water, for example, oxygen (O), with an outer shell of six electrons obtains the stable number of eight by sharing each of the single electrons of two hydrogen (H) atoms. In the resultant molecule (H_2O), no electrons abandon an atom to join another—they are mutually shared (Fig. 2-4). A carbon atom, which has four outer electrons, may share each of these electrons with four other carbon atoms. All these atoms achieve outer stability without becoming charged—ions. The resultant intimately bonded crystalline structure is diamond—the hardest natural substance.

A few elements such as krypton, argon, and helium have neutral atoms with full outer shells. Being geometrically and electrically satisfied,

James Dwight Dana (1813–1895) *A leading American geologist, Dana strongly influenced thinking on many subjects including the origin of mountains, continents and ocean basins. He is commonly remembered for his textbook of mineralogy which, after numerous editions and revisions, is still used today.*

these "noble" gases do not ordinarily enter into chemical reactions. If you have been exposed to chemistry, all this discussion has probably been too elementary, and if you have not it has probably been hard to follow. But, with a smattering of atomic structure and substances in mind, we are set to tackle the minerals and rocks of the lithosphere.

THE EARTH'S CRUST

The earth is composed of naturally occurring chemicals, called rocks and minerals. Rocks are the larger masses which are most evident in the land around us. On closer examination, it can be seen that rocks are composed of minerals. Since rocks and minerals are substances and mixtures, they have been studied by both chemical and physical means. Chemical analyses of several

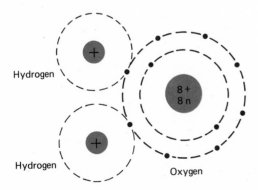

Fig. 2-4 *Water molecule.*

thousand rock samples show that two elements, silicon and oxygen, compose almost 75% of the materials in the earth's crust. Adding the six next most abundant elements, to give a total of eight, accounts for almost 99% of the material in the crust. These elements in order of abundance by weight are as follows:

oxygen	46.6%
silicon	27.7
aluminum	8.1
iron	5.0
calcium	3.6
sodium	2.8
potassium	2.6
magnesium	2.1
TOTAL	98.5%

The other 84 naturally occurring elements comprise a bit more than 1% of the earth's crust. Their overall rarity does not mean that these other elements are unimportant. Economically and scientifically, some of these elements may be of great value and importance; for example, gold, silver, uranium, copper, and lead. But, in a study of the materials which form the bulk of the earth's crust, they may be ignored. This greatly simplifies the problem of understanding earth materials because the great variety of rocks can be considered as combinations, into different forms, of only eight abundant elements.

Properties of minerals

Composition Minerals are natural inorganic elements and compounds having crystalline structure. Being pure substances, relatively speaking, they have characteristic chemical compositions and physical properties. By definition, only naturally occurring substances are minerals. This rules out manmade things such as artificial rubies or the compounds in an ordinary brick. Even some natural substances are not, strictly speaking, minerals because they are organic instead of inorganic. That is, they are compounds of carbon with hydrogen and oxygen which are usually formed by living organisms. Coal, for instance, is formed of substances originating in plants, so is not classed as a mineral by the geologist.

The elements in various minerals can be determined by chemical analyses which range from some that are rather easy to perform to others which are very difficult. Rather simple qualitative tests, which merely indicate the elements present, have been developed to aid in identifying minerals. These are useful mainly to prospectors and amateur mineral collectors. Quantitative analyses, which determine precisely how much and in what proportions elements are present in minerals, are difficult and require elaborate laboratory equipment and highly trained personnel. However, a great many such quantitative analyses, performed in geochemical laboratories, have provided most of the knowledge of the precise composition of minerals as well as the abundance of elements in the earth's crust.

Minerals may consist of a single element. Gold, silver, copper, and sulfur are elements which occasionally occur in native form, pure and uncombined. However, most minerals are compounds because atoms or ions of the abundant elements in the earth have a strong tendency to combine. As examples, silicon combines with oxygen to form silica (SiO_2), the mineral quartz; both together may combine with the abundant metallic elements to form a number of complex minerals called silicates.

Crystal Structure Minerals are solids with a definite internal structure, i.e., crystalline. Thus, of the three states of H_2O, ice is generally considered a mineral, whereas water and steam, being liquid and gas, respectively, are not. Some solid substances, such as opal, lack a regular and repeated internal arrangement of atoms (better ions), so are properly called *mineraloids,* rather than minerals.

The crystalline structure largely determines a mineral's physical properties, which are extremely useful in mineral identification. In order to understand the nature of earth minerals, the physical properties should be related to the structure of minerals; that is, how atoms are assembled to form different minerals. Although our knowledge of crystal structure is based on advanced physics, chemistry, and mathematics, the fundamental ideas are not difficult to understand. They give a rather neat and orderly starting point for the study of how the earth's materials are put together in increasingly complex forms.

A crystal is a solid, bounded by smooth faces whose orderly arrangement reflects the internal structure of the crystal (Fig. 2-5). This merely means they are such forms as cubes, pyramids, and flat-sided columns, as single forms or in various combinations. Furthermore, these shapes develop because a crystal's building blocks, the atoms, are arranged in a minute three-dimensional pattern which is precisely repeated throughout the whole crystal. A somewhat similar relation is shown in a standard setup of bowling pins. The setup is triangular overall because the individual pins are arranged in the same orderly way throughout. However, the rules of bowling restrict the pins to exactly 10, so a total setup is always the same size. No such rule applies in crystallography, so crystals of the same mineral, though always the same shape, may vary tremendously in size (Fig. 2-6).

You may well inquire how the internal structure of crystals is known. Atoms $1/4{,}000{,}000{,}000$ of an inch in diameter cannot be directly observed even with the most powerful optical microscopes. Yet at the beginning of the nineteenth century, Abbé Haüy, in France, believed that the regular geometric arrangement of crystal faces resulted from the arrangement of "integrant molecules." His concept was developed through sound rea-

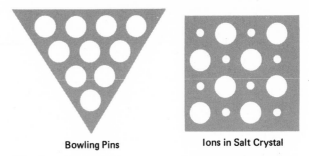

Bowling Pins   Ions in Salt Crystal

Fig. 2-6
Shapes determined by internal geometric arrangements.

soning, based on much careful study of crystal forms, faces, and their arrangements.

This useful concept received final scientific verification in 1912 when Professor Laue at Munich and his two students, Friedrich and Knipping, introduced the use of X-rays for the study of crystals. They reasoned that because X-rays have very short wave lengths, they might be diffracted by particles as minute as atoms. Using equipment which projected a pinpoint beam of X-rays into crystalline substances, they found that regular patterns of dots were recorded on photographic paper placed behind the crystals. The dots resulted because the orderly arrangement of atoms broke up and deflected parts of the X-ray beam (Fig. 2-7). The development of this technique permitted rapid advances in the precise knowledge of crystals, minerals, and solid materials in general. It has also provided a most reliable method for mineral identification.

The crystalline structure of the mineral halite,

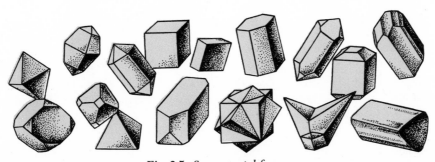

Fig. 2-5 *Some crystal forms.*

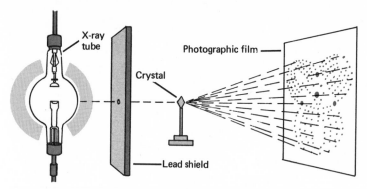

Fig. 2-7
Principle of X-ray diffraction. (After Gilluley, Woodford, and Waters.)

ordinary table salt, was the first to be carefully worked out by the Englishman, W. H. Bragg. Halite, although not an abundant rock-forming mineral in general, is ideal for illustrating the general features of crystals (Fig. 2-8). It has the simplest crystal shape, a cube, and a simple internal structure, compared to most other minerals. The smallest particle which would have the properties of crystalline halite is an orderly cluster of sodium and chlorine atoms [1] about $1/700,000,000$ of an inch across. Its cubic form is an obvious result of the way its atoms are packed together. A visible crystal of salt would simply be a much larger cube made up of a tremendous number of sodium and chlorine atoms, packed, in this same manner, throughout the crystal. The variety of crystal forms which some minerals display results from different packing arrangements, called space lattices, of the atoms. Moreover, several possible crystal shapes may develop from the same space lattice, for there are 14 lattices, but many more external forms. In all of them, the outer crystal form results from an orderly internal packing of atoms, as in the case of halite.

The halite structure is interesting as the first deciphered by X-ray, but geologically another arrangement is far more important—the silicon tetrahedron. It is the basic building block of the earth's crust. Imagine this tetrahedron, chemically SiO_4, as a pyramid of four cannon balls, representing larger oxygen ions, with a golf ball, a silicon ion, tucked inside. Remember, however, that the whole thing is about 2.8 Ångstrom units across (Fig. 2-9). [2]

Silicate minerals, far and away the most common in the earth's crust, are built of silica tetrahedrons with some other ions included. In the mineral olivine, described more fully later, separate tetrahedrons are "glued" together by iron and magnesium ions so that its formula involves SiO_4. In ferromagnesian minerals, another important group, some of the oxygen ions are shared by adjacent tetrahedra, thus building chains of tetrahedra; single chains in pyroxenes, and double chains in amphiboles. In micas, the tetrahedrons form sheets by sharing oxygens. In quartz, SiO_2, all oxygens are shared by adjacent tetrahedra. Put another way, each oxygen ion serves as the corner for two tetrahedra. Thus, in quartz the internal structure can be visualized as a tight framework of overlapping tetrahedra, in marked contrast to the separate ones in olivine. Feldspars have a structure resembling quartz, in which aluminum ions substitute for some of the silicons, and with various additional ions involved.

Cleavage The manner of breaking is a physical property of minerals intimately related to crystal structure. Some minerals, such as quartz, fracture or shatter in an irregular manner. However, many minerals have cleavage. That is, they break along planes which have constant angular relations to each other. In such minerals, the number of

---

[1] Strictly speaking, the sodium and chlorine particles which make up the structure of halite should be called ions.

[2] An Ångstrom unit is one hundred millionths of a centimeter or one four billionth of an inch.

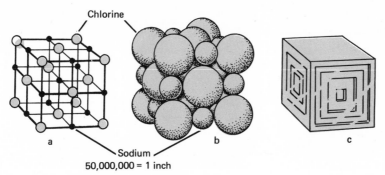

Fig. 2-8
Halite structure showing models of internal arrangement (a) space lattice, and (b) a packing diagram. (c) The external form of a visible crystal.

cleavage planes may vary from one to as many as six. The planes are always parallel to actual crystal faces, or to possible crystal faces, even though a particular mineral may not actually have developed such faces. Cleavage planes result from the packing arrangement of atoms. In a few cases, such as graphite, cleavage planes result where ions are weakly bonded together. However, most cleavage planes are parallel to alternate zones of high and low concentrations of ions. If ions are closely packed in certain directions, they tend to hold together, making a cleavage surface when the mineral is broken. Because cleavage fragments tend to have characteristic shapes for specific minerals, this property is useful in mineral identification, and as a clue to the internal structure of minerals (Fig. 2-10).

Hardness Hardness of minerals is a physical property frequently used for purposes of quick

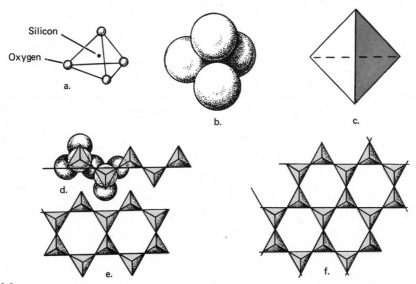

Fig. 2-9
Silicon tetrahedron: a. Lattice diagram b. Packing diagram (silicon ion hidden in center) c. Representation of tetrahedron points are at the nuclei of ions d. Chain structure, as in pyroxene, showing relation of b and c e. Double chain, as in amphibole f. Sheet structure as in mica.

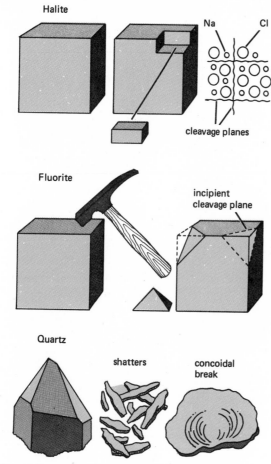

Fig. 2-10
Schematic representation of cleavage and the lack of it in certain minerals.

because adequate determination can be made using certain easily available things of known hardness, such as one's fingernail, a copper penny, knife blade or glass, and a steel file.

Table 2.1 Moh's Hardness Scale

1	Talc
2	Gypsum
2.5	Fingernail
3	Calcite
3	Copper penny
4	Fluorite
5	Apatite
5.5	Knife blade, window glass
6	Feldspar (Orthoclase)
6.5	Steel file
7	Quartz
8	Topaz
9	Corundum
10	Diamond

The factors controlling mineral hardness are rather complex. Involved are the properties of atoms themselves, crystal structure, bond types, and cleavage. However, a clear-cut example of the possible importance of crystal structure is illustrated by two minerals, each composed of the same pure element, carbon. Graphite, the stuff in ordinary pencil lead, is exceedingly soft because its crystals consist of weakly bonded, minute sheets of carbon atoms which easily cleave and slide by each other. For this reason, graphite is frequently used as a lubricant. Diamond, also composed of carbon atoms, is extremely hard because of the interlocking arrangement of the atoms in its crystal structure.

Specific Gravity The weights of minerals also illustrate the relation of physical properties to composition and structure. In most work, "weight" is best expressed as specific gravity. This is the ratio of a mineral's weight to the weight of an equal volume of water.[3] For ex-

mineral identification. Commonly, hardness is measured by the ease with which a mineral may be scratched in comparison to a group of 10 standard minerals, arrayed in a hardness scale. This scale, developed by the German Friedrich Mohs, assigns numbers from 1 to 10 to each of the standard minerals, according to increasing hardness. The softest mineral, number 1, is talc, which is the base for talcum powder; the hardest, number 10, is diamond, which is the hardest natural substance known. The hardness of an unknown mineral may be determined by which of the standard minerals it will or will not scratch. Actually, a standard set of minerals is rarely used

---

[3] Fresh water at 4°C. — The maximum density of water.

ample, the common mineral quartz has a specific gravity of 2.65, which means that a cubic inch of pure quartz weighs that many times more than a cubic inch of water. But remember, in specific gravity, it makes no difference what volume is used so long as it is the same for both. With experience, specific gravity can be estimated by "hefting" mineral samples. However, because many minerals are close to each other in specific gravity, simple laboratory techniques are often used for more accurate determinations.

Specific gravity of a mineral depends on two factors: the weights of the types of atom which compose it, and the closeness with which the atoms are packed in the crystal's structure. Atoms of the element iron weigh over twice as much as atoms of aluminum; therefore, minerals rich in iron have higher specific gravities than those rich in aluminum. The effect of packing is illustrated by comparing two different minerals composed of identical atoms, but having different structures. For instance, diamond has a specific gravity of 3.5 whereas graphite, which has less closely packed atoms, has a specific gravity of only 2.1. In other words, fewer atoms in a unit volume results in less weight, and vice versa.

Color and Luster   Among the other physical properties useful in mineral identification are color and luster. Some individual minerals have one distinctive color; however, others have a range of colors, and sometimes different minerals have the same color. Especially in normally light-colored minerals, minute amounts of foreign substances may strongly modify the mineral's color. Thus, color, although useful and often very obvious, is seldom a reliable means of mineral identification. Luster is the appearance of a mineral in reflected light. It is usually described in non-technical descriptive terms, such as metallic, vitreous or glassy, earthy, etc. Color and luster, which are dependent on a mineral's effect on light, are used mainly in hasty identification of minerals. However, there are other optical properties which, when studied with a microscope, are very important in the precise identification of minerals.

Common minerals

On the basis of physical and chemical properties, some 2000 different minerals have been recognized and described by mineralogists. However, this great number need not discourage us from attempting to understand the earth's materials. Most of the 2000 minerals are rare and of interest mainly to specialists. Actually, fewer than two dozen are abundant, and a knowledge of only ten mineral types is an adequate basis for a generalized understanding of the bulk of rocks which are most frequently encountered (Fig. 2-11).

Feldspar   The most abundant mineral type, feldspar, composes over 60% of the rock materials in the earth's crust. Strictly speaking, the term feldspar refers to a group of closely related minerals having generally similar composition and characteristics. They are alumino-silicates of sodium, potassium, and calcium, which explains why these elements, along with oxygen, silicon, and aluminum, are so abundant in the earth's crust. Potassium feldspar includes the minerals orthoclase and microcline. Plagioclase includes several sodium and calcium bearing feldspars.

Quartz   A very widespread mineral, quartz is the second-most abundant. Quartz is a specific mineral, the only common one of the silica group. Chemically, silica is SiO_2; thus, quartz is a compound composed entirely of the two most abundant chemical elements. In large pure crystals, quartz resembles colorless glass. However, slight impurities may give it a variety of colors, and some minutely crystalline varieties, such as flint, may be opaque and of a waxy luster.

Mica   Mica is the name of a group of minerals which are readily split into thin flexible sheets. This distinctive property results from a single, perfect, cleavage plane, which is repeated throughout the mineral. The minerals are very complex potassium, alumino-silicates with added oxygen-hydrogen combinations. Two common minerals in this group are dark mica (biotite),

Hardness Specific Gravity MINERAL Chemical Composition	COMMON CRYSTALS Color	CLEAVAGE and fragments	USES
H = 7 Sp.G = 2.67 QUARTZ SiO_2	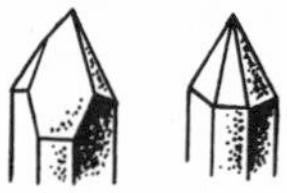 Pure-clean, colorless Impure-pink, purple black etc.	 None-shatters	Crystals in electrical and electronic work Radio quartz Optical lenses & prisms Window glass
H = 6 Sp.G = 2.5-2.9 FELDSPAR GROUP Sodium: Potassium- Calcium Aluminum silicates	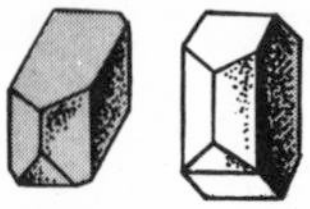 Light colored: white pink, grey, cream	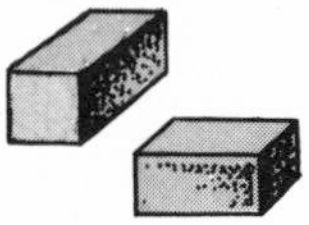 Two directions	Glazes and Flux enamels for ceramics
H = 2-2.25 Sp.G = 2.76-3 MICA Complex: Potassium Aluminum, Iron, Magnesium silicates	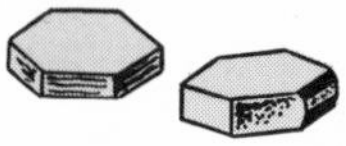 Clear, whitish brown, black, purple	 Parallel, excellent One direction	In electrical and electronic equipment Heat-proof windows
H = 5-6 Sp.G = 29-3.4 HORNBLENDE (AMPHIBOLE GROUP) Complex: Potassium Magnesium, Aluminum Sodium silicates, Iron	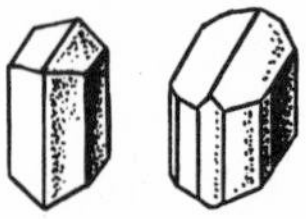 Dark: green to black	Crystal faces 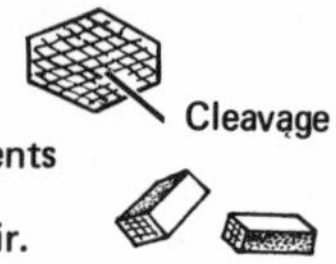 Cleavage Fragments Two dir.	Some fibrous members of amphibole group used as asbestos
H = 5-6 Sp.G = 3.2-3.6 AUGITE (PYROXENE GROUP) Generally like hornblende	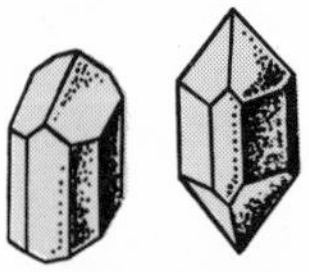 Dark: green,black,brown	Crystal faces 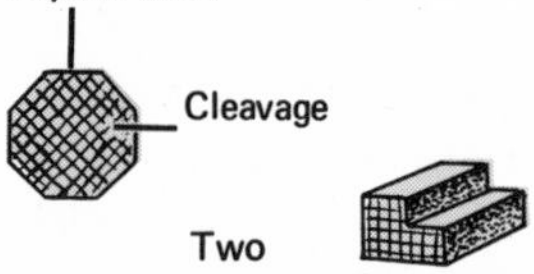 Cleavage Two	
H = 3 Sp.G = 2.72 CALCITE $CaCO_3$	 Usually colorless or white,Other tints common	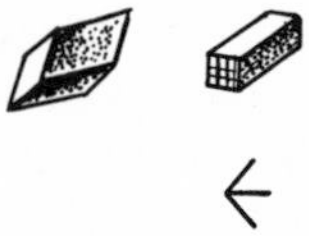 Three	Optical Prisms (transparent crystals) Range finders Microscopes
H = 1-2.5 Sp.G = 2-2.6 CLAY GROUP Complex: Aluminum silicates combined with water	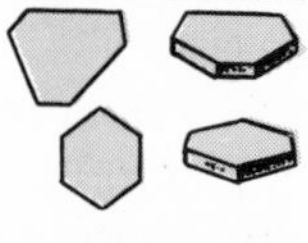 Pure: white Impure: wide range of colors		Bricks Pottery, china Drilling mud Paper slicks

Fig. 2-11
Summary chart of general properties of some of the commonest rock-forming minerals.

which also contains iron and magnesium, and colorless or white mica (muscovite), in which these two elements are absent. The atoms of all these elements are arranged in a complicated manner to produce a loosely bonded sheet-like structure within the crystal. This is responsible for the characteristic cleavage.

Amphibole and Pyroxene A number of silicate minerals and mineral groups are referred to as "ferromagnesians." The name indicates that they contain appreciable iron (from the Latin, *ferum*), and magnesium. Common dark mica is, therefore, in this general class, although the other micas are not. Amphibole and pyroxene are two common groups of related, ferromagnesian minerals. As with most iron-bearing minerals, they are mostly dark-colored and of comparatively high specific gravity. Both groups are rather similar in most properties, but can be distinguished in many cases by cleavage, which results from their somewhat different internal crystal structure.

Olivine In hardness and luster, olivine resembles quartz, but the color and common occurrence in small grains are helpful for identification. Olivine is a ferromagnesian silicate characterized by a green (olive) color. Internally, olivine consists of separate silicon tetrahedra linked by iron and magnesium atoms. It is common in certain dark-colored igneous rocks and may be an important component of the rocks below the earth's crust.

Calcite Calcite is the only common rock-forming mineral which lacks silicon. All others are silicon and oxygen compounds in the form of silica or silicates. Calcite, however, is a carbonate, a class of compounds based on carbon-oxygen combinations. The "calc" in the word calcite comes from the Latin word *calcis* (lime), and indicates the presence of the common element calcium. Calcite has the simple formula $CaCO_3$.

At first glance, calcite might be confused with quartz where both are clear, colorless, and "glassy." However, it is easily distinguished be-cause, unlike quartz, calcite is quite soft, has excellent cleavage, and fizzes when drops of hydrochloric acid touch it. Calcite is a very widespread mineral in certain common rocks and in the shells of many organisms.

Clay Clay minerals are important and abundant products of the slow chemical breakdown of rocks. Especially susceptible to this "rotting," or weathering, are feldspars and ferromagnesian minerals in rocks exposed at the earth's surface. Pure clays, with some exceptions, are white or gray, but they usually contain impurities which stain them to blue, red, or other colors. Chemically, clays are complex aluminum or aluminum-magnesium silicates with added oxygen-hydrogen combinations. Clays, in bulk, have the property of being plastic and moldable when wet. This results because they consist of minute particles, less than $1/10,000$ of an inch across, which resemble mica in form and cleavage. Structurally, these particles are made up of sheets of atoms which become plastic when water particles slip between them.

GENERAL CONCLUSIONS

An exposure to elementary mineralogy should point up several fundamental aspects of science in general; foremost, that science is a search for explanations about nature based on careful observations. The concept of the internal structure of crystals is such an explanation. The existence of crystals was known in antiquity. But, interest in them did not become scientific until certain people, who were willing to accept a natural origin for such things, asked themselves, "What causes the beautiful and regular arrangement of crystal faces?" Following up the question with detailed observations, logical thinking, and a bit of inspiration, led to the explanation relating external crystal shape to an invisible internal structure.

An introduction to mineralogy should also suggest the importance of the development of instru-

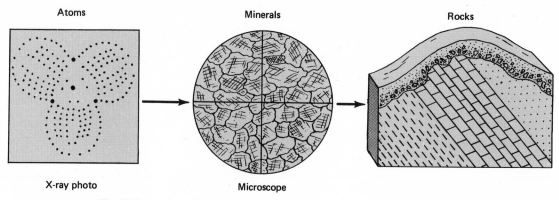

Fig. 2-12
From the ultra-microscopic to the megascopic—atoms to minerals to rocks.

ments to advances in science. The idea that crystal form depended on internal structure was developed in the early nineteenth century. The next major advance in knowledge of crystal structure did not occur until the early twentieth century, because precise information about the arrangement of atoms within crystals and the explanations of related properties were impossible to obtain until research in physics led to the development of X-ray equipment and techniques.

Mineralogy is geologic because its general objective is an understanding of the earth; but, because its special interest is in minerals, it requires the application of principles and techniques from chemistry, physics, and mathematics. Thus, mineralogy gives an excellent example of the overlapping nature of the traditional fields of science.

The most pertinent reason for a knowledge of elementary mineralogy is to give the necessary foundation for the study of geology in general. One must understand what minerals are, how composition and internal structure determine their properties, and the use of properties in mineral identification. Minerals are the substances which make up rocks, and rocks provide the evidence for most of the ideas encountered throughout geology.

SUGGESTED READINGS

Compton, Charles, *An Introduction to Chemistry*, Princeton, N.J., D. Van Nostrand Co., Inc., 1958.

Holden, A., and Singer, P., *Crystals and Crystal Growing*, Garden City, N.Y., Doubleday & Co., Inc., 1960 (paperback, Anchor Books).

Keller, W. D., *Chemistry in Introductory Geology*, Columbia, Mo., Lucas Brothers, Publishers, 1957 (paperback).

Pearl, R. M., *Rocks and Minerals*, New York, Barnes and Noble Inc., 1956 (paperback).

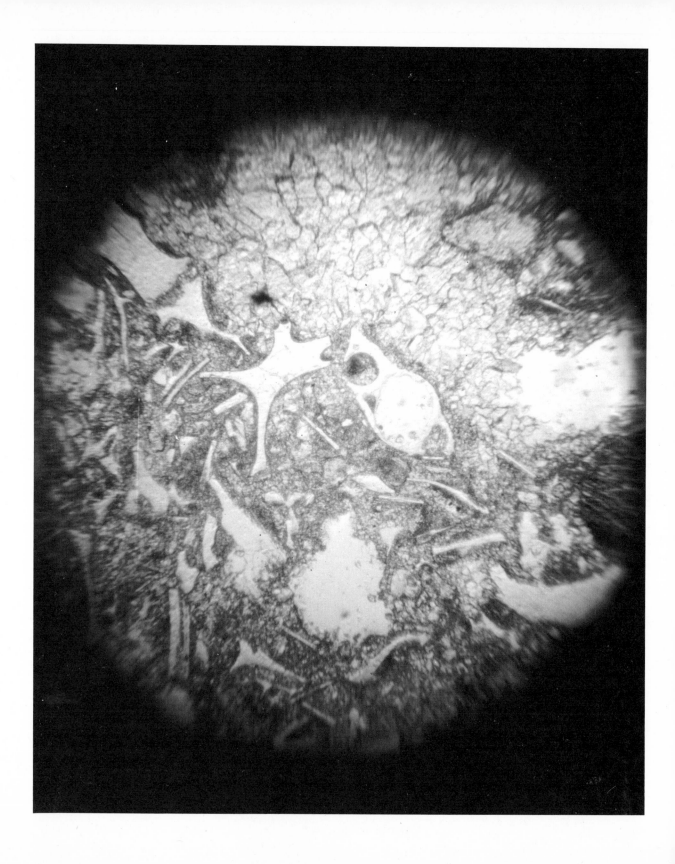

three: Rocks

Rocks are the documents of geology. The facts, principles, and explanations of geological studies are based on careful observation of the rocks, for they alone can preserve the evidence of forces and processes working in and on the lithosphere.

Rocks are natural aggregates of mineral matter. Most are mixtures. For example, a close look at granite, a very common rock, shows an interlocking mass of quartz, feldspar, and ferromagnesian particles. The individual particles are usually small and their crystal outlines often unrecognizable, but they can be identified because their physical properties are the same as in larger specimens. Some rocks are mainly composed of a single mineral. Limestones, for example, are sometimes almost entirely calcite. A few rocks, such as coal, are not composed of true minerals. So, we hedge our definition and say that rocks are mineral matter, not just minerals. Thus, rocks include all natural masses forming appreciable parts of the lithosphere.

In the laboratory, the petrographic microscope has been extremely useful to geologists. Many rocks are so fine-grained that their minerals are difficult or impossible to recognize without a microscope, and even in coarser rocks significant details of mineral grains are often miniscule. Besides giving strong magnification, the petrographic microscope also enables the study of the optical properties of mineral crystals in polarized light. As the light passes through thin sections of rock ground to transparency, it gives distinctive patterns or colors, depending on the microscope attachment used, which are most reliable in mineral identification. Actually, much can be learned by studying hand specimens with the un-aided eye or a hand lens, but the petrographic microscope greatly extends our normal powers of observation.

The geologic literature is loaded with several hundred different names for rocks. With minerals, we avoided the problem of bringing order to great variety by ignoring all but the very common ones. Scientific classification makes the study of great diversity far easier. A classification should show an orderly relation between things, so that they can be sorted into groups and better understood.

Igneous, sedimentary, and metamorphic—geologically all rocks are sorted into these three great groups. This classification is genetic, that is, based on origins. Igneous rocks result from solidification during cooling of molten rock-forming material. Their origin resembles that of ordinary glass which is made by cooling of a melted mixture. Sedimentary rocks are accumulations derived from older materials deposited as fragments or from solution. They differ from igneous and metamorphic rocks by originating at the earth's surface, where temperatures and pressures are low. They are like concrete, a man-made mixture of rock fragments or sand, bound together by cement. Metamorphic rocks originate from the transformation of solid rock to new types by heat and pressure. The baking of clay to make chinaware is a somewhat similar process.

IGNEOUS ROCKS

Igneous rocks compose about 95% of the volume of the earth's crust, and are the ancestral material from which all other rocks are ultimately derived. The origin of igneous rock is dramatically illustrated in an erupting volcano where flaming lava, flowing over the ground, cools and solidifies into solid rock. Igneous rocks, in general, originate from the solidification of molten rock-forming material. The molten material is called magma when below the earth's surface. It is a hot liquid containing chemical elements which solidify into rock, gases which later escape, and solid particles of rock or mineral (Fig. 3-1).

Description

Texture and mineral composition are two important features observable in igneous rocks. Texture, in general, refers to the arrangement and size of particles in an object. In cloths, burlap has a rough or coarse texture because its threads are large; silk has a smooth or fine texture because its threads are very thin. In the same way, rocks have coarse textures if made up of large crystals and fine textures if composed of very small crystals.

Texture Textures of igneous rocks are described in special terms. *Granular* refers to coarser textures in which crystals are all about the same size and easily visible to the naked eye. *Aphanitic* describes fine textures in which crystals exist but are not readily visible without magnification. In other words, a magnifying glass or microscope is needed to study the crystals. *Glassy* is an apt term for rock which has no crystals. *Porphyritic* describes uneven textures composed of two markedly different grain sizes, where larger crystals are surrounded by a groundmass of much finer crystals or glass. Scientific terminology, such as this, seems like jargon to the uninitiated, but it does save constantly explaining what we mean in ordinary words.

Composition Determining composition of rocks involves recognition of the minerals present and determination of relatively how much there is of each. This can usually be done in granular-tex-

Fig. 3-1
Columnar joints in basalt, a volcanic rock. Photo was taken in Columbia lava plateau in Idaho. Courtesy of U.S. Geological Survey, by H. E. Malde.

tured rocks without special equipment, although a hand lens helps. Aphanitic rocks require laboratory study with a petrographic microscope. In porphyritic textures the large crystals are a clue to the minerals present.

Classification

Volcanic and Plutonic Rocks Igneous rocks are genetically classified in two main groups, depending on their place of origin. Magma, rising through existing rocks in the lithosphere, may erupt upon the surface of the earth; the resulting rocks are classed as volcanic. Some magma may stop rising before it reaches the surface and solidify within the earth's crust; these rocks formed at depth are called plutonic (Fig. 3-2). The terms are well chosen. Vulcan was the Roman god of fire, and Pluto was the Roman god of the underworld. That volcanic rocks originate from magma is clear; the process can be seen. Whether all plutonic rocks originate from magma is a lively issue in geology today because they are observable only after erosion has removed their overlying rock, long after they were created.

A *general classification of igneous rocks using mineral composition and texture* can be approached in a more empirical way. The idea behind this classification is as simple as arranging cards by suit and value in a bridge hand and serves the same general purpose, i.e., it makes their study easier. It uses only names for the most common family groups of rocks. Be not dismayed if you hear specialists using such "jawbreakers" as Troctolite, Shonkinite, and Jacupirangite; they are only trying to be more precise in referring to relatives within our broad family groups. Actually, two names will describe most igneous rocks you are apt to encounter in the field. Among the plutonic rocks, *granitic* types are more common (95%) than all the others combined. Of

volcanic rocks, *basaltic* types are by all odds the most abundant (97%).

Of the three most common granular rock types, granite, diorite and gabbro, all contain feldspar and ferromagnesian minerals. Of these, only granite contains quartz and potassium feldspar. Diorite is mostly plagioclase but may contain abundant "ferromags." Gabbro is mainly ferromags but may have considerable plagioclase, usually dark-colored (Fig. 3-3). Generally, from granite to gabbro, there is a loss of quartz and an increase of ferromags. This results in a corresponding change from light to dark-colored rocks.

Peridotite is a general term for igneous rocks with notable amounts of olivine, and with or without other ferromag minerals. It has little if any feldspar. Being high in olivine, this rock is relatively heavy. Although not a particularly common rock at the earth's surface, peridotite figures prominently in speculations on the sub-crustal zone.

Aphanitic rocks have the same general mineral compositions as their granular cousins. Rhyolite is like granite in containing quartz, feldspar, and some ferromags. Andesite has the same general composition as diorite. Basalt resembles gabbro mineralogically. The aphanitic rocks usually reflect compositional changes by their colors, which range from light color in rhyolite, to intermediate color in andesite, and to dark color in basalt.

Glassy-textured rocks are not truly composed of minerals. They are actually non-crystalline solids in which atoms are randomly dispersed,

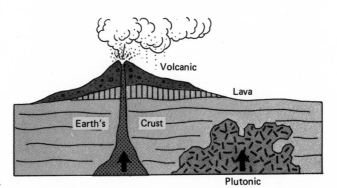

Fig. 3-2
Volcanic and plutonic rocks.

Table 3.1 Generalized Classification of Igneous Rocks

Texture	Composition			
	Quartz, feldspar hornblende dark mica (*generally light colored*)	Feldspar hornblende dark mica *intermediate*	Dark feldspar augite (*generally dark colored*)	
granular	Granite	Diorite	Gabbro	PLUTONIC
aphanitic	Rhyolite	Andesite	Basalt	VOLCANIC
glassy	Pumice	Scoria		
	Obsidian			
pyroclastic	Breccia Tuff			

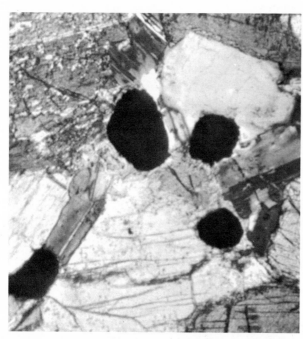

Fig. 3-3
Gabbro (norite) as seen through a microscope. Largest crystals are pyroxene; smaller banded crystals are feldspar (plagioclase); circular, dark masses are crystallized droplets of sulfide minerals (pyrrhotite). Photo courtesy of R. S. Houston.

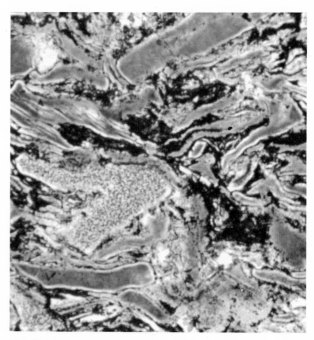

Fig. 3-4
Tuff, much enlarged, viewed through a microscope. Fragments of volcanic ash are flattened and fused together by intense heat of eruption to form a welded tuff. Photo courtesy of R. S. Houston.

instead of being organized into mineral crystals. However, chemical analyses show the same amounts and variations of chemical elements, such as silicon, iron, magnesium, and aluminum, as in related aphanitic and granular rocks. Color is not a clue to composition in obsidians; all are dark, largely because of finely disseminated iron minerals. Pumice and Scoria do not have a glassy look because they are so porous. Since gas-filled magma in eruption behaves like warm, well-shaken soda pop when the bottle is uncapped, pumice is literally a frozen bubbly froth of glass.

Pyroclastic Rocks   Magmas heavily charged with gas may explode, causing volcanic eruptions, showering the area with rock fragments. These accumulate as pyroclastic rock.[1] Volcanic ash is a loose deposit of glass fragments, crystals, or pumice particles which are sometimes no larger than fine dust. Consolidated to light-weight rock, it is called tuff (Fig. 3-4). Volcanic breccias consist of fragments, ranging from pebble-sized to some large blocks ripped from the volcano or surrounding rock. Pyroclastic fragments are unlike the intergrown crystals, or glass, of similar composition, which forms as magma freezes. Pyroclastics are texturally distinctive igneous rocks because they are fragments, heaped together. In fact, some geologists prefer to classify them as sedimentary rocks.

Explanations

Crystal Growth   We can observe the general rule that slow cooling leads to large crystals; fast cooling leads to small crystals or glasses. This can be experimentally demonstrated by controlled cooling of silicate melts in ovens. Also, accidental slow cooling of mixtures used in making ordinary window glass has produced crystals. A great many observations show that plutonic rocks have granular textures, and volcanic rocks have either aphanitic or glassy textures.

In the formation of plutonic rocks, magmas cool slowly. At depth, the surrounding rocks act as

[1] In Greek, *pyro* means fire (igneous), *clast* means fragment.

insulation, preventing the rapid escape of heat, since there is no radiation and conduction is very slow. Thus, larger crystals and coarser textures result (Fig. 3-5). In eruption, magmas are chilled more rapidly because their heat is rapidly lost into the air. Volcanic rocks, therefore, have fine (aphanitic) textures or are glassy if cooling is very rapid. But answering one question in cause and effect leads to another: How does slow cooling cause large crystals?

To explore this basic question, visualize magma as a liquid. This means that its ions are initially evenly dispersed and in contact, but free to move around, like a dish full of ball bearings. During cooling and solidification, ions of the different chemical elements move to randomly distributed centers throughout the magma. There they "freeze" into solid atomic crystal structures which slowly grow, as the liquid disappears, until the magma has become rock (Fig. 3-6). The growth of crystals can be observed by dangling string into concentrated sugar syrup for several days.

Growth of crystals in a magma depends on two main factors: rate of cooling and viscosity. A slow-cooling magma, remaining liquid for a relatively long time, allows many ions to migrate to relatively few centers, so that large crystals can build. We can imagine the centers, or nuclei, as having a magnetic attraction for related ions. In a faster-cooling magma, less time is available during which ions are free to move, so fewer ions gather at more centers and smaller crystals result. If magma chills very rapidly, the mass solidifies before ions can migrate into crystal structures. This produces a glass.

Viscosity of magmas also effects the buildup of ions into crystal structures. Viscosity refers to the "thickness" of liquids. A highly viscous one is stiff and pasty; one with low viscosity is thin and fluid. Differing viscosity of magmas is shown by the flow of lava during volcanic eruptions. Fluid lavas may move quite rapidly; on a comparable slope, highly viscous ones move slowly. High viscosity hinders ion movement through a magma, so crystals grow slowly. Low viscosity

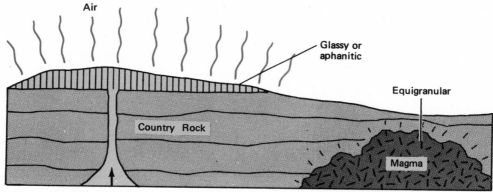

Fig. 3-5
Extrusive magmas cool rapidly in air. Intrusive, being insulated, lose heat slowly.

allows more rapid ion migration into crystal structures. As a rule, therefore, if other conditions are equal, viscous magmas develop rocks with finer textures, and less viscous magmas develop rocks with coarser textures. This explains even textures, but what about the marked difference of crystal sizes in porphyritic texture?

Change of environment is one possible explanation for porphyritic textures. A magma, cooling slowly at depth, would start to develop some large crystals. During cooling, the magma would become a slush, i.e., a mixture of solid crystals and still-liquid magma. Such a magma could start to rise again, for various reasons, and might even erupt at the surface of the earth. In its

new surroundings, the magma would chill more rapidly, so that the remaining liquid would solidify as a fine-textured mass around the larger crystals previously formed at depth (Fig. 3-7).

These explanations about igneous rocks are the barest outline of complex matters. They suggest the sort of reasoning used in attempting to explain what went on millions of years ago, in magmas then miles below the earth's surface, as well as in observable volcanic eruptions of today.

SEDIMENTARY ROCKS

Sedimentary rocks are the most widespread on the continental masses, forming some 75% of their surfaces. However, the volume of sedi-

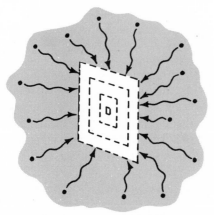

Fig. 3-6
Ions migrating through a magma to build crystals.

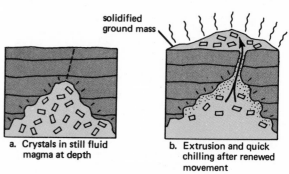

a. Crystals in still fluid magma at depth

b. Extrusion and quick chilling after renewed movement

Fig. 3-7
A possible origin of porphyritic texture.

Fig. 3-8
Panorama of characteristically bedded sedimentary rocks as exposed in the north rim of Grand Canyon. U.S. Forest Service photo by L. J. Prater.

mentary rocks in the outer 10 miles of the earth's continental crust is small, a mere 5%. Yet, this thin rock veneer has given the main clues for the central theme of geology—the history of the earth. Sedimentary rocks are the record of the ceaseless action of air and water on solid rock, through the enormity of geologic time (Fig. 3-8).

Origin

In a large measure, sedimentary rocks are the debris of older rocks. They derive from pre-existing rocks through the workings of weather-ing, erosion, transport, and deposition—the never-ending processes reworking the earth's crust (Fig. 3-9). Weathering is the crumbling of the crust, in place, through exposure to atmospheric "elements." It paves the way for erosion: the carving away of rock by streams and glaciers, wind and waves. Transportation is the carrying of fragments or dissolved particles by moving air or water. Deposition is the settling out, or precipitation, of materials—the defining feature of a sediment. Loose gravel, sand, and silt along a river, the cobbles and sand of beaches, and muds of sea bottoms are sedimentary rocks in the making.

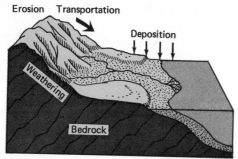

Fig. 3-9
Processes active on the earth's surface that produce sediments and sedimentary rocks.

Many geologists would consider unconsolidated deposits as rock, but to most people a rock is something hard and solid. In any case still another process, lithification, following deposition, can convert loose fragments into solid sedimentary rocks. Sand and larger fragments are bound together by cementation. Water, seeping through sediments, deposits bonding material from solution around individual particles, just as "hard water" leaves a lime coating inside pipes. Calcite, silica, and iron oxides can be seen with a microscope as common cementing materials in the spaces between the original sedimentary particles. Compaction by itself lithifies some sediments. In fine-grained materials, such as clays, the added weight of more and more deposited materials compresses them, squeezing out water until they cohere in a solid mass.

Classification and Description

Sedimentary rocks can be divided into two general groups: clastic, and non-clastic or chemical-organic.

Clastic Rocks Clastic rocks are masses of cemented fragments—like man-made concrete. Their fragments are piled together with much pore space in between. Under a microscope, sandstone, a solid clastic rock, looks like a heap of loose beach sand except that its pores contain cementing materials (Fig. 3-10). Clastic rocks are

subdivided and named according to their fragment sizes.

Conglomerate, the coarsest-textured clastic rock, has easily visible rock fragments ranging from boulders to small pebbles (Fig. 3-11). Fragment shapes vary from rough and jagged to smooth and rounded. Increasing smoothness, along with decrease in size, is a measure of the distance and violence of transport before deposition. In moving water, edges and corners are knocked off as particles strike and grind against each other. This has been demonstrated in rotating drums and other devices that churn particles about.

Table 3.2 Sedimentary Rock Types

Clastic	Chemical-Organic
Conglomerate	Limestone
Sandstone	Chert
quartz sandstone	Rocksalt
arkose	Coal
graywacke	
"Shale"	
siltstone	
claystone	

Sandstone is just what its name implies, lithified sand. Although it can be composed of any sand-sized mineral particle, there are three typical sandstone types. Many sandstones are composed largely of quartz. This mineral is exceed-

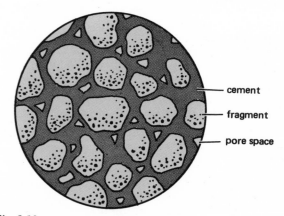

Fig. 3-10
Magnified view of grains and cement as found in quartz sandstone.

Fig. 3-11
Conglomerate. Photo by Rhodes Fairbridge.

ings. Thus, rounded quartz grains are almost indestructible, whereas other common minerals such as feldspar are broken down, dissolved, and winnowed away by extended transport in moving air or water.

Arkose, a second type of sandstone, contains mainly feldspar grains, although it can also contain some quartz and various other mineral grains. Its composition indicates erosion of nearby bare granite whose feldspars have not been completely weathered to form clays. Extended reworking by waves, streams, or wind would remove its feldspars and less resistant minerals, and ultimately produce a quartz sandstone (Fig. 3-12).

Graywacke, a third type, is a hard, dark, "dirty" sandstone. It is a mixture of sand and mud, often containing tuff and particles of rock debris. The appearance of graywacke indicates that it was rapidly deposited in deep submarine basins, so that winnowing of silts and clays by wave action has been minimal.

ingly resistant to chemical change, and quite resistant to mechanical wear in water, after it is reduced to sand size. Experimental work on sand grains shows that angular ones are quite rapidly rounded when blown along the ground in wind, although not during transportation in water; however, once rounded their reduction is very slow as they act like well-lubricated ball bear-

The name shale is loosely applied to the finest-textured clastic rocks originating as muds. Strictly speaking, shale is a rock which breaks into platy chips. If lacking shaly structure, the fine-grained clastic rocks are best called siltstone and claystone, depending on their composition. Silt, greatly magnified, shows angular particles apparently unmodified by transport in either wind or water. Some may be chips knocked

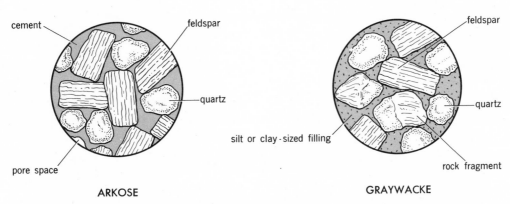

ARKOSE　　　　GRAYWACKE

Fig. 3-12
Diagrammatic magnified views contrasting two sandstones: an arkose and a graywacke.

off sand grains, but of this we cannot always be sure. Clay is produced by the weathering of several minerals, including the abundant feldspars. Its particles are far too small and light to be shaped by impact during transport. These fine-grained rocks often indicate deposition in quiet or protected waters where current and wave action is not too pronounced.

Chemically and Organically Deposited Sedimentary Rocks Besides the clastic group, some sedimentary rocks are deposits of material originally dissolved from older rocks. The particles are carried in solution as ions, which, being too small to be seen with the best optical microscope, are invisible during transport, in contrast to clastic fragments. The lime coating in water pipes and tea kettles is chemically precipitated; the material in a clam shell is an organic deposit.

Textures of chemical-sedimentary rocks are sometimes akin to those formed in cooling magma in that both are crystal masses formed in liquids.

Fig. 3-13
Relatively thin sedimentary stratification is well displayed in Green River lake beds of Western Wyoming at Teapot Rock. Photo taken in 1869 by W. H. Jackson, famous pioneer photographer of the "Old West." U.S. Geological Survey photo in National Archives. Note figure under "spout."

In chemical sediments, crystals form when water becomes saturated with their chemical elements. Fine crystals settle to the bottom of the water forming a loose layer, typical of lime muds in some tropical seas. Later compaction and continued growth of crystals in the layer can produce a dense interlocking mass of crystals.

Chemical-organic rocks generally lack clastic texture, so in a simple classification are named from their composition. There is a considerable variety of such rocks, but a few common ones illustrate their various origins. Rocksalt, composed of the mineral halite, is precipitated from solution as water evaporates. It is a common deposit in and around salt lakes, such as the Dead Sea and the Great Salt Lake of Utah, and in restricted or isolated bodies of ocean water. Gypsum (calcium sulfate) is another common salt deposited in the same manner.

Chert is an abundant sedimentary rock, composed of aphanitic silica which is, perhaps, deposited as a gel or, perhaps, as an ion-by-ion replacement of other materials. Coal, the fuel, is characterized by combustible carbon. It is a non-crystalline rock which often preserves the woody structure of trees or other plants from which it is derived.

Limestone, which makes up about 20% of the world's sedimentary rock, is mainly composed of the mineral calcite. It may be chemical in origin, a direct precipitate from solution in water. Much is also organic, precipitated by animals which take in dissolved ions and convert them to solid shell materials. These progressively accumulate as sedimentary rock as the animals die. The attack of waves along a sea coast may break chemical or organic limestone into fragments which are later cemented into clastic rock — a calcareous sandstone. In any case, limestone is mainly calcite originally removed in solution from minerals in solid rocks.

Sedimentary structures

Layering Stratification (layering or bedding) is the most characteristic structural feature in sedimentary rocks (Fig. 3-13). The rock tends to be separated along bedding planes because of its origin as broad sheets of debris, laid down on the surface of the earth by moving fluids such as in streams, waves and wind. The first sediments laid down cover irregularities in the surface beneath them. Then, sediments are deposited in nearly horizontal layers. Individual layers vary from paper-thin to beds hundreds of feet thick. The pattern is always the same — layer upon layer, like papers piled in order on a table.

The first laid down, the oldest, is at the bottom, and the rest fall in order with the last deposited, or youngest, at the top. These relations, so obvious in stacking a pile of papers, were revolutionary when first clearly stated as early as 1669 by **Nicolaus Steno** (Niels Stensen) of Denmark. The truth is that they are readily seen only if the origin of sedimentary rocks is appreciated. Steno's two laws are stated below.

Nicolaus Steno (1638–1686) A Danish bishop, physician, and naturalist, Steno made important contributions to the knowledge of crystals, including the observation that the angles between comparable faces are always the same — a fact that ultimately led to the concept of orderly internal arrangement of atoms in crystals. His laws of original horizontality and superposition are essential to interpreting sedimentary rocks and deformed structures.

LAW OF ORIGINAL HORIZONTALITY:

Water-laid sediments are deposited in strata that are not far from horizontal and parallel or nearly parallel to the surfaces on which they are accumulating.

LAW OF SUPERPOSITION:

In any pile of sedimentary strata that has not been disturbed by folding or overturning since accumulation, the youngest stratum is at the top and the oldest at the base.

They are the key to unraveling sedimentary layers which have later been folded or broken.

Bedding in sedimentary rocks usually originates from fluctuations and changes during deposition. In some cases, the type of material may change. In a mountain lake, silt and clay, normally carried in by streams, may alternate with sand pebbles and leaves washed in during times of flood, to give a layered sequence. On a larger scale, limestone depositing on an ocean floor may be periodically covered by clays and silts swept far out to sea from the mouths of rivers made especially muddy during major floods. Over great spans of geologic time, shallow seas have advanced and retreated on the continents, leaving blankets of deposits contrasting with the layers laid down on land by streams, wind, and glaciers (Fig. 3-14).

Deposition itself is periodic. A desert lake, a playa, receives water only during rare storms. Most of the time it is dry, allowing the materials washed in to harden. Later, more debris washes in to form additional layers on the older ones. Pauses in deposition range from extremely short, as in the pulses of a continuously flowing stream, to extremely long. For extended periods, areas may emerge from water so that sediments are no longer deposited, and erosion may set in. If deposition is resumed later, the interruption is marked by a surface which forms a bedding plane.

While layering suggests sedimentary origins, it is not proof positive. Successive eruptions give layering to volcanic rocks, and layer-like structures occur in igneous and metamorphic rocks. The recognition that rocks are sedimen-

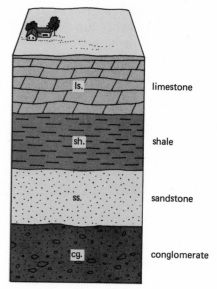

Fig. 3-14
Bedding may result from deposition of a succession of rock types.

tary, and the reconstruction of their origin and environment, depends on the study of minor structures inherited from unconsolidated sediments.

Other Depositional Features *Mud cracks* are common in dried-out puddles, lake bottoms, and marshes where clays and silts shrink as water evaporates (Fig. 3-15). As a muddy surface dries, it can be imagined as shrinking in circular areas towards evenly dispersed centers. Cracks form where contraction circles overlap (Fig. 3-16). Although the causes for the contraction differ, this shrinkage theory of cracking in homely mud applies to far more spectacular forms, such as giant columns of basalt formed by contraction of freezing lava, and large areas of cracks forming great networks on arctic tundras, which result from contraction during intense freezing of water-saturated ground.

Assuming that ancient mud cracks formed like those of the present day, those preserved in solid rock allow us to visualize a geographical setting which disappeared in some long-gone time. Most mud-cracked rocks probably originated in mud

Fig. 3-15
Mud cracks with worm trails. Colorado River, Glen Canyon, Utah. Photo by Tad Nichols.

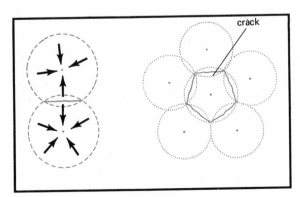

Fig. 3-16
A theory for the mechanics of shrinkage cracks.

flats occasionally covered by shallow water and periodically dry—just as they do today.

Ripple marks on slabs of sedimentary rock are duplicated in modern sediments (Fig. 3-17). They are common on sandy stream bottoms, tidal flats, or beaches, on some parts of the deep-sea floor, and on dunes of windblown sand. Asymmetric ripples with the steeper side to the lee (downwind), called current ripples, develop under the action of water or wind moving in a constant direction. Water, sloshing back and forth, as it does on a lake bottom or near-shore sea floor where there is little current, develops

Fig. 3-17
Ripple marks in sedimentary rocks. Photo by Rhodes Fairbridge.

symmetrical, sharp-crested, oscillation ripples (Fig. 3-18). These features are evidence for the specific movement of water or wind millions of years ago.

Cross laminations are sloping layers within larger sedimentary beds (Fig. 3-19). They reflect

the buildup of sediment, coming from a specific direction. Water and wind spill material down advancing slopes in the same way that bulldozing dumps dirt into a ditch, eventually giving a flat-topped fill (Fig. 3-20). Although cross laminations are often beautifully exposed on rock in

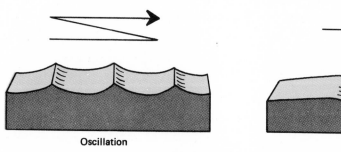

Oscillation   Current

Fig. 3-18
Two types of ripple marks.

Fig. 3-19
Perhaps these are "fossil" dunes or perhaps they were deposited in water. In any case, erosion is now exposing impressive cross-beds in the Sand Creek area, Wyoming. Photo by the author.

cliff faces, their origin in sediments is difficult to observe in progress because they form by burial. However, by running water loaded with sand into glass-sided tanks, their formation can be seen.

Some features of sedimentary rock form within a sediment after it has been deposited. *Concretions* are lumps, or nodular masses, of seemingly different materials from the beds in which they are found. They have a variety of shapes, such as spheres, grape-like clusters, disks, and irregular forms (Figs. 3-21, 3-22).

Most concretions are hard and well-cemented lumps resulting from deposition by water percolating through porous rock layers. Centers of organic materials in sediments may create chemical conditions around themselves which encourage precipitation. Concretions themselves are inorganic in origin although sometimes mistaken for fossils.

Geodes are concretion-like forms, but hollow, and often lined with beautiful layers of calcite or quartz crystals. The crystals are deposits from water filtering into cavities commonly weathered out of limestone. They may resemble concretions until cracked open to reveal their crystal linings.

A lesson from sedimentary rocks

The study of sedimentary rocks introduces a fundamental rule of geologic detective work: "The present is the key to the past." This is the essence of the *Uniformitarian Principle,* proposed about the time of the American Revolution by James Hutton, a Scot. It stems from scientific conviction that the workings of nature are orderly and obey the physical laws of today. For example, ripple marks are caused by moving air or water, which are known physical processes. They are not mysterious special creations.

The great contribution of Dr. Hutton's principle, which we shall discuss more fully in Chapter 10, is that these physical processes have operated in the same way, back through geologic time. Applied to ripple marks, it means that ancient ones on sedimentary rocks were formed in the same way as those on modern sediments. Ripple marks seem trivial; yet, much of geology is based on the careful study of similar minutiae viewed in the light of Uniformitarianism.

METAMORPHIC ROCKS

Origin

Metamorphic rocks, the third great genetic group, form where great heat and pressure have altered solid pre-existing rocks. Lesser metamorphic belts are found along the margins of igneous intrusions. Greater metamorphic masses,

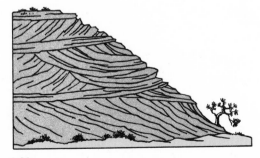

Fig. 3-20
Sketch of several cross-bedding types: inclined planes above and below with curved scour-and-fill in the middle layer.

ranging from relatively small exposures to broad tracts, such as those extending over half of Canada, represent the crumpled roots of mountain ranges now exposed after deep erosion (Fig. 3-23).

In *contact metamorphism,* the heat of an intruding magma is conducted outwards into the surrounding wall rock, which is "cooked" by the heat, and possibly contaminated by hot solutions or vapors from the magma (Fig. 3-24). The heat, in any case, speeds up chemical reactions. *Regional metamorphism,* which involves broad areas, results from crustal deformation wherein surface rocks may sink to great depths in the earth's crust. Here, under tremendous squeezing pressures and high temperatures, minerals of the original rock are altered to types better adjusted to high temperatures and pressures (Fig. 3-25). Flat or platy minerals tend to develop which are oriented perpendicular to the directions of pressure (Fig. 3-26). Many of the rocks develop contorted layers as if the rock had been kneaded like bread dough. At the temperatures and pressures deep in the earth, rocks become plastic and flow. Closer to the surface, the same rocks would be rigid and break under pressure.

Classification and description

Metamorphic rocks range from those with many sedimentary or igneous characteristics, through those with mere vestiges of their parent

Fig. 3-21
A rather weird collection of concretions exposed in the old bed of the Salton Sea. Most, I understand, have now been collected and grace rock gardens in the older parts of Los Angeles. U.S. Forest Service photo by Hutchinson.

Fig. 3-22
Concretions photographed in Antarctic by Larry Lackey.

rock, to those bearing no hint of ancestry. Therefore, although it would be nice to classify them
genetically according to their parents, as altered
igneous or altered sedimentary, this is not always
possible. Moreover, one metamorphic rock type
may result from the metamorphism of several different igneous or metamorphic types. Commonly,
the metamorphic rocks are classified empirically
into two broad textural groups: unfoliated or
weakly foliated, and strongly foliated.[2] Foliation is a rather general term now used to describe

a tendency of metamorphic rocks to part along a
plane or surface.

Unfoliated and Weakly Foliated Rocks Hornfels is a very tough rock produced by contact
metamorphism of shale, tuff, lavas, and other fine-
grained rocks. It is unfoliated, for although the
rock may have relics of bedding or other oriented
structures, it will not break along these structures. Hornfels has a very fine texture, similar to
aphanitic lava. Under a microscope, it is a mosaic
of recrystallized equidimensional grains. Hornfels may contain a variety of minerals (Fig. 3-27).
Quartzites and marbles may have foliation, but

[2] Since most rocks subject to regional metamorphism have
some degree of foliation, we cannot just divide them into
foliated and unfoliated groups—a case of scientific hedging.

Table 3.3 Metamorphic Rock Types

Non or Weakly Foliated	Markedly Foliated
Quartzite	Slate
Marble	Schist
Hornfels	Gneiss

since this feature is not as clearly diagnostic of them as of the strongly foliated group, they are classed with hornfels. Quartzite is a dense sugary-textured rock which is extremely hard because it is almost pure quartz. Quartz sandstone completely cemented by silica is hard to distinguish from metamorphic quartzite. The metamorphic rock, however, has interlocking crystals rather than grains with silica cement between, a distinction which requires a microscope to see.

Marble has clearly visible, interlocking crystals of calcite derived from shell fragments or, originally, from fine grains in limestone. Its

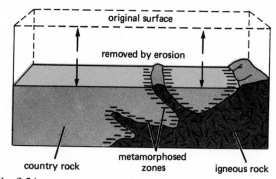

Fig. 3-24
Metamorphic zones resulting originally from alteration of rocks intruded by a magma and exposed much later by erosion.

glistening crystal faces make it a handsome ornamental building stone. Pure marble is white. The wide range of colored marble results from slight impurities in the rock. Marble results from either contact or regional metamorphism of limestone.

Strongly Foliated Rocks Well-foliated rocks are all produced by regional metamorphism. Slates are characterized by excellent, smooth, and par-

Fig. 3-23
Fold in gneiss; specimen about one foot across. Photo by R. B. Parker.

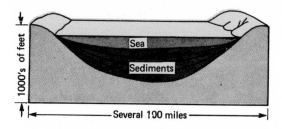

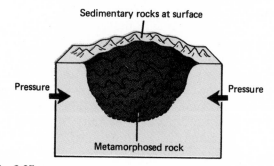

Fig. 3-25
Regional metamorphism resulting when strata (a) are subjected to (b) mountain making forces that alter deeper sediments in the mountain roots.

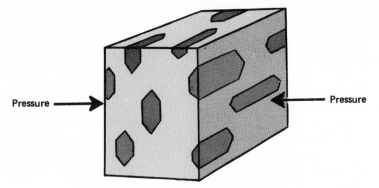

Fig. 3-26
Block shows how minerals tend to be oriented to pressure directions in metamorphic rock.

Pressure → ← Pressure

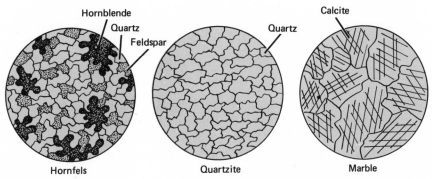

Hornblende
Quartz
Feldspar
Quartz
Calcite

Hornfels   Quartzite   Marble

Fig. 3-27
Diagrammatic views of non- or weakly foliated metamorphic rocks as they would appear under the microscope.

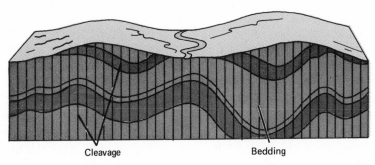

Cleavage   Bedding

Fig. 3-28
The characteristic cleavage slabs of slate are sometimes confused with bedding. Cleavage planes are oriented with respect to directions of pressure applied to the rock and may cross true bedding at any angle.

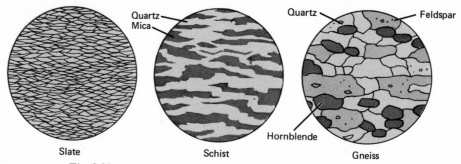

Fig. 3-29
Diagrammatic, microscopic representations of some foliated rocks.

allel foliation, called slaty cleavage,[3] which is largely the result of pressure (Fig. 3-28). Its mineral grains are too fine to be seen with the unaided eye. Good slate has economic value because it can be split along its foliation planes into smooth slabs used for shingles, blackboards, and the tops of billiard tables.

Schist has distinctly visible grains, mostly of platy and blade-like crystals, such as mica and hornblende (Fig. 3-29). The flat crystals have nearly parallel arrangements, giving a finely banded, wavy foliation to the rock. Schists are named according to their predominant mineral; for example, biotite schist and hornblende schist. They originate mainly from further metamorphism of slate, under high temperature as well as pressure, or from alteration of pyroclastic rocks, such as tuff.

Gneiss, a very abundant metamorphic rock, resembles granite in composition and crystal size. It differs in having coarse and irregular streaks and layers of oriented minerals, such as biotite and hornblende, separated by masses of equidimensional minerals, mainly quartz and feldspar. Gneisses, like schists, are differentiated by their composition; for example, granite gneiss or hornblende gneiss. Some gneisses, when traced by mapping into regions of low metamorphism, are transitional into such rocks as shales and sandstones. By and large, it seems that the parent materials of gneiss are sedimen-

[3] Not to be confused with mineral cleavage, which is splitting within crystals, slaty cleavage is determined by parallel arrangement of many crystal faces.

tary. On the other hand, gneisses have been observed grading into granite. So, could granite, that once "classic intrusive igneous rock," be instead the end product of the regional metamorphism of sediments?

Explanations

In volcanic eruptions, muddy streams, and wave-worked beaches, we see igneous and sedimentary rocks in the making. Here, the present is the key to the past. But the origin of metamorphic rocks, like intrusive igneous, is hidden in the depths. It must be deciphered from purely circumstantial evidence.

Alteration How is it established that metamorphic rocks are altered sedimentary and igneous ones? Assume you are having your first field experience with rocks. You examine a buff-colored, fine-grained rock. With a hand lens, small shell fragments can be seen. A drop of hydrochloric acid fizzes on the rock. You conclude it is limestone, composed of calcite. Walking along the bed, the appearance of the rock changes. It becomes whiter and has larger, shiny crystals; examined with a lens, no shell fragments are visible. The crystals can be scratched with a knife; a drop of acid on them fizzes—the mineral is still calcite. Nearby, you notice another rock which you identify as igneous. Recalling the origin of igneous rocks, you can visualize it as originally intruding into the limestone as hot molten magma. From these observations you infer that the magma baked the limestone, recrystallizing the fine calcite grains into a coarser marble texture. Logical reasoning, but does heat recrystallize calcite? You do some reading on the matter and find that as early as 1805, Sir James Hall of England worked on the problem. He experimented by stuffing powdered chalk, which is a soft limestone, into a porcelain tube. He then slid it into a gun barrel, which he tightly sealed and heated. On cooling, he found a rind of granular calcite crystals around the chalk, indicating that heat can recrystallize limestone. From all of your research, it seems logical to conclude that your marble is thermally metamorphosed limestone.

In another situation, hard, dark, aphanitic rock surrounding an igneous intrusion grades into typical shale. We infer that the shale is baked to a natural brick-like rock, a hornfels. Through a microscope the hornfels exhibits small crystals, which are not present in unaltered shale. Analysis shows similar chemical elements in shale and hornfels. Baking shale in an oven reproduces effects of thermal metamorphism. Hornfels, therefore, may be baked shale.

Oriented Crystals Shale may be altered to slate. Slaty cleavage resembles bedding, but close observation shows that cleavage planes cut across fine layers of silt and clay, the original bedding features. Over broad regions, this bedding is usually bent and folded as if the rocks were contorted by squeezing. The cleavage, however, remains generally parallel and constant in direction. Thus, slaty cleavage is not bedding, and is developed in folded rocks.

Although slate appears to be as fine-grained as shale, a microscope shows that it contains minute flaky minerals, mainly micas. Furthermore, the flakes are all parallel to the cleavage planes. The smooth slabs into which slate breaks result from the oriented minerals (Fig. 3-28).

What causes alignment of the mineral flakes? Around 1853, H. C. Sorby of England mixed flakes of iron ore in soft clay. When he squeezed the mixture, the iron flakes became oriented just as the mica flakes in slate (Fig. 3-30). The clay mixture could also be split into slabs, suggest-

ing slaty cleavage. But the mica flakes associated with slaty cleavage are not present in the parent rock, shale. They develop later during metamorphism, so Sorby's demonstration does not reveal the whole story.

In 1906, F. E. Wright of the United States cut several glass cubes having the chemical composition of different minerals. These he compressed at temperatures which allowed the blocks to remain solid, but were high enough to let recrystallization begin. In all cases the resulting crystal fibers were at right angles to the directions of opposing pressure. This suggests that these crystals aligned themselves normal to the pressure directions by growth, rather than by rotation after they had formed. The new orientation favors the development of cleavage planes.

Because schist has easily visible minerals, wavy cleavage surfaces, and often different minerals than slate, these two rocks might seem unrelated. In the field, however, some slates, when followed across country, merge into schist. Chemical analyses of slates and schists show the same chemical elements, even though their minerals differ. Schists result from continued regional metamorphism of slate or other fine-grained rocks. Their larger crystals are the result of a more intense pressure and temperature—a higher grade metamorphism—than that producing slate.

Gneiss may result from metamorphism of granite, a reasonable conclusion where quartz and feldspar grains are streaked and elongated from crushing and deformation. But, many gneisses contain bands and ghost-like remnants

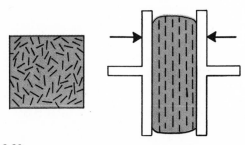

Fig. 3-30
The effect of pressure on clay and mica flakes in Sorby's experiment.

of schist. These rocks appear to be formed from schists penetrated by magmatic juices. The fluids bring new elements which react with the minerals of schist to produce zones of feldspar and quartz crystals characteristic of gneissic texture.

Crystal Growth How can crystals grow, or new minerals form, in solid rock? That metamorphic rocks remain solid is shown by relic structures: bedding planes, fossils, porphyritic textures, and other features inherited from their parent rocks. Complete large-scale melting would obliterate these features; when it does occur, magma forms and igneous rock develops. In igneous rock, mineral growth can be conceived as ion migration to crystal centers in fluid magma. This mental image does not apply for metamorphic rocks.

The regrouping of ions in solid rock to form larger or different crystals requires a solvent. Commonly, rock contains small amounts of water in pores and minute fissures. The water comes from several sources. It may be imprisoned in the rock on burial, be driven from mineral structures such as clay on heating, or have escaped from nearby magmas.

Small amounts of water allow ions to be dissolved from the surface of solid particles. These are then redeposited in crystal structures of new minerals, better adapted to prevailing conditions of temperature and pressure. The process is slow and the water constantly reused, so that the amount required is small. If too much is present, large-scale solution occurs and the metamorphic structure is destroyed.

In the metamorphism of limestone to marble, the ions in calcite regroup into larger crystals. Ions escape more readily from smaller particles and are redeposited on larger crystals. Thus, the rich get richer, and the poor get poorer, until a once fine-grained rock is composed entirely of larger crystals.

SOME CONCLUSIONS FROM ROCKS

It would be wrong to leave the impression that rocks are cut and dried, their story told. They offer many problems, great and small, which challenge imagination, skill, and training. Is granite entirely igneous, formed from magma? Or is it metamorphic, the final alteration of solid rock soaked in juices coming from the depths? Being a scientific problem, the question is naturally argued with all the open-minded calmness of a hot political debate. There are even party labels: "pontificators" for the conservative magma disciples; "soaks" for the metamorphic radicals who believe more in granitization. In part the problem is that what goes on in the depths of the earth can only be inferred from indirect evidence. The making of plutonic rocks is never seen; they come to light only after thousands of feet of rock have been removed—increasing the difficulty of geologic detective work.

Another problem—nature is seldom neat and tidy. Rocks are no exception; they defy easy pigeonholing. Still, most rocks can be easily fitted to our simple classification, which is quite adequate for ordinary purposes. But you would be misled to think that all rock types are separate and distinct. Classifications are man-made distinctions to bring simplicity and order; rocks in nature merge.

Igneous rocks grade in mineral composition from granite into diorite into gabbro, with no sharp breaks. Aphanitic rocks, such as rhyolite, merge imperceptibly into coarse-grained equivalents, in this case granite. In sedimentary rocks, there are clean sandstones and obvious shales. But some are shaly sands or sandy shales. Shale grades into slate, a metamorphic rock, slate into schist, and schist into gneiss.

The problem arises from the nature of rocks. It is in part because most are mixtures—varying assortments of minerals, in all possible proportions, and grading through wide ranges in grain size. Also, rock types are not static and everlasting.

If geology has any message worth remembering after the detailed facts have fled, it is the constant change of seemingly substantial things. Nowhere is this better shown than in rocks, symbols of the enduring. For rocks can be visualized as passing through a cycle of physical processes. In the rock cycle, igneous rocks change to

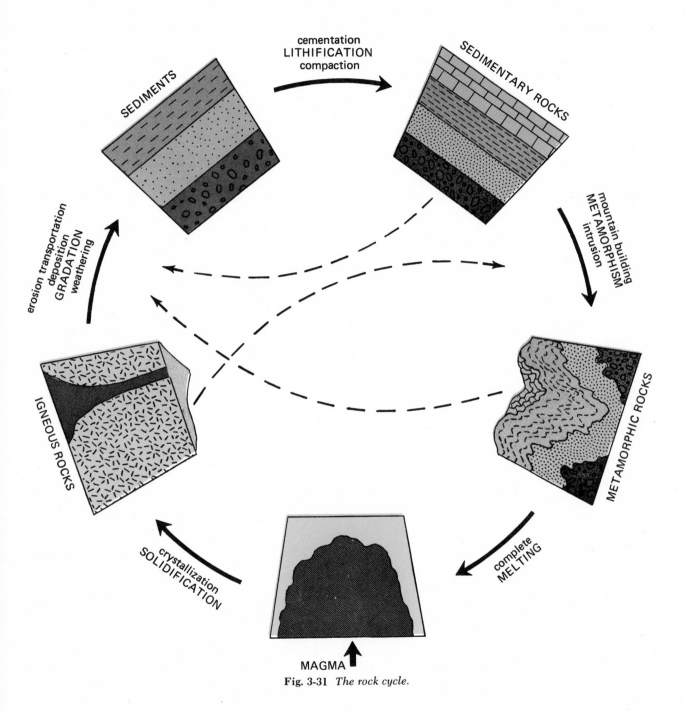

Fig. 3-31 *The rock cycle.*

sedimentary by weathering, erosion, transport, and deposition; sedimentary rocks change to metamorphic by mountain-building and intrusion; if melting is complete, metamorphic rocks go back into igneous. Shortcuts occur, in the large cycle, if metamorphic rocks are exposed to weathering, or igneous rocks are involved in mountain-building (Fig. 3-31).

Change occurs because rocks adapt to new environments. Different conditions of temperature and pressure, in the presence of waters and gases, cause chemical reactions in the minerals of a rock. Feldspar, crystallized from magma, weathers to clay under the low temperature and pressure of surface conditions. Compressed and heated in the depths, clay may alter to mica, which eventually may be melted back into a magma. Throughout the cycle, the atoms, remaining unchanged, are shuffled and rearranged to form new mineral structures, as the chemical elements are circulated from the depths to the surface, and back to the depths.

The rock cycle neatly ties together a raft of seemingly unrelated processes. It has carried us back to where we started; with earth materials, chemistry, and the atomic structure of minerals. It is also an introduction to the surface sculpture and architecture of the lithosphere.

SUGGESTED READINGS

Fenton, C. L., and Fenton, M. A., *Rocks and their Stories*, New York, Doubleday & Co., Inc., 1951.

Pough, F. H., *A Field Guide to Rocks and Minerals*, Boston, Houghton Mifflin Co., 1955.

Spock, L. E., *Guide to the Study of Rocks*, New York, Harper & Row, 1953.

Wear and tear

Antagonistic forces working on rock materials have given the earth's crust its form and structure. The surface is constantly built up by inner forces, while, just as constantly, external forces attack it. Here and there construction or destruction dominate, but overall they are in balance — as highlands are torn down, somewhere else new mountains rise. Yet, if the seemingly substantial scenery is ever-changing, the forces acting on it are not. We now examine how the energy of gravity and the sun working on air and water destroy the "eternal" hills.

four: Decay and collapse

Although the process of rock decay is exceedingly slow in terms of a human lifetime, evidence of its progress is not wanting. An observation in an Edinburgh cemetery was made in 1880 by Sir Archibald Geike, who noted a marked crumbling of a marble tombstone erected in 1792, less than 90 years before. Cleopatra's Needle, a granite obelisk that had survived 3500 years with little change in Egypt's hot, dry climate, was brought to Central Park in New York in 1880. By 1950, some of its deep-cut hieroglyphics were obliterated by the 70 years of damp, cold winters and acid-forming city fumes. The Kamenetz fortress, built of local limestone slabs in the Ukraine in 1632, was abandoned about 1700. In 1930, V. V. Akimtzev reported that the slabs on top of a large tower had decomposed to form a foot of soil in the intervening 230 years.

WEATHERING

Weathering, an important factor in soil formation, is the decay of bedrock, in place, from exposure to the atmosphere. It initiates the surface phase of the rock cycle. Like metamorphism, its counterpart at depth, weathering reflects the adjustment of rocks exposed to new conditions. Minerals in rocks are in balance with the conditions where they originate; if exposed to a new environment, they slowly alter to different forms that are stable under the new conditions. In weathering, rocks and their minerals adjust to low pressures, low and fluctuating temperatures, and the waters that prevail at the earth's surface. Thus plutonic rocks, the products of magmatic or metamorphic processes at depth, are generally most susceptible to chemical changes of weathering (Fig. 4-1).

Weathering is of two sorts that usually occur together, although one may overshadow the other in different climatic zones. *Mechanical weathering* disintegrates rocks into smaller pieces, as when quartzite breaks into smaller quartzite fragments. *Chemical weathering* is a decomposition, or rotting, of rock. New minerals, usually softer, form from the original ones; for example, feldspar alters to clay.

Mechanical weathering

Temperature Change (without water) Rock, like most solids, expands on heating and contracts on cooling. The volume changes are exceedingly small; however, theoretically at least, mechanical weathering can result from such changes in dry bedrock. The mechanism is effective under extreme heat, as in forest fires. Rock, being a poor conductor of heat, spalls off in curved slabs when the surface expands from heating, while at slight depth the rock remains cool and unchanged.

Moderate temperature changes, as between night and day or summer and winter, when repeated over many years, were once thought to be an important cause of the surface breakdown of granitic rocks into a gravelly litter. The different mineral particles in such equi-granular rocks should expand and contract at different rates for several reasons, including their color. Dark minerals absorb heat and expand more than light-colored ones that reflect heat. Thus, uneven

57

Fig. 4-1
A "mushroom" rock about 3 feet high caused by strong weathering on the lower part of a knob of coarse granite exposed in the Laramie Range, Wyoming. The pronounced undercutting develops where moisture — an aid to weathering — lingers around the base of the rock. Photo by Gary Tufford.

stresses are set up, so that individual grains or crystals might be eventually freed, or "pop out," from the bedrock surface. Laboratory experiments, however, cast considerable doubt on this once popular mechanism. Polished granite showed no change, under microscopic examination, after being heated and cooled in a dry oven from freezing to boiling temperatures enough times to equal several hundred years of natural exposure. When the experiment was repeated with the presence of moisture, however, marked disintegration occurred.

Frost Action The freeze and thaw of wet materials is a most important form of mechanical weathering in the colder climates. Broken water pipes, burst milk bottles, and fractured auto engine blocks during a cold spell are compelling evidence of disruption by frost action. A volume increase of about 9% accompanies the freezing of water into ice. Whether the disruptive force is simply a matter of volume increase or is caused by ice crystals, whose growth exerts considerable force, provides an intriguing item for technical debate. In either case, water freezing in cracks and pockets disrupts the most solid rock. The jumble of frost-rived blocks, called felsenmeer, that mantles many mountains above the timberline, is a striking product of freeze and thaw.

Unloading Unloading fractures rock by pressure relief. Rocks deep in the earth are slightly compressed by the static weight of overlying materials. When thousands of feet of overburden are eroded off, a slight expansion in the exposed rock may split off large slabs (Fig. 4-2). Evidence of this action occurs during granite quarrying. The removal of a large block is sometimes followed by a sharp shock which jostles heavy equipment, and accompanies the sudden appearance of a horizontal fracture, creating a new slab under the quarry floor. Rock bursts from the walls of deeply drilled tunnels, and actual measurements of quarried blocks, also demonstrate expansion from pressure relief. The resultant fractures, or sheeting joints, are roughly parallel to the ground. Unloading gives a characteristic rounded appearance to the hills in many granitic and crystalline terrains. *Exfoliation domes,* like Stone Mountain in Georgia, and the domes of

California's Yosemite Valley region, are the most spectacular landforms from this process.

Organisms Charles Darwin suggested that incredible amounts of earth have passed through the alimentary tracts of worms—an interesting cause of rock diminution. Plants are also important agents of both mechanical and chemical weathering. Roots of the ordinary garden pea, grown experimentally between glass plates, create impressive forces equal to 15 or 20 tons per square foot. Individual roots may seem trivially small, but the work of countless ones—including the sizeable roots of trees—probably causes much rock disintegration; moreover, some plants encourage chemical weathering by creating acid soil waters. Overall, mechanical

Fig. 4-2
Curved slabs of granite, resulting from unloading and marked by weathered rills, have slid or crept into a jumble in the valley bottom in the Vedauwoo area of southeast Wyoming. Photo by the author.

weathering assists chemical processes by breaking rocks into progressively smaller particles, thereby greatly increasing the surface area available for chemical reaction.

Chemical weathering

All outdoors is a chemical laboratory, albeit the reactions there are exceedingly slow. Water is essential for chemical weathering reactions. Most outcrops are periodically wet, and water, in addition to its well-known solvent action, is a very reactive chemical.[1] The chemical equations of weathering are usually exceedingly complex, but four broad groups of reactions can be observed.

Hydration Water may combine with compounds to form new compounds. The process is not a mere soaking or absorption of water, as in a sponge, but rather a chemical change in which water enters into chemical reactions producing new products. Hydration is important in chemical weathering, for it acts on the very abundant feldspar and ferromagnesian minerals whose decomposition results in clay.

Desilication Various complex chemical reactions cause desilication, the removal of silica from silicate minerals. In the process, the original silicate minerals decompose, SiO_2 is leached, and the insoluble clays and iron oxides that form are left behind. Desilication produces the deeply weathered soils characterizing tropical rain forests. Strangely, quartz, which is pure SiO_2, is little affected by desilication. The process is restricted to silicate minerals, such as ferromags and feldspars, whose silicon tetrahedrons are associated with a variety of other elements.

Carbonation The reaction called carbonation yields soluble carbonates. It affects rocks whose minerals contain calcium, such as calcite and certain feldspars, and is most active in regions

where ground waters are slightly acid. Carbonic acid forms when carbon dioxide gas from the air, and from plant activity in soils, becomes dissolved in water. The acid then reacts with calcium-bearing minerals. Although limestone is already composed of calcite, which is a carbonate, this mineral is relatively insoluble in pure water. Groundwater, if weakly acid, reacts with calcite to form calcium bicarbonate, a different and far more soluble carbonate. Caves, sink holes, and many of the other solutional features that abound in humid regions underlain by limestone result from the corrosive effect of carbonation. Whereas limestone is subject to weathering and erosion in humid regions, in arid regions it is often a resistant ridge former. Where vegetation is sparse and acid waters are lacking, carbonation is at a minimum, and limestone is little affected by other types of chemical weathering.

Oxidation The rusting of an iron pipe results from oxidation. Chemists would define it a bit more broadly, but, for our purposes, oxidation is simply described as the union of oxygen with other elements, a process which requires the presence of water. The general importance of oxidation in weathering is less than the other methods, since iron is the only element of any abundance in rocks that is affected by this process. Oxidation produces hematite and limonite, minerals giving a dark red or brown color to many soils and rocks. Where locally forming large deposits, these two oxides have furnished much of the better grades of iron ore.

Weathering products

Because chemical weathering creates both soluble and insoluble products, it initiates a sorting of the crustal elements. Sodium, potassium, and calcium become tied up in soluble mineral compounds, largely carbonates. Potassium, an important plant food, tends to be absorbed and held on the surfaces of clay particles; the others are constantly leached and carried off in waters flowing eventually to the sea. Here, much calcium, compounded with carbonate as

[1] We may not ordinarily think of it as a reactive chemical because our bodies, being largely water by volume, are not corroded by it.

calcite, is eventually deposited as chemical or organic limestones. The more soluble sodium tends to remain ionized, in solution, adding to the "saltiness" of the oceans.

Waste Mantle The insoluble weathering products form a part of the waste mantle, or regolith,[2] the unconsolidated material that blankets most bedrock. Except in artificial excavations, steep mountain slopes, rugged coasts, or glacially scoured terrains, outcrops of bedrock are often few and far between (Fig. 4-3). The waste mantle is of two kinds. *Transported mantle* is the debris dumped on bedrock by streams, glaciers, wind, and waves. Its fragments may be exotic, unlike the rock on which they lie, because they have been carried from sources some distance away.

Weathered bedrock that remains in place forms the *residual mantle*. Its bulk is largely disintegrated bedrock fragments in deserts, arctic tundras, and above timberline where mechanical weathering dominates. In humid regions where chemical weathering prevails, it consists mainly of insoluble weathering products. The chemically inert quartz commonly forms sand and silt-sized particles. Clay, minerals, decomposition products of feldspars, and other silicates, compose most of the finer fraction of waste mantle. Limonite and hematite are insoluble residues of iron-bearing bedrock's minerals.

The Soil Whether weathering should be defined as a destructive process is a matter of opinion. In the gradation of the earth's crust, a central geologic theme, it clearly destroys bedrock; yet from another point of view, weathering is constructional because it creates soil. Soil provides food for plants, plants are food for vegetarians, and vegetarian animals are food for meat eaters. So, fundamentally, land life, as we know it, could not have developed on bare rock or even unrefined waste mantle; it ultimately depends on chemical elements extracted from the soil.

[2] Mantle is frequently used, but since an internal zone of the earth is also called the mantle, the cumbersome terms "waste mantle" or "regolith" may avoid confusion.

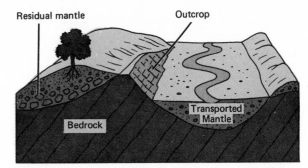

Fig. 4-3
Mantle and bedrock relations.

To civil engineers concerned with excavations and the bearing strength of earth materials, soil is any unconsolidated rock material—essentially waste mantle or regolith. But the soil, as we shall consider it, is not just weathered bedrock. It also contains decayed and living organic matter, moisture, and some gases that play important roles in making it a medium for plant life. Strictly speaking, soil is formed, in place, by further modification of waste mantle that results in a characteristic profile of three layer-like horizons, roughly parallel to the surface of the ground.

The uppermost, or A, horizon contains decayed plant particles forming a dark-colored humus (Fig. 4-4). This is a zone of leaching wherein seeping waters carry soluble substances and insoluble clays downward, at least in humid climates. In the B horizon, materials removed from above accumulate to make a denser horizon, usually enriched in clays. Together, the A and B horizons form the true soil. The C horizon lying directly on bedrock is waste mantle, or parent material, as yet little affected by soil-forming processes.

Aside from generally similar horizontal zonation, soils differ considerably in the development of their horizons, and in their chemical, physical, and organic makeup. The variety in soils, as first suggested by the Russian Dokuchaiev in the late 1800s, results from the dynamic interplay of five main factors: climate, organisms, topography, parent material, and time. The *parent material,* waste mantle of the C horizon, was once thought

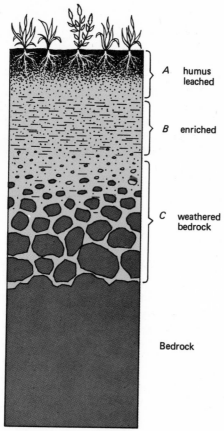

A humus leached

B enriched

C weathered bedrock

Bedrock

Fig. 4-4
Soil horizons as ideally developed in a cool humid region.

all important in controlling the kind of soil that develops. Bedrock is important, in some conditions, and its weathered products form most of the bulk of soil; however, Russian soil scientists found that similar soils extend across different rock types in a given *climatic zone*. Thus the same soil, given enough time, tends to develop on a variety of igneous, sedimentary, or metamorphic rocks in the same climate. In contrast, on similar bedrock (granite, for example), broadly different soils will develop that characterize deserts, tropical rainforests, humid temperate regions, and arctic tundras, respectively.

The *organic factor* includes such things as vegetation and the micro-organisms that live in

the soil. Soils in the forests are usually more acid and leached than those in adjacent grass-covered areas. In tropical jungles, micro-organisms are so active that plant debris is destroyed before any significant humus, which is common in cooler temperate zones, can accumulate. *Topography* causes local variations in soils. Those on uplands tend to be thick and well drained. Soils on valley sides are generally thinner and poorly developed because less water seeps into the ground, and the greater surface runoff removes loose material. In valley bottoms, thick and poorly drained soils contrast with those on steeper slopes and rolling uplands.

The factor of *time* is most important in soil development. The time required to produce a mature soil, in equilibrium with surface conditions, ranges from a few hundred to thousands of years depending on differences of weathering rates in various climates and other factors. As to when waste mantle becomes soil, there is no general agreement. Some workers hold that fresh waste mantle is new-born soil, just beginning to develop. Others insist that material is not soil until weathering and other soil-forming processes have created noticeable horizons. In any case, there are immature soils whose horizons are in the process of developing, for until a soil is mature it is constantly changing. A mature soil is the end product of the slow adjustment of rock to the environmental conditions at the earth's land surface.

Thus weathering is involved in many geologic phenomena. It initiates the chain of events that wears down the crust. For once bedrock is disintegrated and chemically decomposed into softer products, the active processes of erosion, transportation, and deposition are accelerated. These processes, in turn, expose fresh rock to atmospheric corrosion in an unending attack on the earth's solid crust.

LANDSLIDES AND RELATED MOVEMENTS

Between the Canadian towns of Crow's Nest and Pincher Junction, the highway passes

Fig. 4-5
Falling rocks still raise dust 10 days after the Montana quake of 1959. U.S. Geological Survey photo by J. R. Stacy.

through a great jumble of rock blocks marked by this sign erected by the Province of Alberta:

FRANK SLIDE:
Disaster struck the town of Frank at 4:10 A.M., April 29, 1903 when a gigantic wedge of limestone 2100 feet high, 3000 feet wide and 500 feet thick crashed down from Turtle Mountain. Ninety million tons of rock swept over a mile of valley, destroying part of the town, taking 70 lives, and burying an entire mine plant and railway in approximately 100 seconds. The old town was located at the western edge of the slide where many cellars are still visible.

Gravity is the great leveler. Indirectly, it works through the erosive geologic agents, such as streams, glaciers, wind, and waves. Working directly, it creates mass movements whenever surface materials lose support beneath or become less rigid and are subject to flow. Mass movements include a multitude of phenomena, ranging from the fall of a minute grain weathered from a slowly rotting boulder to the sudden collapse of a mountain face (Fig. 4-5). The many kinds of mass movement, the landslides and related phenomena, were classified by C. F. S. Sharpe in 1938. The bases of this generally accepted classification are: the type of movement, rate of movement, the kind of material, and the water content involved.

The movement is classed as *slippage* if mate-

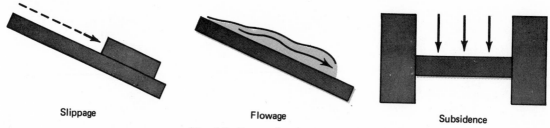

Slippage

Flowage

Subsidence

Fig. 4-6 *Types of mass movement.*

rials move on a definite shearing plane, and the particles in the moving mass retain the same position relative to each other, as in a brick sliding down a board. In *flowage* movement, a distinct slip plane is lacking, and the particles within the moving mass shift in their relative positions, like tar spilled on a sloping roof. Slippage and flowage require a free slope, such as a hillside or cliff. *Subsidence,* which can occur in flat land, is settling: a dominantly vertical sinking exemplified by the surface collapse over some abandoned mine workings (Fig. 4-6). The rate of mass movements grades from the rapidity of a free-falling boulder to movements so slow they are imperceptible. The moisture content, as water or ice, influences the type of mass movement, as some require saturation to a mud, and others can occur even if the material is perfectly dry. Also important is the type of material involved, whether bedrock, coarse rock debris, or finer waste mantle. Let us examine a few mass movements to see how the classifica-

tion is set up, and something of the variety of phenomena caused by the direct action of gravity.

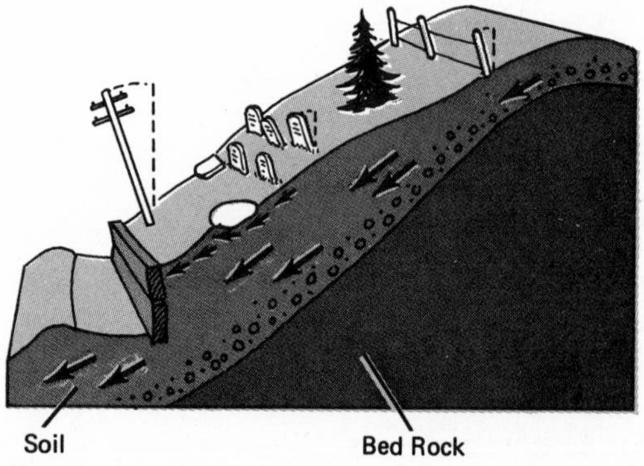

Flowage

Slow Phenomena Soil creep is a very slow downslope movement of rock waste. Although the actual movement is imperceptible, its effects are observable after a period of years (Fig. 4-7). Telephone poles, fence posts, and other originally vertical objects become tilted, and tombstones have toppled on hillsides undergoing creep. Trees are tilted like poles, but since trees tend to grow straight up they develop curves in their trunks.[3] Retaining walls and house foundations may buckle and crack, and, in general, man-made structures may be damaged if the subtle evidences of creep go unrecognized and suitable provisions are not made. *Rock creep* affects bedrock, especially shales. Often where the beds are vertical, their eroded tops will slowly bend downhill under the constant pull of gravity.

Rapid Phenomena In contrast to the imperceptible action of creep, flowage movements are moderately rapid, or even precipitous. *Mudflow* is a rapid flowage of a stream-like mass of saturated waste mantle (Fig. 4-8). Mudflows are common on moderate to steep slopes having a sparse vegetational cover that ineffectively anchors the earthy materials. They are common

Soil   Bed Rock

Fig. 4-7 *Soil creep (after C. F. S. Sharpe).*

[3] The same effect is sometimes caused by snow load crushing down young trees that later recover, so other things should be taken into account as evidence of creep.

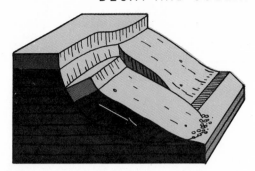

Fig. 4-9
Diagram of larger slump block showing curved slip plane and backward rotation of top.

Fig. 4-8
Mudflow emerging from canyon mouth onto a valley flat.

in semi-arid and volcanic regions where rain, which may be heavy at times, soaks into unconsolidated ash, silt, or clays which are rapidly converted to mud. In the Mediterranean climate of California, mudflows are frequent on canyon walls whose brushy vegetation has been destroyed by flash fires. Here, the occasional heavy rains on bared slopes churn up mud that descends to the valley bottoms where it concentrates into rapidly flowing streams of mud. These often come crashing out of canyon mouths spreading the mud, broken trees, and even large rafted boulders over any farmland or city streets beyond.

Mudflows are a frequent by-product of volcanic eruptions. The heated air and steam, rising over an erupting volcano, can generate thunderstorms whose heavy rain, pelting down

through ash-filled air and onto ash-covered slopes, creates fluid masses of mud. In the famous 79 A.D. eruption of Vesuvius, the town of Herculaneum was buried under mudflows, while the nearby city of Pompeii was overwhelmed by hot clouds of falling ash.

Slippage

True landslides are the slippage phenomena wherein the material may be relatively dry. Three distinct types of slippage are distinguished: slumping, sliding, and falling.

Fig. 4-10
Terracettes, or "cattle walks," common on many steep hillsides.

65

Fig. 4-11
Point Firmin landslip. Slump along California coast. Courtesy of Spence Air Photos.

Slump If an intact block slips to a lower eleva-tion along a curved surface, which usually causes backward rotation, the movement is classed as slump (Fig. 4-9). Slump blocks in bedrock are often very large; those in unconsolidated mate-rials may be quite small. Where sandstone or other massive rock rests on weak rock, such as shale, the blocks may be several miles long and several hundred yards wide, as along the Echo Cliffs, north of the Grand Canyon of Ari-zona. In the waste mantle on steep hillside slopes, small step-like terraces, referred to as "cattle walks," are multiple slump blocks (Fig. 4-10). Whether they result from the stamping of cattle is a debatable point because they are not normally located in the choicest grazing spots;

it seems most likely that the steps originate first and any cow paths on them come later. Large-scale slumping in bedrock often accom-panies basal excavation of a slope, either by natural agencies, such as streams and wave ac-tion along a rugged coast, or by ill-advised en-gineering activities of man (Fig. 4-11).

Slides Although rivaled by some mudflows, *rock slides* are generally the most devastating mass movements. A rock slide is a rapid movement of bedrock that commences as a massive slab slid-ing down an inclined plane of weakness. Usually the slab breaks up into a churning jumble of large blocks. More recent than the Frank slide was the Rock Creek slide along the Madison

Fig. 4-12
Slide in Madison River Gorge under which 19 people in the Rock Creek campground are believed to be buried. Quake Lake, foreground, resulted from the slide blocking the river. U.S. Geological Survey photo by J. R. Stacy.

River Gorge, west of Yellowstone Park (Fig. 4-12). Here, on August 17, 1959, 35,000,000 cubic yards of rock, jarred loose by an earthquake, shot down the valley wall, crashed across a public campground, and climbed 400 feet up the steep opposite wall. Behind the resulting natural dam, a lake formed that was several hundred feet deep, and extended several miles back into the gorge. The causes of slides are many. The Rock Creek slide occurred because of the geologic conditions when the earthquake struck. Schist and gneiss, weakened by weathering, were supported by a strong mass of relatively unweathered dolo-

mite.[4] When the shaking broke the dolomite mass, the mountain face slid off.

The Turtle Mountain slide at Frank, Alberta is a "textbook" case of the conditions responsible for rock slides in general (Fig. 4-13). The setting was precarious. The offending mountain front was precipitous, steepened by the carving of an Ice Age glacier. Structurally, the mountain was a large mass of heavy limestone that had been forced over weak shale, along a great internal plane of slippage, called a fault, millions of years

[4] Similar to limestone, or marble, except that its carbonate minerals contain magnesium as well as calcium.

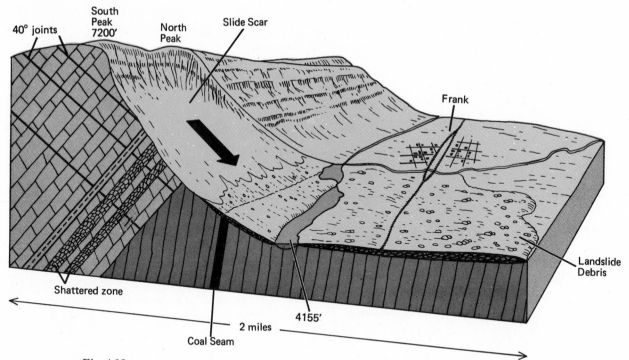

Fig. 4-13
Rockslide on Turtle Mountain that swept across Frank, Alberta, in 1903. (After Canadian Geological Survey cross-section.)

before. Moreover, because an extensive set of cracks in the limestone mass, called joint planes, sloped more steeply towards the town than did the topography, the joints intersected the steep mountain face. Thus Turtle Mountain consisted of a series of inclined slabs, held only by friction, that were poised above the town beneath.

The actual sliding was triggered by a series of late events. An earthquake in 1901, two years earlier, could well have set it off, but instead the jarring merely loosened the whole mass. Just before the slide, frost had caused further loosening, and spring rains and melting snow had lubricated the surfaces of the limestone slabs. Finally, the collapse of an abandoned mine shaft in the underlying shale administered the *coup de grace*. Thus, the Frank Slide is classic because its multiple preconditioning and triggering causes neatly summarize the principal reasons, any one of which would be adequate, for most rock slides.

Fall Perhaps it merits a separate designation (for a slippage plane is absent) but *rock fall* is classed as a type of slippage in which rock masses mix free-fall, bouncing, and sliding down cliffed faces. In the Swiss Alps, in 1881, the collapse of the Plattenbergkopf, a mountain near the town

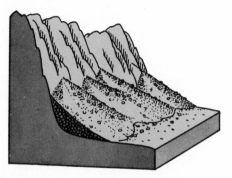

Fig. 4-14
Talus piles accumulating at cliff faces, mainly from rock fall.

Fig. 4-15
Great talus piles at the foot of the 1000-foot cliffs of the Snowy Range above Lake Marie, Wyoming. Photo by the author.

of Elm, sent three great rock falls into the valley, only minutes apart, killing a score of people and destroying three houses and an inn. In Norway, fishing villages have been washed away by waves set up by the plunge of large rock masses into narrow steep-walled embayments that characterize its glaciated coast. Probably much rock fall is of isolated blocks loosened by weathering, at sporadic intervals. Although hardly rivaling the spectacular falls and rock slides, it is quanti-

tatively important, as measured by the aprons of fallen rock, called *talus*, at the foot of many barren cliffs (Figs. 4-14, 4-15).

Subsidence

Loss of volume in material underground produces subsidence. Shallow dish-shaped depressions may result on the surface of the ground

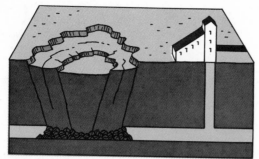

Fig. 4-16
Subsidence resulting from collapse in a mine.

So much for mass movements that are evident and discernible. Today an intriguing controversy revolves around the possibility of great creeping landslips in which sedimentary rocks peel off from the cores of actively rising mountain blocks. The rocks involved form folded, sliced, and generally contorted structures in many mountainous regions. The problem, which relates to mountain building, is that, logical though it seems, the present movement of such masses is not demonstrable, directly or indirectly, in contrast to that in unquestioned mass gravity movements. If the creeping landslips do occur, their progress must be slow, or else the rocks would be a chaotic jumble of blocks, like a rock slide. Admittedly, the contorted mountain structures can be explained by a tremendous vise-like compression between great crustal masses. However, this widely accepted explanation is as problematical as that of slow sliding under the pull of gravity.

when a swamp is drained because of compaction and settling as the materials dry out. The collapse of natural cave passages may cause subsidence. Large funnel-shaped depressions sometimes result from the planned techniques of underground mining, and sometimes, unintentionally, city streets, water lines, and foundations crack and break from the collapse of abandoned mine workings under cities (Fig. 4-16).

SUGGESTED READINGS

Eckel, E. B., Editor, *Landslides and Engineering Practice*, Highway Research Board, Special Report 29, National Academy of Science, National Research Council Publ. 544, 1958.

Jenny, Hans, *Factors of Soil Formation*, New York, McGraw-Hill Book Co. Inc., 1941.

Keller, W. D., *Principles of Chemical Weathering*, Columbia, Mo., Lucas Brothers, Publishers, 1957 (paperback).

Sharpe, C. F. S., *Landslides and Related Phenomena*, Paterson, New Jersey, Pageant Books, 1960.

five: Seas of air and water

A dust devil ruffles a prairie, a rainstorm notches plowed ground, a wave-lashed cliff collapses. Some incidents seem trivial, and more impressive ones may be forgotten during long intervals of little change. Yet every day the Mississippi River dumps into the Gulf of Mexico about two million tons of dissolved salts, silt, and sand—the equivalent of 40,000 freight car loads [1] carved and carried from the land. Rivers alone carry off enough to lower the whole face of the United States about one foot every 9000 years. Wind-blown dust, whose volume is hard to calculate, adds appreciably to this figure.

Through geologic time, moving air and water have attacked the earth's face. Unlike passive weathering and direct gravitational reduction, wind, waves, glaciers, and streams are sculpturing agents that actively carve, carry, and eventually lay down materials from the crust. *Erosion,* whose Latin root means to gnaw away, is a carving action. *Transportation,* which is difficult to separate from erosion, is the carrying of materials whose ultimate end is *deposition,* their dropping.

WIND

Solar energy stirs the sea of air, the atmosphere, into rising and descending currents, as well as the movements parallel to the ground, called wind. In one way or another, all the destructional mechanisms actively sculpting the land are related to wind. It blows away dry soil, sandblasts rock, lays down blankets of dust, and makes shifting hills of sand, called dunes (page

[1] Assuming open railroad cars carrying 50 tons apiece.

72). However, its greatest importance is indirect. Wind sets the oceans and other standing water bodies in motion, creating erosive waves. Perhaps most important, it carries water vapor inland, that condenses and falls as snow or rain and then drains back to the oceans in highly erosive glaciers and streams. Let us briefly review the origin of winds.

Mechanics of wind

Uneven heating of the earth's surface sets air in motion. Although the sun provides the energy that eventually heats the atmosphere, the direct source of heat is the earth's surface. The atmosphere is heated like a greenhouse, or a car with the windows closed, whose glass lets solar energy through to warm the interior, but will not let heat out (Fig. 5-2). Incoming solar radiation has relatively short wave lengths that readily penetrate the transparent atmosphere adding only a little to its heat. The incoming waves strike and heat the opaque ground; the ground then re-radiates less penetrating, longer heat waves that are trapped and absorbed by water vapor and carbon dioxide in the air, thereby adding to its heat.

Air over warmer regions is heated and expands. Being lighter, it rises in vertical currents to the top of the lower atmosphere, where it spreads beneath a boundary [2] that acts as a lid. In cooler regions, air contracts, becomes denser, and descends. To replace the rising air, cool air flows in along the ground surface as wind; at the top of the lower atmosphere, warmer air moves out

[2] Called the tropopause. It separates the troposphere beneath from the stratosphere.

Fig. 5-1
Advancing front of dust storm in Union County, New Mexico. Soil conservation photo by Al Carter.

to replace the descending air. Thus, uneven heating of the ground sets air circulating in convection cells.

Theoretically, if the earth did not rotate, there would be two global convection cells with air rising along the equator, where the sun's rays strike most directly, descending over the chilly poles, where the rays strike most obliquely, and blowing back towards the equator in prevailing polar winds.[3] But because of the earth's rotation, bodies or fluids in motion in the northern hemisphere are deflected to the right of their courses, and those in the southern hemisphere to the left (Ferrel's Law). Hence the northern and southern hemispheres each have three belts of prevailing winds: low latitude Trades blowing east, middle latitude Westerlies, and polar Easterlies (Fig. 5-3). These belts, which do exist over the larger oceans, are in turn disrupted into centers of action over the continents, whose surfaces heat and cool more rapidly than those of the oceans.

Thus, in summer, winds tend to be sucked into the warm continental interiors, while in winter they reverse and spill outwards towards the

[3] Winds are named by the direction *from* which they blow.

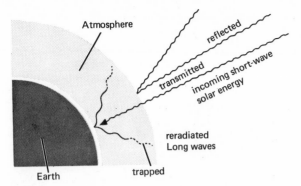

Fig. 5-2
Greenhouse effect in heating of the atmosphere.

warmer oceans—a phenomenon known as the monsoon effect. Further mechanics of planetary circulation need not concern us; let us turn to the geologic work of wind.

Geologic work of wind

Quantitatively, the direct action of wind is less significant than any other gradational agent. It affects unconsolidated materials where vegetation is sparse, as in dry deserts, or locally in humid regions where vegetation is absent, as on beaches, peripheral to glaciers, on exposed stream bottoms, and—unfortunately—on plowed

ground (Fig. 5-4). Wind's landforms are comparatively minor, and even deserts are largely sculptured by running water. Here the rare rains are torrential thunderstorms that radically modify the barren ground.

Blowing Sand and Dust Although wind can blow well over 100 miles an hour in a hurricane, it usually transports only dust and sand, and, at best, only pebbles, because the density of air is so low, 850 times less than that of water. Hence, wind is a good sorting mechanism that leaves larger particles behind as lag gravels, and carries away dust and sand. Blowing sand moves close to the ground, rarely over 6 feet above the surface. Some desert travellers, caught in sandstorms, have been engulfed in stinging sand to shoulder height while their heads were above the cloud.

Pioneering studies of sand movement and dunes were made in the Sahara, during the 1920's and 1930's, by Lt. Colonel R. A. Bagnold of the British Army. Later, he supplemented his desert observations, using a home-made wind tunnel. Bagnold found that sand moves mainly by a hopping or skipping motion, called saltation, wherein sand grains fly through the air, drop to the surface, and either carom into the

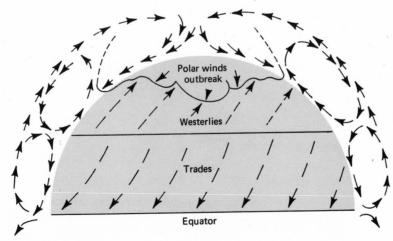

Fig. 5-3
Pattern of ideal wind belts as they would be if the earth's surface were homogeneous (that is, not diversified into land and water).

Fig. 5-4
Dust Bowl. Wind-blown soil trapped by obstruction on a deserted homestead. Soil Conservation Service photo by McLean.

air again, or hit other particles that take up the motion (Fig. 5-5). Over a pebbly surface, sand grains bounce to a maximum height; over a sheet of sand, they fly lower because their landings are cushioned by the loose grains. Here, the impact of saltating grains shoves the surface sand along in a slow surface creep.

The movement of dust, those particles finer than sand, is a different matter. Dust is transported to great heights and distances by the turbulence of winds and currents. In the drought of the 1930's, material from the Dust Bowl from Oklahoma to Colorado was carried to the New England states where it created a dirty cover on

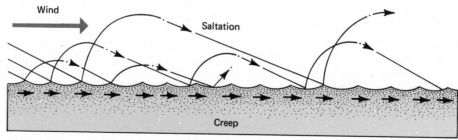

Fig. 5-5
Movement of wind-blown sand after R. A. Bagnold.

Fig. 5-6
House undermined by deflation of sand in Nebraska. U.S. Forest Service photo by C. A. Taylor.

Fig. 5-7
Wind-abraded sandstones near Tuba City, Arizona. Photo by Tad Nichols.

snow. In 1883, when the eruption of Krakatoa pulverized the volcano, dust rode up thousands of feet into the atmosphere on heated air currents to be carried completely around the world.

Erosional Landforms   Wind erodes by *deflation,* the blowing away of loose materials, and by *abrasion,* the natural sandblasting of rock surfaces (Figs. 5-6, 5-7). Deflation in the Dust Bowl stripped the valuable top soil, exposing the less fertile, but better consolidated *B* soil horizon beneath. The principal landforms of deflation are *deflation basins,* wind-scooped depressions ranging in size from a few feet to several miles in diameter. The Big Hollow just west of Laramie, Wyoming, is an elliptical deflation depression, 9 miles long, 2 miles wide, and as much as 120 feet deep.

Desert pavements are layers of closely fitted, polished pebbles often naturally cemented to give a resistant surface. They develop where fine materials are deflated, and the coarse pebbles that lag behind are jostled by wind into a tight mosaic. Once formed, such pavements armor desert floors from further extensive deflation (Fig. 5-8).

Wind-blown sand abrades most effectively a foot or two above the ground, a fact demonstrated by wind-carved notches or grooves on fence or telephone poles in sandy deserts. Above 3 feet the erosion is much less because the saltating grains reaching this height are too light to strike with much impact. Wind abrasion—natural sandblasting—forms relatively minor features. Hard rock surfaces may acquire *wind polish* resembling that on highly polished building stones. *Ventifacts,* wind-blasted pebbles and cobbles, have faceted surfaces that may join in sharp edges. *Yardangs* were first recognized in Chinese Turkistan, and have since been found in other deserts. They are sharp-crested ridges, or small flat mesas, separated by wind-scoured troughs. Yardangs range from a few inches to tens of feet in height, and develop in soft rock where wind blasts along the sides of pre-existing ridges.

Fig. 5-8
Desert pavement in Death Valley, California. Watch in center gives scale. Photo by John H. Maxson.

Depositional Landforms   Sand dunes are the most impressive landforms made by wind. Most dunes move slowly downwind, although some, which purists prefer to distinguish as sand drifts, remain stationary in the lee of fixed obstacles. Characteristically, dunes have a gentle windward slope and steeper leeward side, called the slip face, that averages about 33° or 34°. Sand blows up the windward side, across the crest, and spills down the slip face; thus, dunes migrate, because sand is progressively stripped from their windward face and deposited on the downwind side (Fig. 5-9).

Although dunes are most common in deserts, they can occur wherever vegetation on sandy materials is breached or absent (Fig. 5-10). Sand covers over 400,000 square miles of Arabia, a sizeable tract, but still only one third of that country's desert surface. In the Sahara, some 300,000 square miles are mantled by sand, which is a little over 10% of the total desert area. Thus, Hollywood movies to the contrary, deserts are not completely covered by sand. Smaller dune

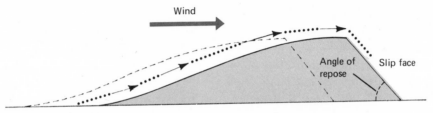

Fig. 5-9
Cross-section illustrating dune migration and position of slip face.

Fig. 5-10
Gleaming gypsum sands form over 140,000 acres of dunes, some 30 feet high, in the White Sands National Monument, New Mexico. Photo by Tad Nichols.

areas appear in humid regions along beaches, and in river bottoms of semi-arid lands.

The distinctive *barchans* are crescent-shaped dunes whose horns point downwind. They move slowly, from 25 to 50 feet a year, and may reach 100 feet in height, and, perhaps, 1000 feet in width. Barchans often occur in fields, or clusters, whose individual dunes are moving across bare rock surfaces (Fig. 5-11). *Transverse dunes* form in seas of sand where bedrock is completely buried. They resemble giant ripples or coalescing barchans whose crest lines are at right angles to the prevailing wind (Fig. 5-12). *Longitudinal dunes* are elongate in a downwind direction. They may be drifts in the lee of an obstacle, or true, free-moving dunes. They are locally abundant in the desert of the Little Colorado River and in a broad expanse of central

Australia. The Australian "sand ridges" average 40 feet in height, and may be hundreds of miles long. These dunes, lying about a quarter of a mile apart, are separated by rocky desert floor.

The *seif dunes,* named from the Arabic word for sword, are large spectacular features, originally described by Bagnold in the Libyan desert. They are complex dunes of irregular shape, as much as 700 feet high, three quarters of a mile wide, and 60 miles long. Chains of seif dunes may trail across the desert for several hundred miles. Fundamentally, seif dunes are great longitudinal dunes controlled by a prevailing wind, but modified by intermittent strong winds from other directions. All the dunes discussed so far are free dunes, little affected by vegetation.

The *parabolic dunes* resemble barchans in

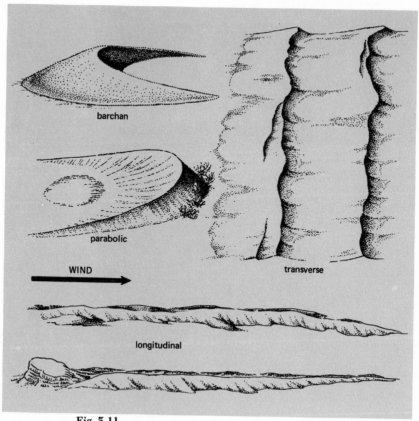

Fig. 5-11
Some types of sand dunes (not proportional in scale).

Fig. 5-12
Complex transverse dunes near Colorado River Delta, Sonora, Mexico. Photo by Tad Nichols.

being crescentic; however, the horns of parabolic dunes point upwind, and the steep slip face is on the outside of the crescent. These dunes are influenced by vegetation that partially anchors their sand. They originate around blowouts, where deflated sand is trapped by vegetation on the downwind side. Parabolic dunes sometimes acquire hairpin shapes, because the dune funnels the wind, so that sand moves most rapidly over the central part, while the sand in the horns lags behind.

A dominance of vegetation stabilizes dunes. The Sand Hills of western Nebraska, and adjacent states, covering some 18,000 square miles, are old dunes now anchored by grass. When dunes become stabilized by vegetation, soil eventually forms, and thereafter sheet wash and creep slowly reduce them. Regions, such as the Sand Hills, indicate a climatic change from more severe conditions associated with shifting sand in free dunes, to a more benevolent climate favoring a mantle of vegetation.

If the wind direction is fairly constant, the type of dunes developed are a function of three main factors: wind velocity, sand supply, and vegetation. Longitudinal dunes prevail where moderate-to-strong winds work on a relatively small sand supply. Barchans develop where both the wind velocity and sand supply are moderate. Transverse dunes form where sand is very abundant. Parabolic dunes reflect the influence of vegetation.

Fig. 5-13
Sea cliff near LeHavre, France. "The Cliff at Etretat" by Claude Monet. Courtesy of The Metropolitan Museum of Art, bequest of William Church Osborn, 1951.

Loess Loess is a deposit of wind-blown dust. Typically, it is a buff-colored, unlayered deposit of angular silt-sized particles consisting of various common minerals. Long-continued dust storms sweeping from barren source areas have deposited great loess blankets up to several hundred feet thick in downwind regions where the vegetation is adequate to hold the settling fine material in place. Some 200,000 square miles of the Mississippi Valley and its tributaries are underlain by loess. In eastern Washington, Alaska, southern Germany, Russia, and China, extensive areas of fertile soil are developed on loess.

The Chinese loess is derived from the Gobi Desert, and is carried eastward, to be deposited in the more fertile parts of the country by great dust storms that continue to the present day. The sources of loess, in the Mississippi Valley and Europe, were great barren areas traversed by meltwater streams, issuing from receding continental glaciers. Such loess deposits reflect a change to more amicable climates, during the fluctuating cold periods of the Ice Age.

WAVES AND SHORE PROCESSES

Coastal dwellers need not be convinced that the ocean shapes the edge of the land. Crashing storm waves topple cliffs, alter beaches, and destroy great concrete breakwaters. Even in fair weather the sight and sound of ordinary breakers, and the swash and backwash on a beach, suggest the timeless gnawing of waves upon the continental margins (Fig. 5-13).

Dynamics

Wind, blowing over standing water in oceans and lakes, initiates the waves responsible for the major sculpturing of the shores. Some waves are created by volcanic explosions and earthquake shocks on the ocean floor, and some currents are caused by tidal changes or different densities in water masses; but by and large, most coastal

modification is the work of waves that are generated by wind blowing across open water.

Waves of Oscillation The friction of moving air ripples a glassy sea. Pushed on their backsides and dragged along by air spilling over their crests, the ripples grow into waves. Waves are moving ridges in water. Their height is the vertical distance between a crest and the lowest point in an adjacent trough. Wave length is the distance between successive crests. Forced waves are actively impelled by wind. They may reach considerable heights during storms and travel hundreds or thousands of miles beyond their breeding grounds. Swells, breaking along a beach on a windless day, are free waves that may well have originated in a distant storm.

Although the shapes of waves rush across a water surface, the water particles do not. They move in orbits whose paths are shown by a floating cork (Fig. 5-14). With each orbit, the water particles make a slight advance beyond their starting point; that is, they drift downwind. Surface particles have the largest orbits, of a diameter equal to the wave height. Orbital motion dies out rapidly downward, being negligible at a depth equal to one half of a wave length. This depth, called wave base, is the lowest limit at

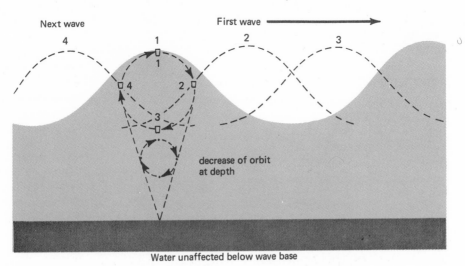

Next wave

First wave ⟶

4   1   2   3

decrease of orbit at depth

Water unaffected below wave base

Fig. 5-14 *Orbital motion in waves of oscillation.*

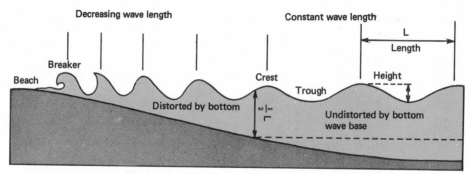

Fig. 5-15
Cross-section of waves breaking on a beach.

which wind-blown waves stir sediments on the sea floor.

Most of the geologic work of waves occurs where oscillatory waves move from open waters onto a shoaling bottom. As the water becomes shallower than wave base, the drag along the bottom causes wave lengths to decrease and the waves to steepen. At a critical point, the waves fall forward in breakers, sending masses of water surging onto the shore (Fig. 5-15). Erosion of hard rock results from the crashing impact and hydraulic pressure of the water masses, along with the abrasive grinding by gravel and boulders carried along as tools.

Wave Refraction Rugged, embayed coasts are strongly modified by wave refraction. Advancing waves are first slowed off promontories, where the shallow bottom projects further seaward, while wave fronts continue their unimpeded advance in the deeper waters of adjacent bays. As a result, the waves wrap around the headlands, and rise into powerful breakers, often 10 times higher than those in nearby bays. Thus, wave energy is concentrated in an attack on the headlands, while it is lessened in bays (Fig. 5-16). As a result, wave refraction straightens an initially irregular shoreline.

Beach Drifting Inside the line of breakers on a beach, water surging onto the beach as swash, and returning downslope in backwash, transports sand parallel to the water's edge when

waves strike the shore at an angle. The swash drives sand particles obliquely up the beach, and backwash receding directly downslope carries them straight towards the water's edge (Fig. 5-17). Thus, sand grains migrate laterally, in looping paths, along a beach.

The Longshore Current Outside the line of breakers, the longshore current moves sand along the ocean bottom (Fig. 5-18). The current

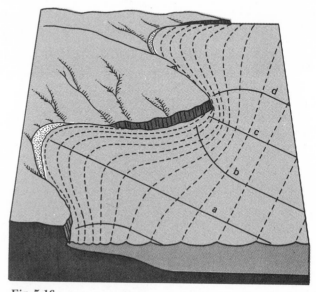

Fig. 5-16
Wave refraction on rugged shore. Dashed lines represent wave crest; solid lines a, b, c, d divide wave fronts into units of equal energy which concentrate on the headlands.

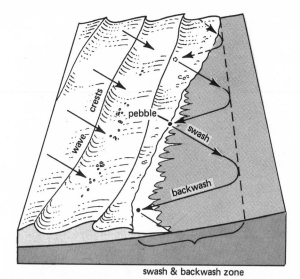

Fig. 5-17 *Beach drift.*

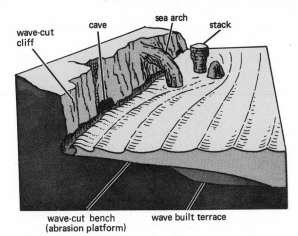

Fig. 5-19
Erosional features on a rugged cliffed coast.

originates when winds, blowing obliquely on-shore, create a slight "piling up" of water because its shoreward drift is impeded by the shoaling bottom. The excess water escapes by setting up a current parallel to the shore. The combination of beach drifting and the longshore current transports sand laterally along the shore, and thus is an important mechanism for extending beaches that lie against the land into sand bars which project into open waters.

Coastal topography

Erosional landforms Sea cliffs and abrasion platforms are the principal landforms cut on a steep coast. They appear on promontories of

embayed coasts where wave refraction is active; along straighter coasts they may extend for many miles, broken occasionally by estuaries. The evolution of cliffs and platforms begins when waves cut a small horizontal notch into a sloping shore. As the notch is eroded deeper, the land is undermined, producing a cliff of progressively increasing size. Accompanying the retreat of the cliffs, a platform is cut, at sea level or slightly above, in the zone of strongest wave attack. Wave action sweeps debris, carved from the land, across the expanding platform and deposits it off the lower end, thereby combining the wave-cut platform with a depositional, or wave-built, terrace.

Where the terrace is narrow, beach deposits are absent or temporary, being present when waves are running normally, but stripped away

Fig. 5-18 *Longshore current.*

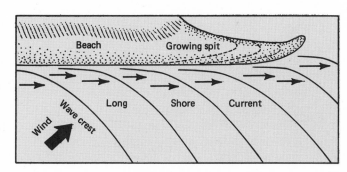

during storms. With widening of the platform by cut and fill, the energy of waves is consumed in friction across the shallow terrace; thus waves reaching the landward margin of the platform are weakened, allowing permanent beaches to develop.

The development of sea cliffs and wave platforms produces a variety of lesser landforms (Fig. 5-19). Hanging valleys form where the wave-attacked cliff recedes more rapidly than streams flowing to the shore can deepen their valleys. Sea caves result where waves, pounding on a cliff face, exploit fractures or other zones of weakness in the rock. Narrow headlands attacked on two sides may develop into sea arches, roughly resembling a flying buttress. Stacks, detached relics marking the former extent of a cliff, are pillar-like islands standing above the wave-cut platform (Fig. 5-20). Some result from the collapse of a sea arch.

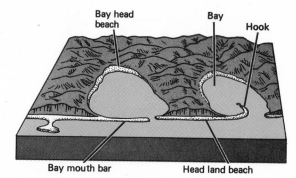

Fig. 5-21 *Depositional beach forms.*

Depositional Landforms Beaches, the most characteristic depositional landforms along a coast, consist of sand and, sometimes, wave-worn cobbles (Fig. 5-21). Technically, a beach lies along a coast, from the low-tide line, to an inland limit marking the highest point reached

Fig. 5-20
Stacks and island remnants along United States west coast. Courtesy of Chicago Museum of Natural History.

Fig. 5-22
The great spit with a smaller secondary one forming the tip of Cape Cod around Provincetown, Massachusetts. Photo by John S. Shelton.

by storm waves. A variety of sandy reefs extending from promontories into open waters are called spits, bars, and barriers. They are all, essentially, extensions of beaches whose sand has been transported parallel to the coast, by beach drifting and the longshore current.

Great offshore sand bars, or barrier beaches, characterize the eastern seaboard of the United States, where the near-flat coastal plain slopes gently out, beneath the sea (Fig. 5-23). The development has produced extensive protected lagoons and marshes lying between the barrier beaches and the shore (Fig. 5-23). The main source of material for these barrier beaches has long been controversial. Many seem to be composed of deposits drifted from headlands by beach drifting and the longshore current. However, some workers maintain that the material is largely scoured from the bottom, seaward from the barriers. The action of waves breaking well offshore could toss sand into submarine bars that

eventually build up above sea level. The barrier beaches off Cape Hatteras, being isolated islands, could have originated from bottom scour. On the other hand, it has been suggested that

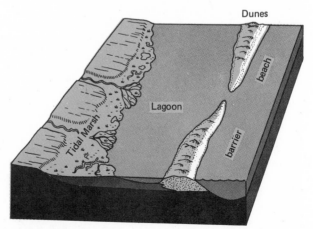

Fig. 5-23
Offshore bar as found along the Atlantic coastal plain.

they, too, were once headland bars, cut off from their original source by violent storm waves or a long-term rise in sea level.

Evidence of shifting shores

Once land forms at the water's edge are appreciated, similar features can be recognized, some of which are high and dry, and others drowned beneath the sea.

Emergent Features The coasts rimming the Pacific Ocean, and on its islands, are cut into giant steps (Fig. 5-24). The California coast near Santa Barbara, for instance, has 17 terraces, ranging from a few feet to a thousand feet above the present sea level. The lower terraces are clearly former wave-beveled platforms, preserving minor shore features such as stacks. The higher terraces are more stream-dissected, and partly masked with slope wash and stream deposits from higher slopes, but nonetheless are of marine origin (Fig. 5-25).

Ancient shorelines are also preserved along the broad, gentle, coastal plain of the eastern United States. The coastal terraces here are less obvious than those of the Pacific shores, for they are as much as 40 miles wide, and bounded by scarplets only a few feet high. Two such scarps, the outer one 20 to 30 feet above sea level, and the one further inland 90 to 100 feet above sea level, extend from New Jersey to Florida, thence westward along the Gulf Coast.

Abandoned shorelines are also common around inland seas and lakes as, for example, the Baltic Sea in Scandinavia, the Dead Sea in the Holy Land, the large lakes of East Africa, and the Great Lakes and Great Salt Lake in the United States.

Although emergent shore deposits, being largely unconsolidated, are less enduring than wave-cut features, elevated beaches, bars, and deltas are sometimes preserved. For example, Trail Ridge, four miles wide, 80 miles long, and 100 feet high, rises prominently above the generally flat plain of southern Georgia. Originating as an offshore bar in a former shallow sea, the ridge was built by the northward drift of sand, from islands in what is now north-central Florida.

Submergent Features Although drowned landforms are more difficult to locate and may be masked by later deposition, a number have been found. For instance, the Franklin "Shore" is a submerged scarp that can be traced at least 200 miles along the bottom, parallel to the present shoreline of the east coast of the United States. Terrestrial features, those made on dry land, have been drowned as well. Surveys of the ocean floor off Alaska, north of the Aleutian Islands, reveal submerged hills and valleys very similar to those on land. San Francisco Bay on the west coast and the Chesapeake and Delaware Bays on the east coast are estuaries, submerged valleys of stream systems that once flowed to more distant shores (Fig. 5-26). Drown-

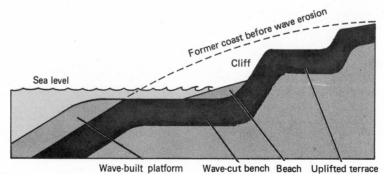

Fig. 5-24
Origin of emergent wave-cut terraces either from sea level changes or coastal deformation.

Fig. 5-25
Uplifted marine terraces in Palos Verdes, California. Courtesy Spence Air Photos.

ing of these main valleys dismembered the stream systems, so that their former tributaries now empty as separate rivers, directly into the salt water of the estuaries.

The marked shifting of the shore indicated by both emergent and drowned landforms has two possible causes: either the volume of the oceans, and that of inland lakes, has changed; or the water level has remained the same while the land itself has risen or subsided. In some instances, a combination of both is probable.

Worldwide fluctuations of sea level, called eustatic changes, are intimately related to the geologically late Ice Age. The water, locked in the former great continental ice caps, came originally from the reservoir of the oceans. Sea level fluctuated, falling in periods when the great glaciers expanded storing water on land, rising as the glaciers melted and their waters flowed back into the sea. The crust of the earth, as will be discussed in more detail later, is far from stable. In earthquake areas of active mountain making, such as the rim of the Pacific Ocean, the coastal rocks are, locally, rising and being depressed. In these restless areas, many shoreline terraces have been cut, then warped, so that traced any distance, the terraces have markedly different elevations above the present sea level. Around the Baltic Sea and Great Lakes, warped and elevated shorelines reflect the rise of land freed of its glacial load by the melting and disappearance of the continental ice caps.

Fig. 5-26
Drowned topography along the east side of Chesapeake Bay, Maryland. Photo by John S. Shelton.

Thus in late geologic time, whatever the cause, the topographic evidence indicates a continuous fluctuation of the shores. Crossbedding, fossils, and other marine features of sedimentary rocks also make it clear that, through much of geologic time, the continental interiors have been flooded by migrating seas far more extensive than those of the present day, and that shore processes are responsible for the characteristics of rocks, remote from existing seas.

SUGGESTED READINGS

Bagnold, R. A., *The Physics of Blown Sand and Desert Dunes* (reprint, Methuen and Co. Ltd., London, 1942).

Bascom, Willard, *Waves and Beaches.* Anchor Books (paperback) Doubleday and Co. Inc., Garden City, N.Y., 1964.

Russell, R. J., "Instability of Sea Level," in the *American Scientist*, Vol. 45, No. 5, pp. 414–430, 1957.

Sheppard, F. P., *Submarine Geology*, 2nd edition, New York, Harper & Row, 1963.

six: The hydrologic cycle

"All streams run to the sea, but the sea is not full. To the place where the streams flow, there they flow again." Whether the author of Ecclesiastes (1:7) envisioned a hydrologic cycle, we do not know. But the concept of a continuous circulation of water from the oceans to the land and back may date back to the Babylonians and certainly dates at least from 650 B.C. At that time, Thales, the Greek philosopher, proposed that sea water is driven into rocks by wind and pumped by the pressure of rock into the mountains where, emerging in springs feeding streams, it flows back to the sea. Subterranean passages and various ingenious explanations for desalting the water and forcing it into the mountains were later added to this basic scheme which, in a way, is still with us in the "underground water seams" of water witches.

The problems of salt and lift were avoided by Aristotle (384–322 B.C.) who, observing evaporation and condensation, held that heat from the sun changes water into air—which would leave salt behind in the sea—and that chilling changes air back into water. He attributed rain to the cooling of air, and observed that some percolates into the ground and some runs off in streams; however, the main nourishment of streams, he held, results from the conversion of air to water, in cool caverns inside mountains which act like great dripping sponges. Thus, Greek thinking contributed a cycle, evaporation and condensation; they erred in insisting that rain alone could not feed streams, and, despite the views of Aristotle, that rock is generally impervious to water.

Though the Greek theories dominated educated thought for well over 2000 years, there were dissenters whose views were essentially correct and modern. Marcus Vitruvius, in the time of Christ, Leonardo da Vinci (1452–1519), and Bernard Palissy, in the sixteenth century, all realized that precipitation infiltrates the ground and makes surface streams. Finally, the true path of the global water system was established in the seventeenth century, when grand theorizing was subjected to the test of careful measurement.

Pierre Perrault (1608–1680) determined the amount of water flowing down the Seine over a period of three years. For the same period, he calculated the volume of rain and snow falling on the slopes leading to the river by multiplying the average depth of precipitation by the ground area, which he had obtained from maps. Rain and snow had six times the volume of water discharged by the Seine. Edmè Mariettè (1620–1684) verified Perrault's findings, and further demonstrated that infiltration feeds springs. He showed that seepage into the cellar of the Paris Observatory corresponded to the rainfall. The English astronomer, Edmund Halley[1] (1656–1742), after experimenting with salt solutions, calculated that evaporation from the Mediterranean Sea could easily supply the water returning to it in streams. Although crude by modern standards, these various measurements established the proper mechanism of the hydrologic cycle.

Heated by the sun, water evaporates from the ocean surface as invisible vapor that mixes with

---

[1] Of Halley's comet fame.

Fig. 6-1
Falls of the Iguazu near the Argentine-Paraguayan border rival Niagara Falls. They are 200 feet high and 2 miles long. Photo by E. A. Carter.

the air above (Fig. 6-2). Vapor-ladened air moves inland in currents and winds, rising and expanding in the higher and thinner reaches of the atmosphere. Expansion causes cooling[2] that de-creases the air's ability to hold water vapor. When a certain temperature, the *dew point,* is reached, the air is saturated; further cooling expels water in liquid form, condensing it into countless minute droplets or, if the temperature is below freezing, ice crystals that form the visible clouds. As the cloud particles grow too

[2] Noticeable if the vapor from an aerosol spray touches your hand.

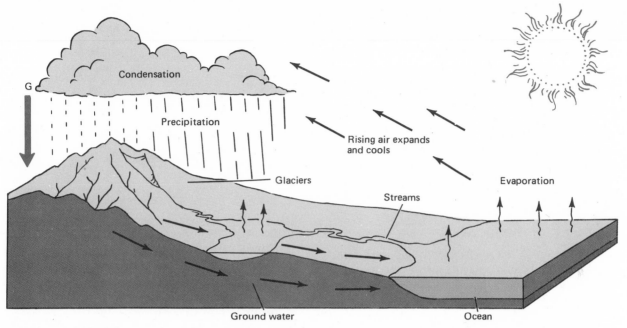

Fig. 6-2
Powered by the sun and gravity (G), the hydrologic cycle keeps water in constant circulation from ocean to land and back to the ocean again.

heavy to be held aloft on rising currents, gravity takes over and they fall as rain or snow.

Of the water reaching the ground, part evaporates or is transpired—used and given off as vapor by plants—returning to the cycle without ever reaching the sea. Part runs overland, in thin sheets that soon concentrate into the linear channels of streams, and part sinks to a level of saturated ground, forming a supply that nourishes springs and streams. This is the essence of the hydrologic cycle.

Although precipitation varies widely from place to place, overall budgets for the hydrologic cycle have now been estimated from a wealth of instrumental readings. The face of the continental United States, for example, receives 30 inches of precipitation each year, averaging data from all climatic zones. Of this total, 70% is recycled by evaporation and transpiration. The remaining 30% feeds streams, and replenishes one of our most important natural resources—ground water.

WATER IN THE GROUND

The economy of ground water, which we obtain from wells, is like a bank account. What goes in, and what comes out, determines the balance. In arid regions, such as parts of Arizona and California, with growing populations, swimming pools, air-conditioning units, and extensive irrigation, the ground-water situation is becoming acute. It might seem obvious that more water could be obtained by drilling more wells. But as more wells are drilled, the level at which water is obtained goes deeper. Deeper drilling chases the water table downwards, and with great depths, the return decreases. The water account dwindles because replacement comes only from rain and melting snow—a fact not appreciated by the many people of this modern day and age, who are ignorant of the nature of ground water and the hydrologic cycle.

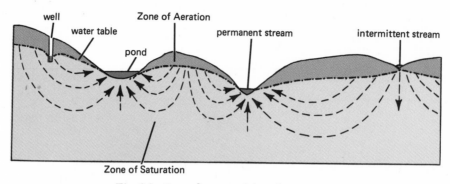

Fig. 6-3 *Groundwater zones and movement.*

Some general principles

Infiltration   If water is slowly poured into a bucket already filled with sand, up to a quarter of a bucket of water may disappear into the sand before water spills out. The water is stored in voids, the spaces between sand grains. *Porosity* is a measure of the total void space, and all mantle and bedrock in the upper two miles or so of the earth are porous to some degree, because of cracks, pores, and other minute channels. Rock porosity ranges from 1% or less, in granite, to well over one-third of the total volume of some clastic rocks. The ease with which ground water flows through rock, called *permeability*, is not a function of porosity alone. The kind of openings, their size, shape, and interconnections, determine permeability. Shale usually has a greater porosity than sandstone; however, it is far less permeable, because its voids are minute and poorly connected. Even dense, massive granite may transmit a fair amount of water if the rock is well fractured.

Ground-Water Zones   Studies of wells and other excavations indicate two main zones of ground water: an upper *zone of aeration* where voids are not completely saturated and considerable air is entrapped; and a lower *zone of saturation* whose pores are water-filled. The *water table* separating the two zones is generally a sloping surface, roughly parallel to the ground.

Water is moving beneath the ground, albeit slowly (Fig. 6-3). It normally sinks through the zone of aeration down to the water table, except in times of drought or in desert regions where capillary action may carry water up to the surface where it evaporates. The level of the water table fluctuates, as is evident in wells, in response to additions from infiltration and losses of water to the surface at springs, into stream bottoms, removed by plants, and pumped from wells.

The movement of water in the zone of saturation has been studied, in wells, by mapping water levels; i.e., introducing special dyes and waiting for their appearance in adjacent wells or springs. Ground water flows slowly, a few feet per day, or as little as a few feet per year. The direction of flow beneath the water table is not a simple downslope movement. Water migrates downward from the water table, in roughly curving paths that bend and rise into stream bottoms. Thus, deeper waters are replenished and replaced, and do not become stagnant.

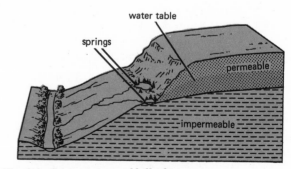

Fig. 6-4 *Common type of hillside spring.*

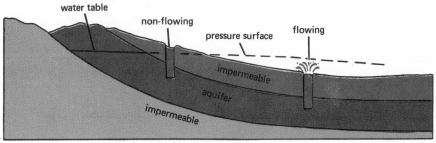

Fig. 6-5 *Elements of an artesian system.*

Water from the Ground Water seeps out wherever the water table is cut. A well, for instance, is a hole punched through the water table. Lakes and swamps fill basins intercepting the water table. Permanent streams, flowing year round, are nourished by ground water emerging in their channels, even when rain and surface runoff have long ceased. The channels of intermittent streams, which are periodically dry, lie above the water table. Thus, they carry water

Fig. 6-6
Mammoth Hot Springs of the Yellowstone. Baroque depositional forms deposited by hot springs charged with calcium carbonate. Photograph by the author.

only when directly fed by surface runoff from storms or melting snow, or when the water table temporarily rises to the channel level. In arid regions especially, water flowing in the channel may be lost by downward seepage to the water table.

Ordinary springs are natural seepages on a hillside. They appear where ground water is deflected to the surface along impermeable rock barriers or along fractured zones (Fig. 6-4). Pressure forces water to the surface in *artesian springs,* a special sort. They require special conditions: sloping strata containing an aquifer, or permeable rock layer, sandwiched between impermeable beds. Water entering such a system flows downward in an enclosed system and emerges under pressure, like water from a faucet in city waterpipes fed from an elevated tower. In both cases, the weight of water extending to the higher source gives a hydrostatic head that drives water through the confined system (Fig. 6-5).

Hot springs result where surface water descends to magma, or hot rock, at depth, and is then recirculated to the surface (Fig. 6-6). *Geysers*

are a spectacular variety of hot springs that periodically erupt boiling water and steam. They are common in the recently volcanic regions of New Zealand, Iceland, and Yellowstone Park in the United States. Geysers, according to the Bunsen theory, occur where ground water fills irregular systems of fissures and cracks in hot rocks. At depth, the higher pressure raises the water's boiling point. On slowly heating, the deeper waters expand and flush water out the geyser mouth, thereby reducing the weight of the water column. Pressure decreases, until the deep, superheated water flashes into steam, setting off an eruption that empties the fracture system. After the force is spent, water slowly seeps back into the geyser plumbing, and the whole process is eventually repeated.

Subterranean topography

The subterranean world is a realm of total darkness, containing permanent ice, labyrinths of baroque magnificence with flocks of bats, and underground pools and streams inhabited by

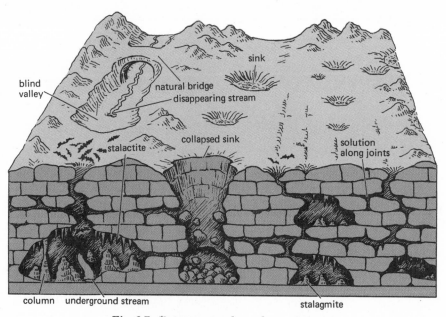

Fig. 6-7 *Karst topography and cave features.*

Fig. 6-8
Stalactites and stalagmites of Carlsbad Caverns, New Mexico. National Park Service photo.

blind fish and salamanders. Extensive caverns, with a few exceptions, are restricted to regions of limestone, a structurally strong rock which is, however, strongly susceptible to weathering by carbonation, in acidic ground waters filtering through its ever-present cracks. The Greeks, being familiar with such limestone caves, as-

sumed them typical of the whole underworld, and, as a result, arrived at their erroneous generalizations about the origins of springs and streams.

In humid climates, limestone develops a surface topography, known as karst, from a typical locality on the Adriatic Sea in Yugoslavia. Karsts, as in the Causses of France, and Yucatan in Mexico, contain dry valleys, holes called sinks, natural bridges, and disappearing streams that flow into sinks (Fig. 6-7). Downward seepage, and water moving slowly beneath the water table, corrodes out the cavern systems.

Limestone caves are ornamented by a variety of intriguing features, largely evaporation deposits of dripping water, highly charged with lime. Most impressive are stalactites, icicle-like limestone pendants from cavern roofs, and stalagmites,[3] mounds built beneath a dripping spot on the cavern floor. Stalagmites and stalactites may grow together, forming grooved and fluted columns (Fig. 6-8).

Because such dripstone features evidently formed in air-filled cavities, it has been proposed that caves are created by undergound streams, flowing above the water table. However, some caves, lined with sharp calcite crystals — resembling super-geodes — must have been water-filled when such crystals formed. Thus the origin of caves is still in doubt; locally one or the other theory may be correct, but as with many geologic problems, the answer, in many instances, may be a compromise involving elements of both.

[3] To help remember which is which: stalactite has a *c* for ceiling and stalagmite, a *g* for ground.

Fig. 6-9
The Grand Canyon of the Colorado River. Photo by J. H. Maxson.

John Playfair (1748–1819) Playfair, mathematician and phi-losopher at Edinburgh, demonstrated the erosional origin of valleys by streams in his Law of Accordant Junctions. An even greater contribution was his Illustrations of the Hut-tonian Theory of the Earth *in which he clearly restated and explained the brilliant ideas which might well have been lost in James Hutton's confusing and difficult style of writing.*

RIVERS

Grand Canyon is an awesome gash, a mile deep and more than 10 miles wide, cut through thick beds of colorful sedimentary rocks, forming cliffs and slopes that recede from a somber inner gorge of crystalline rocks. At the bottom the Colorado River is glimpsed as a tiny brown thread (Fig. 6-9). A park ranger, concluding his lecture to a group on the rim, called Grand Canyon "a monument to erosion by the Colorado River." One tourist asked, incredulously, "Do you really believe that little river cut that great big canyon?" The question echoes a debate between scientists in an earlier day. Do streams make their valleys, or are valleys created separately, and later occupied by streams?

In the eighteenth and nineteenth centuries, conservative geologists, defending the ruling doctrine of Catastrophism, believed valleys were formed suddenly, in tremendous floods or violent rendings of the ground. Streams then spilled into the newly formed valleys, which suffered little change thereafter. The opposing view, that most valleys are slowly excavated by their streams, represents the principle of Uniformitarianism, a cornerstone of modern geologic thinking. In 1802, **John Playfair,** friend and follower of Hutton, stated the Uniformitarian view in his Law of Accordant Stream Junctions. Its essence is that streams flow in valleys proportionate to their size, and that streams in a drainage network are so nicely adjusted to each other that their junctions are accordant, joining at the same level. This, he held, would be most unlikely, unless each valley was carved by the stream in it.

Gullies, tens of feet deep and hundreds of feet long, forming within a few generations, as well as the load of mud and gravel moving in turbid streams, do indicate the erosive power of running water (Fig. 6-10). But in fairness to the early Catastrophists, such indications are inadequate to account for a major valley like Grand Canyon —if the earth is only a few thousand years old, the age that theologians had established from Biblical research. The Uniformitarian philosophy demands an appreciation of the immensity of geologic time.

Stream systems

Rain striking the earth flows off in thin sheets that soon concentrate into linear rills on the uneven ground. Rills combine as brooks and creeks that feed rivers which, in turn, join in ever-enlarging streams.

Drainage Networks Most drainage networks are *dendritic,* having a tree-like pattern of a trunk river, with branching tributaries. Dendritic patterns characterize either near-horizontal layers, or homogeneous rock, of the same resistance to erosion throughout. In the *trellis* pattern, which resembles a lattice work, short tributaries are at right angles to long axial streams. This pattern prevails in eroded rock folds, where the main streams follow the axes of weak beds in valleys,

Fig. 6-10
In parts of Georgia, gullies such as these in Stewart County have expanded notably in a few generations threatening roads and farms.

and the short tributaries flow down the slopes of more resistant beds. The *rectangular* pattern has right-angle junctions like the trellis, but lacks dominant long trunk streams. Both tributaries and main streams have sharp bends along their courses. The pattern develops where streams are controlled by weak zones along fractured rock. A *radial* pattern of drainage characterizes streams flowing outward from the high point on a volcano or structural dome (Fig. 6-11).

Thus, the distinctive drainage patterns allow the prediction of bed rock and structure from ex-

amination of maps and air photos, before visiting a region on the ground. From the broader view of drainage systems, let us turn to the individual streams.

Stream Volume Stream discharge is the amount of water flowing through a cross-section of the channel in a given time, and is usually measured in cubic feet per second. Some streams have a constant discharge throughout the year; others are variable, commonly high in spring and low in fall; and some, especially in arid regions, are intermittent, flowing during, or immediately after, a rain or when fed by melting snow, but at other times being completely dry.

Climate controls the discharge of streams, both directly and indirectly. Expectably, relatively constant rainfall throughout the year tends to give streams a regular discharge, while periodic or seasonal rainfall leads to fluctuating flow. Climate also affects the ground-water nourishment of streams. In humid regions where the infiltration is great, high water tables slope towards and intersect stream channels. Continuous seep-

age into the channels insures a constant flow, even after many clear bright days. Water tables in arid regions are usually below the channel bottom. Streams flow intermittently when charged by surface runoff, but ground water adds nothing to sustain the stream between periods of rain. Here, water from the channel seeps down to the water table, diminishing the volume of the stream.

In well vegetated humid regions, streams have a more constant flow because plants impede sheet flooding, and encourage seepage to the

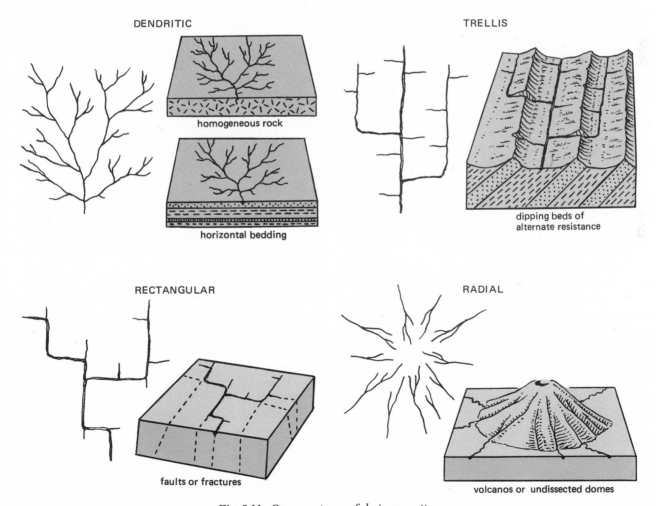

Fig. 6-11 *Common types of drainage patterns.*

Fig. 6-12
Removal of vegetation by over grazing of California range land caused this gullying, except in the spot protected by the oak tree. Rapid runoff during storms actively erodes the bare slopes. U.S. Forest Service photo by N. W. Talbot.

water table. Less water from storms or snow-melt runs overland, and more slowly soaks into the ground, to augment the streams in dry spells. On the barren slopes of desert regions, most rain runs off rapidly on the surface, swelling streams during storms, but adding little to the underground reserve (Fig. 6-12).

Rock also influences stream flow. Impervious clays and shales allow little infiltration, and cause flashy runoff, so that stream discharge is irregular or intermittent. Streams on permeable rock, such as sandstone, have a more constant

flow, since much of the rainfall penetrates the ground.

The Work of Streams The obvious function of streams is to drain the land; in the process, they act as the major gradational agent. Waves and currents work only on the continental margins. Wind erosion is limited by the low density of air and by protective covers of vegetation. Glaciers are restricted to cold regions of relatively abundant snowfall. Streams, however, dissect the ground, in deserts as well as in humid regions, from the arctic to the tropic climate zones. An estimated three million miles of channels, from rills to major rivers, scar the face of the continental United States.

Streams erode in three main ways, the first of which is by the force of moving water alone. Although this *hydraulic action* is most effective on loose material—sand, gravels, boulders, and clay—it also quarries large fractured blocks from solid bedrock (Fig. 6-14). In *abrasion,* which effectively erodes gorges in solid rock, a stream uses cobbles and boulders as tools, to pound and grind the channel deeper. *Corrosion,* the chemical solution of rock, is most important in eroding limestone and other soluble terrains.

The ability of a stream to transport is defined in two ways. *Capacity* refers to the total amount of a given size of material that a stream is capable of transporting. *Competence* relates to the largest particle that a stream can move. Thus, a mountain torrent capable of moving great boulders has high competence, yet if the stream is small, its capacity would be far less than a slower-flowing river, carrying a much greater total load.

Material moves along a channel bottom in the *bed load.* Larger fragments move by *traction,* a

Fig. 6-13
Hydraulic action during flood in Whatcom County, Washington, destroyed farm land and undermined this barn on the Ray Syre farm. Photograph courtesy of U.S.D.A. Soil Conservation Service.

Fig. 6-14
Boulders in Tantalus Creek corraded its channel. Photo by J. K. Hillers, photographer for Major John Wesley Powell, the first geologist to descend the Colorado River by boat. U.S. Geological Survey (National Archives).

dragging or rolling along the channel bottom. Some smaller material is transported in *saltation,* a hopping or jumping of particles along the stream's floor. It is the material carried as *suspended load* that gives a muddy look to a river. Fine sands and silts are held in *simple suspension* by the pulsing and swirling, characteristic of the turbulent flow of streams. Clays, the finest clastic particles, travel in *colloidal suspension,* held aloft by the constant jostling of water molecules (Brownian movement) which never ceases even in still, standing waters. The finest particles of all, the invisible ions dissolved from rock, are transported in *solution.*

Bed load and the suspended sands and silts are deposited when the velocity of flow decreases, as when a mountain torrent emerges on a flatter valley floor, or when stream flow is completely checked by flowing into the standing water of ponds, lakes, or the oceans. When a stream recedes from flood, the gradual decrease in velocity tends to sort clastic material, because coarser particles drop out first, and progressively finer materials settle in the higher layers.

Colloidal material settles by the process of *flocculation.* Clay particles remain suspended, in fresh water, because each miniscule particle carries a negative electric charge. Since like charges repel each other, clays remain dispersed. But on entering the sea, they are neutralized by positive charges in the salt water. No longer repelling each other, the clay particles come together, or flocculate, forming clots that sink to the bottom.

Dissolved substances remain in solution, adding to the saltiness of lakes with no outlets and, on a grander scale, to the salt of the sea. However, when water is completely evaporated, ions deposit in a salt crust. Salts may also be precipitated from concentrated solutions by changes in temperature, or other physical-chemical conditions, before evaporation is complete. Some ions are extracted from the water by animals like clams, oysters, and coral, that convert them into relatively insoluble shell materials, a major constituent of many limestones.

The Well-Adjusted Stream To attribute human qualities to other things is anthropomorphism, which is frowned on in proper scientific circles. Yet, in their dynamic action, streams show one almost human quality. They tend to do their job with the least possible work—a condition of equilibrium characterizing graded streams, whose capacity is nicely balanced with the load they transport. Normally, however, no stream remains in perfect equilibrium. In floods, the increased velocity and discharge give a stream excess energy to scour and deepen its channel while in low-water stages it deposits along the channel bottom. Thus a graded stream is like a

tight-rope walker, out of balance in one direction and then the other, but keeping a general equilibrium.

The long profile of a stream, from mouth to source, has many local irregularities, yet, overall, it approaches a concave curve of increasing steepness upstream (Fig. 6-15). Why should the profile steepen if the stream is generally adjusted along its length? Of the many complex factors involved, three seem most important. The Mississippi, and other rivers as well, shows a progressive downstream decrease in the size of particles transported. Streams have a greater capacity for fine material than coarse; therefore, a lesser gradient should suffice to keep the stream in balance. Also, the discharge of a river increases downstream, as the number of its tributaries grows.

Careful measurements show that downstream velocities remain constant or even increase, which is surprising, for water should logically flow more slowly in a gentler channel gradient. The key to the paradox lies in the number, shape, and size of channels. When small tributaries unite in a single channel, the water surfaces are accordant; however, the single, large channel is deeper.[4] The frictional drag on flowing water is proportionately less, because a single, deep channel carries water more efficiently than several small ones. Hence, the combined water volume continues flowing at the same rate, or even accelerating, on the gentler gradient, and its

[4] It is apt to be much wider, too, but this does not seem to have such a direct connection.

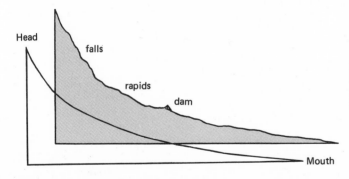

Fig. 6-15
Idealized long profile of a stream from source to mouth represented by the smooth curve as compared to the less regular profile found in actual streams.

Fig. 6-16
Photograph shows the erosion protection given by rocks, twigs, and leaves on the ground. Each rock, leaf, and twig is supported by a little pedestal of dirt. The surrounding soil has been washed away by rain. South Portal Canyon, Saugus District, Angeles National Forest, California. Taken by L. E. Berriman, August, 1954.

capacity remains adequate for the overall load.

Most graded streams have been disturbed at some time in their history. Of the various possible causes, a change in load is often important. Increased load commonly results from weakening or destruction of vegetation by forest fires, excessive timbering, improper farming, and other geologically short-term factors. Accelerated erosion on the unprotected slopes supplies an overload to streams in the affected part of a basin. The ultimate return of vegetation would reverse the process (Fig. 6-16). The effects of climatic fluctuations, which have been pro-

nounced in the last million years of earth history, are most important, widespread, and long-lasting. Such changes not only alter vegetational patterns, but may markedly upset streams by increasing or decreasing their discharge.

Overloading of a graded stream starts a sequence of cause and effect that eventually leads to a new and more steeply graded profile. A stream whose capacity is exceeded deposits the extra load, back-filling its channel and the valley bottom. As the channel steepens, the stream flows faster, and its capacity increases. The increasing capacity eventually comes in balance with the load again, in a more steeply graded profile. A decrease in load leaves a once-graded stream with excess energy for downcutting. As the channel deepens, its gradient decreases. As a result, the stream's velocity and capacity also decrease, until equilibrium with the lesser load is achieved in a new, graded profile, downcut to a less steep gradient.

The dynamic behavior of streams is a matter of practical importance. For example, when the

Hoover Dam was completed in 1935, it upset the equilibrium of the Colorado River. Flowing through a desert, the Colorado is a heavily loaded stream that deposits a delta on entering artificial Lake Mead. As was anticipated in the planning, the growing deltaic deposits will ultimately fill the lake — in 400 years by a recent estimate — ending the dam's usefulness. The dam, however, will more than pay its cost through the sale of electrical power. The water returned to the chan-

Fig. 6-17
The Canyon of the Yellowstone River shows a youthful stream marked by a steep V-shaped valley, falls and rapids. Geological Survey photo taken in 1871 by W. H. Jackson (National Archives).

nel behind the dam is clear, its sediments trapped in Lake Mead. Freed of its load, the Colorado River deepened its channel from 2 to 6 feet, for a distance of 10 miles downstream, within 6 months of the dam's completion. Thereafter, the scouring lessened as a newly graded profile was approached. In other cases, where irrigation water comes directly from a river below a dam, channel deepening has economic consequences: irrigation becomes expensive, if pumps must be installed to lift water into a ditch system.

Stream sculpture

A landscape is a mosaic of smaller forms of two genetic types: erosional features carved in bedrock, and depositional ones built from rock debris.

Erosional Landforms Valleys are cut by streams, yet, if streams were the only process involved, all valleys would be vertical slots, since a stream channel, like a saw, works only in the valley bottom. The familiar retreating slopes of valley walls result from weathering, mass movements, and sheet wash, all of which supply part of a stream's load. Throughout their evolution, streams both deepen and widen the valley bottoms. The importance of vertical or lateral cutting varies, however, with a stream's phase of development.

Before reaching the "well-adjusted" condition of equilibrium, the stream has waterfalls and rapids, and excess energy that is largely devoted to downcutting. In this phase, valley walls slope directly to the channel, giving a V-shaped cross profile (Fig. 6-17). On reaching equilibrium, the

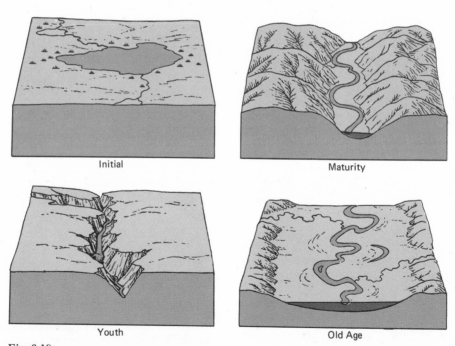

Initial

Maturity

Youth

Old Age

Fig. 6-18
Stream evolution described in stages of a "life" cycle. Initial stage lacks a valley, has swamps and ponds. In youth, downcutting produced a valley and eliminated swamps and ponds as it drains more efficiently. The mature stage has a continuous flood plain indicating the dominance of lateral cutting when stream achieves equilibrium. The stream cycle has reached old age when the flood plain is very broad and marked by abandoned river meanders forming ox-bow lakes.

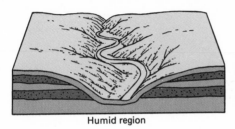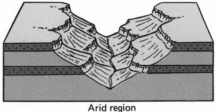

Humid region   Arid region

Fig. 6-19
The softer slopes of valleys mantled by soil in humid regions, whatever the underlying strata, contrast with the sharper outlines of arid canyons especially where rocks have differing resistance to erosion.

marked irregularities in the channel disappear; the stream is graded, its load matching its capacity. The stream may still downcut slowly, but these effects are masked by the now-dominant lateral cutting that undermines the valley walls, creating a flat-floored valley bottom. This low, flat strip, inundated at high water, is a flood plain, and is commonly floored by alluvium. The flood plain is a narrow strip in its early evolution, but, with time, it characteristically broadens considerably through the retreat of valley walls (Fig. 6-18).

Valley walls in humid regions are smooth slopes because thick soil and waste mantle, anchored by abundant vegetation, mask inequalities in the resistance of underlying rock. The canyon walls of arid regions commonly have step-like outlines, with cliffs of resistant strata, like sandstones and lava flows, that alternate with gentler slopes on softer beds, such as shale (Fig. 6-19).

Widespread · erosion of near-horizontal rock layers, some hard and some soft, produces *mesas* and *buttes* (Figs. 6-20, 6-21). A mesa[5] is a flat-topped hill, usually capped by a resistant layer that often protects weaker rocks beneath. A butte is simply a smaller residual pinnacle, lacking an extensive flat top (Fig. 6-22). *Hogbacks,* or homoclinal ridges, are the typical erosional landforms developing on tilted strata of alternate resistance (Fig. 6-23). They are common where mountain-

building forces have buckled rocks into folded structures. *Water gaps* are notches cut through hogbacks by streams; *wind gaps*, despite their name, have a similar origin, but have been abandoned by their parent stream.

The *pediments* of arid regions are smooth surfaces beveled impartially across hard and soft bedrock. They slope gently away from an angular junction at a mountain foot, and are usually blanketed by gravels that are thin, or absent, along the mountain front, but thicken considerably into adjacent valleys (Fig. 6-24). Though conspicuous desert landforms, the origin of pediments is still in question. According to one hypothesis, they develop through lateral planation, where streams emerging from a mountain valley are so nicely balanced that they neither downcut nor deposit extensively. Rather, they swing back and forth, carving the pediment by undercutting the mountain front.

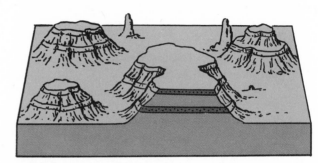

Fig. 6-20 *Mesas and buttes.*

[5] The word in Spanish means table.

Fig. 6-21
1822 lithograph by Carey and Lee, showing mesas just east of the Rocky Mountain front. Courtesy of the Library of Congress.

Depositional Landforms Unlike the erosional features carved into bedrock, depositional landforms are built from unconsolidated materials, the load being dropped by streams when their capacity is reduced.

Where streams flow into standing water, *deltas* of various shapes develop. The delta of the Nile is arcuate, roughly triangular in plan view, suggesting on a grand scale the Greek letter from which all these landforms are named. The Mississippi delta with its projecting fingers exemplifies the bird-foot, or lobate, type. The Tiber delta, a less common variety, is cuspate, suggesting a sharp tooth. Estuarine deltas, such as the one at the mouth of the River Seine, are confined by narrow bays (Fig. 6-25).

The shape of a delta is influenced by many factors, including the configuration of the shore, the material being deposited, and the action of shore processes. Arcuate and cuspate deltas reflect the deposition of loose sandy material, which is readily reworked by waves and shore currents. The intricate bird-foot deltas that develop usually contain much flocculated clay, which is relatively tough and cohesive. Where a river empties into a narrow bay, the outline of the shore becomes the major factor in producing the estuarine type of delta.

Alluvial fans are aprons of stream debris laid down where canyons open onto a broader valley floor (Fig. 6-26). Deposition here results from the decrease in a stream's velocity and capacity on

Fig. 6-22
Monument Valley in the Colorado Plateau along the Utah-Arizona state line.

reaching a more gently sloping floor. Since the stream's position is fixed in the valley, but free to migrate on the flat beyond, it swings back and forth, building the fan-shaped deposit of alluvium.

Flood Plains The most characteristic depositional landform of graded streams, flood plains, contain a wealth of associated features (Fig. 6-27). Although most streams are sinuous to some degree, those on flood plains often have meanders,

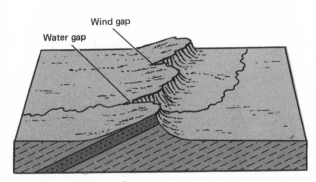

Fig. 6-23 *Hogback ridge.*

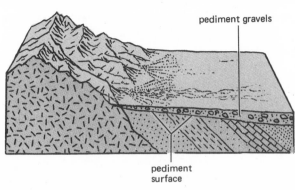

Fig. 6-24 *Pediment.*

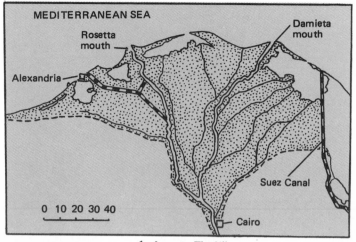

1. Arcuate: The Nile

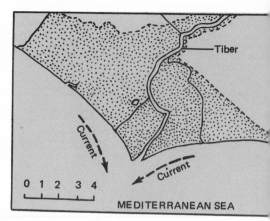

3. Cuspate: The Tiber

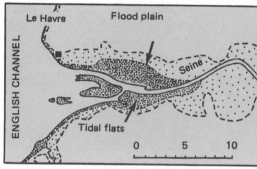

4. Estuarine: The Seine

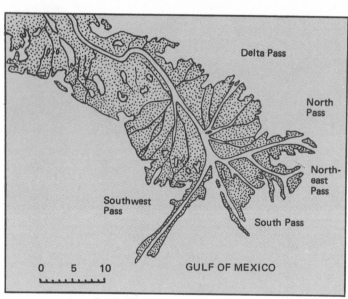

2. Birdfoot or Lobate: The Mississippi

Fig. 6-25
Types of deltas: arcuate, lobate, cuspate, and estuarine. Scales in miles.

symmetrical bends that shift and grow. Like many other geologic phenomena, the commonplace meandering is not easily explained. It has been described in great detail, without leading to general agreement concerning its cause.

Studies by the Mississippi River Commission, using very large models, suggest that streams meander because they flow in easily eroded material, which would be mostly alluvium. Observations indicate that slight bends in a channel throw the strongest thread of current against the outside bank. Caving, along this bank, supplies material that moves a short distance down the same side of the channel, and is then deposited,

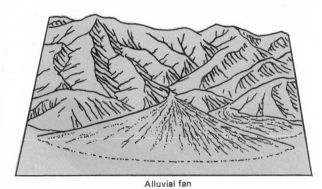

Fig. 6-26 *Alluvial fan.*

by undercutting their outer banks, while depositing in the slack water on the inside of the bend, where they build a gradual "slip-off" slope, or point bar.

Reasonable as the mechanism seems, it may not be the whole answer, because streams flowing on glacial ice, where there is no bank caving, also meander. A theory that accounts for such meandering, and perhaps meandering in general, dates from the late nineteenth century. Water has a helical, or "corkscrew," flow in bends because the more rapidly flowing surface water is thrown to the outside of a bend by centrifugal force, causing a slightly higher water level there. Water on the channel bottom is displaced towards the inside of the bend. As a result, material eroded in the more turbulent and faster-flowing outer side of the bend moves toward the inside of

thus deflecting the current there against the opposite bank, which is in turn undermined, as the process is repeated down the course of the channel. Once started, the meanders expand laterally

Fig. 6-27
Meandering course of the Laramie River across a flood plain marked by the scars of older abandoned meanders. U.S.G.S. photo by J. R. Balsley.

the bend, where it settles out in the quieter water, thus building the point bar. This mechanism may be a more general explanation, for it accounts for meandering in wide and relatively shallow rivers where the banks are far apart.

Whatever their basic cause, meanders do not grow indefinitely, for as they expand, the neck of land projecting into the bend is narrowed. Eventually a short-cut forms, either when flood waters jump the neck forming a channel in which the stream remains, or the neck is gradually cut through by bank erosion on either side. Once formed, the shorter route through the cutoff gives the channel a steeper gradient. This increases the stream's velocity and, consequently, bank erosion downstream, encouraging the growth of a new meander. *Oxbow lakes* are abandoned meanders, whose mouths are gradually sealed off by silt and mud expelled from the faster-flowing water in the new cutoff. Overall, a meandering stream keeps a relatively constant length, and a graded profile, because meander growth is balanced by cutoffs (Fig. 6-28).

The Regional Erosion Cycle Individual landforms are existing details in a broader, and—in the perspective of geologic time—ever-changing scene. The regional erosion cycle, proposed by William Morris Davis (1850–1934) of Harvard, is the most complete presentation of the concept that a landscape gradually evolves through time. A cycle begins with an uplift, caused by mountain-making forces within the earth, and streams start downcutting. Through time, the affected land mass is worn down through a distinctive sequence of stages, culminating in a *peneplain*, a low rolling surface of broad extent near sea level (Fig. 6-29).

Early development, the stage of *youth*, is characterized by high, flat areas, remnants of the uplifted surface between deepening valleys. The region stands high, and much rock must be removed before the cycle is completed. As time goes on, valleys deepen, and the land mass becomes more intricately dissected, as the upland flats are gradually destroyed.

A region in the *mature stage* is largely cut into

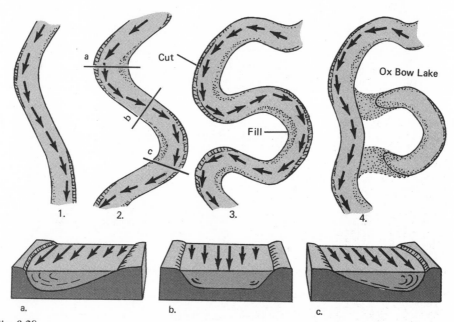

Fig. 6-28

Meander development, ending with the creation of an oxbow lake. Arrows in drawings 1–4 show thread of fastest current. Overall water movement is shown by arrows on cross-sections a, b, and c, location of which are marked on drawing 2.

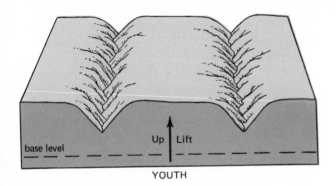

YOUTH

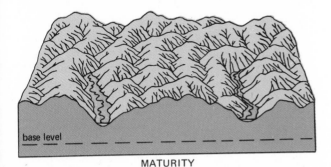

MATURITY

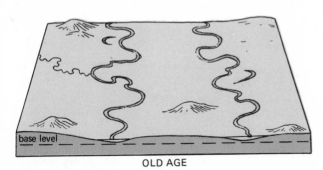

OLD AGE

Fig. 6-29
Diagrams of Davis' Regional Erosion Cycle in an area of homogeneous rock.

slopes, the original high flat has disappeared, relief is at a maximum, and in general the scenery is most rugged. Landslides and other mass movements are active on steep valley walls. As time progresses, the relief decreases and low flats—flood plains—appear in valley bottoms.

Subdued topography distinguishes the *old-age stage.* Broad valleys are floored with thick

alluvium in flood plains, whose meandering streams lower the land at exceedingly slow rates. The bedrock in the subdued divides, between stream valleys, is deeply weathered. Low hills, called *monadnocks,* after the mountain in southern New Hampshire, are scattered relics of the once impressive mountains. Eventually the surface becomes a peneplain, near sea level, the ultimate base level to which streams can erode the land.

At any stage, renewed uplift may set the cycle back. The result is a complex landscape, marked by landforms of disturbed streams, and features of both cycles, until the rejuvenated streams finally obliterate the last vestiges of the earlier cycle.

The concept of the erosion cycle is most valuable in bringing home the gradual evolution of a land mass, in Uniformitarian terms, through the constant flow of water in the hydrologic cycle. Moreover it is very useful in classification, for youth, maturity, and old age are terms that create a strong visual image of topography, without resort to detailed and often tedious empirical descriptions which treat every landscape as if it were somehow different from all others. Yet the Davis concept has been criticized generally in recent times, in part because it is an oversimplification, a nice device for elementary teaching—which it is—but also, because it is hard to apply to actual topography. Most landscapes have had a far more complex history than the scheme suggests. Certainly, as Davis realized, a relatively rapid initial uplift of the earth's crust, followed by an unbroken period of standstill, is most unlikely, because nowhere is the crust completely stable, and certainly not in regions of mountain-building, which is a prolonged process. Some geologists object to the scheme's pronounced anthropomorphism.

A different model of regional development, recently proposed by John T. Hack and others, envisions topography as rapidly adjusting to differences in the bedrock of uplifted masses. Thereafter, the landscape changes little in form because a dynamic equilibrium exists between material being supplied to streams by weathering and mass movement and the materials being carried away. Thus, a "mature" topography of the Davis cycle develops in resistant rocks whose coarse debris requires steep slopes for its removal. "Old" topography develops on shales and other soft rocks whose fine debris can be moved on gentle slopes by streams of low gradient. Unlike the Davis scheme of the continuous gradual change in landscapes, dynamic equilibrium, once established, produces continuous removal of material without gradual evolution of a region through various different stages. Since rugged mountains and broad lowlands in uplifted regions often appear adjusted to the type of bedrock, the dynamic equilibrium theory seems a better model than the regional erosion cycle.

Landforms of Disturbed Streams Many landforms record events in earth history that have interrupted the steady gradation of the crust by external processes. Uplifted and submerged shore features are of this sort, and so are various erosional and depositional landforms of streams. Some, being carved in hard rock, are relatively long lasting, and many record older events; others in unconsolidated alluvium are less permanent, but are more sensitive indicators of the effects of climatic change on streams.

Terraces in general are step-like surfaces; flat bench-like strips bounded on one side by a steeply rising slope, and on the other by a steeply descending slope (Fig. 6-30). They may be developed in bedrock or unconsolidated materials, and are common on many coasts, mountain

Fig. 6-30
Terraces along the Madison River Valley, Montana, just west of Madison Gorge. U.S. Geological Survey photo by J. R. Stacy.

Fig. 6-31
Structural terraces developed in near-horizontal rocks of alternate resistance. Grand Canyon from Desert View, South Rim. U.S. Forest Service photo by B. W. Muir.

Fig. 6-32
Cyclic terraces cut in resistant rock.

fronts, and valley walls. They have many origins. Some stream-made terraces, such as the cliffs and broader slopes, in hard and soft rock layers of barren canyon walls, result from continuous downcutting (Fig. 6-31); but others, not structurally controlled, indicate dynamic changes in streams.

Cyclic terraces, cut in homogeneous resistant rock, give a "valley-in-valley" cross profile in many mountain regions. They form when a stream, flowing in a broad-floored valley, is rejuvenated and cuts a V-shaped inner valley, above which the flatter terrace tread is a remnant of the original valley floor. Cyclic rock terraces indicate that after a region was uplifted, it remained generally stable long enough for a stream to reach the equilibrium, or graded, stage, and form a broad-floored valley. Then, later uplift set the stream to downcutting again, which initiated the inner valley (Fig. 6-32).

Entrenched meanders may also indicate rejuvenation wherein a stream at equilibrium, and meandering broadly on a flood plain, has been disturbed. As a result, a winding V-shaped valley

is incised along the old meander course (Fig. 6-33).

Alluvial landforms of disturbed streams normally record a history of alternate cutting and filling. Flood plains with thin or moderately thick alluvium are a normal feature of valley widening by graded streams; however, many flood plains, from those of nameless creeks to rivers as large as the Mississippi, have deep alluvial fills recording a history of major upsets in normal stream development. These flood plains indicate periods of aggradation, i.e., backfilling of a valley by overloaded streams. On an aggrading flood plain, streams commonly have a braided pattern of many small channels that split and join, because they are constantly being clogged and diverted by excess debris.

Alluvial terraces usually record at least three main geologic events. First, a stream downcuts to form a valley; next, the stream becomes overloaded and back-fills the valley, forming a thick flood plain; finally, the stream returns to normal downcutting, and starts excavating the alluvial fill. Remnants of the thick flood plain now be-

Fig. 6-33
Gooseneck of the San Juan River. Photo of entrenched meander by J. H. Maxson.

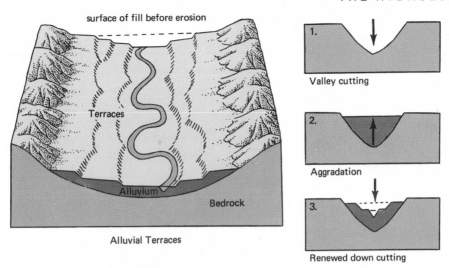

Fig. 6-34
General sequence in creating alluvial terraces.

come terrace surfaces, on either side of the downcutting stream (Fig. 6-34).

Unpaired terraces, which lie at different levels along opposing valley walls, develop during uninterrupted downcutting by a stream into the alluvium. Each terrace surface represents a former level of the river, as the whole channel migrates back and forth across the valley, while it cuts progressively deeper into the fill. *Paired terraces*, whose surfaces have comparable levels on both sides of a valley, have two general origins. They may represent spasmodic downcutting, in which case they are similar to cyclic

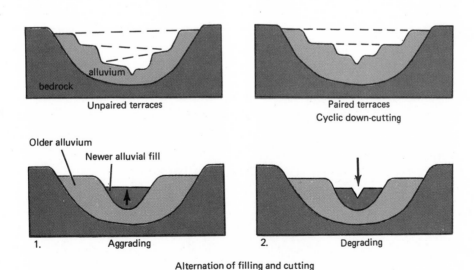

Fig. 6-35
Unpaired terraces and two possible origins for paired terraces.

rock terraces, except for the unconsolidated material in which they are formed (Fig. 6-35).

In other cases, however, paired terraces are formed by several alternations of downcutting and back-filling, a repetition of the three-fold sequence of events producing alluvial terraces. In other words, a stream cuts a valley into its alluvium, until its equilibrium is again upset and it commences to back-fill again, creating a younger aggrading flood plain within the valley in alluvium; if the stream once more returns to downcutting, the surface of the younger flood plain becomes a terrace. Many rivers, especially in the western United States, have a series of such terraces that result from recurrent changes in regional vegetation, stream discharge, and load. These terrace-making changes are in turn the results of a more basic cause—the marked fluctuations of climate during the last million years of earth history, the time of the most recent Ice Age.

Fig. 6-36
Glacial tongues pouring from the ice-locked heart of Greenland. (U.S. Air Force photo, by permission of the Royal Danish Navy.)

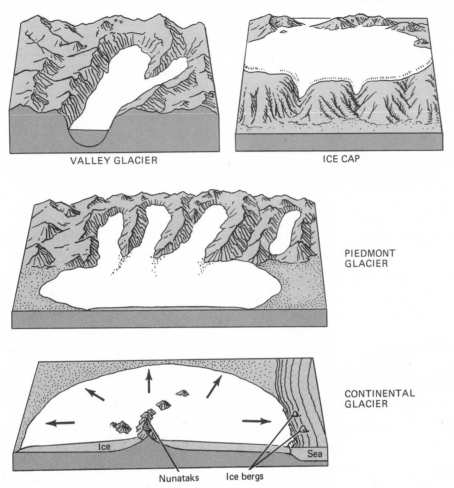

VALLEY GLACIER

ICE CAP

PIEDMONT GLACIER

CONTINENTAL GLACIER

Ice

Sea

Nunataks   Ice bergs

Fig. 6-37
Kinds of glaciers, not to the same scale. The valley glacier might be one or two miles wide whereas the continental glacier would cover hundreds of thousands of square miles.

ICE ON LAND

We live in an Ice Age, a mild phase but, nonetheless, an Ice Age. Today 10% of the earth's land surface, almost six million square miles, lies under glacial ice. The largest part is in the inhospitable Antarctic, much of the rest is in Greenland, and the remainder is widely scattered in high mountains more noted for their scenery than population (Fig. 6-36). In the not too distant past, in a time called Pleistocene, 30% of the land, about 18 million square miles, was blanketed by creeping ice caps that rasped and gouged bedrock, dumping their debris around their fluctuating margins in ill-sorted bouldery ridges. One great glacier buried North America as far south as the Missouri and Ohio Rivers; another spread over most of northern Europe and part of Siberia. Were such glaciers to come again, Moscow, Dublin, New York, Chicago, and many other major cities would be overwhelmed. Far beyond the ice, streams were upset, alternately back-filling and downcutting. Modern deserts were hospitable when the now-populous regions

123

lay under the ice. Sea level fluctuated, from 100 feet above to 300 feet below its present elevation, because water moving through the hydrologic cycle was alternately locked in ice on land, and then released to the ocean as glaciers waxed and waned.

Some glaciology

A glacier is a large mass of flowing ice that originates on land from recrystallized snow. Thus, the ice surrounding the North Pole is not a glacier but, rather, the frozen Arctic Ocean, as the passage of nuclear submarines beneath the Pole has demonstrated.

Kinds of Glaciers The shape of a glacier is controlled by the topography over which it flows and the thickness of the ice (Fig. 6-37). *Valley glaciers* are narrow tongues, hemmed in by the valley walls of mountainous regions (Fig. 6-38). *Ice sheets* develop where relief is slight, or the ice buries topographic irregularities. They may be *high-level ice sheets*, where they spread across plateau-like surfaces until concentrating in marginal valleys. *Piedmont glaciers*, such as the Malaspina glacier in Alaska, form where valley glaciers, emerging on broad flats at the foot of mountains, spread and merge in a broad sheet. The two existing *Continental glaciers*, the

Fig. 6-38
A main valley glacier joined by two tributary valley glaciers. South Sawyer Glacier, Alaska. U.S. Forest Service photo by L. J. Prater.

Fig. 6-39
View toward the interior of Greenland showing the margin of the continental glacier. U.S. Air Force photo, by permission of the Royal Danish Navy.

Greenland ice cap, over one-half million square miles in area, and the much larger Antarctic sheet, of about five million square miles, bury all but the highest mountain peaks beneath ice up to 2 miles thick (Fig. 6-39).

The Origin of Glacial Ice Glaciers form where winter snowfall exceeds the summer losses from melting and evaporation over a long period of time. As a result, each year a layer of snow survives and is added to that below (Fig. 6-40). Newly fallen snowflakes are delicate, feathery ice crystals. With time, the flakes lose their sharp, intricate outlines as water molecules melt from the edges, then migrate towards the center of the crystal and refreeze. Eventually, the snowflakes become grains of ice, called firn or névé. As the mass thickens, the weight of

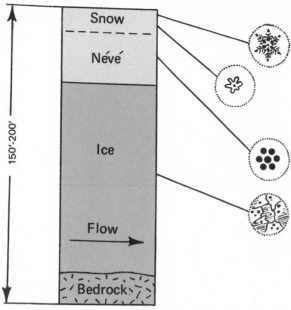

Fig. 6-40
Formation of glacial ice from snow. Thickness of zones is not to scale.

the accumulation compacts the loose névé, and expels air to form solid crystalline ice. When the ice reaches a thickness of about 150 feet, its static weight squeezes out the lower ice, causing it to flow as a glacier. The upper brittle part of a glacier is broken by large cracks, or crevasses, which close and disappear at the depth of flowage.

Macabre evidence that ice flows was provided by some unlucky mountaineers who fell into crevasses of glaciers in the Alps. Some 40 years later their remains appeared at the glacier's end, several miles down the valley. As evidence of flowage, however, boulders from distinctive outcrops will do as well. The plastic flowage of solid ice is thought to result from slippage along minute atomic planes, within the individual ice crystals, so that the motion is somewhat like the slippage in a tilted deck of cards. In valley glaciers, the flow is gravitational down the sloping floors; in continental glaciers the static weight of overlying ice apparently squeezes the deeper ice out over sometimes flat, sometimes uneven rock floors.

Glacial movement is exceedingly slow, ranging from a few inches to, at most, several tens of feet per day. The flow of valley glaciers has been studied by driving a straight line of stakes across the surface. In a few days or weeks, the line bulges downstream, indicating a faster movement in the center, away from the retarding friction of the valley walls. Movement at depth is shown by driving iron pipes into the glaciers. Pipes in valley glaciers slowly tilt downstream, showing that the surface ice moves faster than that below (Fig. 6-41).

The Glacial Economy Glaciers are dynamic. They expand and shrink, thicken and thin, in

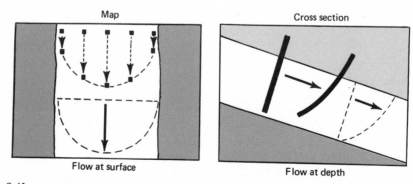

Fig. 6-41
Flow in valley glaciers. Map view shows shifting of points on surface with time. Cross-section shows movement of pipe indicating lesser rate of flow at depth.

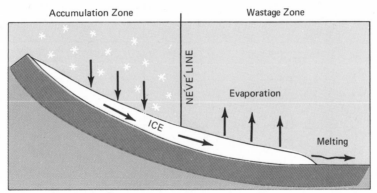

Fig. 6-42
Economy of valley glacier. Névé line is the lower limit of névé (firn) at maximum of summer melting.

response to a delicate balance of nourishment by snow in their upper ends, and wastage by melting and evaporation towards their lower ends (Fig. 6-42). The ice moves forward whether the glacier's front is advancing, retreating, or relatively fixed. If accumulation of snow exceeds wastage, the front advances; if wastage predominates, the front retreats, because the forward flow of ice does not replace the loss. A perfectly stable front requires a balance of accumulation and wastage that is rare because of variations in snowfall, and in average summer temperatures, from year to year. Thus, glaciers are sensitive indicators of climatic change.

Glacial topography

Erosional Features Glaciers erode by *abrasion*, the scraping or rasping action of debris-laden ice, and by *quarrying*, a lifting out of blocks from well-jointed bedrock (Fig. 6-43). Knobs overridden by ice are smoothed by abrasion on the side facing the ice's source, and roughened by quarrying on the lee, or downstream side (Fig. 6-44). When loaded with fine debris, ice may buff down hard rock to a finish resembling highly polished building stone. Sharp cobbles, dragged over bedrock, make striations, or grooves, which are useful in reconstructing the direction of ice movement long after the glaciers have disappeared (Fig. 6-45).

The erosional landforms created by conti-

nental glaciers are generally unimpressive, because the land, being completely buried by ice, is planed and smoothed as if by a great sanding block. The smaller valley glaciers carve and undermine the mountain masses rising above them, producing a rough, spectacular topography, that contrasts markedly with the full, round-bodied forms of unglaciated mountains, modified by streams, weathering, and mass wasting. *Horns*, classically illustrated by the Swiss Matterhorn, are sharp pyramid-shaped peaks formed where encroaching *cirques*, broad glacial valley heads, converge towards a central summit. *Aretes* are sharp knife-like ridges between glacial troughs (Fig. 6-46).

Glacial valleys originate in distinctive cirques: broadly rounded basins, having an arm-chair shape. Cirques are actively cut back into mountains, especially during times of alternate freeze and thaw, such as spring and fall. During the day meltwater coursing down between the ice margin and the adjacent rock wall penetrates the cirque floor, while at night the water freezes causing intense frost-shattering at the floor's edge that undermines the headwall (Fig. 6-47).

Glaciated valleys are characteristically U-shaped troughs, quite unlike the V-shaped cross-sections of stream valleys, and are produced when ice moves down pre-existing stream valleys, gouging out the valley bottom and planing off the ends of interlocking spurs in the process. Actually, the U-shaped glacial trough corre-

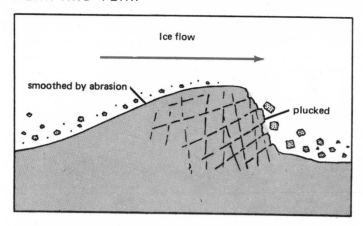

Fig. 6-43
Glacial abrasion and quarrying, or plucking, reflect the direction of ice movement.

sponds in function to the infinitely smaller channel of a stream. However, a far larger trough is required to drain an area of creeping ice than of fast-flowing water (Fig. 6-48).

Streams in previously glaciated mountains seem a notable exception to Playfair's law. Tributaries, flowing into larger glaciated troughs, commonly emerge from *hanging valleys* whose lips create rapids and falls (Fig. 6-49). However, the lack of accordant stream junctions reflects the fact that the streams occupy abandoned glacial troughs, rather than valleys which they have cut. Glaciers widen and greatly deepen earlier stream valleys into the troughs, adjusted to the flow of ice. The ice surface at the junction of glaciers is usually accordant, hence conforming to the law, but the greater volume of ice in the main glacier requires a larger trough, whose bottom is cut far below that of its tributaries.[6]

U-shaped valleys, with less precipitous walls, develop beneath continental ice sheets moving down old stream valleys. Such troughs, in upper New York State, are now occupied by the Finger Lakes, including Lakes Seneca and Cayuga. *Fiords,* which are deep narrow bays, typical of the spectacular glaciated coasts of Alaska, Scandinavia, and New Zealand, are U-shaped valleys that have been flooded by the sea (Fig. 6-50).

[6] Stream channels have the same relations, but they are not so clearly shown because the channels are so much smaller.

Depositional Features A glacier acts like a great conveyor belt. Material scraped from its underlying floor and, in the case of valley glaciers, cascaded onto the ice of valley glaciers from precipitous slopes above, is constantly carried to the glacier's end, and dropped.

Erratics are individual blocks, some as large as a small house and weighing many tons, that are foreign to the bedrock on which they rest (Fig. 6-51). Trains of erratics stemming from a distinctive bedrock source have been used to reconstruct the direction and pattern of ice movement. The unconsolidated material forming the depositional landforms of glaciers is collectively called *drift,* a term inherited from the earlier misconception that it was rafted in and dropped by melting icebergs, when the land was submerged. Drift includes two sorts of deposits: *till* deposited directly by the ice, and *stratified drift* laid down by meltwater.

Till contains a wide range of particle sizes; for ice, being unselective in its transport, deposits clay, sand, cobbles, and boulders in an unsorted jumble. The cobbles and boulders are often striated, like the bedrock floors, and may also be snubbed, or flattened, where they were dragged across a rock floor. Stratified drift is better sorted, because the fine materials are washed out of it, while the boulders and cobbles, too large to be washed along by water, are not carried into them. The washed deposits of stratified drift include those laid down along melt-

Fig. 6-44
Outcrop smoothed and striated by glacial action. U.S. Forest Service photo by C. A. Duthie.

Fig. 6-45
Glacial grooves, Flathead National Forest, Montana. U.S. Forest Service photo.

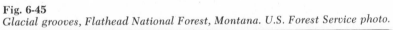

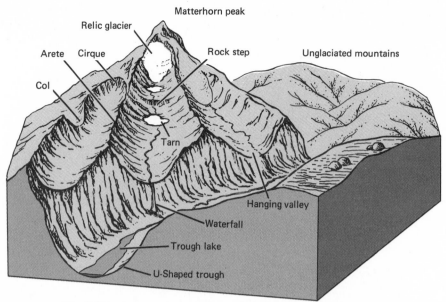

Fig. 6-46
Erosional features left by valley glaciers when the ice disappears.

Fig. 6-47
Steep-walled cirques in the high Wind River Mountains, Wyoming. Photo by Austin S. Post, University of Washington.

Fig. 6-48
U-shaped glacial trough on south side of Tracey Arm, Alaska. Small glaciers still surround aretes and horns of adjacent peaks. U.S. Forest Service photo by L. J. Prater.

water streams, and those carried into lakes or ponds, and the sea.

Moraines are the major landforms composed of till. *Ground moraine* forming low plains, generally, is a thin veneer that accumulates under a glacier, and prevails where a glacier's front was continuously advancing or retreating. *End moraines* are prominent ridges formed around glacial margins and are largest where a glacial front was essentially in equilibrium, so that debris was dropped in the same place.

The topography of end moraines tends to be smoothly rolling if the till is largely clay. A hummocky terrain of knobs and basins, which may contain small ponds called kettles, characterizes coarse, gravelly and bouldery tills, common in valley glaciers (Fig. 6-52). The end moraines of valley glaciers may form a loop a few miles across, whose curved end is called a *terminal moraine*. It often merges with *lateral moraines* extending back along valley walls. (Figs. 6-53, 6-54, 6-55)

The end moraines of continental glaciers form broad sweeping arcs, often traceable for many miles, that are usually lower than those of valley glaciers. Moraines of the former great Pleistocene ice sheets in North America and Europe are

Fig. 6-49
*Old lithograph of Yosemite Falls cascading into the glaciated trough of the Yosemite Valley.
From the Library of Congress Collection.*

rarely over 150 feet high, whereas those of valley glaciers may be 500 to 900 feet high. The reason for the difference seems to be that glacial tongues in mountains flow relatively rapidly down steep valley floors; hence, they erode more actively, and acquire a greater load from their floor, as well as receiving additional material falling from the higher valley walls.

Drumlins are streamlined hills of till, resembling giant inverted teaspoons, that appear in swarms behind an end moraine. Boston's historic Bunker Hill is a drumlin, in a field along the Massachusetts coast. Other drumlin fields occur in upper New York State, south of Lake Ontario, and in Wisconsin, west of Lake Michigan. Drumlins apparently form beneath glacial ice, heavily choked with fine debris. The load is initially deposited on irregularities in the rock floor and then plastered on in successive crude layers, building the hill which may reach a mile or two in length, and as much as 200 feet in height (Fig. 6-56).

Outwash plains, the most extensive landforms of stratified drift, usually extend outward from moraines as broad aprons, deposited by loaded meltwater streams issuing from glaciers. The south shore of Long Island, New York, is a flat outwash plain, bounded on the north by hilly moraines of the former continental ice sheet. Valley glaciers, also, develop distinct, but smaller, outwash plains. *Valley train* consists of meltwater deposits, fillings that give flat-floored

Fig. 6-50
West arm of Fords Terror Fiord, Alaska. A waterfall spills from a hanging valley into the head of the fiord. Photo by L. J. Prater.

Fig. 6-51
Glacial erratics on Moraine Dome, Yosemite National Park. U.S. Park Service photo by R. H. Anderson.

bottoms to originally U-shaped glacial troughs (Fig. 6-57).

Eskers are long sinuous ridges of washed gravels and sands, frequently providing a natural route through swampy land whose drainage has been disrupted by glacial deposition. Forming behind moraines, eskers may lead into outwash plains. They originate as deposits from streams flowing through tunnels in the glacier; when the ice disappears, the esker remains as a natural cast of the former stream channel.

Ice ages

Since the early nineteenth century, when geology was first emerging as a science, glaciers have stimulated controversy and speculation. It started with the concept of an Ice Age.

The Glacial Theory That the valley glaciers of the Alps had once been far more extensive than in recent times has long been recognized by Swiss peasants, whose farms and pastures contain abandoned moraines, scratched and polished bedrock surfaces, snubbed boulders, and other features like those developing around active glaciers. From just such a comparison of landforms and deposits around living glaciers, with those now remote from the glacial ice, the geologic concept of an Ice Age became established. The former expansion of valley glaciers had been appreciated by several Swiss naturalists in the seventeenth century, and was first formally proposed at a scientific meeting in 1821 by Ignatz Venetz-Sitten, a Swiss civil engineer.

The more startling idea, that vast ice sheets had recently overwhelmed much of Europe, was first suggested by Professor A. Bernhardi, who wrote, in 1832, that glaciers had once extended from the polar regions well into Germany, on the basis of the patterns of moraines and erratics there. **Louis Agassiz**, a colorful Swiss zoologist, is often considered the father of the Ice Age; however, his main contribution—which is important—was to force the existing concept into the mainstream of scientific acceptance. Agassiz, originally a skeptic, became an enthusiastic convert to glacial expansion after touring the Rhone Valley glaciers with a Venetz supporter, in 1836. In a paper the next year, he proposed a great period of ice, with a sheet extending from the polar regions to the Mediterranean (a slight overstatement as the Alps were a southern island of valley glaciers). He attributed this glaciation to climatic change.

Causes of ice ages

Today, Ice Ages are acknowledged, and healthy controversy revolves around their causes and the more general problem of past climatic changes. Any satisfactory theory must encompass a number of geologic findings, most important being the fluctuations from warm to cold intervals during the late Ice Age and the spasmodic

Fig. 6-52
Knob and basin topography of valley moraine in Jackson Hole, Wyoming. Photo by Herb Pownall.

occurrence of glaciation far back through geologic time.

The Pleistocene Ice Age began a million or more years ago, and ended about 10,000 years ago. During the Pleistocene, the European and American ice caps had not one, but four, distinct advances, separated by warmer intervals when these glaciers disappeared. As each interglacial time lasted more than 10,000 years, the present could well be an interglacial interval, to be followed by still another advance.

Other Ice Ages have occurred at random through geologic history. About 200,000,000 years ago, in late Paleozoic time, glaciation affected much of the Southern Hemisphere, including India, Africa, Australia, and South America. There is scattered evidence of at least one very ancient glacial period, 700 million years ago, in late Precambrian time, on every continent but South America. Moreover, glaciation reflects only the extremes in a continuous pattern of climatic change. For even in long periods be-

tween Ice Ages, when the earth's climate was largely sub-tropical, there were climatic fluctuations.

Of the many mechanisms proposed, none provides a generally accepted explanation for climatic change. The problem is complicated by the largely circumstantial nature of the evidence, and interpretations require a synthesis of fact and theory from astronomy, archeology, botany, meteorology, zoology, chemistry, and physics, as well as geology.

Solar Variations The sun being the original source of heat for the atmosphere, variations in solar radiant energy should change air temperatures, so that a period of lesser output might cause an Ice Age. Perhaps more significant are sun spots, which change the kind of solar radiation. When sun spots are abundant, the weather in the middle latitudes gets colder, the moisture-bearing storm tracks shift southward, and glaciers expand. Periodic variations in sun spots have

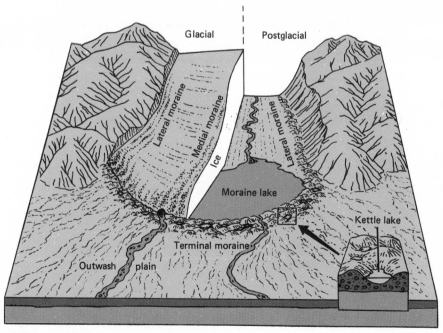

Fig. 6-53
Depositional features of valley glaciers schematically shown with and without ice (after W. M. Davis). Inset shows detail of knob and basin topography.

Fig. 6-54
Looping end moraine of valley glacier confining a lake in Jackson Hole, Wyoming. Photo by Herb Pownall.

been recorded since the mid-eighteenth century and, although insufficient to account for an Ice Age, larger, long-term variations might well be an adequate cause. Most solar theories account for glacial periods by the cooling of the atmosphere. Some, however, attribute Ice Ages to increased solar radiation, which would accelerate evaporation from the ocean surfaces, causing increased cloudiness and precipitation. Critics of this scheme point out that the increased precipitation would be largely rain, which does not nourish glaciers.

Planetary Motions Periodic variations in the motions and path of the earth in space are also considered a cause that shifts the distribution of heat at the earth's surface. Using known variations in the earth's orbit, the tilt of its axis of rotation and other factors, a complicated graph has been constructed showing the changes in solar heat received at various latitudes through time. The curve, most fully developed by the Yugoslav, Milankovitch, does not provide a cause for Ice Ages, as its variations are regular and cyclic, whereas the times of glaciation have been sporadic; however, it may well reflect the causes for lesser climatic variations. The curve has received support from a different line of study. Recent techniques allow the determination of the temperatures at which sediments in

Fig. 6-55
Mount McKinley, Alaska. Lateral moraines which become medial moraines within the ice tongue where two glaciers join. (National Park Service photo by Lowell Sumner.)

the ocean bottoms were deposited. Changes in ocean temperatures, determined from bottom cores, do correspond to the theoretical Milankovitch curve.

Changes in Atmospheric Components Some theorists stress variations in the amounts of carbon dioxide and water vapor, important in atmospheric heating because of their "greenhouse" effect. If these insulating gases decrease, thus locking carbon dioxide in rocks, as would be the case during periods of extensive limestone deposition, less re-radiated heat would be trapped in the atmosphere, leading to climatic refrigeration. Increases and decreases of these gases do occur, but their quantitative importance, based on observed effects of the carbon dioxide released by burning coal and fuels since the Industrial Revolution began, seem totally inadequate to bring on a glacial epoch.

A more geologic hypothesis also involves substances in the atmosphere. Suspended volcanic dust reflects the relatively short incoming waves of solar radiation, but readily allows the escape

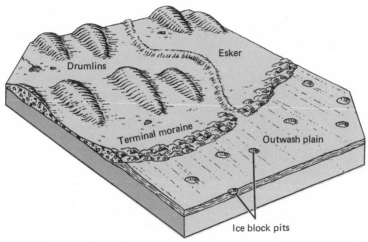

Fig. 6-56
Depositional landforms of continental glaciers.

Fig. 6-57
Valley train extending from the ends of two ice tongues issuing from the margin of the Greenland Ice Sheet. U.S. Air Force photo, by permission of the Royal Danish Navy.

Louis Agassiz (1807–1873) *Agassiz, originally trained in medicine and zoology, wrote several major publications on fossil fish. He began his work on glaciers and the Ice Age concept in Europe. Later, as a professor at Harvard, he organized the Museum of Comparative Zoology, extended the glacial concept to America, and gave exceedingly popular lectures.*

of longer re-radiated heat waves from the ground (which is the reverse of the effect of the insulating gases). For three years after the eruption of Krakatoa in Indonesia, the incoming radiation at a solar observatory as far away as France was decreased by 10%. However, there is no geologic evidence suggesting continuous periods of excessive eruptions lasting for the thousands of years needed to create an Ice Age.

Geologic Factors Through geologic history, Ice Ages have been notably absent when continents are low and extensively flooded by the sea; and they do seem to correspond to times of extensive mountain building and general emergence of the land. Such is the case for the latest Ice Age, was probably true in the late Paleozoic glacial period of 200 million years ago, and could well have been true in the earliest glaciation although its record is scant. The reason seems twofold. High mountains are breeding grounds for

glaciers, and extensive emergence of the continents prevents ocean currents from spreading warm water into higher latitudes where it creates milder climates. The effect becomes even more pronounced, once glaciation starts, by the locking of water in ice on land.

The theory of polar wandering, which has had its ups and downs, now seems rather firmly established. Advocates held that glaciation results when the earth's poles migrate onto land. In the late Paleozoic glaciation, the South Pole apparently lay in Africa; today it lies in the Antarctic continent whose tremendous volume of glacial ice is largely responsible for the present lowered sea level, and the resulting worldwide emergence of the continents.

In their recent hypothesis, William Donn and Morris Ewing assume the Pleistocene Ice Age began when the North Pole moved into the generally land-locked Arctic Sea. The sea lies in a basin that opens to the Pacific through the narrow Bering Straits, and into the Atlantic at Hudson Straits, Baffin Bay, and across a broader expanse around Iceland, all of which are underlain by shallow platforms. Donn and Ewing propose that the Arctic Sea is ice-free during glacial times, but freezes over in interglacial periods. This supposition, coupled with the effects of eustatic changes on ocean currents, provides a shutter mechanism, closing and opening the Arctic basin to warm waters as the adjacent glaciers wax and wane.

When the Arctic Sea is unfrozen, evaporation from its surface leads to increased snowfall on North America, Europe, and Eurasia, and creates continental glaciers. The growth of the continental ice caps, storing water on land, lowers sea level. As the sea falls, the circulation of warmer waters from the major oceans into the Arctic is eventually cut off by the emergence of the basin rims, with the result that the Arctic Sea cools and freezes over. With the sea no longer a great evaporating pan, snowfall decreases, starving the glaciers which recede and eventually disappear.

But the waning glaciers then release water that starts sea level rising until warm currents from the Atlantic once more spill into the Arctic basin. This melts the frozen lid, opening the Arctic Ocean so that once again glaciers grow and advance. Thus, a natural thermostat regulates glacial and interglacial alternations in the northern hemisphere, and will probably continue to do so until the Antarctic ice melts, raising sea level to a point where the Arctic basin is permanently accessible to warm ocean currents.

Neat and plausible though it sounds, the case for the Ewing–Donn hypothesis is not proven. The evidence for an ice-free Arctic Ocean during glacial maxima is scanty: a very few cores from the Arctic sea floor that may indicate warmer water during the maxima; and a few boulders dredged from the bottom that might be erratics deposited by glaciers flowing into an open sea. R. W. Fairbridge suggests that they have overlooked the tremendous volume of Antarctic ice that could be the deciding factor. Some doubt that the shutter can account for the many minor fluctuations within the main glacial advances. And so it goes. As is so often the case with new hypotheses—more evidence is needed.

Ultimately, the explanation for Ice Ages, and the broader problem of climatic change, may well involve elements of many theories. Today, changing climates and Ice Ages remain a challenging scientific puzzle.

SUGGESTED READINGS

Drury, G. H., *The Face of the Land*, Baltimore, Md., Penguin Books, 1959 (paperback, Pelican Book).

Dyson, J. L., *The World of Ice*, New York, Alfred A. Knopf Inc., 1962.

Leopold, L. B., "Rivers," in the *American Scientist*, Vol. 50, No. 4, pp. 511–537, 1962.

Leopold, L. B. and Langbein, W. B., *A Primer on Water*, U.S. Geological Survey, Miscellaneous Report, 1960.

Sharp, R. P., *Glaciers*, Condon Lectures Publications, Eugene, Ore., University of Oregon Press, 1960.

Shimer, J. A., *This Sculptured Earth*, New York, Columbia University Press, 1959.

The structure and architecture of the earth

Having considered minerals and rocks, and the destructive forces wearing down the land surfaces, let us now examine the structure of the Earth. First we shall consider earthquakes and what they tell of the Earth's internal architecture; next volcanoes and related features, the igneous structures and phenomena; then deformational structures, folds and fractures and their relation to the framework of continents; and lastly enter the realm of "fantastic" geologic theories regarding the origin of mountains.

seven: The vibrant earth and its interior

The earth quivers. Its constant vibration, detectable only by sensitive instruments called seismographs, consists of microseisms that reflect storms and atmospheric pressure changes, as well as random "noise" from nearby blasts, falling objects, moving vehicles such as trucks and trains, and even stamping feet. Rising above this muted background are frequent earthquakes, distinctive ground tremors noticeable to anyone near the source.

EARTHQUAKES

Earthquakes reflect the deep-seated forces that break and crumble the earth's crust into deformational structures; moreover, their instrumental records have helped provide the only satisfactory information about the earth's internal architecture. Hundreds of thousands of earthquakes occur each year. Most, being small or from distant sources, are indiscernible except by seismographs; about a hundred are capable of damaging any nearby buildings; and perhaps one or two of these are potentially devastating.

Statistics can only suggest the terror, destruction, and personal tragedies in populous areas visited by a major earthquake. Lisbon, Portugal, in 1775, suffered 60,000 fatalities and many injured. The earthquake of 1906 in the San Francisco Bay area of California was the most destructive in the history of the United States (Fig. 7-1). Some 700 people were killed. The financial loss from the fire that followed was $400,000,000. In 1908 the cities of Reggio and Messina in southern Italy and Sicily were devastated with a death toll of some 100,000. The list is long, including Kansu in western China, where 100,000 were killed in 1920 and an equal number in 1927 (mostly in collapsing cave dwellings cut into soft deposits of wind-blown silt called loess). In Japan, the 1923 earthquake in the Tokyo-Yokohama region left 142,809 dead or missing, 103,733 injured, and destroyed 576,262 buildings. Fortunately, most earthquakes are of less intensity, and many occur in sparsely populated regions, or on the ocean floor. Some of the devastation caused by the "Good Friday" earthquake in Alaska (March 27, 1964) is shown in Figs. 7-2 through 7-5.

The cause of shaking

The Elastic Rebound Theory All stronger earthquakes are attributed to "elastic rebound" along deep fractures in the earth, called faults. This mechanical theory was proposed by H. F. Reed of Johns Hopkins University from studies following the San Francisco earthquake, which apparently originated in the great San Andreas fault. He noticed that a series of carefully surveyed points, and such reference lines as fences and roads crossing the fault at right angles, became warped during a period of years free of earthquakes (Fig. 7-6). He assumed that the ground was being strained by stresses within the earth, but no slippage occurred because of the tremendous friction between opposing rock masses, pressed tightly together along the fault. Ultimately the stresses increased to a point

Fig. 7-1
San Francisco, following the great earthquake of 1906. Note damage to buildings from the shaking on the right. The great fire resulting can be seen down Sacramento Street. Library of Congress Collection.

where they overcame the friction and allowed a sudden slippage. Fences and other reference lines were sheared and offset as the ground snapped to a position of no strain (Fig. 7-7). Rock masses grinding by each other during the displacement generated vibrations that moved out as earthquake waves.[1] Thereafter the stresses, which were temporarily relieved by the slippage, slowly accumulate over the years, and the process continues causing sporadic earthquakes.

Surface effects

A strong earthquake is, to say the least, unnerving. The "psychology of the observer" should always be considered in evaluating the

[1] Something like the vibration in your hands when two coarse files are drawn across each other.

accounts of survivors, which often blend fantasy with fact. What phenomena can be expected?

Buildings   Well-built modern buildings withstand most earthquakes with little damage. Structures on solid bedrock receive less shaking than those on soft or swamp ground because the different materials behave like a bowl of jelly. Tapped on the outside with a spoon, the solid bowl transmits the shock but it is not thrown into waves, such as pass across the soft jelly surface.

Earth materials react to strong vibrations in much the same way (Fig. 7-8).

Chances of survival during an earthquake are better indoors, under stairs, doorways, or stout tables, for the death toll soars when people rush into the streets and are crushed by falling masonry of old or poorly bonded stone buildings. Fires following an earthquake are often more destructive than the shaking. Tremendous losses accompanied the initial shocks in San Francisco and Tokyo.

Fig. 7-2
"Good Friday" earthquake in Alaska. Partial collapse of new J. C. Penney store in Anchorage. Note adjacent glass building still intact. U.S. Coast and Geodetic Survey.

Fig. 7-3
Good Friday quake. Settling of this Anchorage Theater left the marquee at street level. U.S. Coast and Geodetic Survey photo.

Fig. 7-4
Slumping caused by the earthquake destroyed many homes in the Turnagin area of Anchorage. U.S. Coast and Geodetic Survey photo.

Shocks The duration of an individual earthquake shock is surprisingly short considering the damage it can do. The actual period of shaking ranges only from a few seconds to about a minute, or in the case of the Tokyo disaster a minute and a half. However, a major shock is usually followed by sporadic aftershocks that may continue for months, with decreasing intensity and frequency until several hundred or perhaps a thousand have occurred; the majority of the later ones are usually detectable only with seismographs.

Scarps and Cracks Frequently the ground is suddenly offset by the appearance of a scarp, where one side of a fault has moved up relative to the other (Fig. 7-9). A single displacement in Assam, India, in 1897, created a scarp 35 feet high, and others about 20 feet high have been fairly common. Rumors persist of great cracks opening and swallowing people or even whole villages. Cracks do form, but they are relatively shallow features caused by the shaking of unconsolidated soil or dirt (Fig. 7-10). Solid rock does not gape open in abyssal chasms; certainly the

Fig. 7-5
Great ocean waves, called tsunamis, generated by the earthquake severely damaged the rail-road yards at Seward. U.S. Coast and Geodetic Survey.

Fig. 7-6 *Elastic rebound mechanism.*

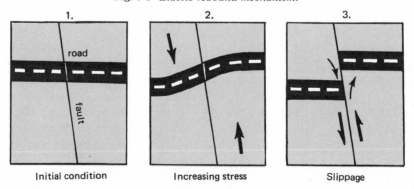

Fig. 7-7
Fence offset 8½ feet horizontally by the main fault during the 1906 San Francisco earthquake. U.S. Geological Survey photo by G. K. Gilbert.

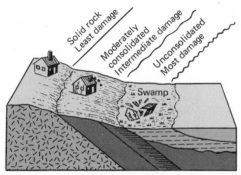

Fig. 7-8
Relation of earthquake damage to foundation material.

faults, which constitute major bedrock fractures, must remain tightly jammed together to produce the quaking. Fear of burial is real enough, however, at the base of mountain slopes, where rocks may be dislodged or landslides triggered.

Ground Roll and Sounds Waves a foot or so high have been reported moving across the ground during earthquakes. Although these are a possibility on loose or swampy ground, one scientist observed such waves moving through a concrete basement floor that was uncracked after the shaking ended. Thus some ground roll is now con-

151

Fig. 7-9
Fourteen-foot fault scarp formed during the 1959 earthquake around Madison Canyon and West Yellowstone, Montana. The trees remained upright although their roots were cut. U.S. Geological Survey photo by I. J. Witkind.

sidered an optical illusion resulting from vibration of the fluid in the eye. Some earthquakes produce sounds because their seismic waves emerge from the ground in an audible frequency range. Loud snappings are reported near the center of an earthquake; farther away the sounds are like the rumbling of heavy traffic or distant explosions.

Distribution

Strength The strength of an earthquake is measured by various scales. Some are based on instrumental readings, but because the number of seismograph installations is limited, qualitative scales based on readily observed phenomena are commonly used to give better coverage in mapping earthquake intensity (see Table 7.1). These scales, printed on postcards, are sent after a shock to reliable citizens, often the postmaster, in the affected area. On their return, intensity zones are plotted on a map using the reported surface effects. Ideally the zones should form a bull's-eye pattern of decreasing intensity outward from a center. However, the effects of seismic waves are strongly influenced by local differences in the consolidation of bedrock, and other complicating factors, so the pattern is irregular. Two centers of maximum strength are determined for an earthquake. The *epicenter* is the point of apparent maximum intensity at the ground surface. The *focus,* the actual point of greatest magnitude, is at depth within the earth, hence must be instrumentally determined (Fig. 7-11).

Regional No region is immune to earthquakes. Even Boston, Massachusetts, a city noted for stability, has experienced a strong seismic disturbance which, by a peculiar historical coincidence, centered near Cambridge, in 1775.

Table 7.1 Modified Mercalli Scale of Earthquake Intensities (after Trefethen).

I. Instrumental: detected only by instruments.

II. Very feeble: noticed only by people at rest.

III. Slight: felt by people at rest. Like passing of a truck.

IV. Moderate: generally perceptible by people in motion. Loose objects disturbed.

V. Rather strong: dishes broken, bells rung, pendulum clocks stopped. People awakened.

VI. Strong: felt by all, some people frightened. Damage slight, some plaster cracked.

VII. Very strong: noticed by people in autos. Damage to poor construction. Alarm general.

VIII. Destructive: chimneys fall, much damage in substantial buildings, heavy furniture overturned.

IX. Ruinous: great damage to substantial structures. Ground cracked, pipes broken.

X. Disastrous: many buildings destroyed.

XI. Very disastrous: few structures left standing.

XII. Catastrophic: total destruction.

Fig. 7-10
Fence compressed by shifting ground along small fracture marked by shovel. U.S. Geological Survey photo by J. R. Stacy.

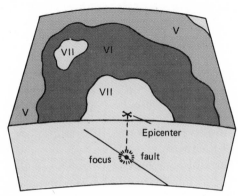

Fig. 7-11
Earthquake centers and intensity zones.

However, when epicenters are plotted on a map for any length of time, well-defined earthquake belts become apparent.

The continental margins and associated arcs of islands completely rimming the Pacific Ocean are especially active. The great circular belt coincides with the Andean mountain chain along the west coast of South America, then passes through the Isthmus of Panama, with a somewhat isolated branch through the West Indies, into the coastal ranges of North America. It continues through Alaska and the Aleutians to the islands of Japan, the Philippines, New Zealand, and eventually to the Antarctic. Another active belt, branching from the circum-Pacific zone at the Celebes, extends through Indonesia and the great Himalayan–Alpine mountain ranges into the Mediterranean region.

One system of extensive seismic activity is largely submarine. It starts at the north in Iceland and follows a continuous system of submarine ridges (which apparently mark global fractures) through the mid-Atlantic Ridge, around Cape Horn, into the Indian Ocean. Here one branch passes into East Africa and the Middle East along a great system of fault valleys; the other trends off into the Pacific Ocean. These major seismic belts clearly correspond to major zones of mountain building and deformation, where the earth's crust is being fractured and folded.

THE EARTH'S INTERNAL ARCHITECTURE

Instrumental observations

Seismographs Seismology, the science of earthquakes, blossomed in the late nineteenth century after the Englishman, John Milne, while in Japan, developed the first useful seismograph for recording earth vibrations. Subsequent improvement of the instruments has resulted mainly from the efforts of Wiechert in Germany, Galitzin in Russia, and Benioff in the United States.

A seismograph is essentially a pendulum, and no matter how complicated by mechanical and

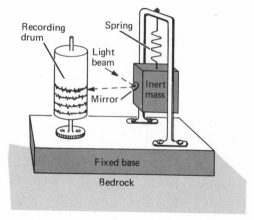

Fig. 7-12
Elements of a simple seismograph. In this case, recording is done by a pin-point light beam on photographic paper, a system used on many modern instruments.

electrical gadgets, it contains three basic elements: a fixed base, an inert mass, and a recorder (Fig. 7-12). In larger installations, the fixed base is a concrete pier set in bedrock to form a single solid unit. The inert mass is merely a heavy weight, the pendulum, suspended from the concrete pier on springs or a pivoting boom. The recorder is a slowly rotating drum wrapped in a paper strip that, in the simplest seismograph, is marked by a pen connected to the inert mass (Fig. 7-13).

When earthquake waves are received, the fixed elements vibrate with the bedrock. The suspended mass remains motionless in space because of its inertia. When the base and inert mass are moving in relation to each other, the recorder plots a "wiggly" line as the marking device moves up and down on the rotating paper strip.[2]

Seismic Waves Modern ideas of the internal architecture of the earth became possible in 1897, when R. D. Oldham of Great Britain distinguished three fundamental types of seismic wave. In the case of earthquakes, infinitesimal

[2] If the motion were large enough, it would seem to you that the suspended mass was moving and the concrete pier was stable. This may sound confusing, but remember that you would be moving with the ground.

Fig. 7-13
*Three units containing inert masses (the single and split cylinders) mounted on a single concrete
pier in modern seismograph installation. University of Wyoming photo by Herb Pownall.*

vibrating particles in rock pass the energy along
in waves. Although the motion of the particles
is at most only a small fraction of an inch, their
quick trip-hammer action can cause the far
larger and potentially destructive swaying of
the ground. The different waves result from the
kinds of motion affecting the particles.

The types originating at the earthquake focus
are called body waves and they radiate in all
directions through the earth. *Primary, P,* waves
are also called "push–pull" waves because they
are compressional. Their motion is like the
"bump" that passes through a string of railroad
cars when another unit is added to the train. In
rock, a particle is driven into its neighbor and
bounces back, the neighbor strikes the particle
beyond and rebounds, the next particle is disturbed in the same way, and so on *ad infinitum*

as the wave speeds away from the focus. The primary are the fastest waves, travelling at about 3
miles a second in the earth's outer rocks. Their
speed increases in the materials, at depth, so
that 1800 miles below the surface, they travel
at about 8½ miles per second.

The *secondary, S,* called shake, waves have
transverse motion. The rock particles move up
and down. This motion can be demonstrated by
tying a rope to a door handle, extending the
rope, then snapping the free end so that waves
roll down the rope. Secondary waves also move
at rates of miles per second, but only about two-
thirds as fast as *P* waves. The paths of both *P*
and *S* waves, passing through the earth's body,
tend to curve upward towards the surface, in
response to changing properties of materials at
depth. Significantly, the waves may be bent (re-

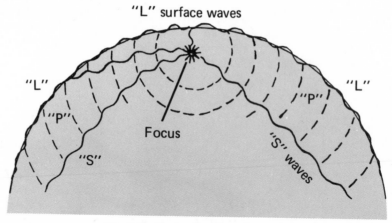

Fig. 7-14 *Types of earthquake waves.*

fracted), or bounce (reflected), when they encounter a boundary between layers in the interior.

The *Surface, L,* waves are complex and have at least two different simultaneous motions producing a "shimmy." They originate where body waves (the *P* and *S*) from the focus reach the earth's surface. Because they move around the outside of the earth, following the crust at rather shallow depths, they are classed as surface waves. They are the slowest and broadest of the three wave types and travel at a nearly uniform speed. Each wave type creates distinctive jogs in the lines being continuously recorded on the seismograph paper, to form a seismogram.

Locating Earthquake Centers Finding the epicenter of a distant earthquake requires cooperative effort among at least three seismograph stations. At each, the distance from the earthquake is first determined by using the difference in the time of arrival of the first *P* and the first *S* waves. Because both waves start from the focus at the same time, and because the *P* travels faster than the *S*, the time interval between their arrivals becomes progressively greater the farther they travel. Thus the interval recorded at a station can be referred to a travel-time table that gives the distance to the earthquake (Fig. 7-15).

Next, the direction to the epicenter is determined. A circle is marked on a globe, using the position of the local station as the circle's center and the known distance as a radius. The epicenter must be somewhere on the circle's circumference. Then, using data obtained from a second station, another circle is constructed which should cross the first one at two points that are both possible epicenter locations. An arc, based on a third station, should cross one of these two points, giving the location of the epicenter (Fig. 7-15).

A major accomplishment of seismologists was the establishment of reliable time-travel tables. About 1940, Jeffreys and Bullen in England, and Gutenberg and Richter in the United States, independently derived tables in close agreement. Such tables to which the arrival times of seismic waves are referred are necessary for the accurate location of foci, as well as epicenters, of earthquakes. They are essential for studying the variations of velocity in *P* and *S* waves, at depth, in relation to the earth's deep internal zones.

An earth model

The Major Zones Various workers have suggested models of differing detail for the earth's internal architecture; however, most envision the following three theoretical zones. A central

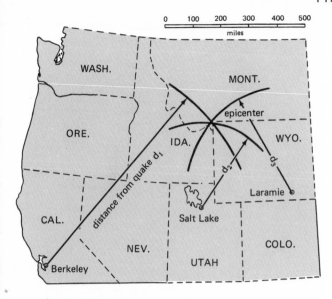

Fig. 7-15
Locating the epicenter of an earthquake.

core is of nickel-iron, a little over 2000 miles in radius, whose density increases to the earth's center and averages about 10.7. The core's outer part is liquid and the inner part is solid (Fig. 7-16).

The mantle surrounding the core is about 1800 miles thick, composed of heavy iron silicate minerals, peridotite or eclogite, whose density increases with depth and averages about 4. The mantle is plastic, except for its outer 400 miles or so, which is solid.

The solid crust, or lithosphere, ranges from 7 to 25 miles in thickness extending deepest under the continents and shallowest under the ocean basins, and is composed of common surface rocks. The crust consists of a continuous lower basaltic layer, density 2.9, that rests upon the mantle. A granitic layer, density 2.7 "floating" on the basaltic one, forms the continental masses. Any such model of the earth's hidden interior must be human interpretation. So how have the bumps and squiggles of lines on a seismogram been supplemented by various logical deductions to produce our present ideas about the core, mantle, and crust?

The Core A major discovery in the exploration of the earth's interior was made in 1906 when

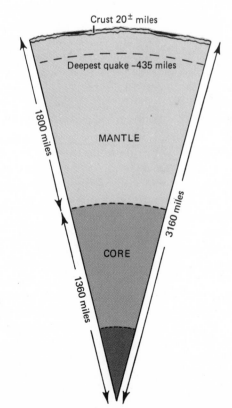

Fig. 7-16
Internal zones of the earth. Depth of continental crust is shown greatly exaggerated.

157

Oldham demonstrated that the earth has a large central core. Its size was determined in 1914 by Gutenberg, who calculated that the outer boundary of the core lay 1800 miles below the earth's surface, which gives the core a radius of about 2160 miles.

The core was discovered from the seemingly anomalous behavior of body waves. Up to a distance of 7000 miles from an epicenter, both P and S waves have well-ordered travel-times. Beyond this distance, the S waves disappear and are not recorded by seismographs because such transverse waves are damped out and not transmitted through a liquid, this must be the physical state of at least part of the core. The P waves, which also disappear at a distance of 7000 miles, reappear very strongly at seismographs more than 10,000 miles from the epicenter, but their arrival is as much as 3 minutes late. The intervening Shadow Zone can be explained by an inward bending of compressional waves, caused by entrance into a medium where their velocity is less. Thus, it is assumed that the core bends and concentrates the P waves, in the same way, and for the same reason, that a glass lens focuses light (Fig. 7-17).

Two lines of evidence suggest that the core is nickel-iron. First, the overall average density of the earth is 5.5 compared to the average density for surface rocks of 2.7. Thus, the interior must have some materials of higher density than the overall average to compensate for the much lighter surface rocks. If the volume of the core, which can be calculated from its radius, is assumed to contain nickel-iron, then the density relations are nicely explained. A second totally different line of evidence bears on the case. Meteorites, which some believe are fragments of a shattered planet, are mainly of two types: stoney ones that are high in iron silicates, not too different from the assumed compositions of the mantle and simatic part of the crust, and nickel-iron ones that indirectly suggest a possibly similar composition for the core of the earth. Neither line of evidence proves a nickel-iron core, but they are the best existing circumstantial evidence.

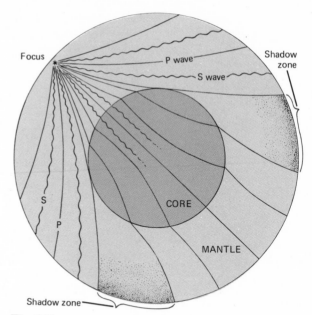

Fig. 7-17
Effect of the core on seismic waves.

The "Moho" The sharp boundary between the mantle and crust is called the Mohorovicic discontinuity, the "Moho" for short, in honor of its discoverer, a Croatian (Yugoslavian) seismologist. He noted that two distinct sets of both P and S waves were recorded from earthquakes originating less than 500 miles away. From records of earthquakes at various distances within this range, it was evident that one set moved more slowly but directly through the outer part of the earth. Within 100 miles or less, this set arrived first; but beyond that distance fell behind the other, arrived progressively later, and died out about 500 miles from the source (Fig. 7-18).

The explanation of this behavior is best introduced by an analogy with auto travel, on direct local roads or superhighways, a moderate distance away. For short trips, the necessarily slower rate of travel on the more direct local roads saves time. But on longer ones, the time lost getting to and from the superhighway is more than gained back by the faster rate of travel there, so that despite a longer trip in miles you reach your destination sooner.

Mohorovicic applied similar reasoning to the travel of seismic waves. Once they reach a certain depth their speed increases, so that the deeper-moving waves, although they lose time getting to and from their "superhighway," soon pass their slower-moving surface counterparts. Thus, he deduced a boundary, called a discontinuity, above and below which the rates of travel differ considerably. Because the velocity of seismic waves is influenced by the elasticity of the materials through which they move, a crust and mantle of different physical properties must exist.

The Mantle Laboratory experiments on physical properties, as they would affect the transmission of seismic waves, indicate that only three rocks could possibly compose the mantle: dunite, which is largely olivine (high in iron and magnesium); peridotite, containing olivine and pyroxenes; or eclogite, of garnet and pyroxene. All these rocks have densities greater than 3.2.

If the mantle is peridotite, a possibility suggested by the similar composition of some stoney meteorites, the "Moho" reflects a change of chemical composition. That is, the minerals in its rocks contain more iron and other heavier elements than occur in the basaltic rocks of the overlying crust. However, if the mantle is eclogite, the "Moho" represents a phase change.

Phase changes from one mineral to another in the solid state, called polymorphic changes, are used by the General Electric Company in making commercial diamonds. The loose packing of carbon atoms in graphite can be converted into the dense compact arrangement of diamond at pressures of 100,000 atmospheres and temperatures of 15,000°.[3] At depth, in the earth, basalt or gabbro, rocks with a specific gravity of 2.95, may convert to eclogite, a denser rock having a specific gravity of 3.3.

Although the minerals in basalt and eclogite are different, chemically the rocks are very similar. That is, the elements in each are the same, but are grouped in different combinations. Thus, high temperature and pressure could rearrange ions in the basalt minerals into the minerals comprising the denser eclogite which, being a more compact rock, is better adjusted to conditions at depth. The process is reversible. An increase of heat, or a decrease of pressure, would cause a phase change, from eclogite to the lighter and more voluminous basalt.

Recently the theory has received experimental support. In a high-pressure laboratory, George C.

[3] One atmosphere is a pressure of 14.7 pounds per square inch, standard sea-level pressure; °K means degrees Kelvin, a temperature scale like the Celsius except that zero is equal to −273° Celsius.

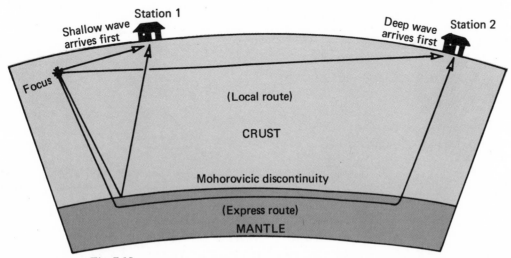

Fig. 7-18
Evidence and interpretation leading to the discovery of the "Moho."

Kennedy of U.C.L.A. has converted basalt glass into crystalline gabbro, and then, with still greater pressure, converted some of the gabbro minerals into minerals typical of eclogite. The pressure and heat required correspond to those calculated as existing at the "Moho." Moreover, basaltic magmas erupting in lava flows are in some cases thought to come from the upper part of the mantle. In any case, the debate about the composition of the mantle may well be settled if the present "Mohole" project, to drill completely through a thin part of the crust, is completed; for the present, however, the project has been temporarily suspended.

Until recently, the Moho was considered the main boundary in the outer part of the earth, separating the crust from a relatively homogeneous mantle. Intensive study of the upper mantle has changed this simple mental image, or model. Beneath the eastern United States, P wave velocities are distinctly faster in the outermost part of the mantle than beneath the mountainous regions of the western United States. Thus materials of the outer mantle differ between one region and another. Moreover, the mantle seems to change with depth, for discontinuities (marked by changes in wave velocities) are re-

ported at about 250 and about 400 miles below the earth's surface. These boundaries, where the upper mantle gives way to the lower mantle, may represent either changes in the chemical composition of the mantle or phase changes resembling the basalt-eclogite transition (but involving rocks containing other minerals that change crystal structure at higher pressures).

Recent interest has centered on a low velocity seismic zone extending from about 40 to about 150 miles below the earth's surface. The zone was suggested by Beno Gutenberg of the U.S.A. from earthquake records in the 1920's, but many seismologists then were skeptical of the evidence. The zone was confirmed by seismic records from nuclear bomb tests whose strength, location, and time were accurately known and gave more clear-cut results.

Gutenberg had originally noticed that P waves were markedly weakened when received at stations from about 60 to about 600 miles from an earthquake center. The waves had much stronger records at distances up to 60 and beyond 600 miles. The behavior was interpreted as indicating a partial shadow zone, like the more pronounced one associated with the discovery of the earth's core. Bending of the waves into a low

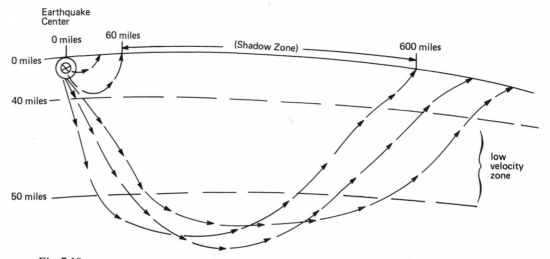

Fig. 7-19
Paths of points on fronts of P waves, illustrating the origin of the upper mantle shadow zone. Based on D. L. Anderson.

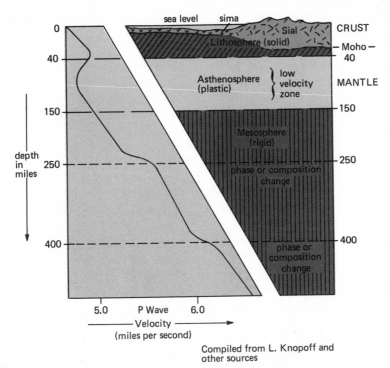

Fig. 7-20
Structure of the crust and mantle as interpreted from the velocity of P waves.

velocity zone was thought to produce the shadow, although in this case weak waves did emerge in the shadow because of inhomogeneities of the rocks and irregularities of the wave paths in the zone. The low velocities were attributed to a change of mantle rock from a solid to plastic state, with possibly some degree of melting.

The plastic state has both liquid and solid properties. Shoemaker's wax and some candy bars are plastic for they break if suddenly snapped, but flow if slowly squeezed. As the mantle transmits both primary and secondary seismic waves, it responds like a solid to sudden shocks but under long-continued stresses it apparently flows like a highly viscous liquid. That rocks do flow under temperatures and pressures at depth in the earth is amply demonstrated by the contorted structures in metamorphic rocks. The velocity of seismic waves is dependent in part on the elasticity of rocks, or the readiness with which they return to their former shape after deformation. Thus the crustal rocks, which are

rigid and more elastic, transmit waves faster than a plastic material which tends to flow and not return to its original shape when deformed. Increase of temperature tends to lower strength as a material approaches its melting point; on the other hand, increasing pressure increases strength by raising the melting point.

At about 40 to 50 miles depth, temperature apparently dominates so that the rock material becomes plastic—and hence the velocity of seismic waves decreases and they are deflected. Deeper than 150 miles, pressure increase is thought to more greatly influence the rock materials so that they become more elastic, and the waves beneath the low velocity zone speed up again with marked changes at the 250 and 400 mile depths of the deeper mantle. Recent theories on mountain building and movements of continental blocks related to large-scale warping and breaking of the earth's crustal plates give considerable emphasis to the plastic nature of the low velocity zone (Chapters 7 and 16).

The Crust The crust is of insignificant thickness when compared to the mantle and core. Taking its lower limit as the Moho, the crust ranges from as much as 30 miles thick under the continents to as little as six miles thick under the ocean basins. The crust has been assumed to have a mirror image—being deepest under mountains of the continents and shallowest under the ocean basins. Formerly, the crust was thought to contain two distinct layers called *sial* and *sima.* In the sial, an upper layer found only in the continents, the velocity of seismic waves theoretically agrees with the known transmission rates in granite. The sial is directly observable in the hearts of continents or in deeply eroded mountains where it is stripped of the widespread but relatively surficial sedimentary and volcanic rocks that veneer the continental surfaces. Sial is thick in continents, and thickest under mountain masses, but is absent from the major ocean basins, where seismic velocities indicate only basaltic sima beneath thin ocean-bottom sediments. The sima was once assumed to be a homogeneous basaltic layer forming the ocean basin floors and extending as a distinct zone under the sial of the continents. Recent work makes the picture much more complicated. Although the granitic sial is char-acteristic of the continental masses, basaltic and granitic rocks seem so intermingled at depth under the continents that a continuous and distinctly basaltic foundation of sima can no longer be assumed for the continental blocks.

The older simpler view of crust and mantle has also become more complicated. The crust might be considered the earth's outer skin above the Moho, although in places under the continents this discontinuity is not easily defined. The Moho probably represents a change in chemical composition or a phase change; however, as related to events shaping mountain ranges, continental blocks, and ocean basins, it is probably far less significant than the top of the low velocity seismic zone in the upper mantle. Thus the crust is best viewed as the upper part of the lithosphere which also includes the solid uppermost part of the mantle. Beneath the solid lithosphere lies the plastic, possibly partly molten, asthenosphere (*asthenes* is the Greek word for weak) which corresponds to the low velocity zone. In turn, the asthenosphere is underlain by the mesosphere, a more rigid zone, where seismic velocities reach and then exceed those of the lithosphere. This deeper zone is even less well known than the upper parts of the mantle.

SUGGESTED READINGS

Anderson, D. L., "The Plastic Layer of the Earth's Mantle," in *Scientific American*, Vol. 207, No. 1, pp. 52–59, 1962.

Bullen, K. E., "The Interior of the Earth," in *Scientific American*, Vol. 193, No. 3, pp. 56–61, 1955.

Hodgson, J. H., *Earthquakes and Earth Structure*, Englewood Cliffs, N.J., Prentice-Hall Inc., 1964 (paperback).

Knopoff, L., "The Upper Mantle of the Earth," in *Science*, Vol. 163, No. 3873, pp. 1277–1287, 1969.

eight: Volcanism

Spectacular, often violent, and sometimes catastrophic eruptions give volcanos a special interest. Besides being newsworthy, they clearly show geologic forces in action, in contrast to the more subtle and slower processes, such as rock decay and the work of streams and glaciers. Moreover they are windows to the earth's interior, for magma, erupting at the surface, gives tangible evidence of the rocks and processes at depths far below any probed by the deepest drilled holes, or brought to light by long erosion into the roots of former mountain ranges.

OBSERVATIONS

Volcanos and related structures

Volcanos and lava plateaus are the principal structures composed of extrusive igneous rocks: the rhyolites, andesites, and basalts. Volcanos are hills or mountains built around pipe-like openings, or conduits, through which magma erupts from the depths. Ordinarily the conduit mouth forms a funnel-shaped crater at the top of the volcano. If the central depression is especially large, and several times wider than it is deep, it is called a *caldera* (Fig. 8-2). Calderas occupying a large fraction of the structure result from former violent explosions and internal collapse when supporting magma is blown out or drained away at depth. They mark decapitated volcanos (Fig. 8-3).

Volcanic Ejecta Liquid lava and solid particles of various sizes compose volcanic structures;

however, ejecta during eruptions also include abundant gases (Fig. 8-4). Nitrogen, hydrogen, rotten-smelling hydrogen sulfide, acrid sulfur dioxide, and a variety of other gases, many highly poisonous, are expelled. Volcanic exhalations also include large amounts of steam. Some may represent surface water that has seeped down to magma bodies; however, there is good evidence that much is an original component of the magma and has come from the earth's interior.

Lava, the liquid ejecta, flows from an eruption until it cools and hardens. Dark basaltic lavas are typically fluid and may flow considerable distances, even on gentle slopes, before congealing, whereas rhyolitic and andesitic lavas are usually quite viscous, and harden before moving very far. The rock of frozen lava flows often gives evidence of its molten past (Fig. 8-5). Many lavas are shot through with vesicles, the frozen holes left by gas bubbles, to such an extent, in the case of pumice, that this rock is light enough to float on water. Many basalts are broken into polygonal columns, in some case several feet across at the top, and a hundred or more feet in length. These structures are bounded by large, deep, contraction cracks, produced by shrinking of the basalt mass as it cools and hardens. Other basalts, looking like a jumbled mass of pillows, are evidence of eruption under water (Fig. 8-6). Here, rapid chilling quenches lava outpourings, producing rounded, frozen skins on successive lava tongues, as they continue to pile over each other.

Solid ejecta, the pyroclastics, are thrown into the air by explosions (Fig. 8-7). The fragments may be smashed or pulverized rock from the volcano, or clots of lava, which become at least

Fig. 8-1
Eruption of Mt. Mayon in the Philippine Islands. Photo from U.S. Information Agency (U.S. National Archives).

partially solidified in the air before falling to the ground. Larger fragments are called blocks and bombs; cinders, ash, and dust include the progressively smaller particle sizes. Although some of the terms might imply that volcanic rocks have burned like coal (and, in fact, volcanic eruptions were attributed in earlier days to burning subterranean coal) such is clearly not the case.

Types of Volcanos Consistent explosive eruptions of pyroclastics produce *cinder cones* which

are, literally, steep-sided conical piles of solid ejecta around the central vent or crater (Fig. 8-8). Although the cones may grow on top of lava—and lava may break out from their bases— the cones themselves contain only pyroclastics. They are the smallest type of volcano, rarely exceeding a few hundred feet in height, and may occur in swarms, producing volcano fields. Mount Suribachi on Iwo Jima, Sunset Crater in Arizona, and the Mexican volcano Paricutin, in its early development at least, are representative cinder cones (Fig. 8-9). Most are basaltic

Fig. 8-2
Crater Lake, Oregon. Water-filled caldera with small more-recent volcano (cinder cone), Wizard Island. Spence Air Photo.

in rock type although some consist of rhyolite.

Most impressively beautiful in their size and shape, and also the most violently explosive, are *strato-volcanos*, sometimes called composite cones (Fig. 8-10). Their deep erosion exposes layers of pyroclastics irregularly interspersed with lava flows. The pyroclastics erupt largely from the main crater, or in parasitic cones on the main volcano's flanks; however, lava may erupt on the sides from deeply penetrating cracks. Fujiyama, the sacred mountain of Japan, Mayon in the Philippines, and the great volcanos of the

A	B	C
early eruption	removal of magma in violent eruptions	collapse & crystallization of magma

Fig. 8-3
Formation of a caldera such as Crater Lake (after H. Williams).

Fig. 8-4
Night view of glowing lava fountains caused by bursts of gas in the caldera of Halemaumau, Hawaii. Bursts reach 300 feet in height and average about 75 feet. National Park Service Photo.

Cascade Mountains in the western United States are examples of these impressive structures which often reach many thousands of feet in height. They are composed mainly of andesite and rhyolite.

The *shield volcanos,* whose profile suggests a Greek warrior's shield, are largely great outpourings of mainly basaltic lava which, because it flows and spreads, produces gentle slopes (Fig. 8-12). Though their flanks are not precipitous, shield volcanos may rise to great heights. Mauna Loa, on the island of Hawaii, rises 30,000 feet above the surrounding ocean bottom, and nearly 14,000 feet above sea level. Thus the Hawaiian islands are the greatest volcanic pile erupted upon the earth's crust. The alignment of the Hawaiians and other island groups in the central Pacific Ocean suggests that they are

localized upwellings of lava, along extensive rifts or cracks in the ocean bottom (Fig. 8-13).

The structure of volcanos reflects their nature of eruption and, because some change their habits, *compound volcanos* are produced that are combinations of the three basic types. Mt. Etna, on the island of Sicily, represents a large shield volcano that is capped by a later, and exceptionally large, cinder cone, which is at least 1000 feet high (Fig. 8-14).

Although not strictly volcanos, because they lack central conduits, *lava plateaus* are eruptive structures. They are volcanic table lands, often of tremendous expanse, that develop where fluid magma erupts along extensive cracks of fractures in the crust (Fig. 8-15). Fluid basaltic magma flows out in a succession of nearly horizontal sheets. Individual flows may be only a few tens of feet thick, but where many flows are periodically erupted upon each other, over a long period of time, lava plateaus thousands of feet thick, and covering hundreds of thousands of square miles, have developed. The Columbia Plateau of northwestern United States, and the Deccan Plateau of India are among the most extensive volcanic features on earth.

Distribution of Volcanos Today some 450 volcanos are active. These, along with many more so little eroded they cannot be long extinct, lie in definite belts corresponding generally to the major earthquake zones. Great andesitic stratovolcanos of the "Circle of Fire" rim the Pacific. An offshoot from this belt passes through Indonesia, and thence, with many sizeable gaps, along the Alpine-Himalayan mountain belt into the Mediterranean region. Volcanic activity is also prominent along the global system of largely submarine ridges, extending from Iceland along the Atlantic ocean floor, and into the Pacific. Other largely submarine belts in the Pacific are marked by islands, notably the Hawaiian group. In contrast to the circum-Pacific and its offshoot to the Mediterranean, the submarine systems of volcanos seem dominantly basaltic.

Intrusive or Deeper Magmatic Structures Many igneous structures formed at depth are exposed only after prolonged erosion. Long after a volcanic cone has disappeared, its former existence is recorded in a *volcanic neck,* composed of solidified magma in the deeper part of a volcanic conduit (Figs. 8-16, 8-17). *Dikes* and *sills* are tabular, or sheet-like, igneous intrusions into older rock. Dikes are discordant, meaning that they cut across the structures in the older, or country, rock (Fig. 8-18). Before solidification, they may have fed lava flows or other igneous structures including sills. Sills resemble dikes except that they are concordant, following the structure of the country rock. They may be horizontal, or nearly so, as in the Palisades sill along the Hudson River across from New York City, but they can have any attitude, so long as they conform to the surrounding structure. Both

range in size from a few inches to many feet in thickness. *Stocks* are vertical plug-like masses of igneous rock extending from depth. They are formed by magma masses that bow up the rocks into which they are intruded. *Laccoliths* are concordant igneous masses of lenticular shape, like

Fig. 8-5
Smooth ropey-surfaced basaltic lava (pahoehoe). Kilauea crater, Hawaii. Photo by Tad Nichols.

169

Fig. 8-6
Pillow lavas west of Othello, Washington. Photo by Vernon Anderson.

a giant blister, that have bowed up the rocks into which they were intruded (Fig. 8-19). They may be fed by a dike or a sill, and form a simple flat-bottomed lers, or, in some cases, a more compli-cated structure whose cross-section looks like a Christmas tree. Laccoliths may be offshoots of larger stocks, as in the Henry Mountains of Utah, which are several miles in diameter, and more than 1000 feet high.

Eruptions of Some Famous and Infamous Volcanos

Vesuvius To the Romans, Monte Somma was just a large mountain close by Herculaneum and Pompeii, resort cities on the coast of the Med-iterranean. There was no record in classic times of any volcanic activity, that is, until 79 A.D. During the preceding 16 years the region had received a series of strong earthquakes, and then, in August, Monte Somma awoke with devastat-ing eruptions. Pompeii was overwhelmed by clouds of white-hot ash, and Herculaneum was buried under streams of mud. As Vesuvius, the mountain has been erupting with periodic vio-lence ever since, and has built a modern cone inside the relic rim of Monte Somma's caldera.

During the 79 A.D. eruption, the Roman na-turalist and historian, Pliny the Elder, was admiral of the Roman fleet stationed nearby, in the present Bay of Naples. To satisfy his scientific curiosity and to rescue panicky friends, he went ashore, where he lost his life. The story of his death and an excellent description of the eruption are preserved in letters to the historian Tacitus from the admiral's nephew, Pliny the Younger, who prudently declined his uncle's invitation to go ashore because he had some studies to complete.

Pompeii and Herculaneum, buried by ash and mud, were forgotten for more than 1000 years. Rediscovered, they were excavated to expose Roman cities in excellent states of preservation, along with the story of their violent destructions (Fig. 8-21). Household goods, personal belongings, and even food have been found in Pompeii, and molds of volcanic ash formed around the bodies of people and animals have been recovered and filled with plaster, to form rather macabre statues.

Fig. 8-7
Early morning photo of Paricutin Volcano, Mexico, during eruption (1944). Light streaks are made by incandescent volcanic bombs. Photo by Tad Nichols.

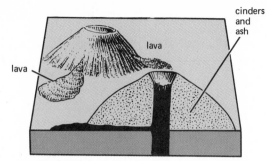

cinders
and
ash

lava

lava

Fig. 8-8 *Cinder cone.*

Pelée Mount Pelée, named for the Goddess of Fire, on the island of Martinique in the West Indies, came to life in 1902 after lying dormant for some 50 years. Eruptions began with explosions in the crater, which eventually ceased, and were followed by periodic eruptions from the flanks that sent dense swirling clouds of incandescent ash, lubricated by intensely heated gases, avalanching down the mountain's sides. Most were directed down valleys leading away from St. Pierre, the capital of Martinique, but on May 8, a flaming outburst slashed through the city, smashing walls, uprooting trees, capsizing ships in the harbor, and incinerating over 30,000 people, almost in an instant. The sole

Fig. 8-9
New lava flow emerging from the base of Paricutin in an early stage of its development. Photo by Tad Nichols.

survivor was a prisoner deep underground in the city jail.

In October, a lava plug was slowly extruded from Pelée's throat to form a spine rising almost 1000 feet above the crater's rim. Within a year, however, the soft rock of the spine, jarred by explosions, was destroyed. Around 1930, the volcano was active again, producing more flaming clouds and lava spines. This time the Peleean clouds all followed a valley north of St. Pierre, sparing the reoccupied city.

Krakatoa The greatest explosion in recorded history was the eruption of Krakatoa in the Sunda Straits between Java and Sumatra in 1883. Dormant for two centuries, it commenced erupting in May, culminating in four tremendous explosions, one of which was heard in Australia, 3000 miles away. The ash-filled air brought total darkness at mid-day in the adjacent islands, during the height of the eruptions. Fine dust, blown high into the atmosphere, encircled the globe,

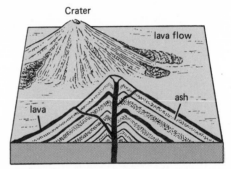

Fig. 8-10 *Strato volcanos.*

bringing exceptionally brilliant sunsets everywhere for some two years after the eruption. Where island masses had stood several thousand feet above sea level, a caldera appeared, whose bottom lay a thousand feet below the sea. The death toll on Krakatoa was zero—it was uninhabited—but over 36,000 lives were lost on Java and Sumatra, where giant sea waves generated by the blast swept the low coastal flats. The

Fig. 8-11
Chilean volcano Osorno from Lake Llauquihue. Photo by E. A. Carter.

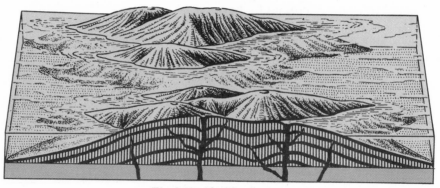

Fig. 8-12 *Shield volcanos.*

Fig. 8-13
Vents of shield volcanos, called calderas, are much broader than they are deep. The caldera of Halemaumau (Hawaii) when photographed in 1952 had a floor of some 150 acres. National Park Service Photo.

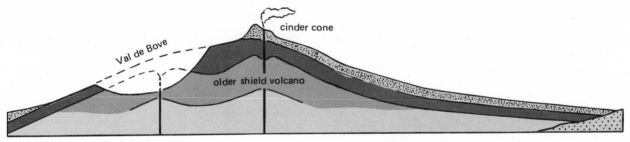

Fig. 8-14
Compound volcano. Cross-section of Mt. Etna (from Sir Charles Lyell).

waves were recorded by tide gauges around the world.

Stromboli Not all volcanos are given to violent eruptions blowing away and collapsing their tops. Stromboli, forming an island north of Sicily, has had almost continuous mild eruptions at intervals from a few minutes to an hour or so apart throughout recorded history. Mild explosions throw clumps of lava into the air where they solidify as volcanic bombs or scoriaceous chunks. The glow of the frequent eruptions in the crater, reflected by steam clouds overhead, make this volcano the "Lighthouse of the Mediterranean."

Hawaiian Islands In the shield volcanos, making up the Hawaiian group, eruptions are comparatively quiet. They are mainly lava flows breaking out the sides of the mountains, or jets and fountains shot up from lava lakes in their craters, which are steep-sided fire pits several miles across. Occasional explosions are caused by steam, when downward-seeping surface waters penetrate to molten lavas.

INFERENCES

The nature of volcanic eruptions

Much is known of the surficial effects of volcanism, but explanations of its origin and causes are tentative at best. The materials and shapes of volcanos are readily observable, and their structures are exposed after deep erosion, although never as neatly as we would like. Eruptions are also observable, but their study poses problems because they are relatively infrequent, certainly uncontrollable, and cannot be summoned on demand like some reaction in a test tube. One must admire such volcanologists as Frank Peray, who stayed in an observation tower high on the western slope of Vesuvius throughout its 1906 eruptions, and also ascended Mount Pelée to study its eruptions from 1929 to 1932. Consider, too, the dedication to their science of Day and Shepherd, who walked out onto the crusted laval over the fire pit of the Hawaiian volcano, Kilauea, to thrust iron pipes into the cracks of flaming blisters above lava fountains,

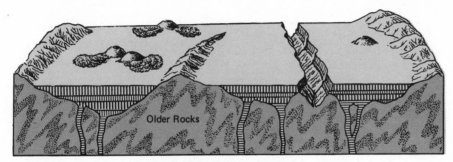

Fig. 8-15 *Lava plateau.*

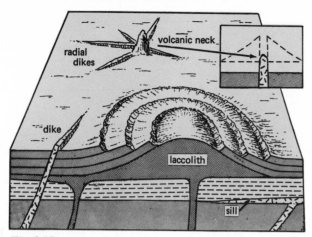

Fig. 8-16
Intrusive igneous structures.

in order to collect volcanic gases uncontaminated by air. Despite all of this, our knowledge of the deeper plumbing of volcanos and the causes of volcanic action remain highly speculative.

Periodic Violence Why are strato-volcanos, like Krakatoa, violently explosive, others less so, and some such as Stromboli rather well behaved? Apparently Stromboli's conduit, which never solidifies, acts as an open safety valve allowing continuous small eruptions, so that dangerous pressures do not arise. On the other hand, violent volcanos like Krakatoa and Vesuvius become plugged when lava in their conduits "freezes," causing tremendous internal pressures to build up. Recall that these volcanos all had long periods when they were seemingly extinct, before their most violent explosions. Moreover, the

Fig. 8-17
Aglathla, a volcanic neck near Kayenta, Arizona. Photo by Tad Nichols.

spine extruded by Pelée is direct evidence that a stout plug had formed in the throat of this malevolent strato-volcano. In contrast to the fluid basalt associated with shield volcanos and lava plateaus, andesitic magmas are notably viscous and gassy. Thus, strato-volcanos are especially prone to plugging with a resultant development of great internal pressures which can be relieved only by breaching the volcano's sides, producing Peléean clouds, or violently decapitating the structure by explosion, and collapse from loss of magma at depth. They are like old steam boilers having faulty safety valves.

Gas Production The generation of gas in volcanic magmas can be explained by a scheme involving the chemistry and physics of magmas. In hot magma, volatiles are held in solution so that little gas pressure exists. As magma cools and starts converting to igneous rock, however, solid crystals form that reject dissolved gases from their structure. Thus, the remaining magma becomes progressively richer in volatiles. When the liquid reaches saturation and can hold no more, some is expelled as free gases including steam. At the high temperatures within a volcano, these confined gases have a strong tendency to expand creating great pressures. The pressures force magma up the conduit in a more normal type of eruption, or if this outlet is plugged, they eventually become tremendous and cause violent explosions.

The deeper structure of volcanos

Magma Chambers Our knowledge of the deeper volcanic plumbing that feeds conduits and fissures is very sketchy. Recent studies of Hawaiian volcanos using tiltmeters, sensitive instruments recording changes in the slope of the ground, show that when an eruption is about to start the mountain surface bulges up appreciably; then as the lava erupts, the ground subsides. Hence at a comparatively shallow depth within the volcano, there seems to be a bladder-like magma chamber which inflates as it fills, and deflates during eruptions. Excessive emptying of such

Fig. 8-18
Vertical dikes cutting sedimentary beds in New Mexico. U.S. Geological Survey photo by N. H. Darton.

chambers, after a series of strong eruptions, probably caused the collapse of those volcanos marked by large central calderas. In any case they probably serve as storage tanks; the breeding ground of magma is believed to be much farther down (Fig. 8-23).

177

Fig. 8-19
Bear Butte, South Dakota. A laccolith surrounded by the eroded edges of upturned sedimentary beds. U.S. Geological Survey photo by N. H. Darton.

Fig. 8-20
Location of some of the earth's major volcanos. Labeled volcanos are open circles. Note the "ring of fire" around the Pacific.

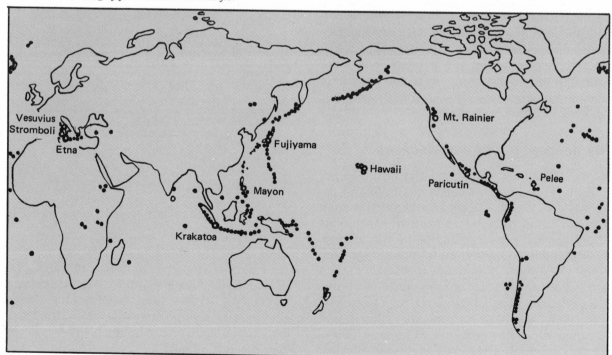

Fig. 8-21
Excavated streets of Pompeii with Vesuvius in the background. Photo by E. A. Carter.

The Origin of Magma Volcanos once seemed good evidence that the earth's interior was entirely molten beneath the relatively thin frozen crust. Geophysical evidence has since ruled out any continuous liquid zones above the earth's core. The core zone is an unlikely source of magma, because of its 2000 mile depth and probable composition of nickel-iron. However, there is evidence of magma just below the crust. Magma, moving in conduits, creates rhythmic vibrations, discernible with seismographs. Newly improved instruments have recorded such volcanic tremors originating about 25 miles below the Hawaiian and a few other volcanos. Thus many present-day workers assume that magma originates in the outer mantle, in local and temporary pockets of unknown shape.[1]

[1] Other theoreticians propose somewhat lesser or greater depths, and relatively thin but extensive magma zones (undetected by seismographs); but let us stick to our story.

179

Fig. 8-22
Mt. Etna in Eruption 1669. (From an old painting in the cathedral at Catania, Sicily.) Monte Rossi threw out a vast volume of lava that destroyed much of Catania, 30 miles away.

Just how solid, or even plastic, rock is converted into liquid pockets of magma poses theoretical problems. For background, consider the temperatures and pressures within the earth. That the earth gets progressively hotter inward [2] is a fact established from temperature readings in deep mines and drilled holes. The pressures also rise markedly with depth as the weight of overlying rock increases. Because of the extreme pressures, rock at depth remains solid or plastic at temperatures well above those which would melt it at the surface.

Volcanos are associated with belts of mountain building and general crustal unrest where local conditions of temperature and pressure could liquify parts of the mantle. Upwarping, or deep fracturing of the crust and upper mantle,

[2] The temperature increase varies widely from place to place, but averages about 150° Fahrenheit per mile near the surface; farther down this geothermal gradient must be less or the mantle would all be melted to a liquid. These are important matters, but they complicate our presentation unnecessarily.

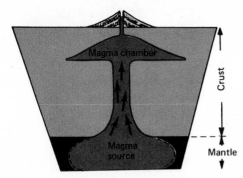

Fig. 8-23
Highly schematic diagram of deeper volcanic "plumbing." The shapes of the chambers and nature of the connections are not really known. Suggested by a diagram by G. A. Mac-Donald.

Leopold Von Buch *(1774–1852) Although Von Buch studied paleontology, alpine mountain structure, and produced the first extensive geologic map of Germany, he is best remembered for his work on volcanos. Originally taught by Professor Werner at Freiberg that the earth's crustal rocks were precipitates from a universal sea, Von Buch reluctantly rejected the erroneous grand theory after his far-reaching travels convinced him of the igneous origin of basalt.*

might relieve confining pressures on "superheated" rock, at depth, to a point where melting would convert plastic mantle of the asthenosphere into magma. Although existing theoretical calculations of internal temperatures do make it unlikely that pressures could ever be sufficiently reduced at the depths where magma originates for melting to occur, the idea cannot yet be ruled out.

Hot zones or pockets caused by localized radioactive heating have been a popular explanation for magma generation. However, geiger counters have shown no excess radioactivity in active Hawaiian lava flows or their associated gas clouds; so the issue remains in doubt. These and other explanations are little more than informed guesses, reflecting our present inadequate understanding of the earth's interior, a stimulating subject for future investigations.

SUGGESTED READINGS

Bullard, F. M., *Volcanos in History, Theory, and Eruption,* Austin, Tex., University of Texas Press, 1962.

Williams, Howell, "Volcanos," in *Scientific American,* Vol. 185, No. 5, pp. 45–53, 1951.

nine: The deformed crust

If the earth's crust were static, the lands would have long ago disappeared beneath a universal sea. But the external destructive forces of weathering, gravity, and the agents of erosion are counteracted by the internal dynamics of the earth. New rock builds up in volcanic eruptions, and the crust is uplifted by deformational forces. Folded, contorted, and broken sedimentary strata are clearly evidence of past deformation. If the crust were static, mud cracks, ripple marks, and many more features of clastic sedimentary, and other layered rocks, would not be found on steeply sloping surfaces where they often appear today.

Moreover, there is direct evidence of crustal movement in historic time. Most obvious and dramatic is the sudden appearance of scarps and horizontal displacements during earthquakes. Clear-cut examples of slow warping are also common. Abandoned irrigation systems of ancient Near Eastern civilizations now go up and down, over hills that must have risen up to warp the ditches after they were dug. The rise and fall of coastal land is often marked by warped wave-cut terraces that can be related to existing sea level, the ideal reference plane.

The classic example of coastal deformation in historic time is the Temple of Jupiter Serapis, described by **Sir Charles Lyell** in his *Principles of Geology*, the leading textbook of the nineteenth century (and used by authors of elementary geology texts ever since). The "temple" was probably a Roman market place, but in any case stone columns there are pitted by rock-boring clams up to 18 feet above the temple floor. Thus, after the temple was built, the coast must have submerged to allow the clams to attack the columns, and then, later, re-emerged to expose the columns as they are seen today. In Lyell's time the case needed proving, but now the accumulated evidence is overwhelming that solid rocks are deformed in the earth's mobile crust.

LOCAL STRUCTURES

Rocks are deformed by compression, or squeezing; tension, a pulling apart; and torsion, a twisting resulting when two forces act in opposite directions, but not on the same line. Up to a point, solid rocks are elastic, i.e., they regain their original shape and volume when an applied stress is released. Under greater stresses they are permanently deformed by folding or fracturing. Deep-seated rocks, especially in zones of dynamic metamorphism, lose rigidity, and flow into the often highly contorted structures characterizing plastic deformation.

Technical terminology, a bane to many, actually simplifies description for the initiated. Conversations among structural geologists are liberally sprinkled with "dip" and "strike," terms describing the attitude in space of a plane, such as the surface of a rock layer or fractures of various sorts (Fig. 9-2). Dip is the inclination of a plane or bed measured from the horizontal in a vertical plane. Put another way, it is the maximum tilt that can be measured on a sloping plane. Dips are recorded in degrees so that a horizontal bed has a 0° reading, no dip at all; a vertical bed has a 90° dip; and sloping beds various readings in between. *Strike* is the compass

Fig. 9-1
Upturned strata forming the dome at Sinclair, Wyoming. U.S. Geological Survey photo by J. R. Balsley.

direction of a line formed by the intersection of a rock surface and a horizontal plane. It should correspond to a horizontal line drawn on the surface of a sloping bed, and it is always at 90° to the dip direction (Fig. 9-2).

Folds

Geometry Folding warps rocks into upfolds called *anticlines* or downfolds called *synclines*. These two basic fold types are usually adjacent to each other, like wrinkles in a tablecloth. The *monocline,* a different type of flexure characterizing some regions, can be described as "half a fold." It develops where near-horizontal rocks locally dip more steeply and then flatten out again. In size, folds range from minute crinkles, an inch or less across, to structures forming mountain ranges (Figs. 9-4, 9-5).

The diversity of folds in nature is most eco-nomically described by referring to their individual geometric parts (Fig. 9-6). The *axial plane* is visualized as dividing a fold into halves that are approximate mirror images. The *fold axis* is an imaginary line formed by the intersection of the axial plane with the curved surface of the fold. The flanks of a fold on either side of the axial plane are called its *limbs*. Thus, in an anticline the dips diverge from the axial plane, and in a syncline they converge towards the plane.

The tightness of folds varies greatly. In *open folds* the limbs have a gentle to moderate dip (Fig. 9-7). *Closed folds,* resulting from more intense deformation, have steeper limbs dipping more than 45° in relation to the axial plane. Tightly compressed folds with parallel limbs, common in dynamically metamorphosed rocks, are called *isoclinal*. The attitude of folds can be described by reference to their axial planes (Fig. 9-8). *Upright folds* have vertical axial planes, and opposing limbs of approximately equal dips. In *overturned folds*, the axial plane is tilted, and one limb turns under the other (Fig. 9-9). The axial planes of *recumbent folds* are horizontal; the fold lies on its side, and one limb is above the other (Fig. 9-10).

Maps and Cross-sections Folds, and other geologic structures as well, are usually illustrated by means of maps and cross-section. Block diagrams are excellent for simple or generalized representation, but detailed and complex structural relations must of necessity be presented through two-dimensional drawings. A geologic map is essentially a scale drawing of the distribution of outcrops—a floor plan of the rocks. Most are made in the field by plotting contacts, the boundaries between different rock masses,

and recording symbols for dips and strikes and other pertinent data on a base sheet. The map should also include roads, property lines, streams, and other features that help in determining location. As outcrops are often patchy, being covered by vegetation, soil, and other surficial materials, many bedrock relations shown on a map are inferred, i.e., informed guesses. Cross-sections, representing vertical slices, are drawn along selected lines across the map to show the visualized relations of rock at depth. This mild digression seems essential because any worthwhile understanding of geologic structures involves an exercise in solid geometry, requiring three-dimensional thinking.

Outcrop Patterns The surface expression of folds and the outcrop pattern shown on a map are controlled by the geometry of the deformed beds and also the ground surface eroded across them. The interpretation of geologic structures is predicated on Steno's Laws of Original Horizontality, and Superposition. If strata are folded, and the topmost bed is not breached by erosion, it will extend across the area in anticlinal hills and synclinal valleys.

Commonly, however, folds are eroded so that the ground surface is beveled across the structures, exposing a series of beds in banded out-

Charles Lyell (1797–1875) *This Englishman's patient collection of evidence during the 19th century finally settled the violent debate among geologists as to whether slow, observable, natural processes acting through a long time or unobserved catastrophic changes accounted for most of the earth's geologic surface features. Although overemphasizing Uniformitarianism by modern standards, his work established a sound theoretical basis for geology.*

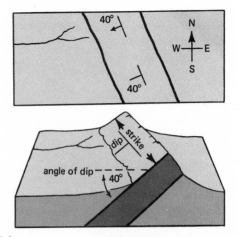

Fig. 9-2
Map and block diagram illustrating dip and strike.

Fig. 9-3
The stream surface gives a reference plane for the dip (toward the left) of these strata on the South Branch of the Potomac River. U.S. Forest Service photo by T. C. Fearnow.

crop patterns. An anticline produces parallel outcrops having the oldest bed in the middle, flanked by progressively younger corresponding beds on either side (Fig. 9-11). An eroded syn-cline has a similar pattern except that the order is reversed, so that the axis in the center follows the youngest bed, which is flanked by progressively older beds on either side (Fig. 9-12).

Fig. 9-4 *Basic fold types.*

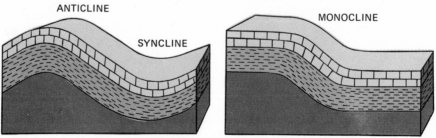

ANTICLINE

SYNCLINE

MONOCLINE

Fig. 9-5
Sheep Mountain in north central Wyoming, an anticlinal fold cut through by the Bighorn River.
Courtesy of Jersey Production Research Company.

Fig. 9-6 *Descriptive nomenclature of folds.*

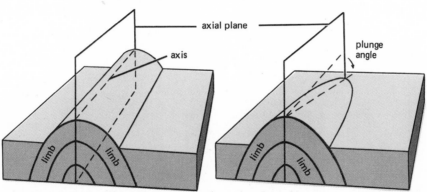

Fig. 9-7
Open and upright fold. Brown's Mountain anticline, "The Devil's Backbone," West Virginia. U.S. Forest Service photo by L. J. Prater.

Fig. 9-8 *Cross-sections showing attitudes of folds.*

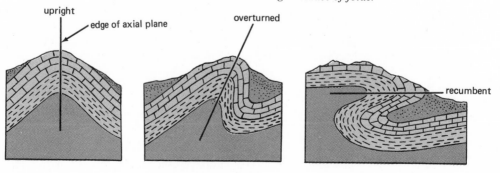

a plunging fold wraps around the axis producing a *nose*. Where many adjacent folds rise and plunge along their axes, a zig-zag pattern may result, somewhat like the wrinkles in a rumpled tablecloth.

Banded outcrop patterns, roughly resembling those of anticlinal and synclinal structures in dipping beds, may develop where nearly flat-lying beds are deeply eroded. A valley, cut through several horizontal beds, creates a map pattern suggestive of an anticline, since progressively older beds are exposed towards the center (Fig. 9-13). A syncline-like pattern can develop on a hill whose sides expose several flat-lying beds (Fig. 9-14). In general, the basic map relations provide the bases for unravelling structural areas where the individual elements are interwoven in complex overall patterns.

Faults

Faults and folds are not mutually exclusive results of deformation as they often occur together and may grade into each other. A fault is a fracture along which rock masses have been displaced. Along many faults, great displacements measuring thousands of feet, or even many miles, are certainly not the result of a single colossal slippage. Instead, such displacements are the sum total of many small slippages over a

Fig. 9-9
Overturned fold, Wind River Mountains, Wyoming. Photo by D. Kisling, courtesy of R. B. Parker.

However, folds do not extend indefinitely. Folded zones may die out where dips decrease, in regions where the deformation was less. Within folded regions, the individual folds plunge where a whole rock sequence goes deeper into the ground. The outcrop pattern of

Fig. 9-10
Recumbent fold in Rheem's Quarry, Pennsylvania. Courtesy of R. B. Parker.

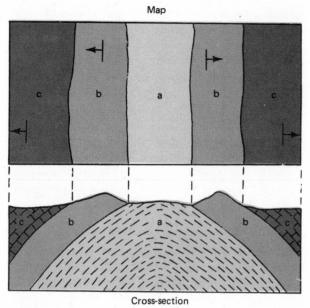

Fig. 9-11
An eroded anticline in map and cross-section. Bed a *is oldest, bed* b *is younger,* c *is youngest.*

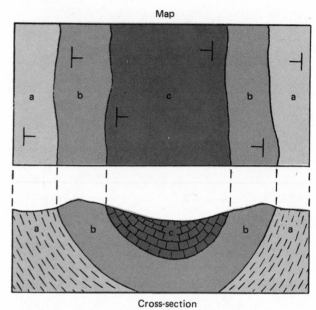

Fig. 9-13
Eroded syncline. Oldest exposed layer is a.

Fig. 9-12
Map pattern and cross-section of deep valley eroded through horizontal strata.

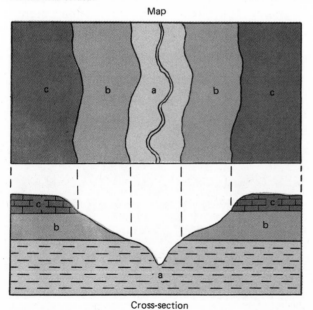

Fig. 9-14
The youngest layer c *reflects an eroded mesa or similar ridge.*

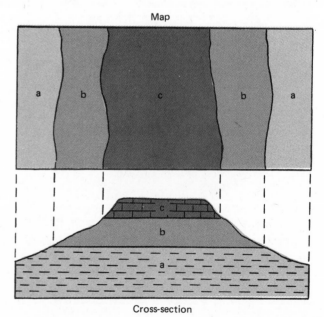

Fig. 9-15
Exposed fault in Johnson County, Tennessee. Crumbling of rocks on fault zone produced gulley and talus in center. Beds on the right dip steeply right parallel to the fault. Beds on the left dip left, except close to the fault where they are bent, or dragged, near vertical because the rock mass on the right moved up. Courtesy U.S. Geological Survey.

great length of time. This pattern of movement characterizes active faults. Their periodic slippages are at most a few tens of feet, and usually much less, as is clearly indicated by the vertical scarps or horizontal offsets appearing during the attendant earthquakes. Moreover, most faults

are now inactive. For example, the southern Appalachians, highly faulted mountains, have few earthquakes, and lack any topographic or other evidence of recent movement (Fig. 9-15). Not all faults show great displacement; some grade into joints, fractures in rock having no

Fig. 9-16
Normal fault of slight displacement. Oak Creek Canyon, Arizona. Photograph by the author.

displacement (Figs. 9-16, 9-17). And, not all faults are distinct planes; in some, the movement is distributed through a fractured zone.

Nomenclature The terms *upthrown* and *downthrown* apply to the vertical movements of opposing blocks along a fault. The terms are relative, as both blocks may have actually moved downward, closer to the earth's center, with one side getting ahead of the other; or both may have risen, but at slightly different rates.

A fault surface exposed on the face of an upthrown block forms a cliff known as the *fault scarp. Key* or *marker* beds are parts of a distinctive unit whose separation indicates the amount of fault displacement. *Hanging wall* refers to the face of a fault block that would form an overhang if the blocks were somehow pulled apart. The *foot wall* is the opposing block's surface that forms a complementary slope. They are old mining terms, originating because tunnels driven through mineralized zones of faults exposed

Fig. 9-17
Well-developed joints in sandstone hogback at Muddy Gap, Wyoming. Photo by Herb Pownall.

these surfaces: the hanging wall sloped overhead; the footwall was underfoot. Although scarps characterize recent faults, erosion often destroys them on inactive ones so that the ground surface extends uninterrupted across both fault blocks. With these terms in mind, an economical description of fault classification is possible.

Classification   Genetic classifications are ultimately the most desirable in geology, and faults can be classed genetically according to the tensional, compressional, or other forces that created them. Unfortunately, such classification is not always possible because the forces producing a given fault are often unknown or controversial. Geometric classifications, being empirical, are the most generally useful and applicable. In these, relative movement, the attitude of the fault plane, and other observable features are used (Fig. 9-18).

Faults are arbitrarily classed as *high angle* if their fault plane dips 45° or more, and *low angle* if the dip is less. Using the direction of movement along the fault plane, three basic classes of faults are recognized. In *strike-slip faults*, like the San Andreas rift, the movement is

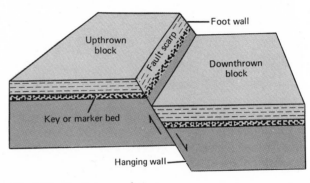

Fig. 9-18 *Fault nomenclature.*

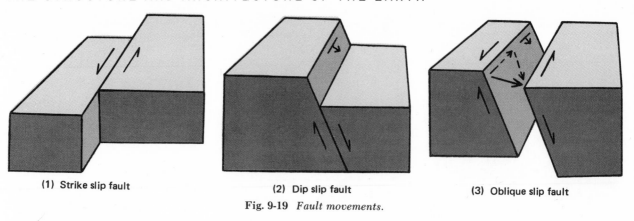

(1) Strike slip fault   (2) Dip slip fault   (3) Oblique slip fault

Fig. 9-19 *Fault movements.*

Fig. 9-20
Normal fault at Coyote Springs, Wyoming. Shale (upper right) is down-thrown against sandstone. Slope (lower right) is shale talus. Photograph by the author. Road cut is 30 feet high.

Reverse fault (low angle)

Fig. 9-21

Reverse fault (normal faults shown in Figs. 9-17 and 9-19, part 2).

largely horizontal, in the direction of the fault plane's strike; as a result no scarp is formed, although a valley may be eroded into the crushed fault zone. *Dip-slip faults* have dominantly vertical motion, in the direction of dip of the fault plane, so that a scarp is likely on active faults. The movement on some faults combines both strike and dip-slip components about equally; hence they are called *oblique-slip* faults (Fig. 9-19).

Three names, commonly used in the field, are applied to varieties of dip-slip faults. In *normal faults,* a common result of tension, the foot wall is upthrown relative to the hanging wall (Fig. 9-20). The name "normal" originated in early European mining districts where such faults were the most common. However in many regions normal faults are not "normal"; the reverse is true. In *reverse faults,* usually a result of compression, the hanging wall is upthrown (Fig. 9-21). Recent reverse faulting might be expected to form an overhanging scarp; actually, such clifflets are almost never formed, because the rocks along joints collapse, producing a scarp resembling that of a normal fault. Because of the mechanics of rock fracturing, normal faults tend to be high angle. Reverse faults show no such preference, and the abundant low-angle reverse faults are commonly called *thrust faults* or simply *thrusts.* Associated thrusts and folds characterize many of the great contorted mountain ranges, which may be the result of major compression with great crustal shortening or,

in some cases at least, the product of gravitational sliding.

Outcrop Patterns In eroded folds, the same beds appear at the ground surface in several different places, but they are always adjacent to beds deposited immediately before or after them, and are of approximately normal thickness. Faults, in contrast, generally play havoc with the sequence of beds, may produce an apparent thinning or thickening of individual beds, and often abruptly truncate the outcrop of a whole sequence of beds. Although there are exceptions, relating to the dip of strata and the character of the surface topography, certain outcrop patterns are characteristic. Thrust or reverse faults commonly cause *omission of beds,* in map view, because the upthrown hanging wall jams older rocks over younger ones that, as a result, do not appear at the surface. *Repetition of beds* characterizes many normal faults (Fig. 9-22).

The line a fault makes across the ground is called its *trace.* The sinuosity of a fault trace, whether it is straight or crooked, is controlled by the steepness of the fault plane where it emerges at the surface, and the nature of the topography. A vertical fault plane has a straight trace regardless of the dissection of the land surface. A low-angle fault, across any but competely flat ground, is sinuous; the lower a fault plane dips, and the rougher the topography, the more irregular is the trace (Fig. 9-23). This elementary

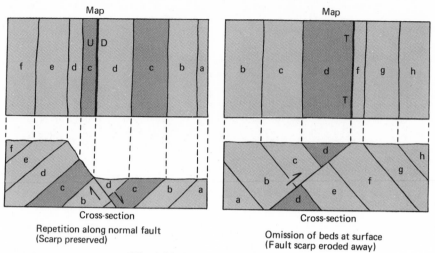

Fig. 9-22 *Repetition and omission.*

discussion may suggest that the geometry of folds and faults can become a complicated matter, especially in contorted mountain ranges. Its study, however, gives clues to the nature of the forces deforming the crust, as well as more practical things such as the search for oil.

Unconformities

James Hutton first comprehended the historical significance of those structural features called unconformities. To his creative mind, they conjured up "vestiges of lost worlds," a dramatic allusion rooted in facts. The appear-

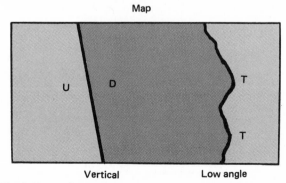

Fig. 9-23 *Fault traces.*

ance of an unconformity is deceptively simple. As seen in many roadcuts, it is soil or rock of one sort lying across different rocks—a buried erosion surface separating rocks of different ages. (Fig. 9-24).

In types called *disconformities*, strata above and below the erosion surface are essentially parallel. Their history is largely one of deposition interrupted by an extended period of non-deposition or erosion, an *hiatus* that produced the buried erosion surface. Because *angular unconformities* involve deformation as well as the processes creating the disconformity, the layers above and below the erosion surface are not parallel, which makes these features easier to recognize.

An angular unconformity indicates at least four major geologic events: (1) an initial period of deposition in which older strata are laid down near-horizontal and in order; (2) a subsequent period of folding and faulting that disturbs the then-existing beds; (3) an ensuing hiatus when the contorted beds are truncated; (4) finally, a period of renewed deposition that buries the erosion surface beneath the younger set of rocks (Fig. 9-25).

The relations in an angular unconformity have been important in dating past deformation where the beds involved can be dated by fossils or

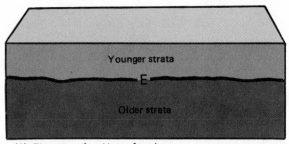

(1) Elements of an Unconformity

E = Buried surface of erosion or non-deposition

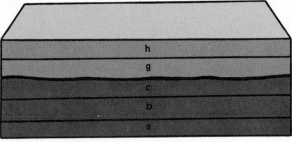

(2) Disconformity

Fig. 9-24
(1) Elements of an unconformity. (2) Disconformity.

other means. The deformation must be later than the youngest layers it affects, and earlier than the first layers deposited thereafter. The precision with which the deformation can be bracketed in time depends on the closeness in age of the dated rocks. If the time interval is long, the deformation cannot be closely dated for it could have occurred at any time within the interval.

The "lost worlds" suggested by an angular unconformity may well involve shifting seas of long duration, the rise of mountains as impressive as the Himalayas, their slow destruction and burial under broad plains of their own debris, and finally a quiet reinvasion by the seas. Angular unconformities record, in outline form, the history of the earth's great chains of deformational mountains (Fig. 9-26).

CONTINENTAL STRUCTURES

Individual folds, faults, and associated unconformities are countless, and often incredibly complex, details in grander structural patterns of a continental scale. Broadly viewed, the continental faces show two topographic elements: vast low interiors of flat or gently rolling land, outside of which lie the high or mountainous regions. Within each element are differing geologic provinces whose arrangement is roughly comparable in all the continents (Fig. 9-27).

Stable interiors

Shields At the heart of each continent is a *shield*, a broad rolling lowland across a largely crystal-

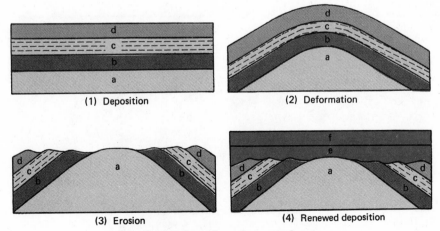

(1) Deposition

(2) Deformation

(3) Erosion

(4) Renewed deposition

Fig. 9-25 *Origin of angular unconformity.*

line basement complex. Its granites and metamorphic rocks belong to the oldest geologic eras, Precambrian time, and are essentially the exposed sial whose generally contorted and metamorphosed nature strongly suggests the deeply eroded roots of extremely ancient mountain ranges.

Interior Plains   The interiors continue as broad plains, underlain by a relatively thin veneer of near-flat, little-disturbed, sedimentary rocks. These rocks bury extensions of the beveled shields, or, in some cases, similar, but younger,

basement rocks. Locally the sediments may thicken considerably into broad basins where the basement has subsided, or they may thin over gently upwarped welts and domes. Such structures are so broad and gradual, however, that associated dips are virtually unnoticeable.

Uplifted highlands

The higher parts of continents lying beyond the stable interiors form plateaus and mountains. Which is which, geologically at least, depends on their internal structure rather than topography.

Fig. 9-26
The angular unconformity at Siccar Point, Berwickshire, Scotland, that suggested "lost worlds" to Dr. Hutton. (H.M. Geological Survey photographs; Crown copyright, reproduced by permission of the Controller of Her Majesty's Stationery Office, London.)

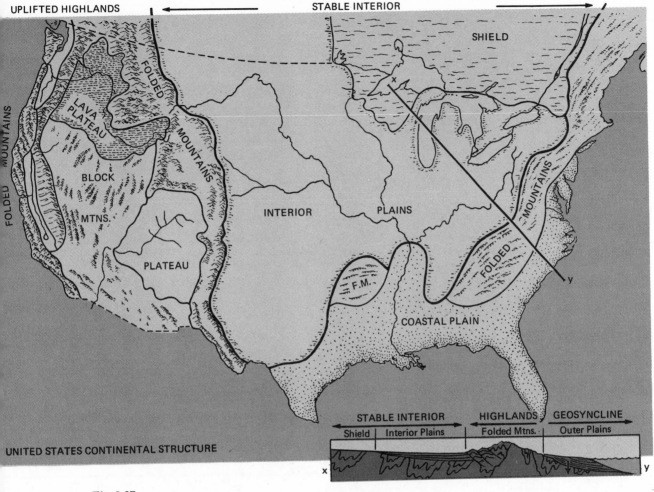

UPLIFTED HIGHLANDS — **STABLE INTERIOR**

SHIELD

LAVA PLATEAU

FOLDED MOUNTAINS

BLOCK

MTNS.

FOLDED MOUNTAINS

INTERIOR   PLAINS

PLATEAU

FOLDED MOUNTAINS

F.M.

FOLDED

COASTAL PLAIN

STABLE INTERIOR		HIGHLANDS	GEOSYNCLINE
Shield	Interior Plains	Folded Mtns.	Outer Plains

UNITED STATES CONTINENTAL STRUCTURE

Fig. 9-27
The United States is part of a rather symmetrical continent having a stable interior flanked by highlands. The Atlantic coastal plain may represent a geosyncline.

Plateaus Structurally, plateaus are highlands characterized by the near-horizontal attitude of their sedimentary or volcanic layers (Fig. 9-28). Most do form tablelands, but when deeply eroded, plateaus have a distinctly mountainous appearance. Many plateaus of great elevation contain fossiliferous rocks deposited in the sea, most notably the vast central plateau of Tibet which lies some 16,000 feet above sea level. Thus they indicate considerable crustal deformation of a remarkable sort; for aside from some high-angle faulting and monoclinal flexing, the uplift of plateaus results in no pronounced folding or crumpling.

Block Mountains Mountains, in general, are those elevated structures—if volcanos are excluded as being a special eruptive type—that are characterized by marked folding and faulting. Although a "saw-tooth" topography is typical, many mountains rise to a plateau-like upland, an erosion surface beveled across their contorted rocks. Structurally, mountains are of two distinctive types.

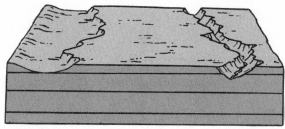 

a. Plateau

b. Mountains having a plateau-like upland

Fig. 9-28
a. *Horizontal strata forming a plateau.* b. *Plateau-like upland eroded across deformed rocks of mountain structure.*

Fig. 9-29
The Panamint Range, near Death Valley, California, is an eroded fault scarp. The mountain is a horst and the valley, an alluvial-filled graben. Photo by John H. Maxson.

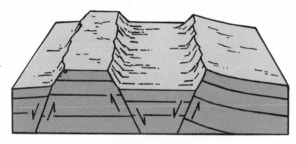

Block mountains

Fig. 9-30
Block mountains produced by high-angle faulting.

High-angle faulting may fracture the crust into angular mountains and valleys bounded by fault scarps (Fig. 9-29). The block mountains are called *horsts* if elongate; the valleys, especially long narrow ones, are called *grabens;* the many long uplifts in the Basin and Range country of the western United States are horsts. Death Valley, California, and the upper Rhine Valley are grabens, and so is the valley containing Palestine's Dead Sea (Fig. 9-30).

Folded Mountains Most attention has centered on the spectacular folded mountains, represented in the modern and imposing Alpine–Himalayan, Andean–North American Cordilleran chains, and in older worn-down ranges such as the Appalachian in America, and the Caledonian and Hercynian in Europe (Fig. 9-31). The modern ranges follow continental margins in world-wide chains corresponding to the Circum–Pacific and Alpine–Himalayan belts of earthquakes and volcanism. It seems possible

that many of the older ranges, when they formed, were also marginal to the stable continental interiors.

Though called folded mountains, these structures also involve much reverse faulting, both high-angle and thrust. Their folds range from open and upright types, to overturned, to recumbent; and in more deformed areas, especially those affected by metamorphism, isoclinal folding is common. *Nappes* are great slabs of complexly deformed rock, often in stacks, that are either great recumbent folds or extensive sheets of rock bounded by thrust faults of very low angle (Fig. 9-32). Nappes have been attributed to tremendous compression in which rock has behaved very plastically, and also to great, slow landslips from high and actively rising mountain masses. Whatever their origin, nappes give incredibly complicated structure to some folded ranges, notably the Swiss Alps.

The deepest parts of folded mountains, exposed only after prolonged erosion, show the effects of great heat and pressure. Here, contorted gneisses, schists, and other dynamically metamorphosed rocks are frequently associated with great masses of granite in *batholiths* (Fig. 9-33). These masses are often hundreds of miles wide and extend to such depths that erosion has never exposed their bottoms. In some places the granites are clearly intrusive, cutting steeply across the surrounding rocks; elsewhere the granites merge imperceptibly into gneiss, or other highly metamorphosed rocks. As a result

Nappes

Fig. 9-32
Complex recumbent folds, of considerable size, forming nappes.

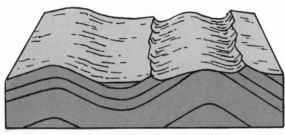

Simple folded mountains

Fig. 9-31 *Simple folded mountains.*

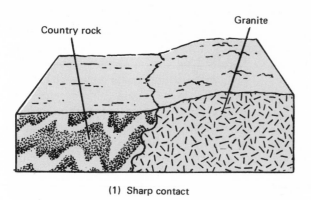

(1) Sharp contact

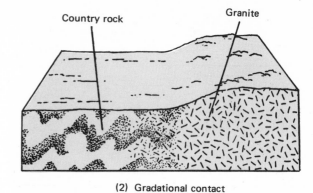

(2) Gradational contact

Fig. 9-33 *Exposed batholith.*

of these relations, and for other reasons as well, the origin of granite and its batholithic structures has created a lively controversy.

Traditionalists consider batholiths as the greatest of igneous intrusions, great bodies of solidified magma. (So, perhaps, batholiths should have been discussed along with dikes, sills, and other clearly igneous structures.) However, many "radical" workers view granite as the end result in metamorphism of sediments and other surficial rocks; if so, batholiths were never magma bodies, but, rather, masses of pre-existing rock that were altered to granite, while remaining largely in a solid or plastic state. In any case, batholiths are safely called plutonic bodies, meaning they were formed at depth; and, significantly, they occur in the roots of folded mountain ranges and nowhere else.

Mobile and rigid elements

Geosynclines One of the most significant facts about continental structure, discovered by James Hall,[3] is that the thickness of sedimentary rocks in folded mountain belts is far greater than in the stable continental interiors. Thus folded mountains originate from deep, sediment-filled troughs, which are filled *geosynclines*. These ideas of Hall, since modified and refined, lead to

the recognition of two main structural elements in continental evolution: relatively rigid and resistant continental platforms, that are subject to erosion, alternating with deposition of thin sedimentary veneers during invasions by shallow seas; and geosynclines, which act as mobile belts along the continental margins.[4] Initially, the geosynclines slowly subside as broad gentle downwarps of the crust, that receive great thicknesses of sediments over a long period of time; later, they are destroyed by crumpling, and their rocks rise into the great folded mountain ranges.

The Atlantic seaboard of the United States is a broad *coastal plain*, the emergent part of the continental shelf, that extends from New England to Florida, thence along the Gulf Coast into Mexico. Unlike plains in the continental interior, it is an outer plain lying, for much of its length, beyond the worn-down Appalachian folds. Moreover, seismic evidence indicates no thin veneer on shallow basement but, rather, tens of thousands of feet of sedimentary rock in what seems a gigantic, linear, crustal downwarp along the margin of the continental platform. Here, some geologists suggest, is a modern geosyncline filling with clastic sediments eroded from the periodically rejuvenated stumps of the Appalachians, and supplemented along the Gulf Coast by

[3] An early geologist in New York State, not to be confused with Hutton's friend, Sir James Hall, the pioneer experimental geologist.

[4] A dress shirt gives a good analogy: The starched front resembles a continental mass, being stiff and resistant although not completely rigid; the rest of the shirt is flexible, wrinkling and creasing from internal forces (the wearer).

materials from the continental interior and limestones that have been deposited in warm seas.

Styles of Deformation Overall, the continental framework exhibits two different styles of deformation. *Orogeny*, which means mountain making, produces the contorted structure of folded mountains in the relatively narrow and elongate mobile belts. *Epeirogeny*, meaning continent making, involves broad, gentle crustal warps that may be accompanied by block faulting and associated volcanic eruptions. This deformation affects the more rigid continental platforms, warping shields and interior plains into welts and basins, as well as cracking them along normal faults, which may create horsts and grabens. Plateaus, whose rocks are not contorted, show that the total amount of epeirogenic uplift can be great.

Epeirogeny usually affects folded mountains after the orogenic phase is complete. Commonly, folded mountains are broadly upwarped in their later history, and their folds and thrusts are offset along younger high-angle faults, frequently accompanied by volcanic eruptions. It seems as if the deformation and metamorphism resulting from orogeny consolidate the sedimentary rocks in mobile geosynclines, which thereafter react as rigid additions welded to the continental plates. Because the contorted rocks of shields have the look of ancient mountain roots, and because new geosynclines, such as the one beneath the coastal plain, come into being along the margins of continental platforms (previously enlarged by orogeny), a grand proposal has been made — structurally, the continents have expanded into the ocean basins through geologic time.

Isostasy Most considerations of mountains, or of continents and ocean basins, involve the concept of isostasy (from the Greek: *isos*, equal; *stasis*, standing). One might assume that the load of high mountains is supported by the strength and rigidity of the earth's crustal rocks. However earth scientists do not hold this idea today. Rather, solid continental blocks and mountains

within them are considered to be "floating" on the denser, plastic mantle beneath — in isostatic equilibrium. Geologic observations and geophysical measurements provide the evidence.

The discovery leading to the concept of isostasy was made in the 1850's. The British, under Sir George Everest (for whom the mountain was named) conducted a survey to locate reference points for the mapping of India. Precise latitudes were determined by triangulation, with plumb bobs used to establish the direction of the earth's center (as in Eratosthenes method). Some points located were in error when checked against independent astronomical observations.

J. H. Pratt, Archdeacon of Calcutta, assumed that plumb bobs caused error because they were gravitationally attracted by the mass of the nearby Himalaya Mountains. Estimating the volume of the mountains and knowing the approximate density of their rocks, Pratt calculated the expectable deflection of the plumb bob, assuming that the earth's crustal rocks were of uniform density. The results showed that the actual deflection was only about one-third of the theoretically expectable deflection. Pratt attributed the difference to less dense rocks in and beneath the mountains than in the adjacent plains. He further proposed that the rocks of the mountains were "floating" on denser material beneath. In Pratt's hypothesis, crustal blocks of the same weight and surface dimensions, but of different densities and thick-

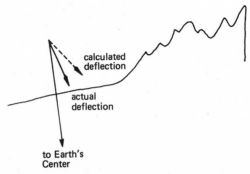

Fig. 9-34
Schematic diagram of plumb bob deflection (greatly exaggerated) caused by gravitational attraction of nearby mountain mass.

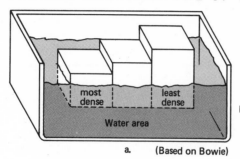

Pratt hypothesis: all blocks same surface dimensions, same weight, but different densities (weight per unit volume).

a.   (Based on Bowie)

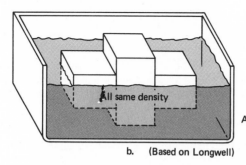

Airy hypothesis: all blocks same density, same surface dimensions but different depths.

b.   (Based on Longwell)

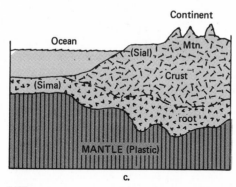

c.

Fig. 9-35
Isostasy models made by floating wooden blocks in water demonstrate the Pratt hypothesis in a, and the Airy hypothesis in b. A schematic diagram of crustal thicknesses is shown in c.

nesses had their bases at the same level within the earth; however, the tops of the less-dense blocks stood higher, forming mountains.

At the same time, in 1855, G. B. Airy, Astronomer Royal of England, made an alternate proposal which accounted equally well for the ob-

served deflection of the plumb bob from the center of the earth. In his view, all the floating crustal blocks had the same density. Assuming comparable lengths and widths, thicker blocks would be heavier hence their bases would be at greater depths to achieve equilibrium while their tops stood higher than thinner blocks. This "roots of mountains" hypothesis has been generally substantiated by twentieth-century seismic studies. They indicate thickest crust under high mountains, thinner crust beneath lower continental surfaces, and thinnest crust under ocean basins; however, Pratt's concept of different densities may well be involved in the contrast between lighter, higher-standing sialic rocks of continents and the denser simatic rocks of ocean basins.

Isostasy is an important geologic concept. Vertical movements probably result where removal of weight by erosion of their tops allows lightened mountain masses to rise and come to isostatic equilibrium, and also where the weight of thickening deposits depress parts of the crust as in geosynclinal basins. Uplifted shorelines in the Great Lakes and Baltic regions probably represent isostatic uplift after the melting and removal of continental glaciers. In such cases vertical movements of the crust are thought to be compensated for by slow flowage of the underlying plastic mantle (Fig. 9-36).

However isostasy is not an orogenic force capable of initiating folded mountain belts. Rather it is a condition of equilibrium responsible for the higher elevation of continental masses in contrast to the denser simatic ocean basins. Where isostatic equilibrium is upset, as by erosion or deposition, epeirogenic movements may result. But the creation of folded mountain belts involves little-known forces within the earth.

ON DEEPER CAUSES

We know less of the earth's internal workings than of the far-distant stars, for spectroscopes can analyze starlight, which is kindled by thermonuclear fires of the sort we have reproduced in bombs. Seismology has determined zones within the earth, and their possible composition has been deduced; yet concerning the earth's internal operations we can do little more than speculate. Their action is manifest in erupting volcanos and earthquakes, and their results are vis-

ible in the cracked, rumpled, and altered rocks exposed at the surface. But internal movements and changes are masked by the outer skin we call the crust.

How is the crust deformed and what makes mountains? We seek a mechanical scheme for the earth's internal forces, like the hydrologic cycle. This mechanism is fairly well understood because the actual sculpturing of the crust by water and air is visible. Gravitational energy and heat working on matter produce the hydrologic cycle. The heat is from the sun, and the matter is the gaseous atmosphere and liquid of the hydrosphere. Internally the earth's mechanisms should be comparable, except that the heat originates within the earth, and the matter acted upon is the crust, mantle, and core.

Recent thinking generally rejects outside forces, such as tidal attraction of the sun and moon, or passing bodies, or rotational forces, as major causes of crustal deformation. The question is just how heat and gravity, acting on internal matter, produce a mechanism responsible for mountain building and the development of continents. The many theoretical mechanisms fall into two broad groups. One assumes that the crust is deformed primarily by horizontal forces acting parallel to the earth's surface. In these, geosynclines are assumed to be crumpled into mountains by vise-like compression; block faulting and volcanism result from stretching. The second group of schemes emphasizes vertical, or radial, movements acting towards or away

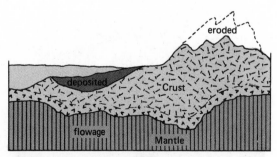

Fig. 9-36   **9-27c.**
Eroded mountains slowly rise and fill basin sinks in isostatic adjustment.

from the center of the earth. Up-bulging or down-sinking of the crust is believed primary, and intensely folded and faulted rocks in mountains are attributed to secondary gravity sliding or compression.

Compressional mechanisms

Contraction The skin of a rotting apple wrinkles around its shrinking interior and the earth's crust may do the same (Fig. 9-37). Giordano Bruno first compared the earth to an apple in the sixteenth century, and later, in 1833, Adam Sedgewick suggested that mountains originated as cooling shrank the earth. The idea was more fully developed in the nineteenth century, by James Dana in America, and Elie de Beaumont in Europe, and ever since the concept of a shrinking earth has had its defenders.

Earlier theories of contraction were based on the assumption that the earth solidified from an originally molten mass and has been cooling by conduction and radiation ever since. Once the outer part of the earth froze, it would no longer contract. Inside, however, the deeper materials, still molten or plastic, would continue to cool and lose volume. Thus, mountains would be compressional wrinkles, developing as the solid crust fits itself to the shrinking interior.

The Pleistocene Ice Age, being a recent geologic event, seemed excellent evidence of progressive global cooling, until the discovery that the earth had undergone other periods of glaciation as far back as 600,000,000 years ago. None-theless, contraction remained the most popular theory, because the earth does slowly radiate heat, and a shrinking earth has much to recommend it as a mechanism for orogeny. A serious challenge to the contraction mechanism developed in the 1930's based on radioactivity. Traces of uranium, thorium, and other radioactive elements are widespread in the crust. Their decay produces enough heat, by reasonable estimates, to account for most of the earth's present heat loss. Furthermore, the earth's solid outer part is good insulation, slowing the escape of heat from depth, and calculations suggest that as a result of these two factors, the earth has lost no original heat from depths below 400 miles, in the last two billion years. In fact, some geologists believe the earth is actually heating up and expanding.

Convection Currents Perhaps the most popular theory of mountain building—until quite recently at least—stems from work by Vening Meinesz, the Dutch geophysicist, in the 1920's and early 1930's. Using a precise pendulum apparatus he developed for determining the attraction of gravity from a submarine at sea, he discovered that in the troughs (which may be geosynclines) adjacent to the Indonesian Island arcs, the gravity values are far lower than anticipated. The observation has since been duplicated in island arcs and troughs of the Caribbean. Meinesz reasoned from this that light crustal rocks extended deep into the denser mantle in elongated pockets, about 30 to 100 miles wide, and 30 to 40 miles deep. These he christened "tectogenes."

The light rocks are maladjusted; they should float much higher on the denser mantle beneath. The depth to which the light rocks extended suggested that, somehow, they were being pulled down. Meinesz proposed that plastic mantle rock descending in slow convection currents was the cause. In any convection mechanism, heat is transferred through liquids and gases by moving material. For example, convection develops in a beaker of water heated by a small burner. Over the flame, heated water expands; hence it becomes lighter and rises as a current to the sur-

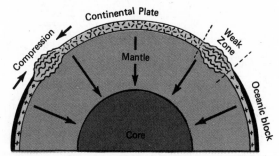

Fig. 9-37
Contraction theory of mountain making.

face. Concurrently, cooler water sinking in a descending current moves in to replace the rising mass. Cells of circulation result as water rises over the heated spot, spreads out and cools at the surface, and then descends on the cooler sides.

The plastic mantle will flow like a liquid under slowly applied and long-continued stresses. Thus convection currents heated by the earth's core could rise beneath crustal blocks, move horizontally, dragging along the continental bottoms, and then descend at the continental margins pulling light sialic material downward, to form the tectogenes which trap geosynclinal rocks (Fig. 9-38). Accelerating circulation pulls the pod of geosynclinal rock deeper and compresses it, producing the orogenic folding and thrusting characterizing mountain structure. Later, the cell dies out when warmer material prevails at the top of the mantle and cooler at the bottom, so that a stable arrangement is achieved. Then the contorted light rocks, no longer being dragged down, bob up, and the mountains rise epeirogenically to their greatest height.

Theoretically, the mechanism just described had much to recommend it, yet many geologists now question the simple model of convection involving the whole mantle. The mantle seems to have a layered structure marked by discontinuities, and it is generally assumed that convection currents would not cross such boundaries. Thus recent theories picture rather flat convection cells limited to the low velocity zone of the mantle (the plastic asthenosphere). What drives the convection cells is not known. They could be heated from below, heated from within, or driven by horizontal temperature differences. It must be admitted that although many earth scientists favor convection in the mantle, the idea is only a concept of how things might be, and needs further investigation and testing.

Continental Drift The jig-saw fit of continental outlines, especially South America into Africa, is impressive as seen on any schoolroom globe. Madagascar fits neatly back into the east side of

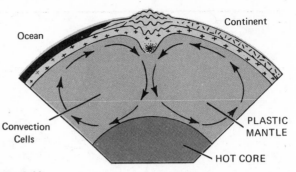

Fig. 9-38
Schematic diagram of convention mechanism for mountain making.

the great African "skull"; Antarctica and Australia can be fitted around India (Fig. 9-39). Led by the German geophysicist, Alfred Wegner, advocates of the theory of continental drift maintain that through most of its history the earth did, indeed, have two closely related super-continents: one included the present northern continents, and the other made up of the southern continents. The rest of the earth's surface was occupied by a single super-Pacific Ocean Basin. Then about 200,000,000 years ago, at the beginning of the geologic era called the Mesozoic, the super-continents broke apart, and their fragments, represented by the existing continents, drifted off. The Atlantic Ocean basin appeared as an ever-widening gap between the Americas and Eurasia-Africa; the Indian Ocean opened between Antarctica and Australia. The Mid-Atlantic Ridge is assumed to mark an old line of junction between the continental masses.

In the original thinking on continental drift, the lighter sialic continental fragments were assumed to have floated over the sima like icebergs in the sea. Mountain chains were attributed to compressional crumpling along the leading edges of the drifting blocks. Thus, the Andean and Rocky Mountain–Cordilleran chain formed along the western side of the Americas; offshore mountains, represented by arcs of islands, rose in front of the Eurasian block. The Alpine–Himalayan chain is attributed to a "bumping-together" of the northern and south-

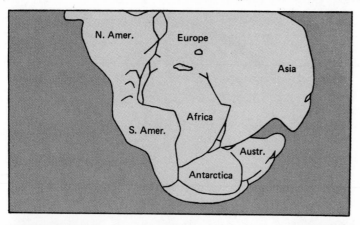

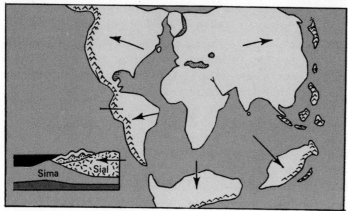

Fig. 9-39
Wegner's idea of continental drift.

ern super-continents that crumpled a great intervening geosyncline. The much-debated pros and cons of continental drift are long and involved. Although fragmentation of super-continents is a possibility, continental drift, as originally conceived, is not a likely mechanism for creating folded mountains. It cannot, for instance, explain ranges such as the Appalachians, which originated before the breakup and drifting of sialic rafts is assumed to have happened.

Until the 1960's most American geologists rejected Wegner's concept of continental drift for generally good reasons — in part because geologic features attributed to it could be explained in other ways, but mainly because the idea of sial drifting like icebergs across a sea of sima seemed impossible because of the friction involved, for the mantle immediately below the Moho is

solid (since seismic waves pass more rapidly through it than through the overlying crust). Today, however, continental drift has won wide acceptance with the finding of a likely mechanism in sea floor spreading (Chapter 16). In the new view of drift and spreading, continents are imbedded in solid oceanic floor to form great slabs of lithosphere that are thought to ride on the asthenosphere (plastic, low velocity seismic zone). Mountain building could result where a slab of oceanic lithosphere is jammed under the margin of a continent-bearing slab to create a downwarp in which geosynclinal sediments collect, and then to be collapsed and crumpled into folded mountain ranges. The scheme can also be related to convection currents in the asthenosphere which might slowly carry along the rigid slabs and bend down their leading

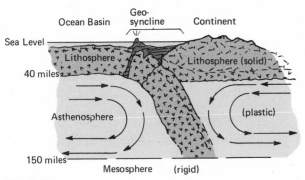

Fig. 9-40
The new view of continental drift and spreading, as discussed in the text.

edges under continental masses where the currents circulate downward.

Vertical oscillation mechanisms

That vertically directed forces cause mountains is fully as old a concept as the contraction theory. The idea went into decline after Dana's advocacy of contraction, probably because vertical forces seemed to have no explanation. Today, however, vertical oscillations are in vogue with avant garde theoreticians. A possible cause for such movements has been found in geochemical processes involving changes of state or phase in matter at depth within the earth. In general, changes of state or phase cause an increase or decrease in the volume of a material. If they strongly affect parts of the crust or mantle, the earth's surface should bulge into domes or ridges, or subside in downwarps forming basins or geosynclines. The contorted structures in folded mountains would be secondary products of up-punched basement blocks, and gravitational sliding of rocks from uplifted masses (Fig. 9-41).

Magmatic Processes In some theories of vertical oscillation, magma becomes the cause rather than the effect of mountain building (Fig. 9-42). The British physicist, John Joly, suggested in 1930 that melting caused by radioactive hot spots inside the lower crust or in the mantle could cre-

ate a magma zone where heat builds up. Based on this assumption, a number of theories have been proposed. In some theories the expansion caused by the change of state from solid to liquid, when magma blisters form, is considered the main cause of vertical uplift. In others, differentiation is assumed wherein lighter granitic magma, on separating from a mixed parent magma, rises and penetrates the crust, causing contortion and intrusion. A theory of this sort was proposed in the early 1930's by R. W. Van Bemmelen from studies in Indonesia. Essentially he followed the earlier suggestion (1929) by the American Bailey Willis that magmatic differentiation was the primary cause of orogeny. He attributed folding, thrusting, and nappe formation to gravitational sliding of plastic geosynclinal sediments down from uplifted welts, as had the German, Harman, in 1930. Building on these basic ideas, Van Bemmelen developed a rather complicated and sophisticated theory that can account for geosynclinal development, orogeny, intrusion, epeirogeny, and volcanism.

Phase Changes A new explanation for crustal deformation, proposed in the 1950's, assumes that solid rock changes volume in response to fluctuating conditions of high pressure and temperature (Fig. 9-43). The fundamental assumption is that the "Moho" discontinuity at the base

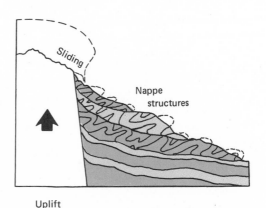

Fig. 9-41
Vertical uplift and downsliding mechanism.

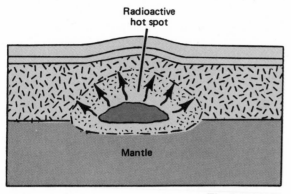
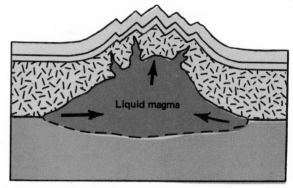

Fig. 9-42
Magmatic theory of mountain building.

of the crust marks a phase change, from basalt to eclogite.

Mountain building could begin when a temperature increase at the base of the crust converts denser eclogite of the underlying mantle into basalt, thereby forming a light mountain root. The deepened buoyant root would cause the overlying crust to float upward, creating an uplift at the earth's surface. Sediments, eroded from the uplift, would initiate a bordering geosynclinal downwarp by creating a load that bows down the crust. The load, in turn, increases the pressure at the "Moho" discontinuity beneath the trough. Here, the light crustal rock, basalt, is converted to mantle rock, eclogite, whose lesser volume causes further sinking and an upward shift of the discontinuity.

Eventually, the process is reversed, because sediments pouring into the trough act as insulation slowing the escape of heat from the depths. If the sediments are richer in radioactive materials, this too would raise the temperature at depth. With warming in the depths of the trough, the "Moho" shifts downward, as low-density roots expand downward at the expense of eclogite. Thereupon the roots would start to bob up, lifting the geosynclinal deposits into mountains. Folding and thrust faulting would result from up-punching of deeper masses, and gravitational sliding of surface rocks from the crest of the uplift.

A general objection to all theories of vertical oscillation is their requirement of gravitational sliding as the major cause for folding and thrust-

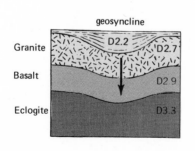
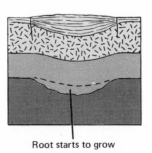
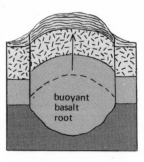

Fig. 9-43
Phase-change mechanism for mountain making.

ing. It has been pointed out that such sliding would necessarily strip rock from the crown of an uplift. Most geologists admit this possibility where a jumbled mass, like the Pre-Alps near Lake Geneva in Switzerland, lies near a high bare core of uplifted crystalline basement. However, many moderately folded ranges, where the basement core is not exposed, show no loss of rock or gaping cracks, expectable if rock pulls away from the crest of an uplift. In such cases, primary compression from horizontally directed forces seems necessary.

Conclusions

The only safe conclusion is — perhaps — that mountains are created by "forces deep within the earth." Many of the elaborate and logical schemes that have been devised would delight Aristotle and the Medieval scholasticists, for the theories are of necessity highly deductive, even though reinforced by mathematical calculations and the latest chemical and physical theories. Explanations are proposed, modified, rejected, and revived. Yet, the clash of concepts gives direction to the search. Better evidence is sought and new tests devised. For example, the "Mohole" project to drill through the crust (when resumed), should yield much valuable first-hand information and, among other things, could end speculation about the composition of the mantle. And, we need more evidence from geophysical instruments that provide precise data for interpreting the earth's physical properties, and our only reliable information on the deep interior. Dana's statement of 1885 still rings true today: "I am led by the conflicting views of the best authorities with regard to the conditions of the earth's interior to hold very loosely to any theory of mountain making. We wait for the physicists ... to give us a theory which will have in view all geologic facts."

SUGGESTED READINGS

Eardley, A. J., "The Cause of Mountain Building—an Enigma," in the *American Scientist*, Vol. 45, No. 3, pp. 189–217, 1957.

Hills, E. S., *Elements of Structural Geology*, New York, John Wiley & Sons, 1963.

Kennedy, G. C., "The Origin of Continents, Mountain Ranges, and Ocean Basins," in the *American Scientist*, Vol. 47, No. 4, pp. 491–504, 1959.

Reconstructing the past

With some notion of physical geology in mind, we are ready to consider earth history. First, we will look at how geologic history is read; then we will discuss the history of life. The proper ordering of geologic events depends, or has until quite recently, on the evolution shown by fossil assemblages. We will consider some major plant and animal groups, then look at them as communities characteristic of particular geologic times.

ten: Some principles and methods for investigating the geologic past

ON THE EARTH'S HISTORY

Conceived as a clot of matter in a swirling cosmic cloud, the earth began to grow as its increasing gravitational attraction speeded the infall of dust and larger particles. Heated by the impact of falling particles, by compression as its mass increased, and by energy from radioactive materials, the earth became a molten mass, churned by convection currents as hot material rose to the surface, cooled, and sank into the incandescent depths. Gradually its materials separated into zones like those in a blast furnace. Nickel-iron filtered downward to form the dense core overlain by the less-dense slag-like mantle, encrusted in turn by the lighter chilled scum forming the primeval crust.

In its molten stage, the earth retained no atmosphere because the heat so agitated lighter molecules that they fled into space. As the earth cooled, the existing atmosphere slowly developed from volcanic emanations of gaseous elements originally compounded with substances inside the primitive earth. Water exuded from the depths and steamed into the atmosphere. However, seas were absent until the simmering crust cooled below the boiling point. Thereafter condensation of volcanic exhalations could produce ever-growing water bodies. With the development of air and ocean, wind, waves, and streams commenced to attack the crust.

Embryonic continents appeared as upwarpings of the crust. Their debris was swept into deepening downwarps and supplemented by that from rising chains of volcanic islands. When sediments in geosynclines thickened to a dozen miles or so, the crust failed, buckling the sediments into mountain ranges. After millions of years the uplifts, eroded to their metamorphosed roots, were welded to the continental margins. Following this pattern through time, the continents progressively expanded at the expense of the crust beneath the ocean basins.

In much of geologic time, the continental platforms have been flooded by shallow, fluctuating seas during world-wide periods of mild climate; however, at intervals mountain building was punctuated by spasms of activity associated with more rigorous climates and sporadic glaciation that overwhelmed large areas with ice.

For hundreds of millions of years the earth was utterly devoid of any living thing, a scene of chemical and physical activity in which reactions between atmospheric gases and water, induced by sunlight and lightning flashes, shuffled atoms into new compounds. Finally, complex carbon compounds were synthesized, making possible the ultimate of chemical reactions—a giant molecule, perhaps a virus, capable of using energy and reproducing itself. Life had appeared on earth. For eons the drama of life was in the seas, where plants and animals proliferated and diversified in myriad forms of increasing complexity. Hard-shelled animals evolved about 600 million years ago, and thereafter, life's record was abundantly preserved. One hundred million years later fish, the first vertebrate animals, appeared and, for a time, were the most advanced form of life.

Through nine-tenths of their history the conti-

215

nents were desolate, barren landscapes of riven rock, jagged cliffs and dissected badlands, beveled plains and debris-filled basins, swept by storms of dust and muddy torrents. Then, perhaps 400 million years ago, land plants appeared and eventually clothed the continents with protective vegetation, slowing the erosive attack of atmospheric agents.

The first vertebrates to invade the land were descendants of fish—amphibians that could never stray far from water. They, in turn, gave rise to efficient land dwellers, the reptiles. Then the land was ruled for 100 million years by dinosaurs, reptiles which included some of the mightiest animals that ever roamed the earth. Suddenly—in geologic terms—the host of dinosaurs became extinct, and were replaced by colateral descendants from an obscure reptilian stock.

Although the mammals who inherited the earth were an unimpressive lot, they evolved more rapidly than the dinosaurs, diversifying into many forms. The present mammal groups, from shrews to elephants, bats to whales, are but the survivors of an evolutionary process marked by many extinct branches. Now man, a mammal, dominates the scene, not because of physical attributes of speed, size, or fearsome jaws, but because evolution produced his advanced brain. Through his intelligence he can use tools, modify his environment, record and accumulate past experience. For better or for worse, he may determine the course of his future evolution. Overall, there has been a progressive development of more complex plants and animals; yet, side by side, simpler forms have prospered, giving a near-infinite variety of life.

Any such naturalistic synopsis of earth history is a story to be revised in light of further investigations: some is established fact, some is well-tested theory, and some is very tentative speculation. The subject of origins and the earliest history of the earth are most conjectural and controversial. Yet, they are not wild speculations, but, rather, possible explanations based on natural law, astronomical and geological ob-

servations. The narrative of earth history is better established after it becomes recorded in existing rocks and can, therefore, be reconstructed by geologic methods. The oldest rocks yet found are metamorphosed sediments which, being products of still older rocks, indicate that, on the continents at least, positive records of the earliest chapters in earth history are lost. Even the record in the rocks is not complete, and becomes progressively less so, back through time. So, before presenting the story in more detail, let us consider the nature of the evidence, and the detective work involved.

A POINT OF VIEW

Successful deciphering of earth history has required careful study of rocks, techniques for dating, an open-minded approach towards grand theories, and above all a faith, long justified, that "the present is the key to the past," the motto of **Dr. James Hutton** (1726–1797). The assumption that processes operating on ancient rocks are the same as those visible today, has brought success. Thus, a sandstone with certain characteristics can be viewed as an ancient beach, a conglomerate with snubbed and striated boulders as a former glacial till, a porous basalt as a former lava flow, and so forth.

From the beginning, Uniformitarianism had the merit of simplicity, a point in favor of any scientific concept. Because rocks could be interpreted in the light of observable processes, there was no need to contrive wholly different explanations for past phenomena. Thus, physical geology, the study of present physical and chemical processes acting on the earth, became a logical foundation for historical geology. Today, Uniformitarianism is firmly established because it has led to great advances, and a large coherent body of knowledge, which is the best measure of the value of any scientific idea.

With time, Uniformitarian thinking has become more sophisticated. "The present is the key to the past," but with qualifications. Catastrophic

James Hutton (1726–1797) *Hutton demonstrated the plutonic origin of granite and recognized the significance of angular unconformities. A few men before him had reasoned in Uniformitarian terms, but it was Hutton and his followers at Edinburgh—though vehemently attacked for decades—who introduced the necessary concept that "the present is the key to the past" into the mainstream of geologic thinking.*

TELLING TIME

It is a mark of Hutton's genius that, unlike most of his contemporaries, he sensed the enormity of geologic time. In his lifetime and after, this necessary postulate of Uniformitarianism was ignored, ridiculed, and violently attacked by many scientists, for telling time has been a major geologic problem. Historians, whose research is largely in musty library stacks, can rely on written documents and calendars to reckon the time of events. Geologists, whose source materials are rocks, have required special methods. The first to be successful dealt only with relative time; reliable techniques of absolute dating are a twentieth-century development.

In general, time determinations are of two sorts: *relative dating*, which merely gives the order of events and is represented in everyday affairs by words like yesterday, Tuesday, April; and *finite dating*, or absolute dating, which is the measure of time either for a duration or an occurrence related to a reference point, as for example June 5th, 1948 A.D., which is a measure in units since the birth of Christ.

Relative time

Geologic Relations In unravelling the physical history of a region, a geologist is usually faced with the end results of many complicated events. He must sort out periods of deposition and erosion, igneous activity, metamorphism, and structural deformation, often from poor bedrock exposures, and put them in a logical order. It takes experience, a certain flare for geometric puzzles, and a grounding in physical geology.

Steno's Laws of Original Horizontality and Superposition are fundamental to any interpretation of rocks originally laid down on the earth's surface. Thus, we assume that sedimentary and also extrusive volcanic rocks are laid down in a near-horizontal, or at least uncontorted, attitude, and in order of their age, with the oldest at the bottom. Folding and faulting, which may shuffle the normal order of beds, or even turn

earthquakes and volcanic eruptions are no problem, for they are present-day occurrences. However, it has become evident that although geologic processes have acted in the same way through time, they have not always had the same intensity. Glaciation, which is widespread at certain times, has apparently been trivial or absent through long spans of geologic time. It is quite possible that erosion was far more rapid before a protective vegetation appeared on land—a relatively late geologic event. Nor is the doctrine a cure-all. The origin of magma, the formation of plutonic rocks, mountain-building forces, all deep-seated processes doubtless going on today, are concealed from view. Nonetheless, Uniformitarianism has been the fundamental guide in establishing the history of the earth. It is a concept that requires some comprehension of geologic time.

217

them upside down, must be later than the origin of the affected beds. Faults are younger than the beds they offset, and older than overlying unaffected rocks. Unconformities, as we have seen, add the element of a period of erosion between older and younger rocks. On the ground surface, certain terraces and other topographic features may be used to determine the order of later geologic events. By using such relations, a sequence of events may be put in relative order in a single area, but something more is needed to fit a local history to broad regional patterns in a master plan of geologic time (Fig. 10-1).

Timepieces Fossils are world-wide timepieces. They can be used for determining order,

but more importantly they date the particular interval of time during the last 600 million years of earth history, when the rocks containing them were laid down.

Fossils come in many different varieties (Fig. 10-2). They may be the actual remains of plants and animals: a mammoth carcass complete with flesh and hair frozen in an arctic tundra (Fig. 10-3); an oyster shell buried in an ancient shore (Fig. 10-4). They may be stone replicas from slow molecule-by-molecule replacement of original animal matter by minerals: an agate log, a silicified bone (Fig. 10-5). They may be impressions, molds left in sediments after organic material has disappeared; or later fillings of such molds forming a leaf or shell reproduced in sandstone or

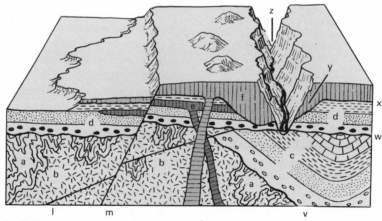

I. Rocks
    a = metamorphosed sediments; schists, quartzites, marbles.
    b = granite
    c = sedimentary rocks, well lithified, cg. ss, sh, ls.
    d = sedimentary rocks, moderately to poorly lithified, cg. ss. sh.
    e = diorite, intrusive igneous dikes and sills
    f = basalt, lava and eroded cinder cones.

II. Faults
    l = thrust fault
    m = normal fault

III. Erosion Surfaces
    v
    w } = buried erosion surfaces of moderate to low relief
    x
    y = broad valley, lava filled
    z = youthful valley of present topography.

Fig. 10-1
Some geologic relations used in relative dating. See if you can determine the order of events represented in this block.

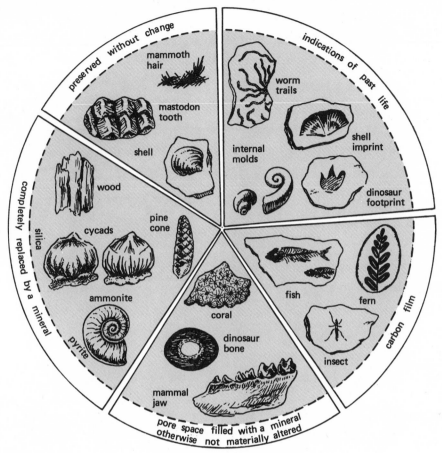

Fig. 10-2
Fossils and some types of preservation. Based on an exhibit in the University of Wyoming Geology Museum.

shale (Fig. 10-6). They may be mere indications that an animal was once there: dinosaur tracks, worm borings in now solid rock (Fig. 10-7). Fossils are evidence of past life, which is the reason they can be used for telling time.

The discovery that fossils date rocks, which paved the way for a coordinated geologic history, was independently made around 1800 by **George Cuvier** (1769–1832) and **Alexandre Brongniart** (1770–1847) working as a team in the Paris Basin, and **William Smith** (1769–1839) a canal engineer in England. These pioneers showed that layers of comparable age in different places have similar fossils, and that fossils in layers above and below are different.

Fossils can be used for dating because the groups of plants and animals living together, the floras and faunas, have gradually changed with time.

Fossils show evolution in the same way that cars, houses, furniture, and clothing date old photographs because of changing styles. If the remains of automobiles were buried in successive layers, as they would be in a city dump, students of Ford cars, for example, could date the layers by the different models. Scraps and pieces of Model T's would be found in older layers, Model A's in somewhat younger ones, simple V-8's above them, and near the top would be bizarre forms with ornate fins, and monsters

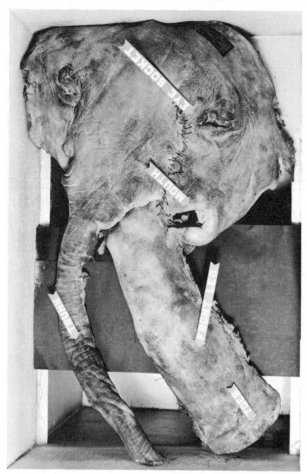

Fig. 10-3
Actual remains of a baby wooly mammoth preserved in frozen ground of Alaska until discovered. Courtesy of the American Museum of Natural History.

Fig. 10-4
Limestone composed of a mass of shell fragments. Photo by Tad Nichols.

Baron Georges Cuvier (1769–1832) The father of vertebrate paleontology, Cuvier recognized that large bones discovered in France were those of extinct animals rather than living types. He and Alexandre Brongniart gave geology an essential technique for unravelling earth history in their discovery of faunal succession. Despite his recognition that fossil groups differed, Cuvier denied the possibility of organic evolution and died a confirmed catastrophist.

with four headlights. Because this make of car is common and widespread, it would be possible to determine which layers had been put down at the same time in widely separated places.

In the case of fossils, dating is based on two fundamental laws: the *Law of Superposition*, that undisturbed strata are in the order of their deposition, and the *Law of Faunal and Floral Succession* (Fig. 10-8). The essence of the latter law is that plants and animals have progressively changed through time, and that each period of time is characterized by distinctive fossil groups. Intensive study has shown that faunas of a given

Fig. 10-5
Partially excavated dinosaur bones from Bone Cabin Quarry, Wyoming. Courtesy of the American Museum of Natural History.

time have never occurred in any other geologic time, and that comparable faunas of a given time have existed on all the continents. That species have not reoccurred has been a major advantage in using the paleontologic "clock."

Some fossils are better timepieces than others. Conservative beasts that persist through ages with little change are of limited value. One stock of marine organisms, whose members are a kind of shellfish called Lingula, has persisted for hundreds of millions of years with scarcely any change that can be recognized from their shells (Fig. 10-9). The best fossils for dating, called *index fossils,* are the remains of rapidly changing, stocks of plants and animals whose members

existed during a short span of geologic history, but at the same time were geographically widespread. They should also be abundant and easy to recognize. Most paleontologists, students of fossils, prefer to work with assemblages of fossils because even if good index fossils are missing, the chances that last, or first, appearances of certain types will be found, is greatly increased. The overlapping of several "tops and bottoms" of life ranges for conservative fossil groups allows a finer time determination than from a single form.

Techniques for dating by fossils have been used for over 250 years to compile an orderly history for the earth's crust. However, they give

Fig. 10-6
Fossil fern from Petrified Forest, Arizona. Photo by Tad Nichols.

relative times only; reliable methods of finite dating are a twentieth-century development.

Finite time

Being so far removed from ordinary experience, the length of geologic time is difficult to comprehend. Saying the earth is at least 4½ billion years old is one thing; sensing the enormity of its history is another. If a dime, one twentieth of an inch thick, were set atop the 1250 foot Empire State Building in New York City, the thickness of the dime would more than equal the span of recorded human history, in proportion to the building, which would represent geologic

time at the same scale. As a scientific revelation, geologic time ranks with astronomical concepts of the distances to the stars in space, and the microcosm of atomic structure.

Older Techniques Attempts have long been made to establish absolute geologic time relations. In 1654 Archbishop Ussher of Ireland proclaimed that the earth was created in 4004 B.C.[1] Such theological determinations were based on the Book of Genesis wherein a careful chronology gives the years of the various periods, from the time of Adam to the building of the Temple in Jerusalem, an event recorded on existing calendars. Scientists also did considerable ineffectual groping.

The saltiness of the oceans was the basis of a late nineteenth-century calculation that the earth was 100 million years old. It was assumed, reasonably enough, that the oceans were originally fresh water and have become progressively saltier, through time, because of the workings of the hydrologic cycle. The salt is derived from weathering of rocks on land, and is carried by streams to the sea where it is left behind, while fresh water is distilled to fall in rain or snow, during the phase of circulation from ocean to land. By calculating the total salt in the oceans and the total salt brought in by streams each year, and dividing the first figure by the second, an age of about 100 million years results. Unfortunately this answer is far too low; somehow the assumptions of this simple, neat, and plausible scheme are astray.

In a somewhat similar way, using simple arithmetic, the rate of accumulation of sedimentary rocks has been tried for the later history of the earth. If an overall maximum thickness of sedimentary beds is totalled in feet, or any suitable units, and the average number of years required to deposit 1 foot, 10 feet, or any particular interval can be determined, then the total thickness multiplied by the number of years it takes to de-

---

[1] Dr. John Lightfoot, vice-chancellor of Cambridge University, arrived at a more precise determination of 9:00 A.M., October 23rd, 4004 B.C.

posit 1 foot gives the time in years for the whole deposit.

The trouble with this scheme, as applied to any considerable length of geologic time, is the difficulty in determining a total thickness of continuous deposition. Unconformities recording hiatuses in deposition are everywhere, and often unrecognized. The rate of deposition varies widely from place to place, and there is good reason to believe it has been far from constant, through time, being rapid during episodes of mountain building, and very slow in the long intervals when lands were low and largely flooded by the seas. So, even if the rate of deposition is well established for hundreds or even a few thousand years in any place, there is no guarantee it represents any sort of average for most of geologic time.

Deposition can be reliably used, however, in special situations where thin layers, or laminae, mark a given length of time. For instance, varves laid down in glacial lakes are paired laminae, forming annual deposits. During the summer when the lake is open, sands and silts washed in by streams settle to the bottom; in winter when the lake freezes over creating a lid, deposition of this coarser sediment ceases, and a thin layer of clay that was in suspension settles out. Thus, a combination of one thicker silty layer and one thinner clayey layer indicates one year; so, by counting varves, the finite duration in years of the former glacial lake can be determined. Some other deposits of non-glacial origin are also varved. The Green River lake beds in western Wyoming and Colorado contain a varved shale, which has been used to obtain an estimate of

Fig. 10-7
Mr. Utterback digging out a Daemonelix *(Devil's Corkscrew) which is a cast of rodent burrow, Sioux County, Nebraska. J. B. Hatcher photo, courtesy of the Carnegie Museum, Pittsburgh, Pennsylvania.*

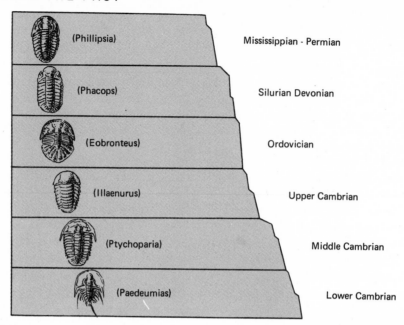

Fig. 10-8

Faunal succession. Selected members of the long extinct group, trilobites—indicating changing styles with time.

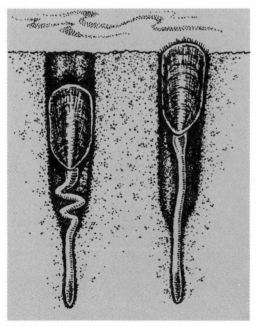

Fig. 10-9

Lingula, a most conservative animal.

6½ million years for the duration of this ancient lake, a figure verified by radioactive methods. Varved deposits are not common, however, and even where they do exist it is not always possible to be sure what time interval each lamina represented.

Just prior to 1900, Lord Kelvin, the British physicist, calculated the age of the earth as, most likely, 20 to 40 million years. He assumed that the earth was originally molten and had progressively cooled to its present state with no addition of heat except from the sun. Using principles of physics he calculated the expected rate of cooling, and, from this, the time required for the earth to reach its present temperature. Many geologists were unhappy, believing that the earth must be far older to account for the great changes and complicated sequence of events in its history, but Kelvin's view prevailed for a while because his scientific eminence and authority were so great. His age determination came to naught, despite the seemingly flawless quantitative reasoning, when his assumptions were invalidated. Heat has been added to the earth by radioactive disintegration of minerals in the mantle and crust.

Radiometric Methods The radioactive minerals provide the most precise geologic clocks, and are the basis for the modern belief in the tremendous length of geologic time, and the great antiquity of the crust. In 1896, Antoine Becquerel, a French physicist, exposed photographic plates by leaving them in a drawer with uranium salts—an accident that revolutionized our understanding of the physical world. Two years later the Curies, in France, isolated radium as a prelude to the discovery of the other radioactive elements. Geology is especially indebted to Bertram Boltwood, an American chemist, working with Lord Rutherford's group of physicists in England. When he found, in 1907, that the ratio of lead to uranium was constant in rocks of the same age, the measuring of geologic time in years could begin.

Although the laboratory determinations require highly sophisticated techniques and exceedingly precise equipment, the general principle of radiometric dating is easily understood. Radioactive elements in minerals are timepieces working somewhat like an hour glass. For example, once uranium atoms are locked in a crystal structure, they start breaking down at a known and steady rate by expelling particles, rays, and helium gas to form new and different radioactive atoms that also decay, until finally, the transmutation ends with the creation of the stable end product, lead.

All of the almost countless radioactive atoms [2] in a newly formed uranium mineral do not start to break down at once; a few disintegrate almost immediately, some follow shortly, others are slow in starting, and in some the breakdown is almost indefinitely delayed. It is impossible to predict when any particular atom will start to decay; however, over a long period of time, the number of transmuted atoms in the total popula-

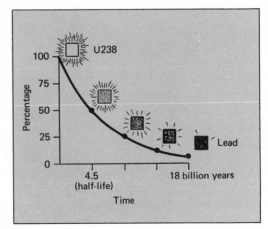

Fig. 10-10
Radioactive distintegration of uranium to lead.

tion increases at a steady and predictable rate, so that the amount of uranium in a sample becomes progressively less, while the lead increases proportionally. Thus by determining the ratio of lead to uranium in the minerals of a rock, its absolute age in years can be obtained.[3] The principle is like that of the life expectancy tables used by insurance companies to determine their policy rates. Their statisticians do not know when any particular person will die, but out of 100,000 people born in a certain year, they can predict what percent will survive and what percent will be dead in each successive year.

Unlike an hour glass, where sand flows at a constant rate, or curves of life expectancy, where the mortality rate increases rapidly after a certain point, the change in the overall proportion of uranium to lead becomes increasingly slow with time (Fig. 10-10). The change is greatest during the time when the first half of the uranium atoms are changing to lead. Then, it takes the same length of time for half of the remaining atoms to break down, increasing the total amount of lead by only a quarter; thereafter, the same length of time for half of the still remaining atoms to break down, increasing the amount of lead by one

---

[2] Actually we should be speaking of isotopes, slightly different kinds of atoms having the same chemical properties but very slightly different weights. There are 2 isotopes of uranium and 4 types of lead.

[3] Perhaps relatively absolute is a better expression. Because of technical problems, dates are usually given with a plus-or-minus factor of so many years; however, the margin of error is usually only a few percent.

eighth, and so on, half of a half of a half, *ad infinitum.* It is virtually impossible to determine when the same is totally "dead." For this reason, the duration of an element's activity is customarily given as its half-life, the time required for half the material to decay. The half-life of uranium is 4.5×10^9 years (4,500,000,000 years) which makes it a very long-lived element.

The uranium-lead method was the first to be used extensively; now, however, other methods have largely replaced it because they may be simpler, more accurate, better for certain ranges of geologic time, or may be used on elements in more abundant minerals. All, however, are based on obtaining ratios between parent radioactive elements and their offspring. Helium, the gas, is a radioactive byproduct of uranium decay, and its ratio to lead has been used in dating. The element thorium, which also produces lead, has been used, and so has the element rubidium, whose stable daughter product is strontium. The proportion of radioactive potassium to its decay product, the gas argon, is now widely used in dating. This method can be applied to the abundant mica minerals and also sylvite, which is a salt occurring in sedimentary deposits. Radioactive potassium is by far the most abundant radioactive element in the earth's crust, and the breakdown is a simpler action involving less chance of loss or addition of critical elements.

Uranium, thorium, rubidium, and radioactive potassium are all elements with long half-lives that are thought to have originated at the same time as the earth itself. They do give rise to radioactive daughter elements such as radium, which are being formed today, but the question arises as to how the primary radioactive elements can indicate anything but the time of their origin, or the age of the earth, because they must have started to break down when they formed. As a matter of fact, the age of the earth has been estimated from the breakdown products. Although all lead has the same chemical properties, there are several kinds of lead atoms, or isotopes, which are slightly different in weight and can be distinguished by certain physical techniques. Non-radioactive lead (Pb^{204}), which is not a decay product, is lighter than the types representing the residues (Pb^{206}, Pb^{207}, Pb^{208}) of uranium and thorium. So, assuming that only non-radioactive lead was present in the earth at the beginning, and its amount has remained the same while the radioactive leads have steadily increased at a known rate through time, a maximum geologic age for the earth has been calculated as 5.6×10^9, or 5,600,000,000 years.

The reason radioactive elements can be used to date rocks formed at various geologic times relates to the way minerals form by crystal growth during solidification of a magma, recrystallization associated with metamorphism, or precipitation of salts. In magmas and solutions, all sorts of atoms (ions, isotopes) may be present, including those of radioactive elements and decay products, and the atoms are randomly dispersed and free to move about. When crystallization occurs, however, they aggregate into crystal structures of different minerals, each having the same chemical composition. The structures of certain minerals would tend to take on atoms of radioactive elements and exclude lead and other daughter products,[4] which would combine in separate minerals. Thus, the sorting action during crystallization, sets the starting time of the radiometric clocks. The oldest rocks dated so far have an age of 3.1×10^9 years, which gives a minimum estimate for the age of the earth.

Radioactive carbon, C^{14}, has a uniquely important spot in finite dating. Having a relatively short half-life of about 5500 years, it is invaluable for dating within the last 40,000 years. The elements with long half-lives cannot be used to date rocks younger than 1,000,000 years because the relative change in proportions of parent elements and daughter products, during that length of time, is too slight to be reliably detected. Unlike the earth's primordial elements and the radioactive elements produced by their decay, C^{14} is continuously created in the air, even today.

Cosmic rays bombarding the upper atmosphere

---

[4] Some lead does get into uranium minerals, but there are ways to handle the problem, and a few minerals, like zircon, are believed to exclude all lead when they are formed, which makes them the most reliable indicators.

convert nitrogen there to C^{14}, which combines with oxygen to form carbon dioxide. This gas, bearing radioactive carbon, becomes mixed in the atmosphere with carbon dioxide containing ordinary carbon atoms, C^{12}. The mixture is taken in and incorporated into living plants and animals (Fig. 10-11). So long as the organism lives, its C^{14} and C^{12} content remains in balance, the radioactive carbon being replaced as fast as it decays to ordinary carbon. After the organism dies, however, no new radioactive carbon is assimilated, and the C^{14} slowly breaks down to the ordinary variety. Hence, the less the amount of C^{14} in such organic materials as charcoal, wood, shell, bones, and teeth, the older the material is. The C^{14} method has been a great boon to geologists, and especially to anthropologists and archeologists studying the "prehistoric" history of man.

Radiometric dating has given such striking results that it may seem a panacea for all problems of geologic time; yet it is not perfect. First of all there is a gap, from about 40,000 to almost 1,000,000 years ago, between the oldest possible C^{14} dates, and the youngest reliable age determinations using long-lived elements, a blind spot inaccessible to present radiometric methods. Clastic sediments present a special problem because their minerals are largely derived from pre-existing rocks. So, although radioactive potassium and rubidium do occur in the grains of many sedimentary rocks, absolute age determinations would reflect the time the parent rock originated, and not the time the fragments were deposited as a sediment. Often where an intrusive mass can be absolutely dated, the age of surrounding rocks must still be determined by cross-cutting relations.

Samples must come from fresh-looking rock and be carefully selected. From a practical point of view the methods are expensive, ranging from around $350 for potassium-argon to about $160 for a C^{14} determination (Fig. 10-12). Although the rate of radioactive decay is unchanged by heat, pressure, and chemical reactions, weathering and leaching remove elements upsetting critical ratios, and metamorphic or igneous action may introduce new materials contaminating a sample. Gases affecting helium ratios may escape if minerals are minutely fractured. Carbon dates may be in error if present-day plant roots and soil organisms are not thoroughly removed from a sample.

Since World War II, however, great progress has been made in techniques and instruments (Fig. 10-13). Most of the earlier measurements are now considered unreliable. Students in the early 1940's were taught that the age of the earth

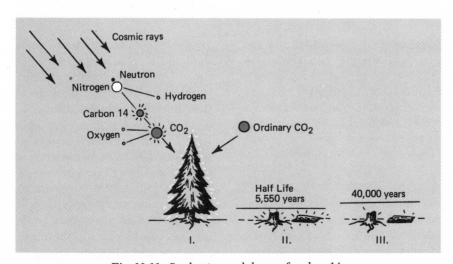

Fig. 10-11 *Production and decay of carbon 14.*

Fig. 10-12
Laboratory equipment used in carbon 14 dating. Sample purification system. Courtesy of Isotopes, Inc., Westwood, New Jersey.

as revealed by uranium-lead determinations was incredibly greater than anyone had thought—two billion years. Now the accepted figure is at least twice that—from 4.5 to 5.5 billion years—on the basis of improved methods, and cross checking of samples, using several different elements.

Correlation

So far we have largely stressed the nature and the reading of geologic clocks to tell the passing of time in a sequence of rocks. Yet if you stop to think of it, time determinations are of two sorts; besides time order, there is the matter of time

equivalence in different places, which is of paramount importance in reconstructing the history of any appreciable part of the earth. Correlation, in general, means to show the connection between related things; however, to geologists it usually means establishing that rocks in different areas originated at the same time, whether locally as between northern and southern New Jersey, or between continents North America and Australia, for instance. In a broader sense, since rocks record geologic events, was the episode of mountain building responsible for the Urals contemporaneous with that of the Appalachians? Was the eastern United States a

Fig. 10-13
Radioactive determination equipment. Sample in central cylinder is surrounded by radio-active counters and the entire apparatus is shielded by paraffin blocks inside steel shields to eliminate outside influence of cosmic rays. Courtesy of Isotopes, Inc., Westwood, New Jersey.

scene of coal swamps at the same time as England? Were equatorial Africa and South America both glaciated in the same ancient Ice Age?

The only reliable means for far-flung correlations are fossils and radioactive minerals, which are essentially synchronized watches; more locally, it may also be possible to use similar physical features of rocks. However, no single method is applicable to all rocks. For instance, fossils, the key to correlating sedimentary rocks, are almost totally absent from igneous and highly metamorphosed rocks. Circumstances determine the method or methods used—we do the best we can with what we've got.

Fossils The major breakthrough in correlation was, of course, made by **William Smith** (1769–1839) when he recognized and applied faunal succession. It soon became evident that not only could separate outcrops be correlated in the relatively limited area of Great Britain, but they could also be correlated across the English Channel with rocks in France (Fig. 10-14). It was eventually realized that the overall succession of life had been similar on all the continents; hence fossils are universal time labels for sedimentary outcrops. However, correlation by fossils is not without some inherent difficulties.

It was fortunate for Smith, Cuvier, and Bron-

William Smith (1769–1839) *"Strata" Smith's first-hand observations while surveying canal routes in England showed him that different rock layers have distinct fossil groups. He used this idea of faunal succession in correlating rocks to produce his remarkable, colored, geologic map of England. His introduction of careful mapping was a major factor in the development of geology.*

gniart—and geology—that these pioneers worked in parts of Europe where the strata were rather neatly laid out and good index fossils were relatively abundant. Had they lived in New England, Switzerland, northern India, and many other localities, geochronology would have been founded by some one else. Even today, it is often difficult to establish the time and order of deposition, where sedimentary strata are metamorphosed, or highly jumbled from deformation. Some thick sequences of sedimentary rocks are notably devoid of fossils, and if fossils are present, there may be complicating factors.

Living groups of plants and animals, which are a basis for Uniformitarian thinking, indicate a problem in correlation by fossils. Modern sea shells on a Florida beach are quite unlike many in New England, and, more locally, those found south of Cape Cod, Massachusetts, are noticeably different from the shells along beaches to the north. Changes are even more pronounced at right angles to a shore, going from land to sea; as a result, the correlation of terrestrial with marine deposits in the geologic record has often been

difficult. The animals entombed in a river flood plain may be quite different from those of the sea (Fig. 10-15). Considering only a single type of marine shellfish, the clam family, those that live in the tidal zone are apt to be mainly burrowing sorts, while in shallow waters further offshore many may be attached forms on the ocean bottom, like oysters, which have a rather different look. Fortunately, there are some widespread forms, such as the swimming and floating animals in the sea which, after death, may be washed onto the beach or settle to the bottom in any one of the several offshore life zones. Fossils reflect different habitats, which has complicated correlation; however, by studying widespread forms, it has been possible to discover which of the local assemblages indicate the same geologic time. Fortunately, marine and continental beds are interlayered in places, and where beds containing marine fossils are sandwiched between beds with distinctive terrestrial fossil types, a tie between the age of land and sea faunas has been established.

The first rocks in which fossils are abundant and varied enough for correlation have been absolutely dated at about 600 million years, whereas the oldest known rocks have an age of about 3½ billion years. Thus some 85% of geologic time, recorded in the Precambrian basement complex, is inaccessible to fossil correlation. Local sequences of events reconstructed from cross-cutting relations, unconformities, and other physical relations in Precambrian rocks had been compiled into relatively simple continental and even world-wide histories based on similarity of events and rock types. However, the recent application of improved techniques of absolute dating has shown some great errors in correlation. For example, two widely separated Canadian granites, which had been considered age equivalents because they looked alike, were found to be two billion years apart in time of origin, a magnificent miscorrelation. Radiometric dating, the only reliable method for correlating basement rocks, indicates that the first three billion years of recorded earth history were far more eventful than previously thought.

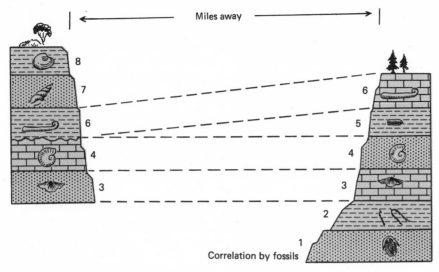

Fig. 10-14
Correlation by fossils. Certain index fossils are keys to matching of sedimentary strata in widely separated outcrops.

Physical Criteria Lacking useful geologic clocks, physical features have been used to establish the time equivalence of rocks. *Continuity,* the simplest and most direct method of physical correlation, is possible where beds can be directly traced from one place to another. It may be a matter of "eyeballing," a sweeping glance along a cliff face, or walking beds out on the ground, or tracing them on an aerial photograph. This method, which is something of a special case, requires continuous well-exposed outcrops—the cliffs and slopes of the Grand Can-

Fig. 10-15
The record of the rocks in a prehistoric Wyoming Lake indicates how quite different fossils are of the same age but from different environments. (Based on an exhibit in the University of Wyoming Geology Museum by P. O. McGrew.)

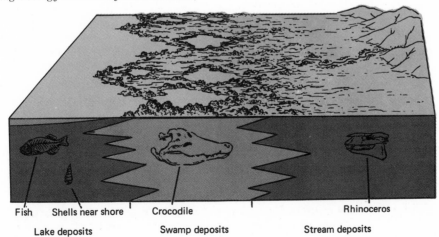

Fish   Shells near shore   Crocodile   Rhinoceros

Lake deposits   Swamp deposits   Stream deposits

yon give a "textbook" example. *Lithologic similarity* is used in correlating isolated samples, outcrops or drill cores, where rock units have rather unique characteristics, such as distinctive minerals, sand grains or pebbles, concretions, cross-beds or similar features, and in some instances overall color. *Similarity of sequence* is often a more obvious clue to rock correlation than the features of a single layer or bed. A gray limestone sandwiched between a red shale above, and a brown sandstone below, might make a distinctive sequence readily identified as the same in scattered outcrops.

Thus, similar physical features can be used like fossils as empirical "trademarks" of certain rocks; however, differences in fossils reflect organic evolution, a one-way process of continuous change. Lithologic features and rock types result from physical processes that, harking back to Uniformitarianism, have operated in the same way and repeatedly formed the same products, through time. So the features of sandstones, schists, granites, and other rocks are distinctive of no one geologic time. Actually most physical methods show the equivalence of rock, but not necessarily of time.

As to whether a particular rock unit is everywhere the same age, the answer is that some are and a good many are not. Volcanic eruptions may blanket wide areas with ash beds which, being the same age throughout, are excellent for time correlation as far as they extend. On the other hand, a beach sand, continuously deposited along the shore of a sea that has slowly spread from a marginal geosyncline over the interior of a continental platform, may well be millions of years younger in the heart of the continent, than where its deposition started. The pitfalls of correlating time by similar lithology of widely separated rocks have already been mentioned in the case of the Canadian granites. All this does not mean that lithologic similarity is useless. It may be the only possible method in certain cases, and used with proper caution in limited areas it may well give a time correlation, but for far-flung correlations, the only reliable indicators of time equivalence are fossils and radioactive minerals.

The universal calendar

Once fossils were recognized as telling time, the next step was to make a universal calendar, a systematic arrangement of time divisions for world-wide dating of events. The geologic time scale is just such a gargantuan calendar whose eons, eras, periods, and epochs are grand and less-grand units for dividing the geologic versions of ancient, medieval, and modern time. The years involved in these various divisions are a late addition from radiometric techniques; the

Table 10.1 Geologic Time Chart

Era	Period	Epoch	Millions of years ago [1]
Cenozoic	Quaternary	Recent	
		Pleistocene	
			1
	Tertiary	Pliocene	
		Miocene	
		Oligocene	
		Eocene	
		Paleocene	65
Mesozoic	Cretaceous		135
	Jurassic		180
	Triassic		
			230
Paleozoic	Permian		280
	Pennsylvanian		310
	Mississippian		345
	Devonian		400
	Silurian		425
	Ordovician		
	Cambrian		
			600
Precambrian			

The 4½ billion years now estimated for the age of the earth makes the length of the Precambrian time far exceed that of later eras.

[1] Absolute time based on J. L. Kulp (1961).

time scale itself was established by purely relative means.

Constructing the Time Scale The modern time scale was a major accomplishment of the nineteenth century based, as things geologic must be, on the record of the rocks. Nowhere is the record complete; so to compile it, north European geologists in England and on the continent had to piece together a master geologic column combining local rock successions from different places. Had the whole column been laid out in some gigantic cliff of fossiliferous and uncontorted strata, unbroken by unconformities, there would have been less of a problem.[5] But the normal order of separate fossiliferous sequences had to be established, originally by walking out barren intervening beds to determine whether datable sequences lay above or below each other. It was a major task because the rocks in places were structurally complicated. There were and are other problems, here glossed over, such as the nature of the boundaries between rock sequences, and the fact that more complete sections have since been found outside the classic areas; nonetheless, with certain modifications, the composite rock column established in Europe provides the worldwide standard.

Thus the time scale is based on a master rock column that is in turn based on local rock units. *Rock units* are the sandstones, shales, and other types forming the observable sequence in any given place. Of the rock units, the most basic is the *formation,* which is essentially a distinct mappable unit and the sort most commonly dealt with by geologists in the field.[6] A formation is a rock mass, most commonly sedimentary, although it can be metamorphic or igneous, which is usually formed by a single process, making it

readily distinguishable from adjacent rocks.

The lithologic features distinguishing a formation could be such things as color, rock type, the presence of coal, or some peculiar concretions — in short almost anything that sets the formation apart. A formation customarily has two names: a geographic one from the place the unit was first described in the geologic literature; the other from its dominant rock type; although if several types are present the word formation is used. The Potsdam Sandstone is a formation named from a city in New York State; the Goose Egg Formation has a type locality near an old Wyoming ranch. In Europe where their usage originated before people worried about consistent naming, famous formations are called such things as the Old Red Sandstone, and the Coal Measures for obvious reasons; to avoid confusion, these names have largely been retained. Although its name comes from a single locality, a formation may be present over vast areas. For instance, the Niobrara Formation, named for exposures in northeastern Nebraska, is also found in the Dakotas, Montana, Wyoming, Colorado, Kansas, and New Mexico. Formations are units, correlatable by lithologic similarity, and as such, like the widespread beach sandstone previously mentioned, are not necessarily of the same age throughout.

Time-rock units, which make up the composite geologic columns of either particular regions or the master world column, are somewhat generalized units representing all rocks laid down during a certain time, as read from fossil evidence. For this reason they are not defined by any lithology since many different rocks, sandstones, shales, schists, basalts, and others, have originated at the same times. Time-rock units are represented by one, several, or parts of physically distinguishable rock units such as formations. Lastly, *time units,* the most abstract of all, are the subdivisions of the geologic calendar, or time scale.

The fundamental time-rock units are called *systems,* and they correspond to the purely time units of the geologic calendar called *periods.* Both are named the same, hence if we speak of

---

[5] Boundaries might have been difficult to select, however, without unconformities in between a wealth of fossiliferous strata because evolutionary changes are characteristically transitional.

[6] Geological "formation" is an almost universal misnomer among the uninitiated who use the term to describe fossils, concretions, stalactites, and other features which do not qualify.

the Devonian System we mean rocks, and if of the Devonian Period we mean time alone. All this doubtless seems boring terminology, unless you have a lawyer's mind, yet it is essential to an understanding of how the universal geologic time scale was constructed, and it is the time scale which holds together the grand patterns of earth history.

The Geologic Time Scale The sudden appearance of abundant and varied fossils, an explosive event in geologic terms, makes a worldwide time line for dividing the geologic time scale into two main parts. These divisions are most disproportionate, in length of years, and in our detailed understanding of each. The first, and by far the longest, is commonly referred to simply as *Precambrian* time. As the Precambrian rocks, most of which are deformed, metamorphosed, and intruded, are relatively barren of fossils, and those fossils that have been found are valueless as timepieces, this part of the geologic calendar has not been satisfactorily subdivided. Radiometric dating may help in the future, but because even a small plus-or-minus factor of long-lived radioactive minerals amounts to a good many million years, it is improbable that Precambrian time can ever be subdivided in any great detail.

Historical geology was founded on the second major division, whose abundant fossils and sedimentary rocks allowed the application of dating and correlation to produce a finely divided time scale. There are no generally accepted names for the two greatest divisions, although it has been suggested that, with appropriate grandeur, they be called eons: Cryptozoic, meaning hidden life for the older; and Phanerozoic, meaning evident life for the younger. Having mentioned these terms, let us ignore them and concentrate on the commonly used divisions after Precambrian time.

The major subdivisions are called *eras*, of which there are three, set apart on their fossil records of dominant life. The first is the *Paleozoic* (from the Greek: *paleo* means ancient; *zoic*, from which the word zoo is derived, means life). In this era, lasting from about 600 million to 200

million years ago, the highest forms of animals were first invertebrates, and later vertebrates including fish, amphibians, and primitive reptiles. The second great era, the *Mesozoic* (meaning middle, or medieval life), extending from 200 million to 70 million years ago is the age of dinosaurs. The third era, the *Cenozoic* (recent life), is marked by the ascendancy of the mammals. Each of the eras is a collection of less-grand divisions called *periods* based, as you recall, on the time-rock units called systems.[7] They are fundamental units because the master column and time scale were largely set up from the study of systems. Their given names, which are the same for equivalent systems and periods, originated in several ways.

Some represent a locality where the rock sequence was first worked out. For instance, Cambria was the Roman name for Wales. A system first studied there by Adam Sedgewick is called *Cambrian*, and rocks throughout the world of the same age belong to the Cambrian System, which records events of the Cambrian Period of time. Other names describe the rocks, such as *Cretaceous* which refers to the dominantly chalky nature of a system of rocks where they were first studied in Europe. *Triassic* is derived from a sequence of rocks that in Germany includes three main divisions. Tertiary and Quaternary are holdovers from an earlier attempt to establish a master rock column. Its "Primary" and "Secondary," which referred to igneous-metamorphic complexes and well-consolidated sedimentary rocks, respectively, are now defunct terms.[8]

As the column became known in more detail, lesser divisions were established. Periods are subdivided into *epochs* corresponding to time-rock units called *series*. Except for the Cenozoic era, the epochs and series cannot easily be ap-

[7] The time-rock units equivalent to an era have no special name and are simply called Cambrian rocks, Mesozoic rocks, or Cenozoic rocks.

[8] It has been proposed to standardize the terminology by getting rid of Tertiary and Quaternary, but geologists are creatures of habit in whom the terms are ingrained. Even if a new system of naming were introduced, one would still have to know the old terms to understand the geologic literature, and the existing patchwork naming has a certain merit in showing how our ideas evolved.

plied from one continent to another, so local names are used. Geographical names are given to these divisions before the Cenozoic; for example, the *Cincinnatian* refers to an epoch, and a series, represented by upper Ordovician rocks in the United States. The only epochs we will be concerned with are those of the Cenozoic because the historical record of these rocks is more detailed and complete than those of any earlier era. Cenozoic epochs and series were originally named by Charles Lyell, according to how recently their fossil populations appeared. The names he coined reflect the observation that remains of modern animal types become fewer and fewer in progressively older rocks. The subdivisions of the Cenozoic, which are used worldwide, all end in *cene* which means recent, and their prefixes are such things as *Pleisto* meaning most, and *Oligo* meaning few; hence Pleistocene means "most recent" and Oligocene means "few recent." So much for how geologists order events and tell time. There is yet another aspect of historical geology, which is to attempt to reconstruct the face of the earth as it was at various given times.

PAST WORLDS

In a large measure, historical geology is geography, because it deals with the face of the earth and with once-living communities.[9] But it is geography of a special sort, a geography in the fourth dimension that involves the patterns of particular by-gone ages, and their progressive change through an enormity of time. As you might suspect, present-day geography is a model for the past, or paleogeographic, reconstructions. Any geography is a composite of many environments, local scenes or surroundings, each influencing communities of life.

As a preliminary to historical reconstruction, the earth's many surface environments which are

[9] Geographers will complain, mumbling something about the effect of physical environment on man, which is a somewhat restricted field of human geography; and geologists, who resent being classed as geographers, will consider the statement a gross oversimplification.

observable today can be viewed as three broad groups. *Continental*, or terrestrial, environments make up the landscapes, which we have discussed in some detail. They occur in mountains, plains, and plateaus, and the lesser features made by the destructional external forces working on them, all of which have certain variations according to their occurrence in particular climatic zones. Geologists are even more concerned with *marine environments* because the sedimentary rocks blanketing three-quarters of the continental surface, and which have been geology's most important historical documents, were largely deposited in shallow seas. For ours is a time of rather notable emergence, and, in the last half-billion years for which there is an adequate record, only the late Paleozoic–early Mesozoic interval, about 200 million years ago, was at all like it. During most of geologic time the continental platforms have been more widely flooded. Marine environments vary with depth from shallow seas to the deep ocean floors and in water temperature from arctic to tropic seas. *Transitional environments* are represented by beaches, deltas, and other features developed by shore processes and the interplay of land and sea.

The same environments are reflected in rocks, but rocks often involve a major correlation problem. Very similar ones have been laid down at widely different times, and those of the same age may not look at all alike because of differences in environments of deposition. The problem is further complicated where rocks have been lost by erosion, and crumbled by deformation. Outcrops are often like scrambled pieces from a hundred incomplete jig-saw puzzles, so, the first chore is to sort out the pieces of a particular puzzle by correlation, then determine their proper places, which can be difficult in areas of structural complication. When this is done, a picture emerges, which is usually presented as a map, showing patterns of different rock types at the particular time in geologic history when they were laid down. But there is still the problem of determining what environments are represented by the various rock types. So historical geology is a geography of a rather difficult sort.

Reading local records

In reconstructing paleogeography, geologists must of necessity start by looking at individual outcrops. Later this local information can be compiled and related to broader patterns; but first, what can be read from rocks at a single place?

Primary Structures Depositional features of sedimentary rocks are often useful indicators of the conditions under which they formed. Mud cracks preserved in shales suggest a former mud flat that was alternately covered by water and then dry. Ripple marks indicate the nature of waves or currents creating them. Cross-bedding may indicate whether beds were formed as wind-blown dunes, stream deposits, or on the sea floor. The largest cross-laminations are generally thought to be formed in windblown sand. Those of streams, if cut across the channel axes, may show a pattern of concave curves cutting across each other. Considerably more needs to be learned about the origin of cross-bedding, but used in conjunction with other evidence it may indicate environment, and it is useful as evidence of the direction, strength, and variability of moving air or water. Volcanic rocks can be used to tell whether eruptions were on land or underwater, for those that cooled in air are frequently jointed into vertical polygonal columns while those cooling in submarine surroundings often have pillow structure. These and similar physical features are records of environments, where we know enough of the processes working on modern sediments to read them.

Color In some cases the color of rocks tells something of environmental conditions. *Black shales* may owe their color to abundantly preserved organic material, which suggests a stagnant ocean bottom of "stinking muds" or rapid deposition, for if long exposed to well-oxygenated waters the dark organic material would be decomposed. These shales contain mainly fossils of swimming and floating organisms that sank to the bottom on death; bottom dwellers [10] are rare, which suggests a rather unhealthy sea floor in a sinking zone of a geosyncline or shelf sea. *Gray shales,* on the other hand, suggest a more stable floor where the water circulation is better.

Red beds include conglomerates, sands and shales whose striking color comes from iron oxide (the mineral *hematite*), which may coat quartz or other clastic grains, or sometimes from abundant particles of red minerals such as red feldspar. In some places red beds are not happy hunting grounds for fossils; however, in others footprints, amphibians, fish, and plant remains have been found, indicating a dominantly continental environment. The red beds are flood plain, alluvial fan, and deltaic deposits, which are sometimes carried into the open sea, in a strongly oxidizing environment. Red beds have posed a classic geologic problem: whether they do or do not represent a particular climate.

Some workers maintain that red beds indicate a desert climate because of their frequent association with layers of salt and gypsum. These precipitated rocks, called evaporites, are thought to form in partially closed basins, where restricted arms of shallow seas are periodically cut off and evaporated to near dryness. Other geologists suppose a semi-arid climate with marked wet and dry seasons, like the Savanna grasslands in present-day Africa. Still others envision the red beds as the red soils, called laterites, of wet tropical areas, the jungles. It may well be that red beds have several climatic origins.

Rock Types Rocks are products of their heredity as well as the environment in which they formed. This is evident in those metamorphic rocks which have not been so drastically altered by deep-seated environments that relic features of original sedimentary and volcanic surface rocks have been obliterated. Slates bear evidence of once being shales, marbles of being limestones, and so it goes. Less directly perhaps,

[10] Swimmers are called *nekton,* floaters *plankton,* bottom dwellers *benthos.*

the composition of sedimentary rocks reflects the regions from which pre-existing materials were derived. For although the only positive environmental record is in rocks at the sites of deposition, we can, from a knowledge of existing erosional landscapes, make informed guesses as to whether the crust was stable, or being actively uplifted in nearby plains and mountains which erosion later destroyed.

Well-sorted quartz sandstones, shales, and limestones suggest relatively stable areas of deposition and source regions of low to moderate relief whose rocks were extensively weathered. The insoluble end-products of chemical weathering are quartz and clays. Wave action, and in some cases wind, winnow these products leaving "clean" sandstones in and near shore surroundings, and carry muds farther offshore where they settle beneath the zone of wave stirring. Pure limestone, derived from the soluble products, suggests precipitation in warm, clear, and shallow seas.

Conglomerate is taken as evidence of relatively rapid uplift, and rugged topography in a source area of mountains drained by swift streams, or of wave-attacked headlands and promontories. Some, however, may represent submarine landslides. A poorly sorted conglomerate containing snubbed and striated boulders could well be a lithified glacial till.

Graywacke, a poorly sorted, "dirty" sandstone containing much clay, silt, and rock fragments, also suggests crustal instability. It has been described as having a "poured-in" look, meaning it accumulated rapidly, with little reworking by waves and currents, which would have removed the finer materials. Thus graywackes indicate rapidly subsiding geosynclinal areas and orogeny, marked by rising mountains or islands and deeply subsiding basins into which sediments were spilled rapidly with almost no winnowing or sorting.

Arkose is literally a "granite wash," a sandstone with notable amounts of feldspar and other grains, suggesting rapid uplift and rugged relief in a source area of granite, little affected by chemical weathering (Fig. 10-16).

Organisms Fossils, as well as being guides to correlation, are important clues to environments. Oysters, a sedentary lot, never left the sea so their shells indicate a marine environment. A lizard's tracks on a lamina of a cross-bedded sandstone [11] suggest a dune sand, rather than one laid in water. Coal, the fossil record of a forest, in the icy wastes of the Antarctic, indicates a far warmer climate when this rock formed. Massive coral reefs, so far as is known, form only in tropical ocean waters. As we have discussed, fossils can be used to reconstruct more-detailed elements within the major environments, as for instance the shore, shallow water, and deeper ocean bottom.

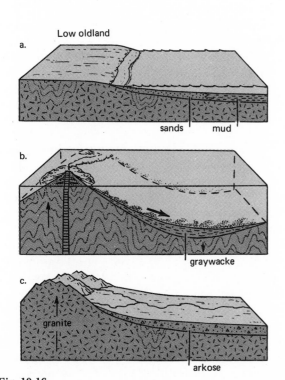

Fig. 10-16
Environments inferred from different types of sandstones:
a. *quartz sandstone,* b. *graywacke,* c. *arkose.*

[11] An uncommon situation, but it illustrates the point.

Leonardo da Vinci (1452–1519) *A near universal genius, da Vinci's notebooks show that he clearly appreciated the nature of fossils, of erosion, transport, and deposition, and of shifting seas and land. Free of dogmatic misconceptions, he was a naturalist far ahead of his times. Unfortunately, his geologic ideas were lost for several centuries.*

A single property of a rock is rarely conclusive evidence of the rock's particular origin; it takes a number of features to make a strong case. One observation, like a statement taken out of context, can lead to erroneous conclusions. For instance, a fossil tree entombed in a rock might well mean a terrestrial environment. Yet the rock could be marine if the original tree drifted to sea before it became waterlogged and sank. In this case, closer examination might disclose clam shells, fish remains, and other evidence of an ocean bottom.

Stratigraphic Columns Although the contacts between rock units in a vertical column may be quite sharp, they need not—as early Catastrophists assumed—represent any sudden flood or drastic change of environment. The slow migration of a sea across a particular area is an adequate cause, in line with Uniformitarian thought. *Transgressive seas*, advancing over an area, would leave a vertical rock sequence such as the

following: Terrestrial red beds at the bottom, overlain by a sandstone laid down at the margin of an encroaching sea, above which is a marine shale of deeper waters (Fig. 10-17). The shifting environments, as a *regressive sea* withdraws over an area, might be marked by a sequence including from bottom to top: a limestone marine facies, a shale of the deltaic facies, and a sandstone of a terrestrial dune facies.[12]

Regional compilations

Restorations Changing patterns of shifting seas, rising mountains, and other episodes in the geologic drama through time are largely reconstructed from restored *cross-sections*. Any cross-section is a geologist's interpretation of what a vertical slice into the earth would show. A restored cross-section is an attempt, after eliminating the effects of later erosion and later structural contortion, to show rock relations as they must have been at the end of some particular interval of time. Because of the spotty nature of outcrops, restored sections must normally be compiled from rock columns measured and described at many separate places across a wide region. They are based on both lithologic correlation, to demonstrate the continuity of particular rock types, and also time correlation, from place to place, to establish time lines marking the slow migration and fluctuation of continental, transitional, and marine environments. For, if traced far enough, rocks of the transitional shore zone, for instance, do tend to cross time lines.

Facies Because of the variety of environments, different sediments are being laid down side by side at that particular time we call the present day. The fact is self-evident; they can be walked (skin-dived, bathyscaphed, or more simply bottom-sampled) from one to another. Boulders and gravels in alluvial fans at the foot of mountains may grade into sands of a beach, the sands may

---

[12] Facies means aspect, or "look." There are also igneous and metamorphic facies, but let's not get involved in these.

Transgressive Sea

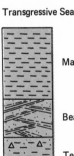

Regressive Sea

Marine shale

Beach sandstone

Terrestrial red beds

Eolian sandstone

Deltaic shale

Marine limestone

Fig. 10-17
Local rock columns indicating advancing and retreating seas.

grade into muds of the offshore bottom, and the muds into limey reefs in clear waters remote from the shore.

Lateral changes in the overall "look" of sediments or sedimentary rock units that reflect different depositional environments are known as sedimentary facies. Thus, piecing together facies relations in rocks—which often takes considerable ingenuity—is important in the construction of paleogeographic maps for a particular time in the geologic past. Such maps, however, are like single frames on a reel of motion-picture film; they are still shots of an ever-changing scene.

There is a noble ring to the story of historical geology, wherein great mountains rise and then are worn low, and the sea comes in and goes out across continental platforms. Such grand episodes are largely read from changing patterns of facies through time, for the geography of the present is not that of the past nor, for that matter, will it be unchanging in the future.

Transgressing Seas An illustration of an advancing sea causing progressively younger rocks to overlap across the older ones beneath is nicely represented in restored cross-sections of the Cambrian, earliest Paleozoic rocks of the eastern United States. The story, to be presented later, is that in early Cambrian time, seas were largely restricted to a geosyncline flanking the low, eroded, continental platform; then the sea spread from the geosyncline, reaching well into the continental interior by late Cambrian time.

The evidence is from restored profiles, which required the unravelling in places of some very complicated structure and piecing together sometimes patchy outcrops, and from some good guide fossils, resembling miniature horseshoe crabs, creatures called trilobites. One called *Olenellus* marks early Cambrian rocks, *Paradoxides* is typical of middle Cambrian, and *Elvinia* of upper Cambrian; they are timepieces showing that these particular rocks cross time lines (Fig. 10-18).

From the east in the geosyncline to west in the continental interior, the local columns of Cambrian rocks lying on Precambrian basement have a striking similarity. At their bottoms are conglomerates and quartz sandstones, above them are shales, and above them are limestones. Using the trilobite clocks, it is evident that deep in the geosyncline the basal sands are early Cambrian, towards the interior they are middle Cambrian, and still farther in the continental interior they are late Cambrian. The picture presented is of seas slowly flooding the continent during a relatively quiet period, free of major mountain building. The sands, derived from Precambrian rocks forming the low continental interior, are well-washed debris carried by streams and worked by wave action. The clays produced by long weathering of the Precambrian Shield were sorted from sands and carried farther from the shore where they could settle below the stirred zone of orbital wave motion. Limestones reflect the clearer waters either well offshore or where streams supplied less mud along the coast.

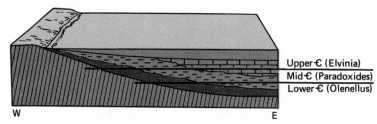

Fig. 10-18
Rock types deposited in the advancing Cambrian sea cross time lines, indicated by fossils.

Clastic Debris Floods. Another instructive case, this one involving active mountain building, relates to changing interpretations in restored cross-sections across New York State, for the Paleozoic period, called Devonian. The geography of the time was different from the present situation, for the state was occupied by a shallow sea with mountains to the east of it. As mountains rose to the east in what is now New England and the seaboard region, the seas withdrew and were replaced across New York by continental deposits, a great wedge of clastics called the Catskill Delta. These rocks are nicely laid out, from the Catskill Plateau just west of the Hudson River, to the western parts of New York and Pennsylvania. Although about 100 different formational names have been locally applied to the New York Devonian, overall, any vertical rock column shows three recurring kinds of rock. At the bottom is a continuous and distinct marine formation, called the Onondaga limestone, which from fossil evidence is the same age throughout. The rocks above are mainly clastic: first sandstones, and gray and black shales (originally called the Chemung group) overlain, where not eroded away, by red beds including shales, sandy shales, sandstones and conglomerates of dominantly continental origin, originally the Catskill group.

The first to work on this Devonian sequence in the mid-nineteenth century was James Hall, father of the geosynclinal concept. He and many competent followers considered each of the broad rock types as time-rock units, that is, deposited about the same time everywhere, and one after another. Thus the red beds were all thought latest Devonian, the dark shale and sand-

stones were older, and the Onondaga limestone as early middle Devonian (Fig. 10-19). In the 1920's George H. Chadwick and G. Arthur Cooper began a classic bit of geologic detective work which showed the lithologies are facies. It turns out that only the basal limestone is the same age across the state; the clastic rock types above were all being deposited at the same time: red beds to the east; to the west the sandstones; and still farther west the shales. With time, the mountain building to the east must have accelerated, for the red-bed facies extends ever farther westward in younger rocks reflecting a retreat of shore and sea environments.

The case for lateral facies changes, which looks so obvious in the restored section, was laboriously built from scattered scraps of both lithologic and fossil evidence. Lithologically, detailed tracing showed that in places certain key beds, such as distinctive limestone layers or conglomerate stringers, extended well into a quite different rock type, say a shale or a sandstone, which lay both above and below. Where such interfingering occurs, rocks of the different facies must be of the same age. Careful study of fossils showed that some had complicated the earlier time correlations by being better indicators of environment than time. As an example, a particular brachiopod,[13] called *Cyrtospirifer,* was a long-lived variety preferring the sandy shale facies of the sea floor adjacent to the deltaic front. However, others, notably a brachiopod called *Hypothyridina,* apparently lived in clear

[13] A shellfish looking superficially like a clam, but attached to the sea floor by a fleshy stalk, and having the shells differently oriented in relation to the body.

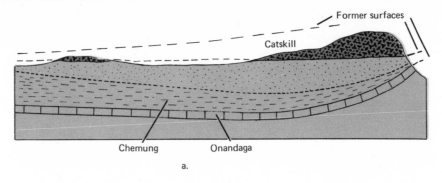

a.

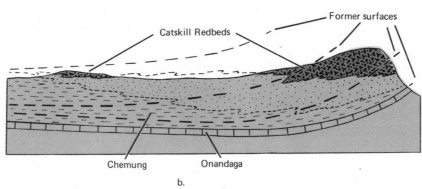

b.

Fig. 10-19
The early a *and present* b *interpretations of the Devonian rocks of New York State.* a *assumes similar rock types are of similar age. In* b, *the "former surfaces," representing time lines, involve sedimentary facies.*

waters of limestone deposition as well as on muddy and sandy sea floors. This fossil is found in a limestone extending from the west into the middle of New York State, then it occurs eastward in a zone of shales, and still farther eastward in sandstones that emerge well up in the Catskill front.

We have dwelt on the Devonian rocks of New York State, not only as an example of how progressively accelerating orogeny can be read from great outpourings of clastic debris and red beds coarsening towards their source, but also because they impressed on American geologists the importance of facies changes and their migration. With some provincial differences, similar patterns have been established in rocks of other places and times.

Time perspective

Enough for how the earth's past is reconstructed; now a word of warning before going on. Short summaries of geologic history almost of necessity have two flaws: first they tend to be pontifical, for the evidence and controversies are largely ignored to make the story flow; second they may leave the impression that the history is like a variety show where scenes and actors whisk on and off. Keep in mind that geologic changes, which can be described in a few words, are almost incredibly slow. Saying that Mount Everest rose from the sea to its existing height of 29,000 feet in Cenozoic time, implies no sudden event in ordinary terms. A rate of uplift averaging $1/100$ of an inch per year would accom-

241

plish it in somewhat less than 40,000,000 years, which is shorter than the allowable time. If the Colorado River deepened its channel 1/32 of an inch a year in cutting Grand Canyon, in 384 years it would down-cut one foot; continuing at this rate the mile-deep canyon would result in something over two million years. A sea, advancing over a subdued continental platform at a rate of about 6 inches a year, would take 2½ million years to reach 250 miles inland. So, when you read that the seas came in and the seas went out, that mountains rose, that great canyons were cut, such changes can be viewed as rapid only in the perspective of geologic time.

SUGGESTED READINGS

Dunbar, C. O., and Rogers, John, *Principles of Stratigraphy*, New York, John Wiley & Sons, 1957.

Hurley, P. M., *How Old Is the Earth?* Garden City, N.Y. Doubleday & Co., Inc., 1959 (paperback, Anchor Books).

Kulp, J. L., "Geologic Time Scale," in *Science*, Vol. 133, No. 3459, pp. 1105–1114. 1961.

eleven: "Dramatis personae" in the history of life

THE PLANT KINGDOM

Plants are broadly divisible into two types: those with a vascular system of vessels and ducts for piping dissolved nutrients and food; and those without. The more primitive non-vascular group, the lower plants, are largely adapted for life in water, where the kingdom originally evolved. The higher, vascular plants are characterized by roots, stiffened stems, and leaves, suiting them for life on land.

Non-vascular plants [1]

Thallophyta A simple body, the thallus, characterizes the thallophytes (phyte means plant). Despite a great diversity of sizes and shapes meriting their division into a number of separate phyla, two main groups are recognized: the algae having chlorophyl, the green protein used for photosynthesis, and the fungi, which lack it.

Most algae live in the sea, some in fresh water, and a few on wet ground, environments where they can absorb water directly into their cells without elaborate piping systems. They include pond scums, simple green algae, and numerous brown marine types, ranging from one-celled micro-organisms to large sea weeds, kelps 300 feet long. Although by far the oldest group and ancestral to all higher plants, only certain types are common in the fossil record.

[1] Plant classification being in something of a turmoil, it seems best not to designate sub-kingdoms, phyla, classes, or the like, but simply refer to groups.

Common fossil algae include various marine species that secrete calcium carbonate within and around their cells to build plates, cylinders, or encrustations with distinctive microstructures. Such algae still live today, and fossil forms are found in rocks as old as Ordovician. In other cases communities of many algal species form filamentous mats which, judging by modern ones, do not precipitate much solid material in their cells. However, they do trap and bind sediment particles to form dome-shaped, laminated structures a few inches to a few feet in diameter and height. Their swirling bun-like masses are relatively common in some Precambrian rocks, but unfortunately of no value in dating and correlation, for modern representatives are almost identical to the most ancient (Fig. 11-1).

Some 15,000 species of diatoms secrete an array of intricate siliceous skeletons. These microscopic plants live in water, mainly in the sea where vast numbers floating as plankton are the foundation of the food chains there. On settling to the ocean floor, their hard remains form diatom ooze—especially in cool waters—and eventually the rock diatomite (diatomaceous earth), some deposits being up to 3000 feet thick. Diatoms are common Cenozoic fossils, occurring in Cretaceous deposits, and are possibly present in Jurassic rocks. Their absence from older deposits may reflect a late evolution of hard parts, or long-term solution of the colloidal, less-stable variety of silica in their tests (shells) by penetrating waters.

The *fungi*, which include bacteria, molds,

Fig. 11-1
Fossil algae of Precambrian age from upper New York State. Courtesy of the American Museum of Natural History.

rusts, toadstools, and such, are probably algae descendants who lost their chlorophyl. In any case, many live on land though usually in moist environments, and all are parasitic on living plants, animals, or organic matter. Through geologic time, the role of bacteria has certainly been of prime importance, else the world of life would long ago have been overwhelmed by its own wastes and dead tissues. There is direct evidence of large fungi growing on trees of the carboniferous coal forests. However, the geologic record of this group is insignificant.

Bryophytes Liverworts and mosses are bryophytes, a minor group of lower plants that are mainly adapted for life in wet places, differ little from thallophytes in lacking a vascular system, and probably evolved from algae. Liverworts have a flat thallus body attached to the ground by thread-like structures called rhizoids. The more familiar mosses, some of which are hardy and adapted to very cold or dry climates, do have very primitive stems and leaves but rhizoids instead of roots, and no vascular system. In common with the higher plants, and unlike thallophytes, the fertilized ovules, or eggs, of bryophytes are retained and protected in the plant's tissues for a time after fertilization, giving them a better chance of survival.

Although mosses are peat-formers, the fossil

record of bryophytes in general, which extends back to the Carboniferous, is too poor to be enlightening. They are interesting as a primitive attempt of plants to adapt to land life; however, they seem a separate line of thallophyte descendants, giving rise to no higher types. The "missing link" between the simpler water-dwelling algae and the vascular land plants is still missing. It was probably a seaweed, like the large *Nematophyton,* that evolved a tube-filled body for conducting water.

Vascular plants

Long ago the algae invaded the swamps and ponds of the wet terrestrial environments, but they lacked the necessary equipment for life on land. In adapting to land life, their progeny, the higher plants, have developed the following:

1. An outer coat, or epidermis, that prevents drying out in air, yet has pores allowing exchange of gases involved in photosynthesis.
2. A fibro-vascular system that supports plants deprived of the bouyancy of water, and serves as a circulatory system.
3. Anchoring roots that tap ground water and mineral nutrients.
4. Leaves for increasing the area of photosynthesis.
5. In the highest types, reproductive systems freed of the need for surrounding water, and producing a protected embryo.

From the fossil record, and the comparative anatomy of primitive survivors and more advanced plants, we can see how plants evolved and met terrestrial requirements.

Psilopsida The fossil record of plants in the early Paleozoic when the land plants were appearing is very poor; yet through a quirk of preservation, Devonian strata of a silicified peat bog in Scotland contain excellent specimens of *Rhynia* which, even if not the actual progenitor of the higher types, is certainly a vascular plant of the most primitive sort. This small,

rush-like plant, a foot or two high, was little more than a creeping stalk with spore cases at the tips; leafless, hence photosynthesis must have occurred in its stem; and rootless, being anchored by a creeping root stock, bearing thread-like absorbing hairs (*rhizoids*) instead of true roots. However, the stem had a fibro-vascular system. Other fossil Psilopsida include slightly more complicated types, whose stems bore scales that foreshadowed the evolution of leaves. Fossil Psilopsida are all of Silurian and Devonian age. No later ones have been found, although two interesting little plants living today in the tropics seem relics of this archaic group, whose fossils provide a good transition to the three main groups of higher vascular plants.

Lycopsida Today the club mosses are insignificant creeping plants of tropic and temperate zones exemplified by the ground pine. They seem descendants of the scaly Lycopsida, because their solid stems are clothed by many spirally arranged leaves. A step up in the evolutionary ladder, they possess true roots which, being adventitious, are essentially downward branches from a root stock. Reproductively, Ground Pines bear small cones filled with a single type of spores. However, one living Lycopsida produces two kinds of spores that develop into male and female plants; and some of the large fossil forms had even evolved a seed habit, a parallel but separate development to that in the higher modern plants.

Questionable remains have been reported in Siberian rocks of Cambrian age, but the heyday of the Lycopsida was in the Carboniferous when they rivalled the size of many large modern trees. These great scale trees, abundantly preserved in coal deposits, were lycopsids which shed leaves from their trunks leaving prominent scales on the bark. The trunks were straight, some varieties having a few branches towards the top. Specimens of *Lepidodendron,* as much as 100 feet high, were scale trees with roots, and almost as large was *Sigillaria.* Why some of these large trees which had evolved a seed habit of reproduction did not survive is something of a mystery.

Sphenopsida   The horsetails, called scouring rushes because their siliceous stems were once used to clean pots and pans, are modern representatives of the Sphenopsida. Horsetails have spore-bearing cones, stout root stocks, and some roots. They are distinguished by vertically ribbed, hollow stems that have bamboo-like[2] joints from which swirls or clusters of leaves radiate. Although a bit more advanced than the club moss group, the Sphenopsida also arose from the Psilopsida stock, had their climax in late Paleozoic time, and are now relatively unimportant in the modern flora. The oldest known representatives occur in Devonian strata; however, the giant of the stock, *Calamites*, an 80-foot tall hollow tree, grew in thickets in the Carboniferous coal swamps.

Pteropsida   Club mosses and horsetails are the remnants of two lineages of Psilopsida descendants, whose late Paleozoic day of grandeur is long past. The third collateral line, the Pteropsida ("fern-like" plants) now dominate the landscape, clothing it in green. The incredibly diverse and prolific Pteropsida are divisible into three groups: *ferns*, the parent stock; and two groups of seed-bearing descendants, the *gymnosperms*, which have naked seeds, and in turn gave rise to the *angiosperms*, whose seeds are inside a case that is contained in a flower. The Pteropsida in general are set apart from other vascular plants by the nature of their leaves.

The *ferns* (technically *Filicinae*), which first appear in Devonian rocks, are the most primitive Pteropsida (Fig. 11-2). Although 40-foot tree ferns still live in New Zealand, the abundant and familiar ones are all relatively small. Their stems are typically inconspicuous, subterranean rhyzomes with adventitious roots. The feathery, lace-like leaves are prominent, and from an evolutionary point of view most important. Unlike

[2] Bamboo, however, is a more advanced plant related to the grass family.

Fig. 11-2
Fossil fern of Pennsylvanian age from Illinois. Courtesy of the Smithsonian Institution.

the horsetail and club moss groups, whose generally small and simple leaves are modified scales, fern leaves evolved from branches. Some of the ancestral Psilopsida have slightly flattened branch tips, foreshadowing things to come. In fossil ferns, transitional stages indicate that the true, or modern, leaf evolved by the continued flattening of small branches, covered with simple, scale leaves. The simple leaves ultimately fused into a single sheet, a superior light-catching device for photosynthesis, which forms the most advanced type of leaf.

Ferns, however despite their efficient leaves, are restricted to shady moist environments, for their reproductive methods are little improved over those evolved in the water-dwelling algae. So, let us review plant reproduction which needed some overhauling—specifically the development of the seed habit—before pteridophytes could complete the conquest of dry land. From a strictly geologic view, spore and pollen, the reproductive cells that plants shed in prodigious quantities, are important fossils, especially useful for dating and environmental studies in younger terrestrial sediments. Pollen is produced by gymnosperms and angiosperms, whereas spores are reproductive structures of ferns and other seedless plants.

Many spores are asexual, single cells, each of which can grow into a new plant under proper surrounding conditions. Algae broadcast theirs in water, and terrestrial plants through the air. So far, the method seems simple and easily adapted to a thoroughgoing land life. But plant reproduction was complicated in the remote past when some ancestral marine algae "discovered" sex. Sexual reproduction involves two kinds of reproductive cells, the gametes, called sperm and egg, that fuse into one which develops into a new individual animal or plant. As a result plant reproduction is more complicated than in animals, for plants lead a double life as alternate sexual and asexual generations. An asexual plant, the sporophyte, sheds only spores that develop into sexual plants, called gametophytes. The gametophytes are sperm and egg producers whose offspring are new sporophyte plants. The typical fern, for instance, is the sporophyte; the gametophyte is an inconspicuous different-looking plant, a thin green sheet attached to the ground by rhizoids. Sperm are loosened on the underside of a fern gametophyte, where they swim through a film of water to fertilize the eggs. Because sperm cannot stand drying out, they are the weakest link in the reproductive cycle of spore-bearing terrestrial plants.

The *gymnosperms* were the first Pteropsida

with seed habit. In seed plants a minute female gametophyte remains and functions inside the reproductive apparatus of the sporophyte. Pollen grains, a kind of microspore resistant to drying, are transported through the air in great quantities. Those reaching a female element generate sperm that fertilize the egg. When fertilized, the egg develops into an embryonic plant surrounded by food housed inside a tough cover —this whole structure constitutes a seed. Thus, the evolution of pollen freed terrestrial plants from the necessity of wet ground; and the seed, being an embryonic plant provided with stored food, has a good start on life when conditions favor germination.

The descent of seed-bearing Pteropsida from ferns is documented by clearly transitional fossils, the extinct *seed ferns* found in Devonian to Jurassic rocks. They had both tree-like and sprawling habits, and are so like the true, or spore-bearing, ferns that unless associated seeds are found, the two groups are indistinguishable. Having seeds attached to their leaves, however, makes seed ferns the simplest of gymnosperms, a group characterized by exposed seeds.[3]

Some late Paleozoic leaves indicate that cycads, palm-like gymnosperms,[4] evolved from seed ferns. Some of the cycads, an extinct group abundant in the Mesozoic flora had stubby, oval trunks crowned with palm-like fronds that bore seed cones. As this group also had primitive flowers, it is thought by some paleobotanists—but not all —to have been ancestral to the angiosperms, the flowering plants. The living cycads are distinguished by cylindrical tree trunks. A rather primitive gymnosperm stock, they are first found in Triassic rocks, and possibly in late Paleozoic.

The ginkgos, which may be found on many college campuses, are reported living wild in Western China. They date back to the late Paleozoic, and were especially common in early and middle Mesozoic time. Superficially resembling angiosperms, they are in fact rather primitive, and their one remaining species is called a

---

[3] Gymno means "naked."

[4] The true palm is an angiosperm.

Fig. 11-3
Miocene leaf from Colorado. Courtesy of the Smithsonian Institution.

"living fossil." Cordaites, a late Paleozoic tree, was common in the Carboniferous coal swamps, but died out before the Mesozoic. Although bearing strap-like leaves as much as 3 feet long, it seems closely related to conifers in most other features.

The *conifers* include most of the familiar evergreens, such as pine, spruce, fir, and those all-time giants of the plant world, the redwoods, reaching 300 feet high and 40 feet through the trunk. Seeds are borne underneath the scales of the characteristic cones, from which the group is named, and the leaves have evolved into needles. Conifers first appeared in late Paleo-

zoic rocks, reached their peak in late Mesozoic time, and are still common.

The *angiosperms* are a tremendously diversified and specialized collection—there are some 135,000 living species—including trees, like oaks, elms, maples, willows, palms, and many others; some smaller woody plants, or shrubs; grasses; garden vegetables, and the flowers. Unlike the gymnosperms, which are all trees or woody plants, the angiosperms have evolved into the rapidly growing soft-bodied forms called herbs. The distinguishing feature of all angiosperms is their reproductive apparatus, the flower. These complicated structures enclose the female elements and, after fertilization, the seed, inside a chamber called the ovary. The enclosed angiosperm seeds are largely insect-pollinated by bees attracted to the flowers, in contrast to the dominantly wind-pollinated exposed seeds of the gymnosperms.

The oldest fossils of angiosperms appear in Triassic rocks. As these first representatives are distinct and well evolved, the group may well have originated from a gymnosperm representative in the late Paleozoic. Unfortunately, a clearly transitional type is yet to be found. Angiosperms have abounded since Cretaceous time when many forms appeared that are quite like those of the present. Geologically, some have been very useful indicators of climatic changes, such as fossil magnolias in northerly climes. The evolution of horses, cows, and other grazing mammals was made possible by the great expansion of the grasses in mid-Cenozoic time. Today, angiosperms are the most important food source for animals and man, by all odds the dominant flora, and the culmination of plant evolution.

THE ANIMAL KINGDOM

The million or more animal species, so far described, comprise about 30 phyla [5] of which only a dozen are common in the fossil record.

[5] Taxonomists cannot quite agree on the exact number.

Arbitrarily, we shall include these phyla in two general, and most unequal, groups based on the kinds of paleontologists who study them, rather than on taxonomic procedures. Invertebrates, animals without backbones, make up all phyla save one. Vertebrates, having backbones or something similar, include the most advanced animal types.

Invertebrates

The geologic time scale—the framework for earth history—is largely based on relative dating using invertebrates. Because of the prevalence of marine rocks, they are by all odds the most common fossils, and their evolution, especially in three phyla, Protozoa, Mollusca, and Arthropoda, makes some of them highly diagnostic index fossils.

There is no direct evidence as to how the invertebrate phyla are related to each other, for the main groups were all distinct and well-evolved, before fossils became abundant, in earliest Paleozoic time. However, their branching from the "Tree of Life" can be logically inferred from the embryology, comparative anatomy, and degree of complexity, of living invertebrates. It may seem pointless to discuss soft anatomy, which is largely internal and rarely preserved in fossils, yet it represents the vital parts of animals, and in a large measure is the basis for arraying the phyla in increasing order of complexity.

Phylum Protozoa The progenitors of all other animals were protozoa, one-celled animals of great abundance.[6] However, as fossils they are virtually unknown, with two notable exceptions: the orders *Foraminifera* and *Radiolaria* of the class *Sarcodina*.

The Foraminifera, living mainly in salt water, have hard tests, or exoskeletons (Fig. 11-4). Most "forams" secrete calcite, a few silica, and some

[6] Classed with one-celled plants, and one-celled things that are hard to class as either plants or animals, in the Kingdom Protista of some classifications.

cement foreign grains together. The tremendous variety of tests makes them very useful to micro-paleontologists, especially for subsurface rock correlation from drill-hole data. Some foraminifera are important rock formers; for instance *Globigerina*, the shells of which make calcareous oozes. "Forams" are typically small, about the size of a wheat grain or less. However, some such as *Nummulites* were "coin-like" forms several inches across, examples of which can be seen in the limestones of the Egyptian Pyramids. The *radiolarians* are saltwater dwellers with siliceous exoskeletons, loosely built and often of a net-like form. Their tests, being extremely small as well as fragile, are not the best guide fossils; however, unlike the calcareous foram remains that dissolve in cold waters, they form characteristic radiolarian oozes and cherts that can exist in cold deep water.

Phylum Porifera For some time taxonomists were not sure whether sponges were plants or animals, as they live attached to the ocean floor, and show little reaction to outside stimulation. They are animals, however, for they feed on organic materials. Despite an exceedingly low level of bodily organization, sponges, being multi-celled animals, are a step above the Protozoa. The sack-like sponge body contains needle-like skeletal parts, spicules often preserved as fossils (Fig. 11-6). Calcareous spicules are common, and siliceous ones are probably the source for some beds of chert. The *archaeocyathids*, a group of extinct reef builders, which may or may not be truly porifera, are important sponge-like Cambrian fossils. In general, however, sponges are a rather dismal group for paleontological purposes.

Phylum Coelenterata Somewhat higher in the evolutionary picture are the coelenterates, jelly fish and the like. They have a digestive cavity—a not particularly attractive one—that ingests food and expels waste through the same opening. This mouth is usually surrounded by tentacles that direct food towards it, and are armed with stinging cells.

Fig. 11-4
Greatly enlarged models of some types of foraminifers. Courtesy of the Chicago Natural History Museum.

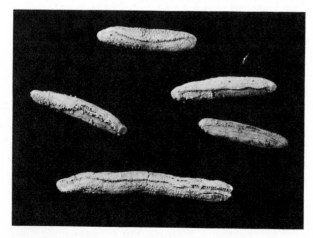

Fig. 11-5
Large foraminifers from Permian of west Texas. Courtesy of Dr. G. A. Cooper of the Smithsonian Institution.

Geologically, the most important coelenterates are the corals because they secrete distinctive calcareous skeletal structures. Some corals are solitary individuals (Fig. 11-7); others grow by budding, to produce coral heads or colonies, fused masses of small coral cups each occupied by a tiny tentacled animal (Fig. 11-8). The cups of many species are braced by vertical plates, called septa, that converge inward from the outer wall. Paleozoic septate corals have four basic septa, and most have secondary additions to the pattern. Mesozoic and Cenozoic corals commonly have six septa and others added in between. The great variety in coral shapes, crowding or loose arrangement of colonial individuals, as well as the arrangement and number of septa, has made them useful guide fossils (Fig. 11-9).

Fig. 11-6
A slab of Paleozoic sponges. Courtesy of the Chicago Natural History Museum.

Colonial corals, aided by other organisms (notably algae), have produced great reefs in tropical seas, past and present. Solitary types, in contrast, are not good indicators of water temperature.

Graptolites As different paleontologists have classed these extinct animals with Coelenterata, Bryozoa, and Hemichordata, it seems safest to treat them separately. Graptolites look like pencil marks on rock (in Greek, *graptos* means written and *lithos*, stone), for they are usually flattened impressions on shale bedding. Their detailed anatomy, which has been largely reconstructed from less common, undistorted specimens in limestones, consists of a central element, surrounded by chitinous [7] branches, bearing many small cups housing the individual animals. They apparently grew by budding.

[7] Organic material somewhat like your fingernails.

Some graptolites were shrub-like forms attached to the sea floor. Many others were floaters, suspended by a chitinous thread from floating seaweed or a gas-filled sack. Graptolites are important index fossils in Ordovician and Silurian dark shales (Figs. 11-10, 11-11). The floating species were widespread; their abundance in dark shales apparently reflects a reducing environment more conducive to their preservation than the better aerated sea floors of limestone deposition. The evolutionary trends making graptolites useful for dating include: reduction in the number of branches, changes in the angle of branches from straight down through straight up, and changes in the shapes of the individual cups.

Worms Several phyla can be treated together as "worms." Their burrows and trails, though generally of little diagnostic value, are preserved in

253

Fig. 11-7
Solitary Paleozoic "horn" coral, a tetra coral. Courtesy of the Smithsonian Institution.

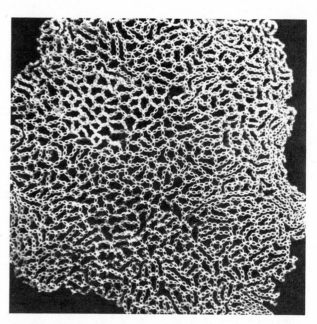

Fig. 11-9
Silurian "chain" coral from Kentucky. Courtesy of the Smithsonian Institution.

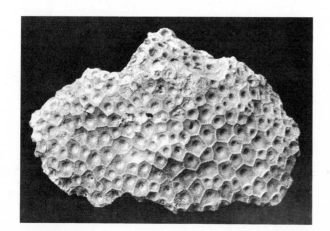

Fig. 11-8
Hexacoral compressed cups. Courtesy of the Chicago Natural History Museum.

Fig. 11-10
Graptolite specimen from Virginia. Courtesy of the Smithsonian Institution.

Fig. 11-11
Graptolite from Quebec. Courtesy of the Smithsonian Institution.

rocks as old as Precambrian, but actual worm remains are rare. If they were important in giving rise to higher phyla, paleontological evidence is lacking.

Phylum Bryozoa The unimpressive Bryozoans are relatively advanced invertebrates, and useful fossils. These "moss animals" are microscopic water-dwelling individuals that build lace-like, twig-like, or mounded colonies of calcium carbonate and chitinous materials (Fig. 11-12). They often appear as encrusting mats on shells and rocks. The bryozoa have rudimentary nerves, a muscle system, and digestive system that takes in material at one end and expels it at the other —an improvement over coelenterates although the gut, being U-shaped, has anal and oral openings adjacent. Bryozoans range from Ordovician, or possibly Cambrian, to recent time. The group as a whole has been abundant, and some forms having a short time range and wide distribution are good guide fossils. However, the individual fossils require microscopic techniques for study, which may be why they have not received the attention they deserve from paleontologists.

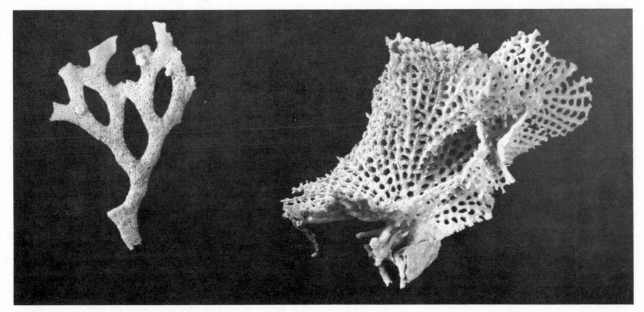

Fig. 11-12
Permian bryozoa from Glass Mountain, Texas. Courtesy of the Smithsonian Institution.

255

Fig. 11-13
Early Paleozoic brachiopods from Ohio. Courtesy of the Smithsonian Institution.

Phylum Brachiopoda The brachiopods are bivalves, superficially resembling clams, which are actually quite different. The two brachiopod shells are usually of different shapes, and one covers the bottom of the animal, the other the top (Figs. 11-13, 11-14). Clam shells, in contrast, are generally mirror images and arranged side-by-side with a hinge at the top; moreover, many clams are mobile. Only the larvae of brachiopods migrate; the adults are all sedentary, commonly attached to the ocean bottom by a fleshy stalk.

Brachiopods, which have calcite, phosphatic, or chitinous-phosphatic shells, are very abundant fossils. Based on comparison with living ones and muscle scars in fossil shells, the soft anatomy of brachiopods was relatively complex with digestive, circulatory, nervous, and muscle systems. Inside their shells, they had fleshy loops covered by minute tentacles that swept microscopic food particles into their mouths. Some "brachs" developed hard supports for the fleshy loops.

Being conservative beasts who never abandoned a sedentary life, brachiopods are all broadly similar in basic plan. They did, however, develop marked differences in shape and ornamentation of their shells. Some are smooth, except for growth lines, but others are strengthened and ornamented with a wide variety of ribs, spines, and such (Fig. 11-15). Thus their details are diverse enough to allow the recognition of 200 living, and some 3000 fossil, species. Among the brachiopods, *Lingula* is a "living fossil"; however, many others of wide distribution and limited time ranges are useful in dating. Unlike many other bottom dwellers, some genera were tolerant to different conditions on the sea floor, hence useful for facies correlation. Overall, the "brachs" have been a most important group. They were the key to much of the Paleozoic history of North America.

Phylum Echinodermata Echinoderms are different. Their five-fold radial symmetry, exempli-

Fig. 11-14
Early Paleozoic brachiopods from New York State. Courtesy of the Smithsonian Institution.

Fig. 11-15
Permian spiney brachiopod from Glass Mountain, Texas. Courtesy of Dr. G. A. Cooper of the Smithsonian Institution.

Fig. 11-16
Mississippian crinoids from Iowa. Courtesy of the Smithsonian Institution.

fied by the starfish, suggests an aberrant branch on the Tree of Life; yet, they may have stemmed from the same ancestor as the vertebrates. The radial symmetry, while reminiscent of the Coelenterates, is a secondary development. Echinoderms are far more advanced in their internal workings with well-developed digestive and nervous systems, and a unique circulatory system. They pump water through ducts or vessels which, in some representatives, have many minute projections called tube feet. This water vascular system serves for food gathering and respiration; in some cases it also serves for locomotion and even grasping, for the tube feet operating by changes in water pressure can be used as suction cups. Echinodermata translates as "hedgehog skin" which describes their leathery body walls, reinforced by loose calcareous spicules or plates which are often intricately fitted.

Two subphyla are recognized: attached forms, and free-moving ones. Of the attached echinoderms, the *crinoids* are most important (Fig. 11-16). These so-called "sea lilies" have been diverse and plentiful, surviving from the Cambrian to the present day, and customarily live in brightly colored swarms suggesting submarine flower gardens. Typical crinoids have a body with a mouth at the top, a set of flexible branch-

ing arms, and a flexible stalk. The bulb-like body, a few inches or less across, protects the vital parts. The arms have furrows throughout their length along which microscopic food particles are wafted to the animal's mouth. The supple stem, usually about 2 feet long, but some as long as 50 feet, consists of button-like discs bound together by animal tissue. At its bottom is a root-like hold-fast, or in some cases coiled or grappling hook arrangements, to anchor the animal to the sea bottom.

In death the binding tissue decays, scattering the body plates and stem buttons over the sea floor. The stem discs, being the most abundant parts, are the main components of some late Paleozoic limestones. The various arrangements of the five or six rows of body plates have allowed paleontologists to describe some 750 genera, and many more species, of crinoids.

The free-moving echinoderms include the common *starfish* that have five stout arms and move along on their many tube feet, and the *brittle stars* who move by wriggling their narrow arms—which they can shed—by means of muscles. Although fossils of these still-living stars date back to the Paleozoic, well-preserved specimens are rare, more curiosities than useful fossils. The *echinoids,* whose name is easily confused with that of the whole phylum, are free-moving, armless echinoderms represented by sea urchins and sand dollars. Their globular, disc, or heart-shaped tests (shells) consist of many well-fitted plates in a radial arrangement. They are protected by sharp spines, also used for locomotion along with their tube feet. Known since the Ordovician, the echinoids have become quite varied and abundant from the Cretaceous to the present day. They would be good guide fossils if they were not so limited in their environmental preferences.

Phylum Mollusca For spineless creatures, molluscs have been a very progressive group. Clams, snails, and squids are modern representatives of this paleontologically most significant phylum. Anatomically they are more complex than any of the animals so far discussed; only arthropods and vertebrates surpass them. Represented in various members of the phylum are circulatory systems including a chambered heart; digestive systems replete with livers and kidneys; sensory systems with nerves, rudimentary brains, and well-developed eyes. Distinctive molluscan features include bilateral symmetry; a fleshy body covering; the mantle that secretes calcareous shells; a rasp-like tongue, the radula, which is a ribbon of many tiny hard teeth for obtaining food, sometimes by drilling holes in other mollusc shells. They also have a single muscular foot, designed originally for crawling but now adapted to other types of locomotion.

Snails and their kin, class *Gastropoda*, are successful and complex animals (Fig. 11-17). Producing some 60,000 species, since early Cambrian time, they now inhabit the ocean bottom from 18,000 feet below sea level to the tidal zone, ponds, and streams; some have even invaded the dry land. Most crawl about on a large muscular foot—albeit at a snail's pace—and some, the pteropods, whose remains make considerable ooze on the ocean floor, can swim. Most are vegetarians; some, with gamier tastes, are scavengers; and a few are voracious carni-

vores, drilling the shells of other molluscs with their file-like radulae. All gastropods have a distinct head with a pair of eyes, one or two tentacles, and most breathe with gills, although land dwellers have evolved lung sacs.

Except for naked land slugs and marine *nudibranches,* snails are protected by a single, coiled shell. Its single opening can be closed with a horny or shelly trap door, in some cases. The shells are commonly screw-like spirals; most being right-handed, or clockwise, although a few spiral to the left. Shell forms range from high and pointed to low, near-flat spires, and some are flat coils with no spire point at all. In some gastropods, abalone and limpets, for example, the single shell is a simple, open saucer or cone having no twisting passage. The surfaces of shells are variously ornamented with lines, grooves, ridges, spines, or knobs.

Although many groups are long ranged and many distinguishing features are not reflected in their hard anatomy, snails are useful fossils. Their variety of form and ornamentation gives them value, especially in fresh water and terrestrial deposits where other fossils are often lacking.

The clams and oysters—a generally tasty lot—have been called "Bivalvia" by Germans, "Lamellibranchs" by the British, and *pelecypods* by Americans. Translating the names in order gives a fair description of these molluscs as two-shelled, having leaf-like gills, and with a hatchet foot. Most move by their wedge-shaped muscular foot, have a shell-secreting mantle, and breathe by fairly complicated gills. Besides extracting oxygen from water, the gills sweep microscopic food particles to the animals' mouths. In contrast to snails, the pelecypods lack a well-defined head, eyes, tentacles, and radula.

Clams are typically bilaterally symmetrical, with each of their two shells a mirror image covering one side of the animal (Fig. 11-18). Internal muscles close the shells, and elastic ligaments along a hinge line at the top open them. The shells are calcareous, usually lined on the inside with "mother of pearl," and pro-

Fig. 11-17
Devonian snail collected in Michigan. Courtesy of the Smithsonian Institution.

tected on the outside by a chitinous film preventing solution by the salt and fresh waters of their environments. Some pelecypods have lost the mirror symmetry of equal-sized shells, notably the sedentary oysters who cement themselves to the sea floor, and the scallops, who swim by clapping their shells. However, most clams are equi-valved, and crawl or burrow. Razor clams are surprisingly rapid diggers. In size, clams range from a fraction of an inch long to one six-footer, the 400-pound South Sea *Tridacna*.

As fossils, clams are rare in Cambrian rocks and relatively common since the Ordovician. Most remains are casts or molds because clam shells are largely composed of aragonite, a mineral like calcite in composition but a less stable form, more readily dissolved. Despite a wide variety of shell forms differing in shape, ornamentation, and detailed hinge structure, the pelecypods are a rather disappointing fossil group for rock correlation—more useful in defining large time units than small ones.

The 55-foot Giant Squid is a living "sea monster," the greatest invertebrate of all time, and a member of the most progressive molluscan group, the *cephalopods*. Modern cephalopods are active swimming carnivors with keen senses. They breathe with gills, have a radula, two beak-like, horny jaws, eight, ten, or more tentacles, and eyes the equal of our own. Naked cephalopods, one of three subclasses, are represented in modern seas by the octopus, which has no skeleton whatever; and squids and cuttlefish which have much reduced internal skeletons (Cuttlebone is seen in canary cages). These unarmored cephalopods are unimportant fossils except for one extinct group, the *belemnoids*. They resembled living cuttlefish, and had stout, cigar-shaped, internal skeletons. Once considered actual thunderbolts, the skeletons are found in late Mississippian through Cretaceous rocks, and are most plentiful in certain Jurassic and Cretaceous formations.

Shelled cephalopods abounded in the Jurassic strata of Britain, where William Smith pioneered the art of stratigraphic correlation.

Fig. 11-18
Devonian clams from New York. Courtesy of the Smithsonian Institution.

Yet, of the bygone hosts of this tremendously important fossil group (10,000 fossil species), only the pearly nautilus survives. It swims in a flat-coiled shell, buoyed up by gas, and partitioned into chambers by cross-bulkheads, called septa. The last, or living, chamber, which is occupied by the animal, connects by a calcareous tube, the siphuncle, to the smaller empty chambers that were vacated as the animal grew. The partitions are visible only when the outer shell is stripped, or in fossils after the chambers have filled with mud and the shell has dissolved away. The junctions of the septa with the outer shell

Fig. 11-19
Cretaceous clam from Tennessee. Courtesy of the Smithsonian Institution.

form lines, called sutures, whose trace-like handwriting identifies species. From the intricacies of the septa, and their resultant suture lines, two groups of armored cephalopods are recognized.

The *nautiloids,* of which the pearly nautilus is a member, are characterized by simple, saucer-shaped septa that make smooth or gently curving sutures. Nautiloids, which first appear in Cambrian rocks, abounded in the time interval from Ordovician to Devonian (Fig. 11-20). The earliest ones were uncoiled; coiled shells are a later evolutionary development. Most had smooth exteriors, although some were bedecked with ribs and spines.

The *ammonoids,* which appeared in the Silurian and became extinct at the end of the Mesozoic, are distinguished by increasingly more complicated septa through time. Most Paleozoic forms had rather simple septa (called goniatitic) whose sutures appear as simple curved and angled lines (Fig. 11-21). In late Paleozoic and Triassic time, a tribe appeared whose more complex partitions were warped into crenulated lobes and rounded saddles (ceratitic type) producing a suture like the teeth of a coarse bucksaw. A third group living from Permian through Mesozoic time had wrinkles on both the saddles and lobes (ammonitic) creating sutures like scribbled handwriting (Fig. 11-22). Most ammonoid shells are flat coils (Ammon was

the Egyptian ram-headed god), little different from their nautiloid kin; however, a few spiralled, like large snail shells, and towards the end of their history, some straight forms evolved with only a small coil in the first-formed juvenile chambers.

Ammonoids are index fossils *par excellence.* They are large and easy to study, had a worldwide distribution—reflecting their swimming habit—were abundant and readily preserved, and had a long history and geologically rapid evolution. Thus they are ideal for relative dating and correlation of both large and small time units, as well as invaluable evolutionary materials. They are delightful fossils.

Phylum Arthropoda Three-quarters of the living species in the Animal Kingdom are insects, centipedes, crabs, spiders, and their close relatives. So, if numbers are the criterion, the arthropods are the most successful of all animal groups. Adapted to all possible habitats, they fly, swim, walk, crawl, burrow, or in the case of barnacles lead a sedentary life. Many are complex animals

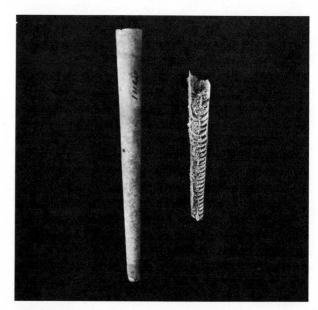

Fig. 11-20
Late Paleozoic straight nautiloid cephalopod from Glass Mountain, Texas. Courtesy of the Smithsonian Institution.

with complicated respiratory, circulatory, reproductive, excretory, and sensory systems including brains and eyes. They are exceedingly prolific; the record egg-producers are arthropods.

The most diagnostic arthropod feature is jointed appendages forming legs, pincers, and in some cases antennae (*arthro* means joint; *pod* means foot). Arthropods have a chitinous exoskeleton, usually segmented for flexibility, that is strong, waterproof, and resilient—witness the grasshopper which strikes a windshield and survives. Yet, a suit of armor presents a problem if the occupant is to grow. The arthropod solution is molting, whereby they periodically shed their suits and replace them with larger ones. From Cambrian onward, arthropods have been a dominant part of the earth's population, through one branch or another.

Most arthropods are insects: flies, mosquitoes, ants, moths, and beetles; they alone comprise two-thirds of the living animal species. Because insect life spans are brief—some live less than a year—many generations develop in a short time. Thus, insects have had a greater opportu-

Fig. 11-22
Cretaceous coiled cephalopod (ammonite) with complicated suture. Courtesy of the Smithsonian Institution.

nity to evolve into diverse and very specialized forms than most other creatures. Wingless insects are known as far back as Devonian time, and flying varieties appear in the Pennsylvanian, a time of dragonflies with two-foot wing spreads and cockroaches four inches long. Unfortunately, fragile insect corpses are not particularly amenable to preservation, so their use in geologic dating and detailed evolutionary studies is almost nil.

The *trilobites*, another group of arthropods, were lords of the Cambrian seas where they represented 60% of the known population (Figs. 11-23, 11-24). They thrived in the Ordovician, but thereafter gradually declined to their extinction at the end of Paleozoic time. Most trilobites were small, from one to four inches long; a giant of the tribe, *Paradoxides*, grew to 18 inches. The name trilobite reflects the division of their chitinous shell, or carapace, into three lengthwise lobes. The central one usually stood in highest relief, set off from the marginal lobes by grooves. The animals also had three transverse parts, from front to back: a head, or cephalon; a body, the thorax, of from 2 to 29 unfused cross-

Fig. 11-21
Late Paleozoic coiled cephalopod (goniatite) with relatively simple sutures. Indiana. Courtesy of the Smithsonian Institution.

261

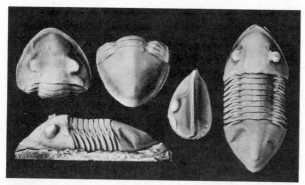

Fig. 11-23
Ordovician trilobites from New York and Ohio. One of the species is flat; the other is enrolled. Courtesy of the Smithsonian Institution.

segments; and a tail, the pygidium, of several fused segments. Some had compound eyes, like the fly, and paired, jointed appendages. The common preservation of their carapaces results because their chitinous shells were impregnated with calcium carbonate.

Fig. 11-24
Ordovician trilobite from Oklahoma. Courtesy of the Smithsonian Institution.

Swimming, crawling, and burrowing in shallow parts of the sea floor, they apparently grubbed in the mud for small animals or organic debris. Though now extinct, hence evolutionary failures, they left 1000 fossil species, exhibiting interesting adaptations to their way of life, and, as we have previously mentioned, are important guide fossils for the early Paleozoic.

The *eurypterids* were most common in Silurian and Devonian time, although species have been found in rocks from Ordovician to Permian age (Fig. 11-25). These extinct "sea scorpions" are the only important fossils in the group of arthropods whose living members include scorpions, spiders, and a "living fossil," the horseshoe crab. All have a fused head and thorax, and lack antennae. The eurypterids had posion glands, stingers, and, in some representatives, large claws. Thus, they were probably active predators. Especially fearsome ones, the largest arthropods known, were almost 10 feet long. Their general plan suggests that the eurypterids may have been ancestral to the scorpions who were the first animal invaders of the land.

Vertebrates

The last major group to emerge on the Tree of Life is the *Phylum Chordata*—creatures supported with an internal flexible rod. Worms, arthropods, and molluscs have been proposed as their immediate forebears; however, good evidence suggests a seemingly unlikely group, the echinoderms of the five-fold symmetry. Their larval forms are bilaterally symmetrical and resemble the larvae of acorn worms, a lowly group of peculiar chordates. Moreover, blood serum tests and the chemistry of muscles suggest the affinity of echinoderms and chordates. Apparently echinoderms evolved along two lines; one acquiring a secondary radial symmetry lead to the star fish, echinoids, and sea lilies; the other gave rise to the chordates.

Chordates include two broad groups: the primitive *Acraniata*, lacking definite heads, brains, or paired appendages; and the *Craniata*, or vertebrates. The former group had several in-

Fig. 11-25
Silurian eurypterid from western New York State. Courtesy of the Smithsonian Institution.

significant subphyla—sea squirts, the acorn worms, and the sea lancelets. The lancelet, *Amphioxus*, occupying an important evolutionary spot, has a front end, but no real head, eyes, ears,

bones, or fins; but it does have a jelly-filled rod stiffening its back, with a nerve chord above and a simple digestive tube below, as well as fish-like gills. Amphioxus is a living prototype—there is no fossil record—of the ancestral vertebrate. For, with certain improvements, amphioxus could become a very primitive fish.

All vertebrates have an internal skeleton with a spinal column of jointed cartilage or bone segments, called vertebrae; a skull housing a brain and various sense organs; appendages, usually paired, forming fins, feet, arms, or wings supported by skeletal girdles; and usually sets of ribs. The subphylum Vertebrata is customarily divided into two super-classes: *Pisces* meaning fish, and the *Tetrapoda* including the amphibians, reptiles, birds, and mammals.

Fish

Primitive Fish Scattered bony flakes, first found in Colorado and Wyoming, tell us that in Ordovician time vertebrates existed, but little more. Better fossils in late Silurian and Devonian rocks allow reconstruction of the first vertebrate animals. They were *ostracoderms* which were jawless, and with one exception finless, bone-

Fig. 11-26
Mass of Tertiary vertebrate bones from Nebraska. Courtesy of the Chicago Natural History Museum.

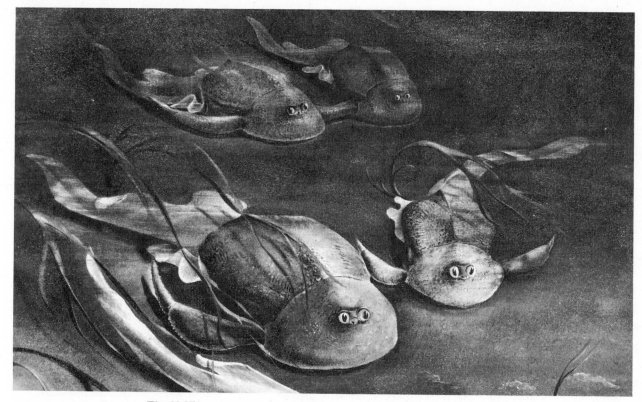

Fig. 11-27
Devonian placoderms. Courtesy of the Chicago Natural History Museum.

headed fish of an archaic sort. The heads were heavily armored, perhaps as protection from eurypterids, but the rest of the skeleton was cartilaginous. As their mouths were mere holes or slits under the heads, and the animals lacked stabilizing fins, ostracoderms were probably bottom-dwelling mud grubbers.

The first improvements in vertebrate design occur in *placoderms,* a rather diverse group of armored fish first appearing in late Silurian and Devonian strata (Fig. 11-27). The placoderms included flat-bodied, full-bodied, and eel-like forms. Their revolutionary development was moveable jaws, evolved from gill arches, as well as paired fins. While placoderm history ended in the blind alley of extinction at the end of Paleozoic time, some of its early members, as yet unknown, spawned a new lineage whose progeny are the living fish.

Higher Fish The higher fish are of two types: those with cartilaginous skeletons, the sharks and rays; and the bony fish. *Sharks* are mainly marine fish, aggressive members of the salt-water community whose record extends back into Devonian time. Having cartilaginous skeletons, their fossil remains are mostly teeth and spines, which are notably abundant in some Mesozoic and Cenozoic formations.

The *bony fish,* now dominating both fresh and salt water, include two groups. The first consists of the ray-finned fish whose primitive members are represented by sturgeons and gars, and whose advanced representatives include such various types as eels, catfish, salmon, sailfish, tuna, and a host of others. These fish, by far the most abundant group of vertebrates, are the culmination of animal adaptation to aquatic life.

The other branch of the bony fish includes the

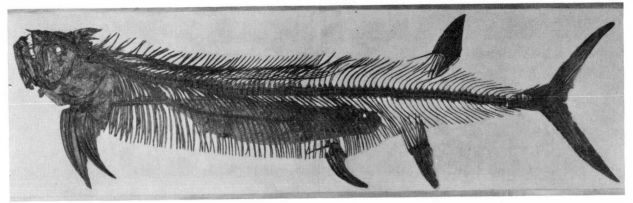

Fig. 11-28
A 14-foot Cretaceous fish (Portheus) with his last meal, a 6-foot fish (Gillicus) inside. Collected and prepared by George F. Sternberg. Photo by E. C. Almquist, courtesy of the Fort Hays Kansas State College Museum.

lungfish and lobe-finned fish which, although subordinate in numbers, species, and adaptation to aquatic living, have a most significant position in the Tree of Life, for some ancient member of the group begat the first land-dwelling vertebrates. Lungfish are today limited to the southern continents of Australia, Africa, and South America. Using their lungs to breathe air directly, they can survive in stagnant pools fatal to gill-breathing fish, and inside burrows in dried-out river bottoms.

Lobe fins, or *Crossopterygian* fish, were abundant in Devonian time, as were the lungfish, but were believed extinct in the Cretaceous. However, in 1938, a 5-foot representative was netted in deep water off East Africa, and more have been caught since. The Devonian crossopterygians may well have been reluctant invaders of the land, literally fish out of water. Equipped with lungs, they could survive in air as they struggled to find new water holes in drought-seared river bottoms. In many ways, the lobe fins

Fig. 11-29
Cast of a coelocanth, a still extant lobe-fin fish. Courtesy of the American Museum of Natural History.

resemble the first land vertebrates. They have lungs, nostril openings, similar teeth and skull elements, and a rather rugged skeleton. Their fins extend from fleshy stalks braced by a single upper and double lower bone, a structure analogous to the limbs of terrestrial vertebrates.

Tetrapods

The high point of animal evolution is reached in the tetrapods, the second broad subclass of vertebrates. Their main stream of evolution involves progressive improvement for life on land. Some of them have gone farther and taken to the air, and some have reverted to water dwelling, but in such cases the structural adaptations are superimposed on a terrestrial reptilian or mammalian body plan. Like the plants, which preceded them, animals faced formidable problems in moving from water to land. They, too, needed skins that would hold in their body fluids, special systems of respiration, new reproductive methods, and stiffer support to counter the increased effect of gravity. Moreover, the strengthening of their skeletons had to include a better design for overland travel.

Class Amphibia Though the amphibians were the first vertebrate land dwellers, they never quite succeeded as terrestrial animals. Amphibians are not completely divorced from life in water. The juveniles are tadpoles, gilled and legless swimmers. The adults must breed in water, except for a few specialized types who use other damp places, and except for toads, periodic swims are a necessity to prevent desiccation. Of existing amphibians, frogs and toads are specialized forms. The salamanders are closer to the basic stock.

Skeletons and tracks of the earliest amphibians, the *labyrinthodonts*, occur in late Devonian rocks of east Greenland. These primitive types were ungainly creatures whose broad flattened skulls of heavy bone insured a better fossil record than most later amphibians which were more lightly built (Fig. 11-30). Abundant in the later Paleozoic, the labyrinthodonts died out in the Triassic. The name comes from the labyrinth-like pattern of their tortuously enfolded tooth enamel, a characteristic of many lobe-finned fish. Their sprawling, stubby legs were most inefficient, but the skeletal structure was stouter than in their fishy forebearers and adequate for overland travel unsupported by the buoyancy of water. If little more than modified fish, these Devonian amphibians were nonetheless the precursors of all tetrapods.

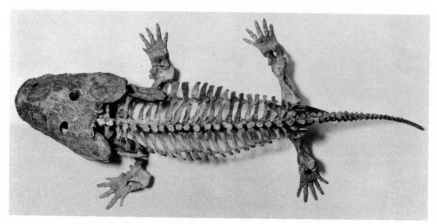

Fig. 11-30
Skeleton of Eryops, a Permian labyrinthodont amphibian, attaining 6 feet in length. Courtesy of the Chicago Natural History Museum.

Class Reptilia Until a suitable means of reproduction evolved, the vertebrates could not become thoroughly terrestrial. It was the development of the amniote egg—a hen's egg is an example—that freed reptiles from life in water. Such an egg allows an embryonic animal to develop in a moist environment, surrounded by food inside a protective shell, until it can survive in air. To complete their adaptation to land living, the reptiles also evolved scaly or platy skins that can stand air indefinitely, improved hearts and circulatory systems for active life on land, and improved legs.

The *cotylosaurs,* ancestors to all other reptiles, abounded from Pennsylvanian to the end of the Paleozoic and lingered on into Triassic time. *Seymouria,* a two-and-a-half foot representative of this group, had the teeth and skull of a labyrinthodont, but the rest of the skeleton was of a more advanced and reptilian design. If Seymouria laid shelled eggs, it was a reptile; if not, an amphibian. As the first known fossil egg is Permian, and reptile skeletons are known from the Pennsylvanian, the exact classification of Seymouria is unsettled. In any case, Seymouria is an ideal connecting link between amphibians and reptiles.

Turtles, snakes and lizards, crocodiles, and rhynchocephalians (whose sole survivor is the small Tuatara, a primitive lizard-like inhabitant of New Zealand) are the living remnants of Mesozoic reptilian hordes that ruled land, sea, and air. The now extinct *thecodonts,* which evolved from the cotylosaurs by early Mesozoic time, are progenitors of the living crocodiles and, also, birds as well a flying reptiles, and the spectacular dinosaurs that left no descendants after holding the Mesozoic limelight for well over 100 million years. One group of thecodonts were four-footed carnivores, called *phytosaurs.* They closely resembled crocodiles except that their nostrils were just in front of their eyes. Despite the resemblance, however, crocodiles are not descendants of the phytosaurs who, although creatures of similar habit, became extinct at the end of Triassic time.

Other thecodonts, called *pseudosuchians* were bipedal reptiles, walking on strong hind legs, whose forelimbs were arms for grasping, and had long narrow skulls. *Ornithosuchus,* found in upper Triassic rocks of Scotland, typified this basic stock that produced the dinosaurs. They had bird-like hind legs, each with three-clawed toes, and the sturdy pelvis essential for animals balancing on two legs. The skeleton and skull were of relatively light construction containing many hollow bones, and a long tail counterbalanced the forward-leaning body. The pseudosuchians, like the phytosaurs, died out at the end of Triassic time but several lineages evolving from them retained basic family resemblances, notably the dinosaurs. Although some of the dinosaurs were to revert to a quadruped (four-footed) existence, the hind legs were always notably bigger than the front, reflecting their bipedal ancestors.

The intriguing *dinosaurs* are the subject of some popular misconceptions. Their name translated means "terrible lizard"; however, they were not lizards, and if some were unquestionably terrible—the largest terrestrial carnivores ever—many were unaggressive vegetarians. Nor were they all giants, another misconception, for they ranged from 85-foot, 40-ton monsters down to adults no larger than a plucked chicken (which they superficially resembled).

The name was given to the lot of them before it was recognized that the dinosaurs include two quite different reptilian orders, markedly different in their hip and pelvic structure. Most higher vertebrates, including you and I, have three main bones in the pelvic girdle: the ilium, ischium, and pubis. In *saurischian* dinosaurs, the downward-projecting ischium and pubis diverge from the ilium above, as they do in most other reptiles, hence these are the "reptile-hipped" group. In the *ornithiscian* order, the two downward-projecting bones are parallel, adjacent and directed towards the back as in birds; hence they are the "bird-hipped" dinosaurs.

The saurischians produced two lines: the only carnivorous dinosaurs, bipedal forms culminating in the great *Tyrannosaurus rex,* and four-footed, unarmored vegetarians including the well-known *Brontosaurus* (Fig. 11-31). The

Fig. 11-31
Skeleton of Brontosaur excavated near Sheep Creek, Wyoming. University of Wyoming photograph by H. Pownall. Mount by S. H. Knight (in foreground).

Fig. 11-32
Duck-billed Trachodon and crested dinosaurs with a squat "reptilian tank" in center. Mural by C. R. Knight. Copyright Chicago Natural History Museum.

Fig. 11-33
Stegosaurus. Mural by C. R. Knight. Copyright Chicago Natural History Museum.

ornothiscians were all herbivorous and of four main types. One group of largely unarmored bipeds included the duckbills, like *Trachodon*, some of which developed bizarre head structures (Fig. 11-32). The other "bird-hipped" dinosaurs were all quadrupeds. The *stegosaurs* were distinguished by erect bony plates rising from their backs (Fig. 11-33). The *ankylosaurians* were "reptilian tanks," heavily armored with overlapping bony plates, and wielded a mace-like tail studded with spikes. The toothless, beaked *ceratopsians* had large heads protected by a bone neck frill projecting from the backs of their skulls, and usually long spear-like horns projecting forward.

Besides the thecodonts which gave rise to the dinosaurs and several other reptile groups, the primitive cotylosaurs spawned *mammal-like reptiles,* a lineage of great interest in subsequent evolutionary developments. The remains of the "sail-backed" *pelycosaurs* (Fig. 11-35) have been found in late Pennsylvanian and Permian rocks of North America. These flamboyant, lizard-like beasts, up to 12 feet long, sported a great flap braced by long spines rising from the vertebrae. The function of the "sail" is not known, but it may have helped control the body temperature of this cold-blooded group. The differentiation of teeth shows that some pelycosaurs were predators and others plant eaters.

Sometime before the appearance of the more bizarre pelycosaurs, offshoots from this lineage gave rise to the *therapsids* whose fossils occur in middle Permian and Triassic rocks on all continents. Although the early therapsids differed little from the ancestral cotylosaurs, later representatives developed distinctly mammalian features. *Cynognathus,* an early Triassic therapsid as big as a large dog, stood well off the ground (Fig. 11-36). Although its body extended

269

Fig. 11-34
Triceratops and Tyrannosaurus. Mural by C. R. Knight. Copyright Chicago Natural History Museum.

well into the tail in a reptilian manner, its legs, vertebrae, skull, and jaws had mammal-like structure. Significantly, the dental array has incisors, canines, and cheek teeth in contrast to the relatively undifferentiated sharp pegs forming the teeth of most reptiles. Cynognathus neatly links the reptiles and mammals.

Class Aves There are and have been flightless birds, such as ostriches and penguins, but anatomically the great majority of modern birds are superbly adapted to the rigorous demands of flight. Feathers, which are highly modified scales, distinguish birds from all other animals. These structures are excellent body insulation, and provide wing surfaces that—unlike the membranes of bats and flying reptiles—are not easily damaged. Birds are warm-blooded animals with a very efficient heart, and high metabolism appropriate for their energetic way of life. Their skeletons are evolutionary masterpieces, combining light weight with superior strength and rigidity

Fig. 11-35
A "sail-backed" lizard from the Permian of Texas. Courtesy of the Smithsonian Institution.

Fig. 11-36
Several representatives of Cynognathus, a carnivorous mammal-like reptile, looking hungrily at a vegetarian relative. Mural by C. R. Knight. Copyright Chicago Natural History Museum.

needed to anchor their strong flight muscles. The pelvis is solidly fused and the breast bone, which anchors the wing muscles, is large.

Despite their specialized structure, birds are clearly reptilian descendants. Their legs are strong, rather like those of the reptile ornithosuchys. They have scales on their legs (note chickens) and around their mouths. Though all modern birds have beaks, there are traces of teeth in embryonic ducks, and birds lay amniote eggs like reptiles. Because their bones are light, porous, and often hollow, bird fossils are rare. However, birds are linked to pseudosuchian reptiles by two excellent specimens. These represent the first known bird called *Archaeopteryx* (Figs. 11-37, 11-38).

The first fossil was discovered, in 1861, in a fine-grained limestone [8] laid down as a calcar-

[8] Quarried in those days for lithographic printing.

eous mud in a Jurassic lagoon near Solenhofen, Germany. Had the skeleton not been completely fringed by the impressions of long feathers, it would almost certainly have been classed as a small reptile. The bones were solid, the neck was long, the hind legs and pelvis were reptilian, the vertebrae extended into a long bony tail, and the front limbs bore three clawed fingers. All in all, a most unbirdlike skeleton, but the feathers meant a warm-blooded animal, and their distribution along the front limbs indicated wings. By Cretaceous time, birds were essentially modern except for the presence of teeth, and since the early Cenozoic when they had evolved horny beaks, birds have shown virtually no basic structural changes (Fig. 11-39).

Class Mammalia Today the lands are ruled by mammals. Their success is largely a matter of su-

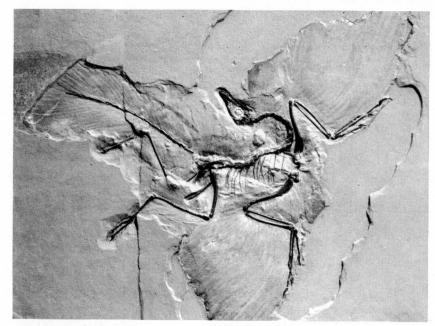

Fig. 11-37
Cast of fossil Archaeopteryx. Courtesy of the American Museum of Natural History.

Fig. 11-38
Restoration of Archaeopteryx. Courtesy of the American Museum of Natural History.

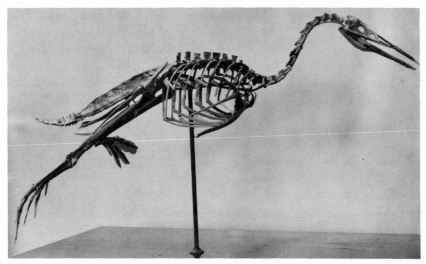

Fig. 11-39
Skeleton of Cretaceous, toothed, swimming bird (Hesperornis) from Kansas. Courtesy of the Smithsonian Institution.

perior physical endowment. Like birds, they are warm blooded, maintaining a constant body temperature that allows a more energetic life as well as relatively constant activity, despite daily or seasonal temperature changes. Cold-blooded animals, like reptiles and amphibians, are handicapped because they go torpid when the temperature is low, and must, on the other hand, seek shade on hot days to avoid sunstroke. The warm-blooded mammals usually have protective coats that help control their body temperature. This insulation may be subcutaneous fat; more commonly it is hair, the mammalian trademark, just as feathers are for birds.

Mammalian reproduction gives their young a better chance of survival. Unlike the embryos of reptiles and birds which often fall prey to egg-loving creatures, those of mammals are carried inside the mother until born. And mammals are superior parents, suckling their infants with milk (*mamma* is Latin for breast), and protecting and training their offspring until they can fend for themselves.

Paleontologists, of course, usually deal only with skeletons, but here, too, the mammals are distinctive. The mammal's well-constructed legs are under their bodies so the bones carry most of the weight, and little muscular energy is wasted in merely supporting the body. Most distinctive is the skull. The larger brain of mammals, marked by a larger brain case in fossil types, gives them a decided intellectual advantage over the other vertebrates. Also, the skull has two round knobs called condyles—typical reptiles have only one—that ride on the uppermost vertebrae. The mouth has a secondary bony palate, missing in reptiles, that separates the food and air intake systems. Whereas reptiles have seven bones in their lower jaws, mammals have only one, and it is hinged differently to the rest of the skull.

But of all the hard parts, mammal teeth are most distinctive. Often a vertebrate paleontologist can tell the type and age of mammal remains from the teeth alone.[9] Reptiles and lower vertebrates develop an indefinite number of teeth during a lifetime, replacing those shed or lost, and the teeth are all roughly similar. But mammals normally have only two sets, the milk and adult teeth, and there is considerable differentiation. Their basic dentition includes incisors, or nipping teeth, followed by a set of canines, or tusks, behind which are diverse cheek teeth, premolars and molars, designed for grinding or

[9] Which is not to say he could reconstruct an unknown animal from one tooth.

273

cutting. This basic pattern shows many specializations. Note how different are the teeth of elephants, horses, beavers, rats, and men, to name but a few.

The incredibly diverse mammals, living and fossil, defy brief summary. Some 34 orders are lumped into various larger cohorts, super-orders, and sub-classes; and on the other hand divided into smaller sub-orders, super families, and families. All mammals are, however, divisible into three basic, but numerically disproportionate groups: monotremes, marsupials, and placentals.

Monotremes The only known monotremes are the duck-billed platypus and two genera of spiney anteaters in Australia and New Guinea. Being egg-layers with other reptilian features, they were once considered survivors of the transitional stock that produced all mammals. Now, monotremes are generally thought to be a completely separate warm-blooded, hairy, milk-producing lineage from the reptiles. Monotremes have no fossil record prior to the Pleistocene.

Marsupials Opossums are "living fossils," very like the ancestral marsupials but a bit larger, whose reproduction characterizes the group. Born in a very immature state, marsupial young climb into their mother's pouch, where the more fortunate ones attach themselves to teats, and grow until ready for life outside. Skeletally, marsupials are rather like placental mammals; however, paleontologists can identify their skeletons from their special pouch-bearing bones, smaller brain cases, and other features. In the Cretaceous they competed successfully with the placentals. In the Cenozoic, except for the opossums, they were largely restricted to an isolated community in South America and another in Australia, where such marsupials as kangaroos, koala "bears," wombats, and carnivorous Tasmanian "wolves" still survive.

Placentals Some 95% of Cenozoic mammals are placentals, the most advanced, intelligent, and

Fig. 11-40
Notharctus, an early (Eocene) primate. Courtesy of the American Museum of Natural History.

successful vertebrates. They range from *a* to *z* (aardvark to zoril), from pygmy shrews no heavier than a dime to 100-foot blue whales weighing 150 tons, from flying bats to burrowing moles, and a host of other living and fossil types, including men.

Small-brained and primitive in dentition, the *insectivores,* exemplified by the mouse-like shews, moles, and hedgehogs, represent the ancestral placental stock. Since their late Cretaceous appearance, insectivores have remained small (the giant of them was about two feet long), and lived on a diet of insects and worms. Bats, edentates, and primates form a super group, or cohort of mammalian orders whose descent from insectivores can be traced.

Bats are essentially flying insectivores whose front limbs are highly modified as wings in which the greatly elongated fingers support a thin membrane. They had mastered true flight by the Eocene, the only mammals ever to do so.[10]

The *primates* are apparently tree shrew descendants whose specializations reflect an active arboreal life (Fig. 11-40). They have five digits with flat nails on feet or hands, adapted for grasping, keen eyes with good depth perception, and a general emphasis on brains. Man, a primate along with lemurs, monkeys, and apes, is the acme of organic evolution in terms of intelligence, but he is certainly not in physical structure. His teeth are degenerate, and his body primitive and obscenely naked — by mammalian standards.

The *edentates*, a peculiar group including sloths, anteaters, and armadillos, may be toothless, as the name implies, or more commonly have simplified teeth devoid of enamel. Although edentates are highly specialized, as exemplified by anteaters, armor-plated living armadillos, and extinct glyptodonts, their descent from insectivores can be paleontologically demonstrated. The same is not true of the remaining mammal groups; the first known cetaceans, rodents, carnivores, and ungulates were already specialized and distinct.

Whales, dolphins, and porpoises are *cetacea*, mammals that, like some reptiles before them, returned to a fish-like existence. Their bodies are well streamlined, their front limbs have become flippers, and the hind limbs are vestigial with no external expression. The first known whales, represented by the fossil *Zeuglodon* of the Eocene, were already highly specialized marine mammals, giving no clues as to their original derivation. Supported by water, whales have evolved the giants of all time, far larger than the brontosaurs.

The prolific *rodents* have more species than all other mammals combined. Rats, mice, gophers, porcupines, beavers, and guinea pigs are among the best known representatives. Rabbits, once classed as rodents, now seem a separate line that evolved rodent-like teeth. Rodents are gnawers, distinguished by two pairs of long, chisel-like self-sharpening incisors that grow throughout life as they are continually worn down. Otherwise, rodents are rather unspecialized, having long skulls with low brain cases, and flexible clawed feet bearing five well-developed toes. Fossil rodents, being generally small, have attracted little paleontological attention.

The *carnivores* and hoofed animals, or ungulates, seem to be descendants from a common ancestor in the late Cretaceous, because their first known and most primitive members of earliest Cenozoic time have a strong "family" resemblance. The carnivores, specializing in agility and intelligence, claw and fang, have preyed on their hoofed cousins. Carnivore bodies are relatively primitive; they are most specialized in teeth. Typically (examine your pet dog or cat) the strong incisors are for tearing and ripping; the canines are daggers for stabbing and killing; and the cheek teeth are efficient bone crushers or meat shears, except in bears, who have reverted to a more general diet. Terrestrial carnivores include all dogs, cats, bears, badgers, and raccoons. Seals, sea lions, and walruses are aquatic carnivores, for despite external appearances, their skulls are very like their land-living cousins.

The *ungulates* are hoofed vegetarians. Unlike the carnivors, which are included in a single order, the very diverse ungulates comprise about 16 different orders, some only distantly related. They have specialized in feet and teeth. Browsing ungulates, eaters of leaves and twigs, such as deer, have low-crowned cheek teeth; whereas grazers, the eaters of silicous abrasive grasses, for example horses, have high-crowned

[10] Flying squirrels merely glide on skin flaps stretched between their legs.

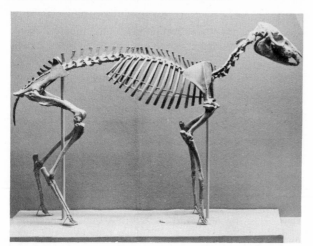

Fig. 11-41
Skeleton of a fossil three-toed horse (Mesohippus) from Wyoming. Photo by Herb Pownall, courtesy of the University of Wyoming.

molars suited for much wear. Their cheek teeth, in general, have evolved towards square-topped grinding mills with distinctive ridges and wrinkled surfaces. Ungulate feet are modified for walking on "tip-toe" with the heel well off the ground (in contrast to "flat-footed" creatures like possums, rodents, and men).

Perissodactyls are the odd-toed ungulates, such as the rhinoceros, which have three toes, and the horses, which having only one functional toe represent the ultimate foot evolution in the line. The functional toes are greatly lengthened and strengthened; the useless side toes (which are not counted in describing an animal as even or odd-toed), no longer touching the ground, are reduced or lost. *Artiodactyls*, those of the "cloven hoof," are the even-toed ungulates like cows and deer. The vertical axis of their foot passes between two central toes. Pigs represent primitive artiodactyls in having a simple stomach and eating almost anything. Advanced artiodactyls are ruminants, vegetarians who can quickly crop and gulp food into the first section of their complicated stomach for storage, later to be regurgitated for further chewing, before passing it back to other stomach compartments for final processing. The stomach mechanism has great advantages for vegetarians harassed by carnivores, and may well be the reason artiodactyls are still thriving, while the perissodactyls with their simple stomach, are not. Today only domestic horses are at all abundant; wild members of the once-great hosts of odd-toed ungulates are perilously close to extinction.

Ponderous ungulates, such as elephants, have evolved pillar-like legs whose toes are pulled together creating a short, broad stump of a foot that is usually "shod" with a shock-absorbing pad. Elephants are *proboscidians*, so called because of their proboscis, or nose, which with the upper lip forms the distinctive trunk. Until near the end of the Cenozoic, the proboscidians were an amazingly abundant and varied stock. They have some rather exotic close kin whose relationship is established from fossil evidence. Sea cows, dugongs, and manatees are aquatic vegetarians that evolved from members of this ungulate group in early Cenozoic time; and so are the conies, primitive rodent-like ungulates mentioned in the Bible. With the ungulates, we conclude the "Dramatis Personae" of some of the important participants in the geologic story of life.

SUGGESTED READINGS

Matthews, W. H., *Fossils*, New York, Barnes and Noble, Inc., 1962 (paperback).

Romer, A. S., *Man and the Vertebrates, Volume I*, Baltimore, Md., Penguin Books, 1954 (paperback, Pelican Books).

Simpson, G. G., *Life of the Past*, New Haven, Conn., Yale University Press, 1953 (paperback).

twelve: A greater genealogy

Having reviewed the different plants and animals important in the fossil record, we now examine them in floral and faunal groups. As such, they are the basis for relative dating of later rocks, and the geologic time scale, as well as glimpses of the changing panoramas of life through the ages.

PRECAMBRIAN LIFE

Better than Pooh-Bah, in Gilbert and Sullivan's *Mikado,* who could trace his ancestry back to a piece of amoebic protoplasm, modern science traces our origin to a virus, a far simpler form—little more than a self-reproducing crystal.

On origins

Speculations Of the various speculations about the birth of life, *creation by a Divine Being* is a theological concept, not demonstrable by fact and observation; hence beyond the realm of science. Among naturalistic explanations, the *Extraterrestrial Hypothesis* requires that the original protoplasm on earth came from somewhere else in space. It has been suggested that carbon compounds recently found in some meteorites are organic. However, the extraterrestrial hypothesis is not generally accepted, in part because it avoids the origin of protoplasm, relegating it to some other planet. The hypothesis of *Spontaneous Generation*— long outdated —states that life is continuously arising in dead matter. Scientists once argued the idea, because of the appearance of flies and micro-organisms

in "sterile" solutions or decaying meat. Some time ago, it was demonstrated that the flies came from minute, maggot-producing eggs, and the idea was finally negated when Louis Pasteur and others, in the mid-1800's, showed that airborne germs caused the "spontaneous generation" of decay bacteria. Today the prevailing scientific view is that life did indeed arise spontaneously —but under different chemical conditions prevailing in the geologically remote past. This hypothesis is at least possible in view of two recent lines of biological investigation.

Some Evidence First, amino acids, the building blocks of protein, have been synthesized in the laboratory. In 1952, Stanley Miller, a University of Chicago graduate student, mixed water vapor, hydrogen, ammonia, and methane (marsh gas), compounds theoretically present in the earth's primitive atmosphere. He then subjected these compounds to electrical sparks, simulating lightning discharges or solar radiation. After a week, the mixture contained traces of amino acids where none were present before. The experiment certainly did not manufacture life from nonliving substances, but in the amino acids it did produce some of the basic materials.

Secondly, the nature of viruses—those disease agents far smaller than bacteria—has finally been established thanks to the electron microscope, which provides magnifications of some 300,000 times. Viruses unite the crystalline substances of the mineral realm with the world of life. They consist of carbon, hydrogen, oxygen, phosphorus, and sulfur, the elements of the geochemical life cycle found in protoplasm. The much-studied tobacco mosaic virus has a dual behavior. In the cells of tobacco plants, it functions as a living disease organism; yet when isolated it forms a minute crystalline structure, like a mineral substance. Admittedly, known viruses require surrounding protoplasm of higher organisms to function as living entities—a possibility denied to the first-formed life. To date no one has created a virus by laboratory experiment; moreover, the evolutionary advance from a virus to the simplest one-celled organism, such as the amoeba, is very great. But the evidence, from viruses coupled with amino-acid synthesis, does suggest that several billion of years ago some chance combination of the earth's existing chemicals created a super-molecule with the attributes of life.

Possible early evolution

Lacking a fossil record we have no direct evidence of how the earliest life progressively evolved in the Precambrian seas. However, armed with the fact of evolution gleaned from later fossiliferous rocks, and by comparing the living organisms from simple to more complex as arrayed in the Tree of Life, we can establish the likely pattern.

Before the Fossil Record The first miniscule specks of protoplasm must have been plant-like, resembling the existing sulfur bacteria in their ability to use inorganic chemicals for food, without relying on photosynthesis. In the first great evolutionary step, protoplasm formed single cells with a nucleus and other special parts. Those cells acquiring a predatory habit, like the amoeba, begat the animal kingdom, and those developing chlorophyl for photosynthesis were the progenitors of typical plants.

The next great advance was the development of multi-celled organisms, probably as colonies of similar cells joined together. Later, colonial masses acquired specialized cells in a "division of labor" for carrying out different bodily functions. Thereafter, tremendous evolutionary changes produced the very heterogeneous thallophytes and most of the invertebrate stocks, by the end of Precambrian time. So far the story is logical speculation; what is the actual record from fossil evidence?

Precambrian Fossils There are sparse but significant indications of well-established life, long before the Paleozoic. Bun-like masses of crinkly laminae in Precambrian limestones are virtually identical to some living calcareous algae. In the ancient rocks of Ontario's Gunflint Formation, black cherts radiometrically dated at about two billion years, microscopic algae and fungi have been authenticated (Fig. 12-1). Although less conclusive, graphite and metamorphosed carbonaceous shales are common in some Precambrian terrains. In later rocks, the carbon in dark shales and graphite deposits is largely organic, so the carbon in Precambrian rocks may be the same.

Fossils of multi-celled animals are periodically reported in Precambrian rocks; however, uncontested finds are exceedingly rare. Burrows and trails of worms were the only generally accepted ones, until recently, when Precambrian rocks in Australia disclosed fossils of jellyfish, worms, coral-like animals, and some previously unknown invertebrates. At best, however, the Precambrian fossil list is very unimpressive, considering that life was probably quite profuse.

Thus until the earth was at least four billion years old, its rocks were virtually devoid of fossils. Then suddenly, geologically speaking, abundant fossils appear worldwide, marking the beginning of Paleozoic time. Most explanations for the delayed and dramatic appearance of fossils are unconvincing. Was life far less abundant in Precambrian times than later? It seems unlikely because of the complexity and diversity of Cambrian faunas. Many Precambrian rocks are highly metamorphosed and intruded; so has the fossil record been destroyed? Possibly, yet fossils of later eras have been found in metamorphic rocks, including high-grade schists. Moreover, some Precambrian rocks are little-

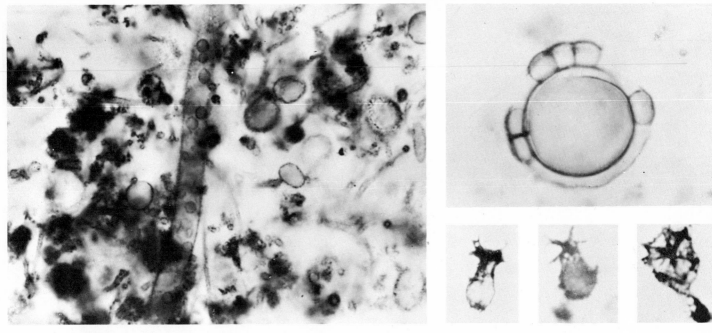

Fig. 12-1
Microorganisms from the Gunflint Chert. Photomicrographs taken in transmitted light through rock thin sections (magnifications: left, 1289×; top right, 1389×; bottom right 1823×). Courtesy of E. S. Barghoorn.

altered sandstones and limestones, virtually indistinguishable from younger fossiliferous strata.

That Precambrian animals lacked hard parts is a reasonable explanation. Most fossils record shell or bone, corruptible flesh being rarely fossilized. Unfortunately, the hypothesis leads to other considerations, as to why hard parts became abundant almost simultaneously. Also, how did muscles evolve without solid areas of attachment? Trilobites, for instance, have complex appendages; how could the muscles controlling them have evolved without a carapace (shell) for anchoring them? Whatever the answers to these questions, for practical purposes the meager Precambrian fossil record is useless for dating and correlation.

ANCIENT (PALEOZOIC) LIFE

Early Paleozoic life

At the dawn of the Paleozoic, all life as far as we know was in the seas, vertebrates were conspicuous in their absence, and the lands were barren. Yet the Cambrian fauna of invertebrates had an advanced development far removed from the original primitive one-celled organisms. The early Paleozoic, encompassing the Cambrian, Ordovician, and Silurian, is rightfully called the "Age of Invertebrates." Beginning in early Cambrian as a rather small bottom-dwelling group of coelenterates, brachiopods, sponges, gastropods, and arthropods, the invertebrates expanded greatly through the Silurian. Thereafter, although still prospering, they had to compete with vertebrate populations which arose in the seas and eventually followed the plants onto the lands.

281

Fig. 12-2
Diorama of mid-Cambrian sea floor showing algae "organ-pipe" sponges, worms and trilobites.
Courtesy of the Chicago Natural History Museum.

The Cambrian All the animal phyla may have been present in Cambrian time; the absence of bryozoans and chordates as fossils could reflect either a lack of hard parts or the vagaries of preservation (Fig. 12-2). Trilobites rapidly reached their all-time peak in varieties and numbers in the Cambrian, for which they are the outstanding guide fossils, then gradually declined to their extinction at the end of the Paleozoic. Brachiopods of a rather primitive sort were second to the trilobites in abundance. Also common were Archaeocyatha, a sponge-like animal forming clusters of tubes on calcareous ocean floors. This particular group is known only in Cambrian rocks.

Minor elements of the population were snails, uncoiled cephalopods, and very rare clams. Graptolites, which were soon to flourish, appeared towards the end of the period. That the fossil sample gives a biased picture of the Cambrian community is illustrated in the dark Burgess shale of the remarkable Canadian locality where many soft-bodied animals, such as jellyfish and worms, are preserved in abundance.

Mound-like calcareous structures reflecting algal activity are the most common evidence of plants. The record of terrestrial plants is exceedingly poor—explicable in North America because known Cambrian strata are almost wholly marine—although possible lycopod impressions have been found in Siberia. Thus higher plants could have been tentatively invading the wet fringes of the land. But, overall, the continents must have been desolate, eroded badlands.

The Ordovician   Marine invertebrates from Cambrian stocks were widespread in the Ordovician seas (Fig. 12-3). Trilobites and brachiopods inhabited limey bottoms of the "shelly" facies of shallow-water deposits, and clams now became relatively common. Nautiloid cephalopods reached their all-time peak; both straight and curved-shelled varieties being present. The giant of the Ordovician was a straight nautiloid, 15 feet in length. After the Ordovician, nauti-

loids progressively declined. Above all, however, this was the "age of graptolites." Preserved largely in black shale facies, they are among the most important guide fossils for the Ordovician, and following Silurian, as well.

New members of the Ordovician community were the corals, both solitary and colonial tetracorals; the bryozoans; and among the echinoderms, crinoids and starfish appeared. The oldest known eurypterid was found in black shales of this period in New York State. Perhaps most significant are the scattered bony plates heralding the first vertebrates. The generally widespread nature of Ordovician seas makes seaweed and other algae the principal plant fossil; al-

Fig. 12-3
Ordovician sea floor of shell facies near present site of Cincinnati, Ohio. Algae, straight shelled nautiloid cephalopods, snails, colonial and solitary "horn" corals, bryozoans, brachiopods, and trilobites are represented. Courtesy of the Chicago Natural History Museum.

Fig. 12-4
Silurian sea floor of coral, sand, and patch reef bottom showing algae, chain coral (foreground), honeycomb coral, organ-pipe coral (right), lacy bryozoans, early relatives of stalked crinoids (cystoids), brachiopods, nautiloids and trilobites. Photo of exhibit in the Smithsonian Institution.

though they may have been present somewhere, we have as yet no record of Ordovician terrestrial plants.

The Silurian Compared to the Cambrian and Ordovician, the Silurian period was relatively short, and its fauna shows few major changes (Fig. 12-4). Brachiopods, molluscs, and corals abounded; graptolites, if less flourishing, produced important guide fossils, until the end of the period, when floating types died out. Trilobites were definitely on the decline. They may well have been meals for nautiloids, as well as placoderms, the first jawed vertebrates, for the progressive decline of the trilobites seems to bear a "sinister" correlation to the rise and expansion of fish.

The Silurian was the "age of eurypterids," the largest arthropods of all time, which became abundant towards the end of the period (Fig. 12-5). The remains of their close relatives, the scorpions, first found in upper Silurian rocks, are of special interest as the first air-breathing animals potentially capable of venturing onto the land. Doubtless, most of the lands were still barren; however, plants were established in swampy lowlands, for the first good record of Psilopsida and Lycopsida is found in Silurian rocks.

Late Paleozoic life

The Devonian, Carboniferous, and Permian periods comprise the late Paleozoic, an interval of profound developments in life. Fish came to dominate the waters, and vascular plants and vertebrates spread over the continents.

The Devonian The Devonian was a most important period in the history of life. Among the established invertebrates, corals, bryozoans, pelecypods, and various echinoderms flourished. Brachiopods, reaching their peak, were to serve as most important guide fossils. Some eurypter-

ids still persisted; trilobites were definitely on the decline. Important new animals appeared on the Devonian scene. The ammonoid cephalopods, which were to become the most paleontologically significant invertebrates, were in the seas (Fig. 12-6). Insects of a wingless type were well established on land.

Most important was the establishment of several major vertebrate lines. Although the primitive ostracoderms became extinct in the period, the Devonian was the "age of fish." Placoderms flourished, producing, among others, the great 30-foot armor-headed arthrodires. Sharks and bony fish were present; in the latter, the lobe-finned crossopterygians were of greatest evolu-

Fig. 12-5
Silurian brackish water environment dominated by eurypterids, also shrimp-like animals and snails. Courtesy of the Chicago Natural History Museum.

Fig. 12-6
Devonian sea floor showing a variety of corals, straight and coiled cephalopods, simple and bizarre trilobites, snails, and brachiopods. Courtesy of the Chicago Natural History Museum.

tionary significance. Towards the end of the Devonian, the first amphibians appeared. In upper Devonian rocks of Greenland, remains have been found that are essentially like crossopterygian fish, except that these animals had very primitive legs, instead of fins.

Vascular plants made considerable progress. Early in Devonian time there is evidence of only small primitive plants, mainly Psilopsida, seemingly restricted to wet coastal marshes and swamps. By the middle of the period, however, the earth's first true forest certainly existed. At Gilboa, New York, for example, stumps up to two feet in diameter are included in a fossil flora of ferns, seed ferns, scale trees, calamites,

and the forerunner of the conifers, cordates. Thus by the end of the Devonian, terrestrial vegetation was prominent, and amphibians held a vertebrate beachhead (Fig. 12-7).

The Carboniferous The North American Carboniferous is divided into the Mississippian and Pennsylvanian periods; in European usage, however, the Carboniferous is considered a single period with an upper and a lower division (corresponding to Mississippian and Pennsylvanian in approximate time). The name refers to the characteristic coal strata, the carbonized remains of vascular plants forming true "forests primeval." Ferns, seed ferns, thickets of large

Fig. 12-7
Devonian forest as painted by C. R. Knight. Copyright Chicago Natural History Museum.

calamites, the giant scale trees Lepidodendron and Sigillaria thrived in lowlands of the great coal swamps. Besides this collection, true conifers, precursors of the trees that would dominate later landscapes, appeared by the late Carboniferous.

The coal forests, like modern swamps, were infested with insects (Fig. 12-8). Although mostly of extinct primitive orders, Pennsylvanian insects were well evolved, suggesting they had been common in Mississippian and Devonian time as well, but their fragile carcasses were not preserved. In any case, coal-swamp insects include, among others, a dragonfly whose wingspread was over two feet, and some thousands of different species of cockroaches with representatives up to four inches long.

Sharks and bony fish continued to dominate the seas. In Mississippian time, amphibians must have ruled the lands for want of competition;

however, their fossils are few because rocks of this period are mainly marine. Pennsylvanian strata have exposed a varied host of peculiar-looking Labyrinthodonts, some being 15 feet long, who held their own with the first reptiles appearing in late Carboniferous time. These ancestral reptiles, the Cotylosaurs, included Seymouria, a transitional form from the amphibians.

Among marine invertebrates, the crinoids were extremely prolific, their plates making up a major part of some Mississippian strata. Brachiopods continued to thrive with the appearance of some new spine-covered types. The *fusulinids*, a most important group of Foraminifera for dating purposes, appeared in early Carboniferous time and were exceedingly common in the Pennsylvanian.

The Permian The end of the Paleozoic era brought a crisis wherein some plants and ani-

Fig. 12-8
Restoration of Pennsylvanian coal swamp. Scale trees and firs (left), giant horsetails (right). Large cockroach on tree trunk (left). Dragon fly (right center). Copyright Chicago Natural History Museum.

mals declined, some died out completely, and others, meeting the challenge, prospered. The decline and fall of many groups is an interesting enigma. It may have related to a pronounced shift in the land–sea ratio. The Permian was a time of widespread continental emergence marked by increasingly extreme climates, and a complimentary reduction in area of shallow, shelf seas. Thus, changing environments may have exerted adaptive pressures on inhabitants of both land and sea.

Crinoids and bryozoans declined markedly. The Permian was the end of the line for two once-great Paleozoic groups: the tetracorals, later to be replaced by modern six-septaed types; and the trilobites which had once reigned supreme. The ammonoid cephalopods were reduced to one small group. On land, the dominant trees of the earlier coal forests approached ex-

tinction, but other groups profited. True conifers became abundant, perhaps being better adapted to the cooler climates. The *Glossopteris* flora, a plant group found almost exclusively in the southern hemisphere, appeared in the Permian, and lasted well into the Triassic. They were "tongue-leaf" plants related to seed ferns, or perhaps angiosperms, that lived in temperate and cold climates prevailing then on the southern continents.

The amphibians, including the large ungainly *Eryops* and the wedge-headed *Diplacaulus*, were still common in the Permian, but amphibians were giving way to reptiles (Fig. 12-10). Notable were the flamboyant "sail-backed lizards," the Pelycosaurs represented in the carnivorous *Dimetrodon,* and the less-common, herbivorous *Edaphosaurus.* The mammal-like Therapsids such as *Mosochops,* a large South

Fig. 12-9
Mississippian "garden" of sea lilies and their kin on sandy mud sea bottom. Courtesy of the Chicago Natural History Museum.

African vegetarian, had appeared in abundance. The late Paleozoic expansion of reptiles foreshadowed their coming days of grandeur.

MEDIEVAL (MESOZOIC) LIFE

The Mesozoic, era of "medieval life," was the heyday of reptiles on land, in the sea, and in the air. The ammonoids, recovering from their late Paleozoic depression, once again flourished. By the end of the era, the flora had a distinctly modern look.

Early and middle Mesozoic

The Triassic Widespread desert, semi-arid, and cool conditions, accompanying the general continental emergence, continued into the Triassic. In terms of life, the period was transitional between the late Paleozoic, and the highly characteristic floras and faunas of the subsequent Mesozoic.

The beginning of Triassic time is marked, in marine rocks, by a resurgence of the ammonoids rebounding from their near extinction at the close of the Paleozoic. The generally ceratitic sutures of Triassic ammonoids contrast with the simpler

Fig. 12-10
Permian landscape in Texas showing primitive lizard-like reptiles, sail backs, and (lower right) some wedge-headed amphibians. C. R. Knight painting. Copyright Chicago Natural History Museum.

goniatite sutures, prevailing in the late Paleozoic forms. By the close of Triassic time, when ammonitic sutures, the most complex kind, were well evolved,[1] these cephalopods again faltered. This low in their racial history marking the period's end was followed—as at the Paleozoic–Mesozoic time line—by another expansion in the ensuing Jurassic.

Among other invertebrates, the belemnoid cephalopods were also widespread in Triassic seas; brachiopods declined in most regions; echinoids, starfish, and various crustaceans including lobsters and shrimp were also present. Corals, seemingly extinct in the early Triassic, reappeared as the new six-septaed types. Al-

though vegetation was rarely preserved in the widespread Triassic redbed environments, the conifers apparently flourished; cycads, ferns, and scouring rushes were not uncommon, but seed ferns and scale trees were rare.

Of land vertebrates, the Labyrinthodont amphibians had a final surge, then passed from the scene at the end of the Triassic. The cotylosaurs and various mammal-like reptiles, other late Paleozoic holdovers, also persisted until the close of the period. Most significant among the reptiles were the newly appeared thecodonts. Of these, the phytosaurs were the crocodile equivalents of the Triassic; the bipedal branch of pseudosuchians, such as Ornithosuchus, were late arrivals during the period. Although 10-foot long, running reptiles would be most impressive

[1] They had appeared in the Permian.

Fig. 12-11
Triassic landscape showing a small dinosaur ancestor (lower right), a mammal-like reptile (cyognathus, lower center), and larger ancestral forms of the Sauropods (middle). Peabody Museum diorama, Yale University.

if living today, the pseudosuchians hardly rivalled their Jurassic and Cretaceous descendants, the dinosaurs (Fig. 12-11).

Still other reptiles readapted a tetrapod instructure to aquatic life. These "sea serpents" ruled the seas, prevailing over the fish until the end of the Mesozoic era. Turtles appeared in the Triassic seas along with a number of specialized marine reptiles that lived only in the Mesozoic. The *ichthyosaurs* resembled sharks and the later mammalian porpoises, externally. However, the fish-shaped ichthyosaurs had a reptilian skeletal structure. The *nothosaurs* had rather stout bodies, limbs and feet adapted as paddles, and long, darting necks for snatching fish. They used their fins as oars, unlike the streamlined ichthyosaurs whose appendages functioned as stabilizers as they swam like fish, using body oscillations and sculling with their long tails.

The Jurassic The marine invertebrates would not look unfamiliar except for the widespread

Fig. 12-12
*Marine reptiles. Plesiosaurs and (leaping) Ichthyosaurs. Mural by C. R. Knight. Copyright
Chicago History Museum.*

abundance of belemnoids and ammonoids. After
their second racial depression, near the end of
Triassic time, the ammonoids once again proliferated. They showed a remarkable evolution
in shells and suture complications, allowing exceedingly detailed dating of marine rocks, for
the rest of the Mesozoic.

In the sea, the fish-like ichthyosaurs were
thriving, and nothosaurs had given rise to *plesiosaurs*, "sea monsters" looking like miscegenation of turtle and snake, though not a member
of either group (Fig. 12-12). Their shell-less,
paddle-driven bodies extended into snake-like
necks, some relatively short and others fantas-
tically long. The *geosaurs*, sea-going crocodiles
with fish-like tails, appeared and died out, all in
the Jurassic. There were dragons, flying reptiles
called *pterosaurs* that were apparently soaring
carnivores. They ranged from the size of a spar-
row to those such as *Rhamphorhynchus*, having
long, toothed skulls, light bones, and a tail like

a child's kite. Pterosaurs were a separate lineage,
not ancestral to birds, because they lacked
feathers, had weak legs, and their wings consisted of a flight membrane stretched over a
greatly elongated "little" finger. The Jurassic
is notable for the first appearance of birds, Archaeopteryx, that probably flew among the conifers
and cycads prominent in the landscape (Fig.
12-13). Another Jurassic first were the true mammals. No complete skeletons have been found;
their presence is indicated, largely, by jaws, and
by teeth differentiated into molars, canines, and
incisors. These animals were an unimpressive
lot about the size of squirrels or rats, a furtive
group relegated to insignificance by the dinosaurs.

The "Golden Age" of dinosaurs began. The
world's greatest land animals were a group of
rather similar dinosaurs, collectively called
brontosaurs. These saurischian quadrupeds, as
much as 80 feet long and weighing an estimated

Fig. 12-13
Jurassic landscape showing the first known bird (Archaeopteryx). Mural by C. R. Knight. Copyright Chicago Natural History Museum.

Fig. 12-14
Jurassic dinosaurs. From left, Brontosaurus, Stegosaurus, the large carnivorous Allosaurus, and (lower right) Camptosaurus, an early "bird-hipped" herbivorous type. Courtesy of the Peabody Museum, Yale University.

Fig. 12-15
Cretaceous sea floor showing algae, numerous types of clams and snails, straight and coiled ammonites, and belemnites (swimming). Courtesy of the Smithsonian Institution.

50 tons or more, may have spent much of their time immersed in swamps and ponds to support their great bulk. The most formidable of Jurassic carnivores was *Allosaurus*, a 40-foot, bipedal saurischian. The ornithischian line produced Stegosaurus, a vegetarian quadruped, 20 feet long weighing, perhaps, 10 tons, whose back sported erect triangular plates and terminated in a tail sprouting formidable defensive spikes. Stegosaurus is popularly believed to have had two brains. The true one, in the head, was the size of a walnut and 20 times smaller than the "second brain," an enlargement of the spinal cord controlling the movements of the hind legs and tail (Fig. 12-14).

Late Mesozoic times

The Cretaceous During Cretaceous time the earth's floras became modern in most aspects. The coming of the angiosperms, our familiar trees and flowering plants, lead to a partial displacement of the cycads and conifers so prevalent in the earlier Mesozoic.

In the seas, belemnoids persisted, and ammonoids continued to evolve in great variety, producing, among others, the giant of the tribe, 9 feet in diameter (Fig. 12-15). Ichthyosaurs, plesiosaurs, and other marine reptiles abounded, and a new group, the mosasaurs, appeared. These fierce-looking, 30-foot marine lizards swam with their long lithe bodies using paddle-like limbs as stabilizers (Fig. 12-16). Though now extinct, the mosasaurs have close living relatives in the split-tongued varanid, or monitor, lizards of the East Indies.

The Cretaceous *Pteranodon*, with a 27-foot wingspread, was the largest flying vertebrate of all time. Unlike the Jurassic flying reptiles, Pteranodon was tail-less, had a long cantilever projection from the back of its skull, and a toothless beak.

Cretaceous birds are known mainly from fossils of *Hesperornis*, an aquatic bird up to 6 feet long having vestigial wings and paddle feet, and the small gull-like *Ichthyornis*. They were skeletally modern except for the presence of teeth.

Dinosaurs were still in ascendency. Among the giant saurischian quadrupeds, the brontosaur group lingered on. The bipedal carnivores culminated in *Tyrannosaurus rex*. This "tyrant king" was the largest flesheater the world has ever seen: 40 feet long, 20 feet high, and weighing an estimated 80 tons. His stunted forelimbs

were apparently useless, but the great head and jaws, armed with dagger-like teeth, were adequate for assaulting the largest dinosaurs (Fig. 12-17).

The ornithiscian vegetarians produced several interesting types. The bipedal trachodons, or "duckbill" dinosaurs, so-called from their flattened lower jaws, had had Jurassic ancestors, but the group reached its climax in the Cretaceous. They were mainly aquatic dinosaurs, some, at least, having webbed feet, and their jaws bore as many as 2000 teeth for grinding swamp plants. Some members of this group evolved bizarre skull structures, capping crests, ridges, and thick domes of bone. Armored ornithiscians were the ankylosaurs. These squat-bodied, "reptile tanks" were protected by heavy, overlapping bony plates and fringed with protective spikes. The tail was a spiked mace, a fearsome defensive weapon.

The last dinosaurs to evolve, appearing in the late Cretaceous, were the ceratopsians. These massive, four-footed ornithiscians achieved

Fig. 12-16
Some Cretaceous marine vertebrates, a mosasaur and giant turtle with flying Pteradon. C. R. Knight painting. Copyright Chicago Natural History Museum.

Fig. 12-17
Cretaceous dinosaurs. From left, Triceratops, Tyrannosaurus, Ankylosaurus, and a duck-billed Anatosaurus. Upper center, the flying reptile, Pteradon. Courtesy of the Peabody Museum, Yale University.

lengths of 25 feet and weighed up to 8 tons. They had large, toothless beaks, and were characterized by a protective bone neck-frill projecting backward from their specialized skulls. Most later ceratopsians sprouted horns from the front of their skulls, from a single one, as in *Styracosaurus*, whose neck-frill was studded with spikes, to as many as three in *Triceratops*.

The Cretaceous period ended with mass exterminations. Dinosaurs, flying reptiles, and most marine reptiles died out completely; invertebrates were not immune, for the hosts of belemnites (some may have lingered into the Eocene) and ammonoids and the fusulinid foraminifera died out as well. Such mass extinctions are, as yet, impossible to explain. All the Mesozoic victims had been diverse, numerous, and very successful animals. Whatever the cause, the disap-

pearance of these many groups produced a distinct fossil boundary between Mesozoic and Cenozoic rocks.

MODERN (CENOZOIC) LIFE

The collapse of the reptilian dynasty must have left the landscape with a vacant look. This was deceptive, however, for insignificant, furtive mammals who had bided their time for 100,-000,000 years were on the scene. Their unprecedented radiation is the major life theme of the Cenozoic, "the age of mammals." Abundant and widely dispersed into every environment, these rapidly evolving vertebrates left excellent guide fossils in terrestrial deposits which, because of their relative recency, are generally less eroded than earlier terrestrial strata.

The early Tertiary

The early Cenozoic includes the Paleocene, Eocene, and Oligocene epochs. In the Old World, it is called the *Nummulitic Age* because the "giant," coin-shaped foraminifera proliferated in a seaway across southern Eurasia. Otherwise, the marine invertebrates were mainly foraminifera, clams, and snails, not too different from today. In the mild climates of early Cenozoic, tropical and sub-tropical floras spread far northward. Magnolias, figs, and palms, for instance, graced the now treeless plains of Wyoming, Montana, and Canada.

The Paleocene and Eocene At the beginning of the Paleocene, terrestrial mammals were all small quadrupeds, at most a few feet high, and of rather similar and primitive structure (Fig. 12-18). They had flat, five-toed feet, and long narrow heads bearing 44 relatively unspecialized teeth. Marsupials, insectivores, and the soon to be extinct multituberculates remained from the Cretaceous fauna. Gradually, new forms appeared: primates, rodents, carnivores, and ungulates. Certain groups evolved rapidly, dominating the early Tertiary in an archaic mammalian fauna, some of whose members achieved a considerable size.

Of the archaic groups, *creodonts* were the earliest abundant carnivores. They were, initially, small animals like weasels having slender bodies and rather short legs. Evolving rapidly, the creo-

Fig. 12-18
Paleocene landscape in Rocky Mountain region where a subtropical flora of modern-type plants existed. With the great dinosaurs extinct, small primitive mammals took over the scene. Peabody Museum diorama, Yale University.

donts diversified into types resembling wolves, lions, and bears. One, with a yard-long skull, represents the largest known predatory mammal. Creodonts are classed as archaic because their teeth were primitive adaptations of insectivore dentition. By Oligocene time, most of these flesheaters were extinct, replaced by the more intelligent ancestors of modern carnivores.

Several orders of archaic ungulates reached a climax in the early Tertiary, then, like the creodonts, gave way to forerunners of modern hoofed lineages. The giant amblypods included *Uintatherium*, which resembled a present-day elephant in size and pillar-like leg structure. Its defensive weapons were impressive: three sets of horns on the top of its head, and two long canine teeth set in the upper jaw (Fig. 12-19).

Coryphodon was as large as a living hippopotamus, hornless, but armed with fierce canines. The failure of these animals to survive may relate to their low-crowned teeth, suitable only for soft vegetation, or, more probably, to their small brains and lack of intelligence.

Condylarths, appearing in earliest Tertiary time, were the first and most primitive of ungulates. The sheep-size *Phenacodus* resembled the early prototypes of later carnivores in having a long skull and tail, conspicuous canine teeth, short legs, and five-toed feet. Although too large and too late to be the direct ancestor of modern ungulates, Phenacodus displayed significant preliminary changes. Its molars were square-topped, and its toes were tipped with individual small hooves instead of claws. Also present in Eocene

Fig. 12-19
Mural of Eocene flora and fauna in western Wyoming. Large animal is Uintatherium. Early members of many mammal lines are shown. Courtesy of the Smithsonian Institution.

Fig. 12-20
Oligocene mammals and flora of North Dakota. Included are Titanotheres, entelodonts (fighting), ancestral horses (left), running rhinos and many other vegetarians and carnivores. Courtesy of the Smithsonian Institution.

time were small, relatively unspecialized ancestors to oreodonts, titanotheres, rhinoceroses, camels, and horses.

Famed *Eohippus*[2] was a slim, relatively long-legged, and long-headed lowbrow about the size of a fox—an unlikely looking forebear of noble *Equus*, the modern horse. Significantly, however, the "Dawn Horse" of the Eocene ran on the tips of its toes, each capped with a little hoof. There were four useful toes on each front foot (and a fifth non-functional toe), and three on each hind foot. Dentally, small incisors and canines were present, and the molars, although low-crowned, were already square-topped. The ancestors of the other future great lines of perissodactyls were as humble, and almost indistinguishable from Eohippus, in Eocene time.

[2] Technically and more properly called *Hyracotherium*.

The Oligocene By Oligocene time, the large archaic mammals had given way to more modern lineages (Fig. 12-20). Small carnivores could be distinguished as dogs and cats. Miniature mastodons, the first elephant stock, roamed the Old World continents. The perissodactyls, odd-toed ungulates, were, generally, the dominant vegetarians. Horses were represented by the three-toed, sheep-size *Mesohippus*. The rhinoceroses had diversified into three lines, from hornless, slim-legged, fleet Eocene ancestors, only a bit larger than Eohippus.

Oligocene rhinos included the following types: larger, running members whose habits differed little from the contemporary horses; large, stout, short-legged amphibious forms outwardly resembling hippopotamuses; and forebears of "true" rhinoceroses. The running and amphibious tribes became extinct about the end of the

299

Oligocene, while the main line continued. *Baluchitherium,* a hornless rhinoceros of the Oligocene and early Miocene, qualifies as the largest known terrestrial mammal. Although not as large as the greatest dinosaurs, it was 25 feet long, and 18 feet high at the shoulders. Having a rather long neck, Baluchitherium was apparently a browser of tree leaves, and, superficially, like a ponderous giraffe.

The Perissodactyls had striking offshoots in the now-defunct *titanotheres.* Theirs was a short spectacular career. From small Eocene forebears, differing little from Eohippus, they evolved bulky giants with large-bone-cored horns on their skulls. Flourishing in the early Oligocene, they were gone by the middle of the epoch. Low intelligence may have contributed to their downfall, but a more fundamental flaw was probably dental. Their low-crowned teeth may have worn out rapidly in chewing the harder, siliceous grasses, that in mid-Tertiary time, were replacing the softer earlier vegetation.

The *chalicotheres,* unique as the only ungulates with clawed feet, were probably diggers, feeding on soft roots along streams. They were "composite" perissodactyls, having three functional toes on each foot, a head like a horse, teeth like a titanothere, and a giraffe-like body with longer legs in front than behind. Never numerous, they were, however, a long-lived group surviving from their Eocene appearance till late Pleistocene.

In early Cenozoic, the artiodactyls of the cloven hoof had not come into their own. Pig-like types, from whose members the diversity of later advanced ruminants probably evolved, did produce an impressive offshoot in the now extinct "giant hogs," better called *entelodonts.* Despite a swinish look, entelodonts differ from existing pigs in being adapted for running. They had a straight back, long legs, and, in later forms, just two toes. Ugly in looks and most probably in disposition, they bore knobs or flanges on their cheeks, and impressive canine tusks. By Oligocene time, some were twice the size of a bear, and they were to become larger still.

Oreodonts were thriving North American artiodactyls from late Eocene until their Pliocene extinction. Judging by their prolific remains in certain Oligocene beds, herds of oreodonts must have swarmed over the western regions at that time. They are, perhaps, best classed as "ruminating swine" for their teeth suggest cud chewers, whereas their legs were short with four-toed feet and their bodies were pig-like. Some were quite small, many were the size of a sheep, and the largest were comparable to a hog.

The late Tertiary

The Miocene Starting in Miocene time, climates on the great landmasses of the Northern Hemisphere became progressively cooler and drier. Grasslands expanded at the expense of forested areas, and, as a seeming result, the hoofed grazing animals proliferated. This was the "Golden Age" of mammals whose rich fauna, if differing somewhat from that of the present, had a generally familiar look. Although impoverished by the disappearance of the titanotheres and some other lines, the perissodactyls were still varied and prominent until the end of late Tertiary when they began a final decline. Their cousins, the artiodactyls, ever diversifying and expanding, became the dominant hoofed vegetarians, a position they continue to hold to the present time.

In the Miocene (Fig. 12-21), horses included several types, one of which was the size of a small pony and ran on a single functional toe. Rhinoceroses of several kinds were still common. The chalicotheres were represented by the relatively large *Moropus.* The entelodonts culminated in the pig-like *Dinohyus,* as large as an American bison and having a yard-long skull. The brains of this particular animal group were never large, which may account for their mid-Miocene extinction. Oreodonts were still present. Camels were a varied and humpless stock; some were relatively small and designed for fast running, while others became large with long necks, such as *Alticamelus,* who could browse on leaves 10 feet off the ground. Giraffes

Fig. 12-21
Miocene menagerie, including Dinohyus, Chalicotheres, horses (Merychippus), camels, antelope, and others. Courtesy of the Smithsonian Institution.

first appeared in the Miocene as a branch from the deer family. The earliest forms were short-necked; the elongation of neck and legs characterizing the living giraffes is a late evolutionary development. Cattle and their close relatives, the antelope, sheep, goats, and pronghorns (American "antelope"), were new arrivals on the Miocene scene. Mastodonts, the elephant stock with low-crowned teeth, some with four tusks, diversified and spread across the Northern Hemisphere. To complete the mammalian array, varied carnivores of the dog and cat families preyed on the multitudes of ungulates.

The Pliocene In the Pliocene, the "autumn" of the Cenozoic preceding the Pleistocene "winter," mammals still prospered, and some increased in size (Fig. 12-22). Oreodonts became extinct; however, cattle and their kindred ruminants were expanding. Mastodons, an Old World stock, were well established in North America, and the true elephants, whose stout, complexly ridged molars adapted them to grazing, appeared. Rhinoceroses and camels abounded and several horse types were present. The ubiquitous carnivores included various dogs, wolves, cats, and bears. A notable development in Africa was the appearance of ape-like creatures whose skulls and bodily structure foreshadowed the advent of man.

The Quaternary

Mammals The last million years of earth history, the Pleistocene and Recent, has been a time of climax and crisis for mammals. As the great ice caps waxed and waned, Eurasia and North America were still populated by a greater diversity of mammals than exists today, including the giants of certain lines. *Castoroides*, a now extinct beaver, was a gigantic rodent as large as a black bear. Buffalo—technically Bison—roaming North America, included some species having a six-foot horn spread, far larger animals than exist-

Fig. 12-22
Pliocene diorama showing large bear, dog, horse (Pliohippus), an amphibious rhino, a "shovel-tusk" mastodon, camels, pronghorn, and the unicorn-like ruminant (Synthetoceras) with a branched horn above its muzzle. Courtesy of Peabody Museum, Yale University.

ing ones. Most impressive were the proboscidians, the browsing mastodons, and true grazing elephants represented by woolly mammoths. The greatest of these was the *Imperial Mammoth,* a hairy giant 14 feet high at the shoulder and bearing tusks 13 feet long. The abundant mastodonts and mammoths left hundreds of skeletons in peat bogs of the United States. In Siberia and Alaska thousands of mammoth tusks have been collected for the ivory trade, and some complete specimens, with preserved flesh and hair, have been recovered in permanently frozen ground (Fig. 12-23).

Horses, including the modern Equus, abounded, and rhinoceroses included a woolly type roaming far north in Eurasia. In north America, carnivores included *Smilodon,* greatest of a now-extinct line of saber-tooth cats, capable of attacking the largest mammals; lions as large as those living today in Africa; and the giant *Dire Wolf,* larger than any modern ones. Living beside the giant extinct mammals were many of today's familiar types.

At various times in the Cenozoic, mammals had migrated between Africa, Eurasia, and North America. The mixing was especially pronounced while Pleistocene ice caps lowered sea level, exposing intercontinental land connections, such as at the Bering Straits. Thus, by the late Cenozoic, emigrants from Africa, such as the proboscidians, ranged over North America; on the other hand, horses and camels, native

North American stocks, had spread as far as Africa. South America and Australia, in contrast, have been isolated continents, where rather exotic faunas evolved. In Australia, the marsupials, free of competition from the more aggressive placentals, have prospered until today, when man is upsetting their natural balance.

South America long had a provincial population of marsupials and archaic placentals whose ancestors reached the continent in early Cenozoic time. In isolation, they evolved a variety of herbivores and carnivores which, if exotic compared to animals in the rest of the world, took on many of the habits and filled many of the ecological niches occupied elsewhere by more progressive placentals. In the Pleistocene, however, a migration route became exposed along the Panamanian Isthmus. Thus the Pleistocene fauna of North America was enriched by South American armadillos, porcupines, and some now extinct forms: the giant ground sloth, *Megatherium*, the size of a small elephant, and *glyptodonts*, unique armored mammals, with mace-like tails, which resembled the "reptilian tanks" of the Mesozoic. North American placentals invaded South America, with disastrous results to the natives there, who were largely exterminated and replaced.

Extermination is a major theme of the Pleistocene, for towards the end of the epoch, most of the giant mammals, and some others, became extinct on the northern continents. Unlike the decimation of the South American animals, which is explicable through competition with advanced placentals, the decline of the great mammals is as mysterious as the end of the dinosaurs. Changing climates with failure to adapt, competition from man (the most devastating predator of all time), and other hypotheses proposed, are not entirely satisfactory. Many of the

Fig. 12-23
The Pleistocene was an era of giant mammals. Mammoths, mastodons, giant bison and sloths, large beaver and wolves, saber-toothed tigers, the modern horse (Equus), as well as the "mammalian tanks," the Glypotodonts. Courtesy of Peabody Museum, Yale University.

Fig. 12-24
Diorama of a Neanderthal family by sculptor Frederick Blaschke. Copyright Chicago Natural History Museum.

victims were large and powerful, extremely well-adjusted animals that had survived the marked climatic fluctuations of the Pleistocene.

Whatever the cause, the herds of mastodons and mammoths, the largest bison, saber-toothed cats, sloths, glyptodonts, and other impressive mammals all disappeared from the northern continents. If horses and camels, which evolved in North America, had not spread into Eurasia and Africa in earlier times, they too would be totally extinct.[3] Had south Asia and Africa not provided a sanctuary, many splendid mammals would be known only as fossils. Africa—where elephants, rhinos, hippos, great cats, and antelope herds roam the grassy Savannas—presents a last glimpse of the "Golden Age" of mammals.

[3] Our modern horses were reintroduced into North America by men, starting with the Spanish Conquistadores.

Even here, they are on the decline. Thus, the existing populations of large mammals are the impoverished survivors of the great dying, in late Quarternary time.

Man　The human population, now at its greatest number and still rapidly expanding, makes latest Cenozoic time the "Age of Man." Structurally, humans are primates, a group having a scanty fossil record, markedly so for the direct ancestors of man. Most primates were arboreal, living in forests where conditions for fossilization are poor; and being generally intelligent, they were not apt to be trapped in bogs, tar pits, or other environments of quick burial. Thus, for want of evidence, the early descent of man is conjectural. He could be a modified ape, branching from the anthropoids in late Cenozoic time; or he may represent a long-separate lineage that diverged from early primates as far back as the Oligocene.

The first known fossils of true men are of early, or perhaps middle, Pleistocene age. They are classified as *Pithecanthropus*, represented by Java and Peking man, who had low heavy brows, jutting jaws, and about two-thirds the brain capacity of modern men. Yet their chins and teeth were human, and they walked erect.

By the third interglacial age, the modern genus of man, *Homo*, was well represented by the *Neanderthals*. Numerous skeletons show them as short stocky people having low brows and more pithecanthropoid features than we possess. Early Stone Age men made tools from chipped flints, and had a relatively complex culture (Fig. 12-24). They were hunters, in a world of mammoths, giant cave bears, wolves, and other non-extinct species.

The modern species of man, *Homo sapiens*, appeared during the Wurm [4] glacial age, and displaced the Neanderthals. He was *Cro-magnon* man, of physically modern appearance, with a brain as large, or larger, than ours. Cro-magnon man developed several rather complex stone-age cultures, and among other accomplishments was a fine artist whose cave paintings still rank as masterpieces.

Human evolution is an Old World phenomenon. Not until the end of the Wisconsin did modern men reach the Americas by way of the Bering Straits. No incontrovertible skeletons of these first Americans are known; their record is in distinctive, well-fashioned artifacts, exemplified by the Folsom type points, with which they hunted the last of the giant bison and mammoths. These first men to "discover" America are called paleo-Indians, although it is

[4] Equivalent to the Wisconsin of North America.

Charles Darwin (1809–1882) *Darwin ultimately gained scientific acceptance for the concept of organic evolution and suggested a reasonable mechanism—a major intellectual achievement of the 19th century. The opposition generated in his time (and in some circles today) was violent, but today the scientific evidence, much from paleontology, overwhelmingly supports the concept, although the mechanism is still being investigated.*

not surely known whether they were ancestors of the Indians living here when the first Europeans arrived.

Geologically, man's ancestors are poor fossils; moreover, their early history has been largely pre-empted by the anthropologists. Still, his arrival on the scene makes an appropriate ending for a geologic account of life through the ages. After all, man—or a few of his more gifted members—developed the awareness and methods, to write and decipher the story.

SUGGESTED READINGS

Carrington, Richard, *A Guide to Earth History*, New York, New American Library, 1956 (paperback).

Rush, J. H., *The Dawn of Life*, New York, New American Library, 1957 (paperback).

Physical evolution

We now discuss the changes in our planet through time—the central theme of the geologic story. The remote and hazy past will be first on the agenda.

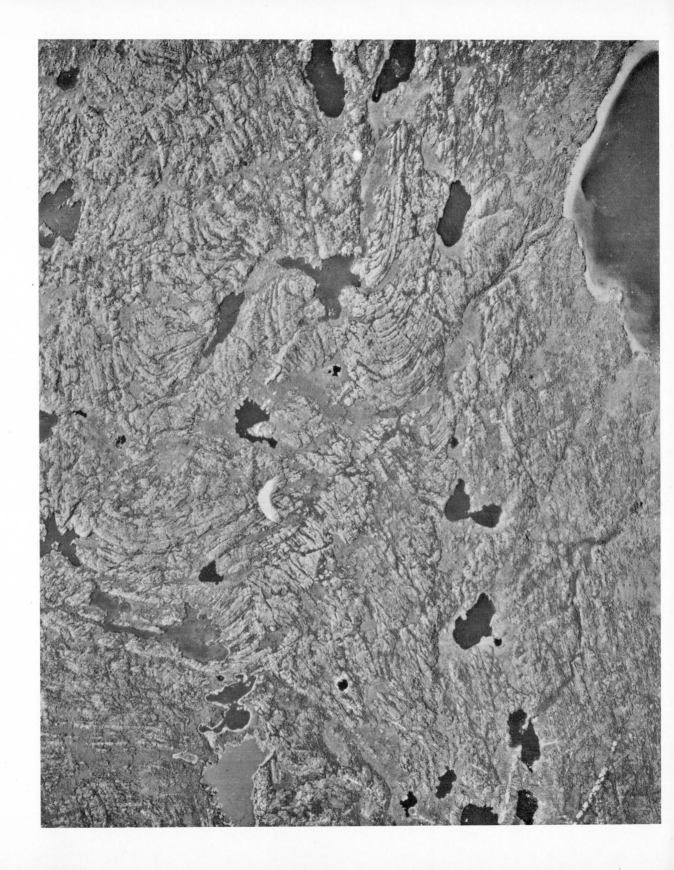

thirteen: Before the Cambrian

Geologic history—like the history of civilizations—becomes progressively more vague as we search back through time. For while erosion, mountain building, and igneous phenomena have continuously added new rocks to the geological record, they have also masked and erased the evidence of earlier events. Thanks to fossils, however, a coherent physical history has been compiled for the last 600 million years, back through the Cambrian period. Our reconstructions, however, before the Cambrian period, are far less certain because of the difficulties of correlating geological evidence. The Precambrian story, representing three-fourths of geologic time, will remain the least known, even though radiometric dating is helping to clarify this most ancient era of earth history.

PRE-GEOLOGIC HISTORY

Since the oldest known rocks are something over three billion years old, and the earth's age is now estimated as over five and a half billion, much of our planet's earliest history is pre-geologic as the events cannot be directly reconstructed from rocks. Thus the birth of our planet, and the rest of the solar system, is in the realm of cosmogony, a speculative branch of astronomy dealing with theories of origin for the Universe. Although in the broad province of geology, the earth's early differentiation into core, mantle, and crust, hydrosphere and atmosphere, can only be deduced by applying chemical and physical theory to the existing architecture and conditions of the planet.

In the beginning

The Origin of the Earth   Perhaps the earth was born in a great cosmic accident, or perhaps it appeared in the normal evolution of a star called the sun. These two schools of thought date back to the beginnings of scientific speculation on the origin of the solar system. In 1749, Georges Louis Le Clerc, Compte de Buffon, suggested the first catastrophic explanation of the Genesis, wherein a comet striking the sun sent blobs of matter into space to form the earth and other planets attending the sun. About six years later, Immanuel Kant developed the first evolutionary hypothesis; that the sun and its planets formed simultaneously by the gravitational accretion of particles in a contracting cloud of cosmic gas and dust. With modification, these basic themes have prevailed to the present (Fig. 13-2).

In 1796, Pierre Simon LaPlace, apparently unaware of Kant's work, developed an evolutionary hypothesis based on a contracting cloud of hot gas, called a nebula. In his thinking, the initial, slow rotation of the cloud was accelerated as it cooled and contracted,[1] throwing off rings [2] that gradually coalesced into planets, while the larger central mass formed the luminous sun. Despite flaws in its special mechanics, the La Place Nebular Hypothesis dominated scientific thinking for a century.

About 1900, T. C. Chamberlin and F. R. Moulton of the University of Chicago, proposed a new

[1] As a figure skater can speed up his spin by drawing his arms close to his body.
[2] It's not recorded, but Saturn's rings could have influenced LaPlace's thinking.

Fig. 13-1
Granite dikes cross-cutting older, contorted Precambrian rocks in Medicine Bow Mountains, Wyoming. Photograph by the author.

hypothesis, reminiscent of Buffon's comet. A comet, we now know, has far too little mass to disturb the sun, but Chamberlin and Moulton substituted a near-collision with a passing star whose gravity pulled great tidal blobs from the sun. On cooling, gas from the arm-like[3] blobs condensed into dust, which gradually aggregated at centers that ultimately grew into planets. This hypothesis, with subsequent modifications, was in vogue until about 1950, when it fell to insurmountable mechanical objections,

[3] The arms may have been suggested by some of the spiral galaxies, which at that time were thought to be gaseous nebulae, rather than great clusters of stars.

the chief one being that incredibly hot masses pulled out of the sun would explode into space and never coagulate.

Two presently contending hypotheses were formulated in the early 1940's. Since twin stars, and stellar explosions producing novae are not uncommon, the British astronomer, Fred Hoyle, envisioned the sun as once accompanied by a nearby star that exploded, with some of its debris coalescing into the planets. About the same time, C. F. Von Weiszacker of Germany, Fred Whipple in America, and others renovated the Kant–LaPlace concept. They assumed a collapsing cosmic cloud of cold dust, wherein turbulent eddies eventually coalesced into knots, whose gravitational attraction swept in more dust, and ultimately grew into the planets. The larger central mass, heated by tremendous internal compression, became the sun. So, reinforced by new facts, deductions, and sophisticated calculations, the catastrophic and evolutionary schools survive to the present.

The evolutionary view that sun and planets formed together has intriguing implications. If it is true, planets should normally accompany stars. Thus, the possibility is good that other planets situated like the earth (not too close, and hot; or too far, and cold, from a star), could have evolved higher, perhaps intelligent, forms of life. Of the catastrophic hypotheses, Hoyle's explosion of a twin star reduces the likelihood of planets, and the possibility of life on other worlds. Chamberlin's hypothesis, considering the incredibly low odds for a chance near-encounter of stars in the vastness of space, makes other planetary systems most improbable, and life on earth a unique cosmic accident.

The embryonic earth

Evolution of the Mantle, Core, and Crust During its pre-geological history, the growing earth must have differentiated into its major architectural zones. Assuming the now-popular view that the planet developed from a cold cosmic cloud, the chemical elements must have initially been distributed evenly throughout the growing mass (Fig. 13-3). Subsequently, the kinetic energy of particles falling into the proto-planet generated considerable heat (added to by compressional heating and the decay of radioactive elements) and the earth's mass grew. As a result, the earth became molten; and as though in a blast furnace, the excess of heavy iron and nickel filtered towards the center forming the core, while the rest, combined with silicon and oxygen, produced the overlying mantle.

The basalt of the crust could represent lighter substances which separated from the molten mantle and floated to the top, like cream on milk; or if the mantle is eclogite, the basalt is a phase change in the outer zone of lower pressure. Whether the earth was ever completely molten is debatable, but in any case the blast-furnace analogy is a generally acceptable explanation for the zonation into core, mantle, and the simatic part of the crust.

About Continents The origin of the granite forming the sialic layer in the continents involves two opposing viewpoints. In the older and still stoutly defended one, granite is a still lighter material that separated from the basalt, floated to the surface and hardened. Thus, ideally, granite should form a world-wide layer on top of the basalt. Early students attributed the interrupting ocean basins to the foundering of great crustal blocks (Fig. 13-4). Aside from the difficulty of explaining how lighter sialic blocks could have subsided into the denser sima beneath, it is now known that the major ocean floors are devoid of granite, and underlain entirely by basaltic rocks.

To account for the absence of granite from the major ocean basins, Sir George Darwin, son of Charles, suggested that while the earth was still plastic, tidal forces tore out a great mass forming the moon and leaving as its scar the basalt-floored Pacific Ocean basin. Thereafter, it can be assumed that the relic patch of granite split asunder and its fragments drifted off until they froze in place forming the existing continents. Subsequent calculations, by Sir Harold Jeffreys, proved tidal forces totally inadequate to remove a mass as large as the moon; so he proposed that while the earth was molten, convection cells stirring the mantle carried granitic magma to the surface, where it concentrated in super blobs, which, later, congealed into the continental platforms.

Recently the whole idea that continental masses of sial were derived from basaltic magma, during the earth's pre-geologic history, has been attacked. Granite, the proponents of the process of granitization believe, is mainly an end product of metamorphism accompanying the continuing action of the rock cycle. To them, the absence of sial from the ocean basins, far from an enigma,

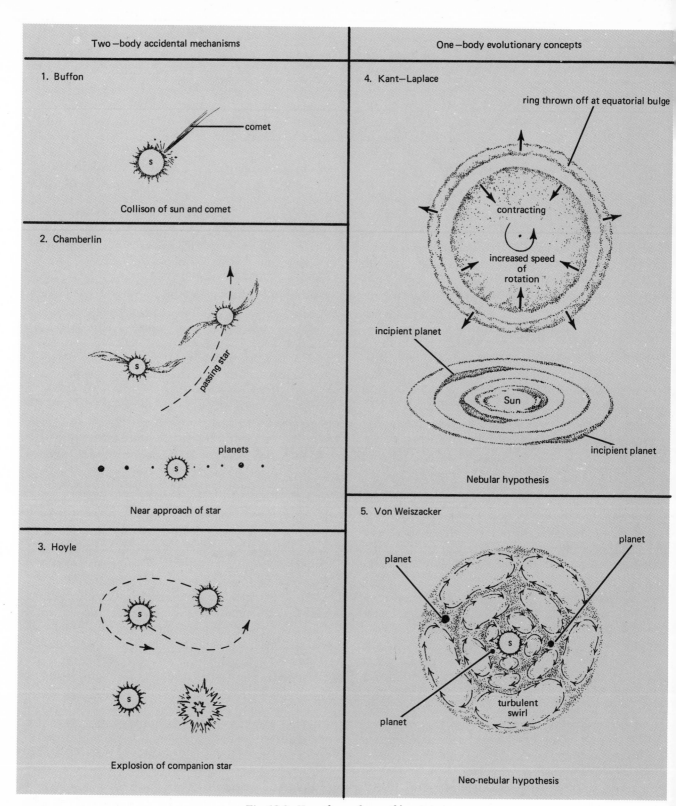

Fig. 13-2 *Hypotheses for earth's origin.*

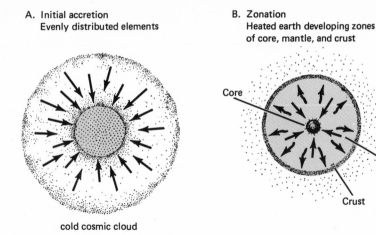

A. Initial accretion
Evenly distributed elements

B. Zonation
Heated earth developing zones
of core, mantle, and crust

Core

Mantle

Crust

cold cosmic cloud

Fig. 13-3
Hypothetical early and later stages in accretion and zonation of the embryonic earth.

is expectable. They assume the initial crust was entirely basaltic, and granite has subsequently been evolving through time, causing an expansion of the continents (Fig. 13-5).

The continents were initiated where upwarps of the original basaltic crust produced elongate fracture zones. Here, slightly less basaltic magma could have originated and erupted on the earth's surface. Thereafter, weathering and erosion would winnow certain of the original volcanic constituents and concentrate quartz and clays in the sediments carried into flanking geosynclines. Chemically, quartz and clay, in sandstones and shales, contain about the same elements in the same proportions as granite. Dur-

ing orogenic destruction of the geosyncline, metamorphism of the deeper sandstones and shales would lead to increasingly granitic material. Thus, the fusion of geosynclinal sediments into relatively rigid blocks produced the embryonic continents. The orogenic destruction of successive geosynclines forming along the margins of the rigid blocks has led to the expansion of the sialic continental platforms at the expense of the ocean bottoms.

This theory—neat as it sounds—is not above criticism. For instance, to make a proper granite by the weathering and erosion of basalt, large quantities of iron, magnesium, and aluminum would have to be permanently removed from the

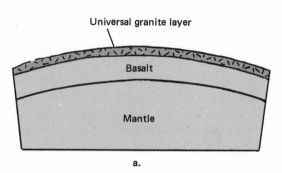

Universal granite layer

Basalt

Mantle

a.

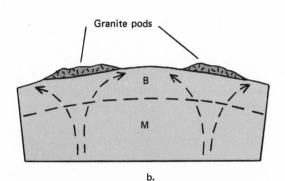

Granite pods

B

M

b.

Fig. 13-4
Hypotheses for an initial granite crust: (a) universal layer; (b) isolated pods.

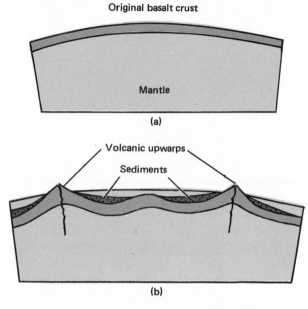

Original basalt crust

Mantle

(a)

Volcanic upwarps

Sediments

(b)

Contorted continental nucleus

Geosynclinal sediments

(c)

Fig. 13-5
Hypothesis of gradual evolution of continent through orogeny and granitization of sediments: (a) crust originally basaltic; (b) warping and volcanism with deposition in adjacent downwarps; (c) early contorted continental plate with newly formed marginal geosynclines.

system. The question is: Where have they gone? The quartz and clay of geosynclinal sediments are highly deficient in calcium, sodium, and low in potassium—all very important components of granitic rocks. Although possible answers have been made for these objections, today we can only say that primary differentiation early in the earth's history, or the growth of continents with granitization, through time, are two basic alternatives for the origin of the continental granites.

Development of the Oceans and Air According to an older view, the newly formed earth had a dense primitive atmosphere charged with water vapor. No oceans existed, initially, however, because rainfall was immediately vaporized by the planet's molten exterior and sent steaming back into the atmosphere. Eventually, when the crust solidified and cooled enough to permit water bodies to accumulate, long-continued downpours—the original "Deluge"—filled the ocean basins, setting the hydrologic cycle in operation. Today there is a new trend of thinking. The original atmosphere, if there ever was one, has been lost, and the existing atmosphere and hydrosphere are secondary features that have slowly emanated from the mantle and crust in volcanic exhalations, hot springs, and the weathering of igneous rocks. The reasoning is based on astronomical, chemical, and geologic data.

Using spectroscopes to determine the composition of the stars, astronomers have calculated the cosmic abundance of the various chemical elements. Assuming the cosmic cloud from which the earth originated was an average sample of matter in the Universe, it would have contained considerable neon, argon, krypton, and some other gases. According to calculations, there should be a million times more of these "noble" gases in the air today if the existing atmosphere had been present from the beginning. The lack of the noble gases is the key to the history of our atmosphere because if they escaped into space, so did nitrogen, carbon dioxide, methane, or whatever other free gases might have originally been present.

What caused the escape of the original gases? We cannot be sure, but they may have been lost from the contracting cosmic cloud, or, more likely, were expelled when the earth became molten. Gas molecules are in constant motion, and if their speed was accelerated by heating, the "excited" molecules could have exceeded the escape velocity and broken free of the earth's gravitational attraction.

Why were not the chemical elements, now forming gaseous molecules, lost with the primitive atmosphere? Apparently they were then locked with the heavier elements. Unlike the "noble" gases, so called because they are inert and do not enter into chemical combination, oxygen, hydrogen, nitrogen, carbon, and the other elements in the present-day oceans and air are reactive. In the cosmic cloud, they were chemically combined in iron oxides, silicates, and other minerals. As the earth became molten, they remained dissolved in the magmas, while the free gases escaped from the surface. Thus, our present atmosphere and hydrosphere have most likely seeped from the interior as volatiles, expelled from crystallizing magmas after the earth's surface had cooled and crusted over. Significantly, analyses do show that volcanic emanations could have produced the present atmosphere and hydrosphere, assuming carbon dioxide has been broken down by photosynthesis to produce the unique abundance of oxygen.

So far, our story of the earth's physical evolution is speculation. It does represent logical deduction reinforced by mathematical calculations. But the deductions are no better than their basic, and often debatable, assumptions. Turning to the history recorded in Precambrian rocks, we do have observable evidence of the geological events, although here too there are conflicting interpretations.

THE PRECAMBRIAN RECORD

Observations

Precambrian rocks, the first positive records of earth history, form the foundations of all the continents. In the large expanses where the continental platforms are blanketed by later strata, Precambrian outcrops are limited to a few deep valley bottoms, such as Grand Canyon, and to the cores of deeply eroded mountains, like the Rockies. By far the greatest accessible Precambrian exposures, comprising millions of square miles of the earth's surface, are in the shields of the stable continental interiors.

Precambrian Shields The Baltic-Russian shield is exposed across most of Norway, Sweden, and Finland. The Angaran shield forms the heart of Asia. Most of Africa south of the Sahara Desert, adjacent Arabia, and Madagascar form one of the world's greatest Precambrian expanses. The Amazon River follows a broad, gentle downwarp, filled with younger sediments, that separate the Guianean shield from the Amazonian shield, in South America. The least known shield underlies most of the eastern part of ice-covered Antarctica. The Canadian shield, of nearly three million square miles centers around Hudson's Bay, and extends into Greenland and the Arctic islands, with projections into the Adirondacks and Great Lakes region of the United States. One of the most studied shields, it illustrates some of the difficulties, as well as some tentative conclusions, in interpreting Precambrian history (Fig. 13-6).

Rocks of the Canadian Shield Vast tracts of the surface of Canada are granites and granite-gneisses. In this "sea of granite" are island-like masses, patches, and infolded pods of metamorphosed sedimentary and volcanic rocks, which are most important in deciphering the history of the Precambrian (Fig. 13-7). From their degree of metamorphism and deformation, three general types can be recognized.

A highly altered and contorted group is characteristically isoclinally folded and intruded. In central and northwestern Canada, a group called the Keewatin–Timiskaming type includes relic graywackes and lavas whose pillow structures indicate eruption underwater. In southeastern Canada, northwest of the Saint Lawrence River, equally metamorphosed marbles and quartzites that were originally well-sorted sandstones and limestones represent the Grenville type.

A second distinctive group, infolded in widely spaced belts, includes moderately deformed slates, quartzites, and marbles. Originally marine sediments, all lie unconformably on the more highly deformed sequences; they range from flat-lying to closely folded. These rocks, called the Huronian type, include the ironstone

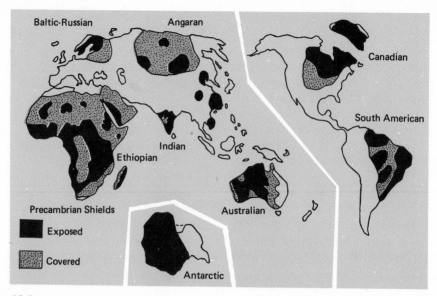

Fig. 13-6
Precambrian shield areas of the world. Dark areas have generally exposed Precambrian rocks. In the stippled areas, shields are generally covered by uncontorted and nearly flat-lying younger strata.

beds which include some of the most productive iron ores in North America. In places, coarse conglomerates are interpreted as Precambrian glacial deposits.

Least extensive is a third group of flat or gently tilted sediments and lavas, lying unconformably across the more deformed groups. The little-altered rocks, known as the Keweenawan type, resemble many Paleozoic and younger rocks in their lack of metamorphism. In the Great Lakes region, where they were first studied, lavas and dark-colored intrusive sheets are overlain by arkosic, continental redbeds.

Older interpretations

Despite the relatively simple summary, the reading of Precambrian rocks is difficult. Many have been so twisted and metamorphosed by successive orogenies that their volcanic or sedimentary origin is hard to determine. The larger part of them has been lost to erosion, not only during their long and eventful Precambrian his-

tory, which is marked by unconformities, but also in the long interval since the end of Precambrian time, during which the stable shield has been largely exposed. At best, the sedimentary and volcanic rocks are mere patches in a deeply eroded complex of gneissic and granitic mountain roots.

The Original Crust In the 1840's and 1850's, Sir William Logan pioneered the study of Canada's complicated Precambrian geology. He recognized, mapped, and named many of the important rock groups. Until 1880, however, the widespread granites and gneisses were considered the original crust, inherited from the earth's molten phase. Then, A. C. Lawson of California, working in the shield, made a significant discovery. The granite was intruded into metamorphosed sediments and volcanics. Clearly, they must be older than the granites. Moreover, the most ancient sediments must have been (in part) derived from and along with the volcanics, also lain on still older rocks, but these have been obliterated by invading granites and mountain building. Further work has nowhere disclosed an original crust; perhaps it will be found under the oceans although recent findings make this unlikely, but in the continents there seem to be no remnants exposed.

The Introduction of Time Units As mapping progressed through the last half of the nineteenth century, confusion arose in attempts to correlate Precambrian rocks, which had been mainly studied for economic reasons, in mining districts of the vast shield area. So, in the early 1900's a committee of Canadian and American geologists was appointed to straighten out the matter. They classified the Precambrian rocks into four divisions, based on the rock types in the Great Lakes region. Shortly thereafter, Chamberlin and Salisbury, in their popular *Textbook of Geology*, proposed that the four divisions represented two great geologic eras. Thus, the Precambrian received time designations, like those previously established for the later part of the geologic calendar.

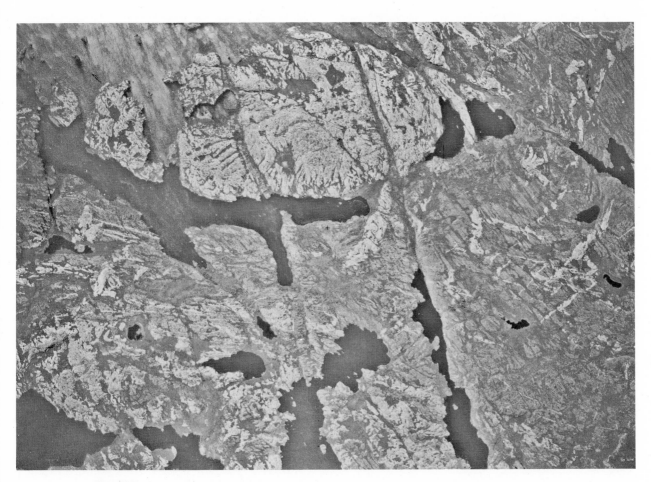

Fig. 13-7
Early Precambrian metamorphosed sediments (dark grey) intruded by granite (light grey) in large bodies, up to a half mile across, and small layer-like bodies. Late Precambrian basaltic dikes (dark grey) cut both meta-sediments and granite. Royal Canadian Air Force photo, courtesy of the Canadian Department of Mines and Technical Surveys.

The Archeozoic era, whose rocks are called Archean, was conceived as a "fiery" era in the earth's early evolution. Although the dramatic concept has slowly disappeared, the name, Archean, has persisted for the most highly metamorphosed and largely granitic rocks. The "quiet" Proterozoic era was based on the moderately and little-altered sequences, resting unconformably on the Archean rocks.

Based on the four rock divisions in the Great Lakes region, the Archeozoic era was divided into the Keewatin and Timiskamian periods; and the Proterozoic era into the Huronian and Keweenawan periods. Three major orogenies, or geologic revolutions, named from intrusive granites were proposed. The Laurentian orogeny, marked by the Laurentian granite, ended the Keewatin period and was followed by erosion, as the Timiskamian period began. The Algoman revolution, starting in late Timiskamian time, closed the Archeozoic era. The Huronian period opened with erosional levelling of the Algoman mountains, and ended with local deformation and erosion inaugurating the Keweenawan period. The end of the Precambrian was marked by the Killarney orogeny, associated with granite emplacement. Major erosion followed, producing a widespread surface of low relief upon which the invading Cambrian seas left the first abundantly fossiliferous strata, marking the beginning of the Paleozoic era.

Such a history depends on the basic assumption that the Canadian shield went through three or four major cycles, each affecting the whole of the shield area, and each, in a grand way, representing the events—with the addition of a granite invasion—that produce an unconformity. The events include: (1) the laying down of sedimentary or volcanic rocks, (2) orogeny deforming the surficial rocks, and the intrusion of granite, (3) erosional levelling of the resultant mountains followed by the onset of a new cycle. Moreover, in designating the Archeozoic and Proterozoic as eras, and the Keewatin and others as periods, these units were assumed to be worldwide time divisions.

Modern views

This relatively simple Precambrian history may well represent the relative order of events in the Great Lakes locality, but it is probably not a universal pattern for the Precambrian of all Canada, and the rest of the world, as well. In the late nineteenth century, Lord Kelvin's decree of 40 million years as the age of the earth, or even the 100 millions years assumed by many geologists, made a relatively simple series of Precambrian cycles seem reasonable. Today, however, radiometric dating of rocks indicates a minimum Precambrian time span of about three billion years. From the complicated history of deposition, eruption, mountain building, and erosion, during the 600 million years since the Paleozoic began, we should suspect an even more complex Precambrian history on Uniformitarian grounds.

The assumption of universal granite intrusion associated with orogenies across the vast expanse of the Canadian shield is not like the well-established patterns of later times. Granite emplacement accompanying the major mountain building since the Precambrian has been generally restricted to long narrow belts; so why should the Precambrian be different?

For want of fossils (or radiometric dating), early correlations were based on the lithology and degree of metamorphism of Precambrian rocks. In widely separated regions, the highly metamorphosed and intruded sequences were assumed to be time equivalents; moderately metamorphosed groups were equated in age; and so were the little-altered rocks. The pitfalls of far-flung correlation based on similar lithology are demonstrated by the work of Lawson. He correlated a granite over a 1000 miles to the west and north with the Laurentian granite in the southeastern part of the shield. Subsequently, radiometric dating gives the true Laurentian an age of 1.1 billion years and Lawson's granite an age of 2.5 billion years, making his an understandable, but magnificent, miscorrelation.

Even without radiometric dating, the dangers of lithologic time correlation are evident. Granites in Idaho that intrude Mesozoic strata are quite like some in the Precambrian. Triassic redbeds in New Jersey resemble the Keweenawan arkoses. Graywackes in California differ little from some in the Precambrian terrains, and, were it not for fossils, might be correlated lithologically. Moreover, in later and well-established systems, highly metamorphosed rocks subject to intense orogeny are known to be the same age as the very little altered rocks away from the active parts of a geosyncline. Cambrian clays in Russia, for example, are the same age as crystalline metamorphics in the British Isles. Thus in light of recent radiometric age determinations, Uniformitarian philosophy, and hindsight, our concepts of Precambrian rocks and history are changing.

Precambrian Provinces Based on recent investigations, the Canadian shield is now considered to consist of broad belts, called provinces, each distinguished by characteristic rock assemblages, and generally similar structural trends (Fig. 13-8). Adjacent provinces have different structural trends, and seem to be separated by zones of faulting. Radiometric age determinations on granites yield different ages for the various provinces. The granites, being intrusive, give minimum dates, probably representing times of orogenies that affected the somewhat older sedimentary and volcanic rocks.

In the Canadian shield, the oldest province, called the *Superior,* contains many narrow curving belts of Keewatin type volcanics and graywackes. These highly metamorphosed rocks of surface origin are surrounded by granites dated radiometrically at 2.5 to 3 billion years. South of the Superior province lies the *Grenville province,* containing vast areas of granite and granite-gneiss, originally named the Laurentian granite by Logan. These rocks have been radiometrically dated as from 1.1 to 0.8 billion years. They are intrusive into strongly metamorphosed sediments that are quite different from the Kee-

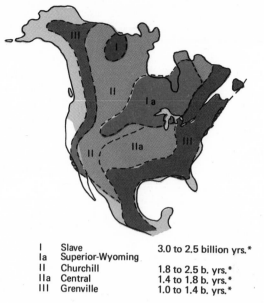

I	Slave	3.0 to 2.5 billion yrs.*
Ia	Superior-Wyoming	
II	Churchill	1.8 to 2.5 b. yrs.*
IIa	Central	1.4 to 1.8 b. yrs.*
III	Grenville	1.0 to 1.4 b. yrs.*

* for most dated samples

Fig. 13-8
Generalized scheme of Precambrian Provinces of North America (after A. E. J. Engel, 1963).

watin and Huronian types of the Superior province. The quartzites, marbles, and schists of the Grenville province must have originated as sandstones, limestones, and shales. They indicate deposition in broad marine basins where they were reworked and sorted by wave action, in contrast to the rapidly "dumped in" graywackes with their associated submarine volcanics. The *Slave province,* in the northwest part of the shield, is comparable to the Superior province although smaller in area. Between these two provinces lies the *Churchill province,* where ages range between 1.0 and 1.4 billion years, containing less lava and more rocks of sedimentary origin than the older adjacent ones. The *Great Bear province,* northwest of the Slave, is comparable to the Churchill province.

The arrangement of the Precambrian provinces has been taken as evidence for the growth of continents (Fig. 13-9). The Superior and Slave provinces could be continental nuclei, relics

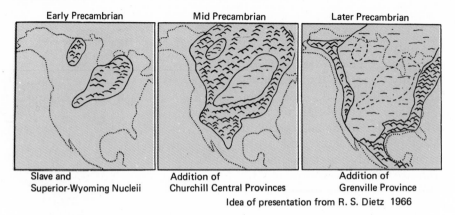

Early Precambrian | Mid Precambrian | Later Precambrian

Slave and
Superior-Wyoming Nucleii

Addition of
Churchill Central Provinces

Addition of
Grenville Province

Idea of presentation from R. S. Dietz 1966

Fig. 13-9
Hypothesis of continental accretion during Precambrian time.

of the first-formed parts. The other provinces could represent later additions produced by orogenic destruction of successive marginal geosynclines, through Precambrian time. The case for expanding continents is not proven—some geologists argue strongly against it—but preliminary work in the Precambrian of Africa, India, and Australia suggests the presence of provinces comparable to those of Canada. Also, in later time, the evolution of the Appalachian mountain system, and the Coastal Plain geosyncline, for example, seem to follow the pattern. In any case, the Precambrian shields appear to be deeply planated complexes of mountain roots, forming the stable continental platforms along whose margins occurred the greatest mountain-building activity of Paleozoic, Mesozoic, and Cenozoic time.

SUGGESTED READINGS

Dietz, R. S., "Passive Continents, Spreading Sea Floors, and Collapsing Continental Rises," in the *American Journal of Science,* Vol. 264, No. 3, pp. 177–193, 1966.

Engel, A. E. J., "Geologic Evolution of North America," in *Science,* Vol. 140, No. 3563, pp. 143–152, 1963.

Jones, H. S., *Life on Other Worlds,* New York, New American Library, 1956 (paperback).

fourteen: North America after the Precambrian

The evolution of continents since the early Cambrian can be reconstructed in some detail, for Paleozoic and later rocks are less complicated by metamorphism, less extensively eroded, and less covered than their Precambrian counterparts. Above all, Paleozoic and later rocks can be dated and correlated using fossils, so that far-flung or structurally jumbled outcrops can be fitted into regional patterns. To understand the ephemeral paleogeographies of the past half billion years, however, one should have in mind the present-day configuration of the lands and the general age and kind of rocks exposed.

INTRODUCTION

North America today

North America is rather nicely symmetrical. Its heart is the broad Precambrian shield, a deeply planated, basement complex. Surrounding the shield are the Interior Plains of younger, flat or gently dipping sedimentary beds, covering the shield's margins. The strata, although up to several thousand feet thick in places, are thin compared to the sequences exposed in the highlands beyond (Fig. 9-27).

The Appalachian mountain system, extending from Newfoundland through eastern Canada to Alabama, is broadly divisible into north-south belts. Farthest inland is the Appalachian Plateau. Its little-deformed sedimentary rocks extend eastward, into the Valley and Ridge province of relatively open folds to the north, thrust faults and tighter folds to the south. The "crystalline" Appalachians extend from the Blue Ridge Mountains and Piedmont in the south to Maritime Canada. Their rocks are strongly metamorphosed and intruded by granite as far north as New England, but become less so in Canada.

Beyond Alabama, the mountain structures veer westward, and, though largely buried by Coastal Plain sediments, do emerge in the Ouachita Mountains of Arkansas and Oklahoma, and in the Marathon Mountains of west Texas.

The Coastal Plain is the emergent part of the broad, gently sloping continental shelf, the largely drowned eastern margin of North America. Its relatively unconsolidated, gently dipping sediments form a continuous outer lowland from Mexico to New Jersey, with emergent patches on Long Island and Cape Cod. No comparable feature borders the Pacific shore, where coastal ranges reach the ocean with only a narrow continental shelf beyond.

The complex Cordilleran region west of the Interior Lowland is far broader and more diverse than the Appalachian system. The Cordillera extends from Alaska to Mexico and, ultimately, down the length of South America as the Andean chain. The Rocky Mountains, forming a western bastion to the Interior Plains, include broad anticlinal ranges with broad intervening basins from central Wyoming southward, and more complexly faulted masses with narrower valleys from northeastern Utah, through Canada into Alaska.

The Rockies are separated from the Pacific Coast mountain system by broad, often rugged, intermontane provinces including the Columbia Lava Plateau, fault block mountains and valleys of the Basin and Range country, and the Colorado Plateau of largely flat sedimentary rocks.

The Pacific mountain system includes the Sierra Nevada, a great tilted block, mostly of granite, which merges northward with the volcanic Cascades, a broad, even-crested warp topped by volcanic cones. Separated by broad valleys from the Sierra–Cascade chain are the Pacific Coast ranges, complicated mountains including rocks as young as Cenozoic. With this barest outline of the present situation in mind, let us return to the earliest Paleozoic.

Early Paleozoic symmetry

North America was also symmetrical in the early Paleozoic, but lacked the flanking Appalachian and Cordilleran mountain systems whose evolution is the major theme of Paleozoic and later history.

Platforms and Geosynclines As the Paleozoic dawned, North America was an emergent continental platform, a subdued or broadly rolling landscape, eroded across the generally contorted and crystalline rocks, recording a long and eventful Precambrian history (Fig. 14-1). The platform, which included the present-day shield, stable interior, and some areas beyond, was bordered by seas where mountain belts lie today. Towards the end of Precambrian time, both the eastern and western continental margins had begun to subside and collect sediments in elongate belts—the initial Appalachian and Cordilleran geosynclines.

Each geosyncline had an inner and outer part. Next to the continental platform, the deepening troughs accumulated sandstones, shales, and limestones—all well-washed deposits reworked by wave action in shallow water, on a stable, or slowly subsiding, sea floor. The outer part of the geosynclines, farther offshore, is characterized by graywackes and other poorly sorted clastics, as well as cherts, often thickly bedded. Significantly, these sediments are interspersed with volcanic rocks, including lavas with the pillow structure, indicating submarine eruption. The rock types in the outer belt suggest a paleogeography of volcanic archipelagos, shedding

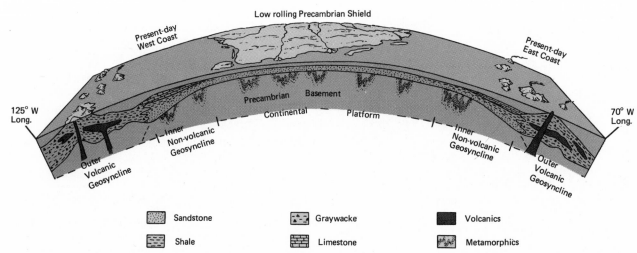

Fig. 14-1
Diagram of symmetrical North America developing through Cambrian and early Ordovician time (data mainly from Marshall Kay).

clouds of poorly sorted debris into rapidly sub-siding basins of an unstable sea floor.

An Early Paleozoic Flood   Early Cambrian seas crept along the axes of both the Appalachian and Cordilleran geosynclines. In time the seas expanded inland, leaving a transgressive se-quence of basal sandstones, overlying shales, and finally limestones indicating clear waters, with younger rocks progressively lapping over the older. Most of the sediments laid down in the advancing seas seem derived from the con-tinental interior where streams carried material out from weathered Precambrian terrains. The advance of the seas continued unbroken from Cambrian into Orodovician time leaving a con-tinuous rock sequence, so that the time change from one period to the other is determined purely from fossil evidence. Two facies of dif-fering fossil assemblages were well established by the Ordovician: a shelly facies character-ized by trilobites and brachiopods in the better sorted rocks nearer shore; and a graptolite facies in dark shales farther offshore. By mid-Ordovi-cian, shallow seas had inundated much of the continental platform, leaving only the heart of the shield exposed.

So far we have treated the continent as a whole, for until mid-Ordovician, when the flood reached its peak and then receded, North America re-tained its roughly mirror image of a central plat-form bordered by geosynclines, from which the seas advanced and merged across the continental interior. Hereafter, we shall discuss the Ap-palachian and Cordilleran regions separately, for from mid-Ordovician onward the events in each were not concurrent.

THE APPALACHIAN STORY

Cambrian and Ordovician rocks preserved in North America are almost entirely marine. Start-ing in later Ordovician, however, continental deposits appear that reflect the rise and fall of mountain systems along the eastern and southern borders of the continent.

The collapsing geosyncline

From the Ordovician to the close of the Paleo-zoic, the volcanic part of the Appalachian geo-syncline was affected by spasmodic orogenies during which its rocks were deformed and meta-morphosed, replaced, and intruded by granite. Mountainous islands arose in the geosyncline and were worn down, shedding clastic debris westward across the more-stable, non-volcanic belt, and onto the continental interior. Finally, the whole geosyncline was destroyed when its inner part was folded and faulted, near the end of the Paleozoic.

Taconic Mountain Building   Pulsations of Ta-conian orogeny commenced in mid-Ordovician, reached a peak at the end of the period, and died out by the Silurian. The orogeny was strongest in the northern Appalachian region and New England. In easternmost New York and adjacent regions, the present-day Taconic Mountains, which are eroded stumps of the Paleozoic ranges, contain black graptolitic shales of the outer vol-canic belt that some geologists believe have been thrust 40 miles westward, onto rocks of the non-volcanic geosynclinal belt.[1] Unconformities in the Hudson Valley give good evidence of the Ta-conian orogeny where folded Ordovician rocks are beveled and overlain by relatively unde-formed Silurian and Devonian strata. Farther east, in the highly deformed rocks of New Hamp-shire's White Mountains, the orogeny is indi-cated by an unconformity, as well as granites that invaded Ordovician rocks, but not Silurian.

Doubtless, the Taconian ranges were majestic mountains, perhaps comparable to the modern Rockies or Alps, for they shed tremendous vol-umes of sediments westward into a new trough, subsiding where the older non-volcanic geosyn-cline had lain. The clastic flood from the rising Taconian ranges is called the *Queenston Delta*, although strictly speaking it was a compound of many deltas, flood plains, and alluvial fans. Their continental sediments grade into marine de-

---

[1] The extent of the thrusts is debated, but they do seem prom-inent in the north while dying out to the south.

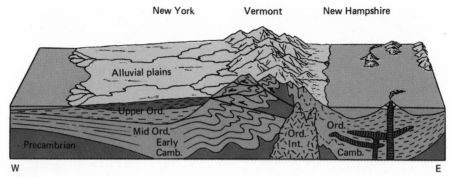

New York   Vermont   New Hampshire

Fig. 14-2
*Diagram of the late Ordovician Taconian Mountains (center) and Queenston Delta (west)
(based on Marshall Kay and other sources).*

posits that extended far westward on the sea floor (Fig. 14-2).

Near the rising highlands, continental sandstones and redbeds predominate, with darker shales beyond representing muds swirled westward and deposited in shallow seas; extensive limestones accumulated on the clear waters of the stable platform. These facies record a retreating sea wherein continental and near-shore deposits expanded ever-farther westward during the accelerating orogeny of later Ordovician time. The spread of the continental sediments fluctuated as seas occasionally advanced slightly eastward, depositing marine shales on redbeds, before renewed deltaic expansion drove the shore westward again. When the Taconian orogeny reached its climax, at the end of Ordovician time, terrestrial redbeds extended to the present-day location of Niagara Falls, almost onto the stable continental interior.

Return of the Seas The Taconian ranges were levelled during Silurian time, while the seas spread back towards the east (Fig. 14-3). That the mountains were still high at the beginning of the period is shown by the lower Silurian deposits which grade from conglomerates on the east, into widespread sandstones thinning westward, and being replaced by shales on the stable continental platform. But by mid-Silurian the mountains were much reduced, and sluggish

west-flowing streams deposited fine-grained redbeds and shales. With time, the region of deltaic clastic deposition contracted, until, by the end of the period, marine limestone was being laid down as far east as the present-day Hudson Valley region. Together, the Ordovician and Silurian clastics form a great horizontal wedge recording the rise and decline of the Taconian Mountains.

In New England and Maritime Canada, geosynclinal remnants persisted through the Silurian. These locally subsiding basins trapped sediments and volcanics over two miles thick, which lie unconformably on the edges of rocks contorted in the Taconian orogeny.

The Acadian Orogeny The northern part of the Appalachian geosyncline, as far east as the beveled Taconian ranges, remained a quiet area of widespread limestone deposition from the late Silurian until early Devonian time. Then, the Acadian orogeny began, which affected much of the region already deformed in the Taconian. Thus, the already contorted and intruded Ordovician strata, as well as previously unaffected Silurian and Devonian layers, were deformed and invaded by granitic masses to produce such complicated crystalline rocks as are now exposed in the White Mountains of New Hampshire. By the end of Devonian time, the volcanic belt of the Appalachian geosyncline had been destroyed

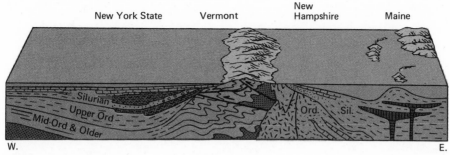

Fig. 14-3
Diagram of the eastern United States in late Silurian time when seas encroached on the eroded Taconian Mountains (based on Kay and other sources).

in the northeastern United States, and eastern Canada. Thereafter, its crumpled rocks formed a solid addition to the continental platform.

The rising Acadian mountains shed a second clastic flood towards the continental interior, during middle and late Devonian time (Fig. 14-4). This clastic wedge, called the *Catskill Delta,* buried the early Paleozoic geosyncline and more recently deposited Silurian and Devonian rocks. As in the preceding Queenston Delta, conglomeratic and sandy redbeds, of continental origin, grade into marine sands and shales in the shallow sea west of the mountains. Strata of the Catskill Delta also coarsen upward, reflecting the spread of debris as the sea was driven westward.

Carboniferous Aftermath Erosion levelled the Acadian ranges of New England and eastern

Canada during the Mississippian. Then, in a typical aftermath of orogeny, the region was epeirogenically uplifted with block faulting. Terrestrial sandstones, conglomerates, and shales derived from the new highlands were laid down in local basins along with some interspersed volcanics. Shallow Pennsylvanian seas encroached the northern part of the area, and left some limestone and evaporites before withdrawing. In eastern Massachusetts and Rhode Island, some terrestrial deposits have the look of glacial tills, and others were coal swamp deposits.[2]

The western Appalachian region, during Carboniferous time, remained a subsiding belt collecting debris eroded from highlands to the east.

[2] Whether these conglomerates are tills is now in doubt; the coals have since been metamorphosed to graphite, suitable for pencil lead but not for burning.

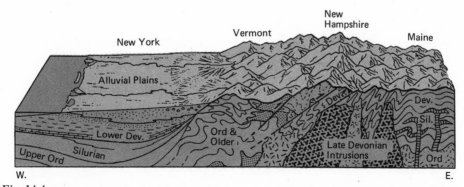

Fig. 14-4
Diagram of conditions at end of the Devonian time. Acadian Ranges on the east and the Catskill Delta on the west (data from G. H. Chadwick, M. P. Billings, and others).

Fig. 14-5
Present-day view of crystalline Appalachians in the Great Smoky Mountains. Courtesy of the Department of Conservation and Development, Raleigh, North Carolina.

In Pennsylvania and Virginia where they are still preserved, lower Mississippian comglomeratic rocks grade into extensive sandstones towards the west. The upper Mississippian rocks are largely deltaic redbeds of sandstone and shale. Although some in Virginia are coal-bearing, the overlying Pennsylvanian strata have the principal coal deposits of the Appalachian region. The coals, formed in forested swamps, are interbedded with terrestrial clastics swept from uplands to the east. Half a mile thick in Pennsylvania, the coal measures become much thicker southward into Alabama, indicating deeper subsidence of the western trough with the creation of a clastic wedge. It, like the older clastic floods to the north, is suggestive of another orogeny, a Pennsylvanian spasm in the Piedmont–Blue Ridge region.

The Appalachian Revolution The western Appalachian region remained undeformed until near the end of the Paleozoic. Beds of the early Paleozoic non-volcanic geosyncline and the overlying clastic deltas are essentially parallel, with no angular unconformities. The end of geosynclinal conditions in the Appalachians came in the Appalachian Revolution, a final spasm of orogeny that created the folded ranges of the sedimentary Appalachians in the Permian. During this orogeny, the crystalline Appalachians were again invaded by granite and parts were thrust westward, overriding and contorting hitherto undeformed strata into open folds in Pennsylvania, and tighter folds and thrust sheets southward into Alabama. (Figs. 14-5, 14-6).

We have dwelt largely on the classic story of

328

Fig. 14-6
Z-shaped folds formed in the Appalachian orogeny as seen today. Photo by John S. Shelton.

the Appalachians. Their extension in the Ouachita belt, from Alabama to west Texas, had a generally comparable Paleozoic history. Originating in the Ordovician, the Ouachita geosyncline was a relatively quiet site of subsidence and deposition until Mississippian time. Thereafter, the destruction of this geosyncline, though telescoped in time, followed the Appalachian pattern. In the early Carboniferous, pulses of orogeny began in the outer, volcanic belt where great thicknesses of graywacke and shale accumulated, while floods of clastic debris were shed northward towards the continental interior. In Pennsylvanian time, the volcanic part of the geosyncline, which had been largely consolidated, was rammed northward, contorting clastic wedges and older non-volcanic geosynclinal rocks of a longer-lasting, inner depositional belt. Orogeny had ended by the Permian.

Thus at the end of the Paleozoic era, North America had lost its earlier symmetry, for the Cordilleran geosyncline still remained in the west, while mountains rimmed the continent from Texas through Alabama and northward to Canada (Fig. 14-7).

Later Appalachian history

When the mobile geosynclines in the Appalachian region were finally destroyed, their rocks became a relatively rigid extension to the continental platform. But if folding, thrusting, and regional metamorphism had ended, the area was still restive.

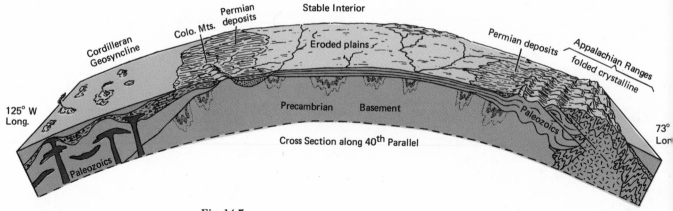

Fig. 14-7
Asymmetrical North America at the end of Paleozoic time.

Mesozoic Aftermath The Appalachian ranges were steadily eroded during the early Mesozoic. Debris from the uplands was apparently swept from the region, which lacked major structural basins to trap sediments, and deposited in the continental interior and the depths of the Atlantic. As the Triassic progressed, erosion reduced the Appalachians to the low rolling surface of a peneplain (Fig. 14-8).

Late in the Triassic, the subdued erosion surface was broadly upwarped with associated large-scale normal faulting and volcanism, an episode known as the *Palisades disturbance* (Fig. 14-9). Rising blocks shed sediments into a series of grabens, following the earlier mountain trends. The fault valleys are prominent today, along the

Bay of Fundy region in Nova Scotia, the Connecticut Valley, and other Triassic lowlands from New Jersey to North Carolina. Drilling through Coastal Plain sediments has revealed buried Triassic grabens as far south as Florida, and in the Gulf Coast region of Texas. The infaulted Triassic rocks include arkosic conglomerates, sandstones, and shales that are largely redbeds in the northern valleys, and dark gray with occasional coal beds in the southern ones. These terrestrial sediments, nearly four miles thick in places, represent coarse alluvial fans near valley walls, with finer sediments of flood plains and lake bottoms beyond. Basaltic volcanism, accompanying the normal faulting, produced lava flows and shallow intrusive sills

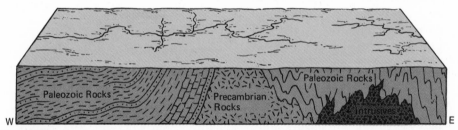

Fig. 14-8
Later history of the Appalachians (based on D. W. Johnson, 1931). Triassic erosion surface beveling Appalachians.

Rejuvenated Appalachians

Triassic
Fault Valley

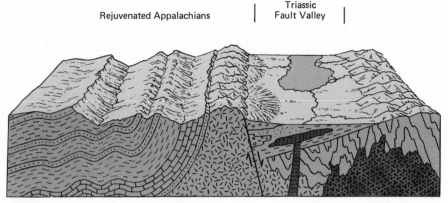

Fig. 14-9
Diagram of late Triassic uplift (Palisades orogeny) with associated block faulting and volcanism (after D. W. Johnson).

that are interbedded with the sediments. A striking example is the 1000-foot thick Palisades still across the present-day Hudson River from New York City.

Following the Triassic epeirogenic rejuvenation of the Appalachian belt, the region stabilized and was eroded during the Jurassic. By early Cretaceous time, a relatively featureless surface called the Fall Zone peneplain was beveled across the Paleozoic mountain roots and the downfaulted Triassic blocks (Fig. 14-10).

Cenozoic Finale The Fall Zone peneplain was epeirogenically arched and eroded, except where it was protected by flanking sediments of the Coastal Plain to the east. Thus, in the early

Cenozoic, another broad erosion surface, called the Schooley peneplain, which is well preserved in New Jersey, was carved across the uplift during an interval of relative stability (Fig. 14-11). This surface forms extensive plateau-like uplands on crystalline rocks from New England to the Blue Ridge, and is responsible for the even crests of the folded Appalachians. The Schooley surface was, in turn, broadly uplifted. Rejuvenated streams incised it until an interval of mid-Cenozoic stability resulted in still another subdued erosion surface (Fig. 14-12). It is developed on less-resistant rocks in the Appalachians, and is called the Harrisburg peneplain from its prominence around the capital of Pennsylvania.

Initial coastal plain

Low rolling erosion surface

- - Fall zone surface

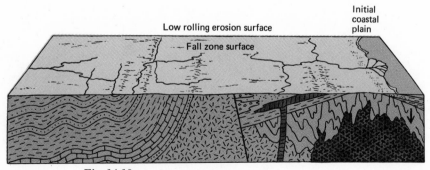

Fig. 14-10
Early Cretaceous erosion surface. Fall zone peneplain.

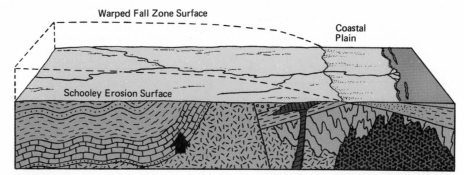

Fig. 14-11
Early Tertiary arching and erosion producing the Schooley erosion surface (after D. W. Johnson).

The Harrisburg surface was also uplifted and eroded, producing another still less-extensive surface on the weakest rocks in the region. Called the Somerville surface, from Somerville, New Jersey, it is now being incised by present-day streams (Fig. 14-13). Thus Appalachian evolution after the orogenic phases of intense folding, which destroyed the Paleozoic geosyncline,

Fig. 14-12
View of early Cenozoic erosion surface, now uplifted and dissected in northwestern Massachusetts. Courtesy of the U.S. Forest Service by L. J. Prater. Photo taken from Whitcomb Summit on the Mohawk Trail.

Fig. 14-13
Dissection of the Schooley surface and cutting of lower surfaces to produce present-day topography. (1) Fall zone surface, (2) Schooley surface, (3) Harrisburg surface, (4) Somerville surface (after D. W. Johnson).

has involved a series of broad epeirogenic uplifts with interspersed periods of erosion and stability—a history recorded in the Triassic grabens and cyclic erosion surfaces.

The Coastal Plain

While the Appalachian saga trailed off into an aftermath of gentle upwarpings and erosion, a new geosyncline was evolving as the Coastal Plain. It first appeared when the subdued mid-Mesozoic surface, beveling the Appalachian and Ouachita belts, began to subside along the continental margins. Thereafter, ever-thickening sediments collecting in the down-warps built a great terrace whose emerged surface is the Coastal Plain.

Along the Gulf Coast—where subsurface relations are well known from intensive drilling and geophysical prospecting for oil—the basement has subsided to produce a trough filled with sediments, as much as 10 miles thick beneath the present shoreline (Fig. 14-14). Geophysical evidence also indicates a basement trough beneath the Atlantic seaboard, where sediments are two or three miles thick. Despite the depth to the basement, none of the sediments in the troughs indicates especially deep water. Older continental clastics and shallow-water deposits (penetrated by deep oil wells) now lie buried thousands of feet below sea level. Thus, this modern geosyncline, like its non-volcanic counterparts in the ancient Appalachian and Cordilleran regions, has subsided slowly as its sedimentary wedges thickened.

Paleogeography At any given time in its history, the Coastal Plain surface had broadly similar geographic belts, as recorded in its sedimentary facies. Flood plains, swampy lowlands, and marshes lay inland behind deltas and beaches along the shore. Offshore, beach and bottom sands merge into muds of progressively deepening waters. Sands, silts, and clays deposited in these environments were carried from the continental interior by existing streams and their predecessors, chief among them being the Mississippi. In clear waters, well away from turbid river mouths, limey muds, shell banks, and chalks were deposited.

The deposits reflect events in the headwaters of streams draining to the Coastal Plain. In the eastern Gulf Coast, for example, Mesozoic rocks are largely sands and other clastics, indicating strong erosion of the Appalachians; whereas Cenozoic rocks are dominantly limestones. In the western part of the Gulf Coast, in Texas, limestones are the most abundant Mesozoic rocks, and the overlying deposits are largely sandstones and shales, reflecting the active rise and erosion of the Rocky Mountains during Cenozoic time. Coastal Plain sediments also reflect fluctuating shorelines, as the sea flooded and ebbed across the continental margins during Mesozoic and Cenozoic time.

Fig. 14-14
Surface of the Gulf coastal plain, east of Sabine Pass, Louisiana. Old beach ridges form stripes parallel to the shore. Photo by John S. Shelton.

Shifting Seas The oldest Coastal Plain strata are subsurface Jurassic rocks known only from drilling along the Texas–Louisiana coast. These red beds and salt deposits lie unconformably over the eroded surface of the Ouachita orogenic belt. The thick salt beds are thought to have precipitated from highly concentrated saline waters, periodically renewed by flooding into enclosed basins along a desert coast. The salt has a special interest, for it eventually punched upward through great thicknesses of younger sediments to form *salt domes,* great subterranean columns thousands of feet in vertical extent. The salt domes, aside from providing a commercial source of salt and associated sulfur, have created some very productive oil-bearing structures.

Late in the Jurassic, seas from the Caribbean flooded over the red bed sequence in the first of some eight advances, each complicated by lesser fluctuations. The Jurassic sea spread as far north as Arkansas before retreating. In early Cretaceous time, the seas returned, spreading as far inland as Kansas and southeastern Colorado. Their withdrawal left a marked erosion surface preserved in an unconformity with late Cretaceous rocks. The late Cretaceous transgression was one of the greatest floodings of North America. It spread Coastal Plain sediments far across the continental margins, and created a great north-south embayment across the stable interior as well.

After the Cretaceous deluge ebbed, the Paleocene–Eocene flooding was the most extensive. Middle and later Cenozoic transgressions of the Coastal Plain each fell short of its predecessor. But while the extent of the marine transgressions declined, the sites of thickest deposition shifted southward, building the continental shelf progressively outward into the Gulf of Mexico.

Summary We have concentrated mostly on the Gulf Coast region. The Atlantic Coastal Plain differs mainly in having a thinner sedimentary wedge, no salt deposits, no known strata older than early Cretaceous, and—influenced by the warpings of the Appalachian axis to the east—strata that extend less far inland and contain more terrestrial clastics. Overall, however, the Atlantic and Gulf Coastal Plains and their underwater extensions, the continental shelves, are a modern geosyncline. But unlike its Appalachian and Cordilleran predecessors, the Coastal Plain geosyncline lacks an outer belt of volcanic islands and deeply subsiding basins where graywackes, lavas, and pyroclastics are accumulating. This may merely mean that there are geosynclines and geosynclines.

Although still quietly subsiding, the Coastal Plain region might soon—geologically speaking—become an active orogenic belt, for crustal subsidence beneath the Gulf Coast sediments now approaches 50,000 feet, the depth of downwarping in the Appalachian and Cordilleran troughs when they began to crumple into mountains. So, if continents do indeed expand through time, orogeny may eventually consolidate and weld the Coastal Plain sediments onto the North America's continental plate.

CORDILLERAN EVOLUTION

To present the highlights of Cordilleran evolution, we must now go back, in space and time. Towards the end of the Paleozoic, North America as a whole had lost its earlier symmetry. The Appalachian and Ouachita geosynclines had been crumpled into mountain belts east and south of the stable interior, while in the west the Cordilleran geosyncline persisted. Then, starting in Mesozoic time, it too collapsed during orogenic storms in whose wake the varied provinces of the Cordilleran highlands emerged. This, then, will be the main thread of the following story.

The prelude

The Colorado Mountains A preliminary episode of mountain making in the western United States—perhaps linked to orogeny in the Ouachita geosyncline—had centered in Colorado, mainly in Pennsylvanian time. However, unlike the Appalachian–Ouachita and subsequent Cordilleran mountains, which involved more typical crumpling of thick geosynclinal depos-

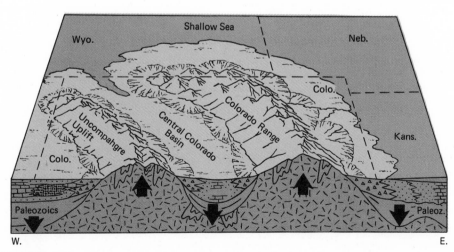

Fig. 14-15
The Colorado Mountains, later destroyed by erosion, originated in a late Paleozoic orogeny in the general area where, much later, the southern Rocky Mountains would develop.

its, the late Paleozoic Colorado Mountains arose on the Continental Platform where Paleozoic rocks were thin or absent. Thus, Precambrian basement was soon exposed in these linear uplifts which shed aprons of terrestrial debris into intervening and adjacent downwarps (Fig. 14-15). The resulting sediments—represented by the Fountain Formation in the Red Rocks west of Denver—formed arkose, a sandstone rich in feldspar as well as quartz fragments, indicating rapid erosion of a rugged granitic terrain and rapid deposition, so that the feldspars were not weathered to clay.

These late Paleozoic mountains have sometimes been called the "Ancestral Rockies," which is a bit misleading because the present-day Southern Rockies, although in the same region, are much later features. After the main uplift in Pennsylvanian time, levelling of the Colorado Mountains is indicated by fine-grained red beds that progressively buried the uplifts and flanking arkoses. Thereafter, Mesozoic seas left thick marine deposits over the site of the Paleozoic ranges, before the existing Rockies emerged during the final orogenic phase in the destruction of the Cordilleran geosyncline.

The Cordilleran Geosyncline Until mid-Mesozoic time, the Cordilleran geosyncline remained, as it had been in the Cambrian and Ordovician, a generally subsiding trough with two contrasting north–south belts. Well-washed sandstones, shales, and limestones were deposited in shallow seas of the eastern belt. Graywackes and other clastics, interspersed with basaltic flows, accumulated in the restless western belt. Here, in what is now the Pacific border region, basins subsided deeply among rising volcanic archipelagos. Across the whole geosyncline, the axes of deepest subsidence and deposition shifted, in place and time. Seas periodically flooding onto the neighboring continental platform and then receding, left a relatively thin sedimentary veneer—measured, at most, in a few thousands of feet.

Yet if the geosyncline seemed tranquil, there were premonitions of things to come. Late in the Devonian a northeast trending arch, called by some the Manhattan geanticline, rose from the eastern margin of the volcanic geosynclinal belt (Fig. 14-16). The arch, which extended as far north as central Nevada, periodically emerged as an island chain during orogeny, and while quiescent was eroded to a platform beneath shallow seas. Its history is recorded in unconformities and coarse clastics, shed eastward into waters of the adjacent non-volcanic belt. West of the Manhattan arch, graywackes and volcanics continued to accumulate, except for early Triassic time when the region was probably emergent.

In the non-volcanic part of the geosyncline next to the continental platform, marine sandstones, limestones, and shales were deposited in a stable region of shallow seas, until late Triassic time, when continental red beds and sandstones spread westward from the continental platform over the marine deposits.

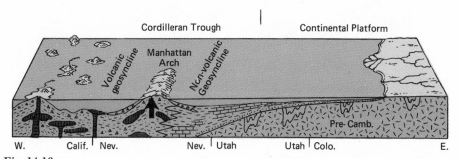

Fig. 14-16
Reconstruction of the Manhattan arch emerging in late Devonian time from the Cordilleran geosyncline.

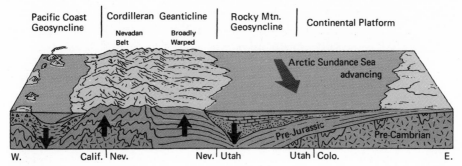

Fig. 14-17
Late Jurassic orogeny divided the earlier Cordilleran geosyncline into two separate troughs.

Expanding orogeny

Cordilleran geography began to change markedly in early Jurassic or, possibly, late Triassic time. Initially, broad warping sent a long, low peninsula northward, from lands in southern Arizona and New Mexico, through Nevada and Idaho, well into British Columbia, far beyond the northern limit of its Paleozoic predecessor, the Manhattan arch. Except for northern Canada, the Cordilleran geosyncline was split in two. Thereafter the structural evolution of the western United States involved: a western trough, called the *Pacific Coast geosyncline;* an eastern downwarp, the *Rocky Mountain geosyncline;* and the intervening barrier of land and mountains, the *Cordilleran geanticline.* We will return to the complicated story of the Pacific Coast geosyncline after discussing the evolution of the Cordillera to its east.

The word geanticline originally meant a broad upward flexure of the earth's crust wrinkled by minor subsidiary folds — a complimentary feature to a geosyncline. At certain times and places the Cordilleran geanticline may have been such, but at others it was intensely folded and faulted. It is now generally considered a complex deformational belt whose broad warps and contorted mountains were notable sources of sediments during active uplift.

Although differing in details, the fate of the Cordilleran geosyncline broadly mirrors the Appalachian pattern. Starting well offshore, the great sedimentary trough collapsed during a protracted spell of mountain-building pulses that progressively enlarged the geanticlinal region as they gradually migrated to the continental platform. Earlier western spasms in the volcanic belt are collectively called the *Nevadan orogeny.* It merges into the *Laramide orogeny,* the later deformational phase that eventually crumpled the eastern non-volcanic part of the geosyncline. In contrast to the Nevadan episode, Laramide orogeny is distinguished by its somewhat later date and general lack of metamorphism and granite intrusions.

Nevadan and Early Laramide Convulsions In the late Jurassic, Nevadan mountain building began in the geanticlinal area through western Nevada and adjacent California. Jurassic and older rocks in the volcanic part of the Cordilleran geosyncline were intensely folded, faulted, and metamorphosed (Fig. 14-17). Today such rocks are exposed in the Klamath and Sierra Nevada Ranges.[3]

Although called Nevadan, this orogeny was no local affair. From Alaska to Mexico, and as far east as Idaho, the older Cordilleran geosyncline crumpled into mountain ranges, invaded at depth by extensive granite batholiths. Nor was the Nevadan orogeny a simultaneous spasm of

[3] The great tilted fault block of the Sierras is a much later development, but the rocks within it are deformed by the late Mesozoic orogeny.

short duration. From late Jurassic until about the middle of Cretaceous time, shifting sites of deformation migrated generally eastward through Nevada to central Utah, and across Idaho into western Montana. Later phases affecting non-volcanic geosynclinal rocks represent the beginnings of Laramide deformation. Overall, the geanticlinal complex was growing at the expense of the Rocky Mountain geosyncline.

The Rocky Mountain Geosyncline In early and middle Jurassic time, when North America was largely emergent, a narrow Arctic sea crept southward through Canada east of the geanticlinal belt. By the beginning of late Jurassic time, while the Nevadan orogeny was active to the west, waters of this *Sundance Sea* advanced far southward into the subsiding Rocky Mountain geosyncline and widely flooded the western margins of the continental platform. Sandstones, shales, and limestones of the Sundance Sea are 10,000 feet thick in Utah where the geosyncline subsided deeply, but thin towards their shoreline margin on the continental platform.

Later in the Jurassic, the sea withdrew. The geosyncline and adjacent platform emerged as a vast swampy lowland—traversed by streams heading in the active geanticlinal belt to the west, and in highlands rising across Arizona and New Mexico in the south. The sands, silts, and clays deposited across the lowland comprise the *Morrison Formation*—a world-renowned burial ground for Jurassic reptiles including the great brontosaurs, and a host rock for major uranium deposits, as well.

Conditions of latest Jurassic continued into the earliest Cretaceous, but then seas reinvaded the Rocky Mountain geosyncline, depositing especially thick sediments in deeply subsiding pockets marginal to the continental platform, in Utah and western Wyoming. These early Cretaceous seas eventually withdrew, northward into the Arctic, and southward towards the Gulf Coast.

During the late Cretaceous, the seas returned in the greatest inundation of North America since the Ordovician deluge (Fig. 14-18). They flooded the Rocky Mountain geosyncline and spread broadly across the stable interior, dividing North America into a broad low island in the east where parts of the Canadian Shield and eroded Appalachians remained above water, and the mountainous geanticlinal belt to the west. While mountains rose in the expanding geanticlinal belt, the Rocky Mountain geosyncline warped downward, notably along the margin of the continental platform, and on the platform itself in south-central Wyoming. Late Cre-

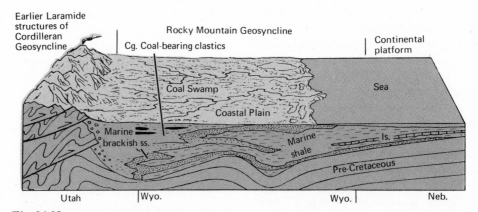

Fig. 14-18
Diagram of late Cretaceous conditions with the subsiding Rocky Mountain geosyncline bound on the west by early Laramide mountains.

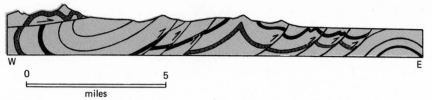

Fig. 14-19
West-to-east cross-section a few miles south of Frank, Alberta, showing multiple thrust faulting and folding, typical of Rocky Mountains, developing from deeper parts of geosyncline (generalized from B. R. MacKay, Canadian Geological Survey, 1932).

taceous sediments, deposited in the unevenly subsiding basins, have a rather constant facies pattern at any given time.

Along the foot of the mountains rising to the west lay coarse bouldery fans that grade into fine-grained sands, silts, and clays of a swampy forested lowland. Farther east, the continental clastics are replaced by marine deposits: beach and near-shore sands of the transitional zone, which, in turn, grade into muds of the sea floor. At times, limestone accumulated in clear waters towards the low-lying interior of the continent.

These facies reflect accelerating western orogeny with time, for as sediments collected in the subsiding Rocky Mountain geosyncline, the fluctuating shore retreated eastward, so that continental deposits progressively overlap marine beds towards the continental interior. As the Mesozoic era drew to a close, the final collapse of the Rocky Mountain geosyncline was imminent, for to the west continuing orogeny had largely converted the site of the Paleozoic Cordilleran geosyncline into an uplifted mountainous belt.

The Laramide Culmination Geosynclinal deposition ended east of the Pacific Border region, towards the end of Cretaceous time, when the Rocky Mountains arose in the climactic phases of the Laramide orogeny. In general, Laramide deformation has two differing styles. Where many thousands of feet of non-volcanic sediments had filled the Cordilleran trough, rocks were intricately folded and broken into multiple slabs by low-angle thrust faults. Such struc-

tures are now exposed in an almost unbroken mountainous terrain extending southward through the Canadian Rockies, Montana, westernmost Wyoming, and adjacent parts of eastern Idaho and Utah (Fig. 14-19). These complicated mountain structures make up the greatest part of the Laramide belt of deformation, and are rather typical of folded mountain belts in general.

East and south where the continental platform was deformed, broad flat-topped anticlines rose between broad synclinal downwarps. These ranges—rather unique as mountain structures—extend from southern Montana through central and eastern Wyoming into Colorado, and as far south as Santa Fe, New Mexico. Let us focus on the history of these ranges in Wyoming, as a sample.

The broad folds first appeared as islands, emerging from the late Cretaceous seas some 70 million years ago. They divided the earlier wide area of Cretaceous deposition in the Rocky Mountain geosyncline into local basins receiving sediments eroded from the rising folds. Close to the upwarps, coarse clastics and unconformities marked the spasmodic rise, but in the centers of the basins deposition was continuous. Thus, no all-embracing unconformity separates Mesozoic and Cenozoic rocks, and the time change from one era to another can be determined only from fossils.

As the eastern ranges grew, they were eroded. Thus, the youngest Cretaceous rocks of the Rocky Mountain geosyncline were the first to be stripped from the anticlinal crests, and were redeposited in the newly formed local basins

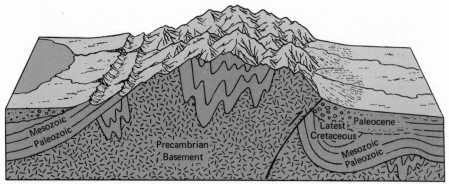

Fig. 14-20
Diagram of the type of early Cenozoic (Paleocene) mountain that emerged in the eastern part of the Rockies from Montana southward through Wyoming and Colorado (after diagrams by S. H. Knight).

to form the latest Cretaceous clastics. Thereafter, older Mesozoics and Paleozoics were successively exposed in the uplifts until, finally, abundant granitic and metamorphic fragments of earliest Cenozoic age show that the ranges had been breached to their Precambrian cores. As a rule then, the oldest rock fragments made up the youngest conglomerates (Fig. 14-20).

The last vestiges of the seas disappeared from the Rocky Mountain region sometime in the earliest Cenozoic. Marine deposition was wholly replaced by alluvial fans, flood plains, coal swamps, and (in western Wyoming and northern Colorado) some exceedingly large fresh-water lakes. Though the mountains, then, were probably as rugged as the present-day Rockies, the region as a whole lay near sea level, for early Cenozoic plant and animal fossils document a wet sub-tropical climate like that of the Gulf Coast region today. The present-day dry Rocky Mountain climate reflects the later evolution of the Cordillera.

Orogenic aftermath

North America regained its symmetry during the Nevadan–Laramide orogeny, which destroyed the earlier western geosynclines. The continental platform had expanded by consolidation of the formerly mobile geosynclinal belts, but the present-day Cordilleran provinces did not emerge until well into Cenozoic time. Then, in the orogenic aftermath when seas were gone, epeirogenic deformation involving broad upwarping with high-angle faulting and volcanism produced the Rocky Mountains, Colorado Plateau, Columbia Plateau, and the Basin and Range. With this introduction to later evolution of the Cordillera, let us continue the eastern Rocky Mountain story, and then discuss the other regions.

The Rocky Mountains Laramide folding and thrust faulting died out towards the end of the Eocene. By then the Rockies had a rather modern look. Existing mountain ranges were established, and local relief—from valley floors to mountain peaks—was impressive. But the region remained close to sea level and had a humid climate. The final shaping of the region during an epeirogenic phase of uplift was yet to come.

Through Oligocene time especially, great clouds of ash from prolonged eruptions to the west drifted into the Rocky Mountains and Great Plains. The exact sources of the ash are not everywhere known, but Cenozoic volcanism occurred at various places in the Rockies—a notable example being in the Yellowstone Park region, of northwestern Wyoming and adjacent states (Fig. 14-21). Although its eruptions seem finished, the Yellowstone is still hot below the

Fig. 14-21
Water-laid volcanic conglomerates and tuffs of Oligocene age in Absaroka plateau, southwest of Yellowstone Park. Photo by Herb Pownall, courtesy of J. D. Love.

surface as indicated by its renowned geysers and other hot-water phenomena. From Eocene until Recent geologic time, however, active eruptions in the Yellowstone region built great lava plateaus, and could well have provided enormous amounts of windblown ash during the Oligocene. Whatever its source, the ash clogged streams, causing them to aggrade and raise the levels of basin floors while back-filling mountain valleys.

The Rocky Mountains and Great Plains region began to rise gradually sometime in the mid-Cenozoic. Unlike the preceding Laramide deformation, involving the sharp folding and thrust faulting characteristic of orogeny, the mid-to-late Cenozoic uplift was epeirogenic—a gentle regional arching accompanied, in the Rockies, by some normal faulting. In places, cobbles and boulders incorporated in a matrix of reworked ash show that the highlands of the Rockies had been washed clean and were being eroded.

Towards the close of the Tertiary period, the Rocky Mountain region as a whole had risen well above sea level, and the rugged local relief of earlier times was gone (Fig. 14-22). Only scattered hills rose above a subdued and rolling

341

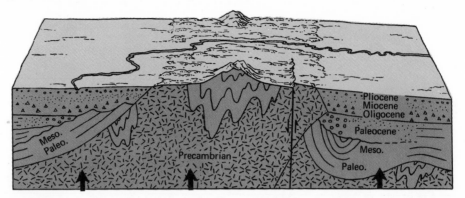

Fig. 14-22
Diagram of late Tertiary (Pliocene) conditions in central and southeastern Wyoming with surface of low relief reflecting filling of intermontane basins and reduction of mountains (after S. H. Knight).

Fig. 14-23
Air view of the Granite Mountain region in central Wyoming bears similarity to the late Tertiary landscape in the region. Courtesy of Paige Jenkins and J. D. Love.

Fig. 14-24
Hogback ridges and Rocky Mountain front in the Pikes Peak region of Colorado, as seen from the lowland excavated east of the mountains in Quaternary time. An 1866 lithograph from the Library of Congress Collection.

landscape, partly cut across resistant rocks in Laramide folds, and partly built up on thick basin fills. The surface across the Rockies merged with the Great Plains, a vast eastern apron of volcanic ash and debris eroded from the mountains (Fig. 14-23).

At the beginning of Quaternary time, or perhaps a bit before, the long Tertiary episode of basin-filling ended. Streams were rejuvenated; possibly because the cooler, wetter Pleistocene climates swelled stream volumes. In any event,

streams scoured out the broad basins, re-exposing the once-buried mountain fronts, and leaving the late Tertiary surface preserved on resistant rocks as a plateau-like upland with scattered higher peaks (Fig. 14-24).

Normally, streams head near divides and flow outward to adjacent lowlands, but many streams in the Rockies are unique in crossing major mountains by way of deep canyons. Notable examples are the Flaming Gorge, cut by the Green River through the Uinta uplift; the canyon of the Wind River through the Owl Creek Mountains; and the Royal Gorge of the Arkansas in the Colorado Front Range (Fig. 14-25). Such special cases represent *superposed* streams whose transverse courses reflect the later Cenozoic history of the region. Streams on the subdued late Tertiary surface wandered through sediment-filled divides on buried Laramide structures. Then, during the Quaternary excavation of the basins, the streams were "let down" across the exhumed folds and maintained their earlier courses by carving the transverse canyons.

Thus, the Rocky Mountains of today are essentially Laramide structures exhumed from a Tertiary burial — but with additions. The normal faults reflect the last broad uplift of the region.

High-level erosion surfaces and superposed streams are inherited from the great interval of cut-and-fill (Fig. 14-26).

The Colorado Plateau The Colorado Plateau has long been a conservative block of the continental platform. Never a geosynclinal region after the Precambrian, its sedimentary veneer is relatively thin — measured in a few thousands of feet.

Through the Paleozoic era, the region was washed by shallow seas migrating from the Cordilleran trough to the west, periodically emergent and eroded, and at times mantled by terrestrial redbeds. In the Mesozoic era, redbeds and dune sands of Triassic and Jurassic deserts were succeeded by somber-colored Cretaceous

Fig. 14-25
*Canyon cut by superposition of the Wind River across the Owl Creek Mountains of Wyoming.
Photo by Paige Jenkins.*

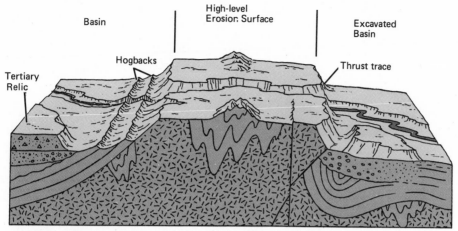

Fig. 14-26
Diagram of eastern and southern Rocky Mountain structure today showing excavated basins, relic erosion surface on mountain core and superposed stream (after S. H. Knight).

sandstones and shales, signalling the rise and erosion of mountains in the surrounding Cordillera.

During the time of the Laramide orogeny, the Plateau developed long, flat-topped uplifts, which are separated by locally sharp, monoclinal flexings from broad intervening basins (Fig. 14-28). In structure as well as age, these great upwarps resemble the broad-backed anticlines in the Southern Rockies. However, the deformation and uplift in the Plateau having been less intense, subsequent erosion has not exposed Precambrian basement (except in the deep inner gorge of Grand Canyon).

Prolonged denudation after the monoclinal flexing stripped weaker Mesozoic rocks from the uplifts. The debris, mingled with that from the Rockies rising to the north and east, was laid down as terrestrial basin deposits, unconformably overlapping the warped margins of the uplifts. As in the Rockies, fossil plants and animals indicate a low humid region until mid-Cenozoic time; then, an arid climate developed as the region was epeirogenically uplifted.

High-angle faulting broke the Plateau during its final rise. In places, volcanic fields erupted onto the surface. A notable example is near Flagstaff, Arizona, where great eroded strato-volcanos of the San Francisco Peaks are surrounded by a swarm of smaller cinder cones, ash beds, and extensive lava flows. Streams, rejuvenated in the general uplift, excavated basin deposits and cut many deep canyons, including

John Wesley Powell (1834–1902) A one-armed Union veteran, Powell was a leading figure in the heroic period of American geology after the Civil War. His two boat trips down the Colorado River and field work in Utah and Arizona contributed greatly to geologic knowledge of the region and geologic processes in general.

345

Fig. 14-27
*Monoclinal flexure in Pennsylvanian rocks of the Colorado Plateau near Mexican Hat, Utah.
Photo by Tad Nichols.*

the Grand Canyon of the Colorado across the Kaibab monocline. Jagged canyons, great retreating escarpments, relic buttes, and mesas all carved from colorful strata, as well as stocks and laccoliths, volcanos, and lava flows of dark rock, today make the generally desolate Colorado Plateau a geologic showplace (Fig. 14-27).

The Basin and Range Province Meanwhile, back where it all began, the protracted storm of Nevadan–Laramide orogeny had subsided. West of the Rockies and Colorado Plateau, a generally mountainous region of crumpled geosynclinal rock was being eroded (Fig. 14-29). Relic patches of latest Mesozoic and earliest Cenozoic depos-

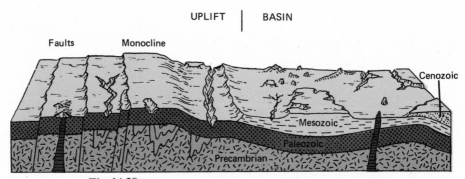

Fig. 14-28
Diagram of Colorado Plateau features (after Powell, 1876).

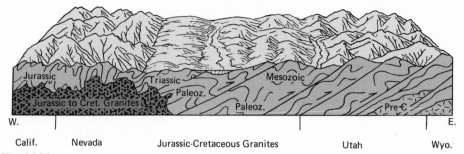

Fig. 14-29
Diagram of late Mesozoic mountainous region of the Nevadan and Laramide deformation where the Basin and Range Province was later developed.

its are largely scattered valley fills, indicating that most of the mountain debris was flushed from the region by streams flowing to the sea.

During the early Cenozoic, the mountains were generally worn low. A subdued upland surface was beveled across the deformed and intruded Nevadan rocks to the west (Fig. 14-30). Tuffs, lavas, and agglomerates erupted upon this surface in Miocene time. To the east, flood plain, swamp, and lake deposits accumulated near the actively rising Rockies of early Cenozoic time.

In late Cenozoic time, mid-Miocene or perhaps earlier, normal faulting began blocking out the characteristic Basin and Range structures. Although the Miocene horsts are now levelled by erosion, their terrestrial debris of thick bouldery fans, overlain by clays and silts with salt and gypsum, resemble deposits in modern grabens. Active block faulting of the region has shifted from place to place, with time, so

that the present-day mountains show varying stages of erosion, ranging from fresh fault blocks to low relic hills (Fig. 14-31). Grabens between the horsts form broad basins, largely filled with coarse clastics shed from the mountains. Where the uplifted blocks have long been stable, the basin margins are broad pediment surfaces eroded at the expense of the mountains (Fig. 14-32).

The Columbia Plateau Tremendous lava floods erupted in the Cordillera north of the Basin and Range from the Miocene onward. Flow after flow of fluid basalt emerging from narrow fissures inundated all but the highest peaks of a rugged topography having up to 2500 feet of relief, and cut across granite and metamorphics of the Nevadan orogeny. The Blue Mountains of northeastern Oregon are Nevadan islands, partly upwarped, standing above the volcanics, as do

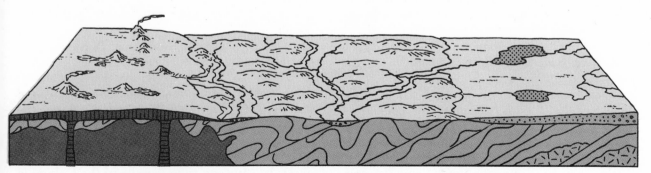

Fig. 14-30
Reduced topography during early Cenozoic time in Basin and Range Province.

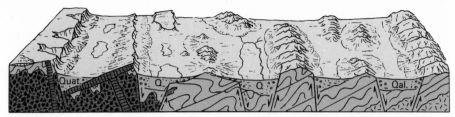

Fig. 14-31
Diagram of late Cenozoic block-faulting producing the present Basin and Range topography.

the Steptoe Buttes, much smaller masses of granite marginal to the Northern Rockies in eastern Washington.

Clay, sand, and gravel beds are sandwiched with the lavas. Between spasmodic eruptions, streams flowing across the surface were dammed by lava tongues to create lakes that persisted, until buried by renewed lava outpourings.

Although largely flat-lying, the Plateau's strata were warped after most of the lavas had erupted. Parts of the region broadly subsided, perhaps from loss of mass erupted from the depths, or perhaps under the load piled on the crust. However, other parts rose, forming broad flexures towards the east and sharper anticlines near the Cascade Ranges, along the western margin of the Plateau province.

Youthful streams, in places cascading over retreating Niagara-type falls, have cut many spectacular canyons whose walls expose the Plateau's structure. By far the deepest is Hell's Canyon, a 6000-foot chasm cut by the Snake River through somber volcanics and deep into the underlying granite. As in the Rockies, stream valleys sometimes cut across uplifted structures. However, such streams in the Columbia Plateau are probably *antecedent*. That is, they were established before the plateau surface was warped and have maintained their courses by cutting canyons across the actively rising folds.

Today erosion prevails in the Columbia Plateau, and the igneous episode seems at an end—although the "Craters of the Moon," a line of prehistoric cinder cones with associated lava flows on the youthful Snake River Plateau of Idaho, seem fresh enough to have erupted yesterday.

West Coast evolution

Let us go back to the region west of the Cordilleran geanticline.

The Pacific Coast Geosyncline While late Jurassic and subsequent events were shaping the inner Cordillera, a restive volcanic geosyncline subsided unevenly along the Pacific border. Thus, eastern and western North America were comparable, from Jurassic onward, in having new marginal downwarps, but contrasted in that the Pacific Coast geosyncline was a less-stable volcanic belt.

From late Jurassic through early Cenozoic time, clastic sediments shed from the Nevadan ranges, along with cherts and submarine volcanics, built strata tens of miles thick on the subsiding floor of the Pacific Coast geosyncline. The region can be imagined as a coastal plain, building from Nevadan highlands into a broad seaway that merged with the Pacific Ocean beyond. The seaway remained a site of shifting volcanic archipelagos and rapidly subsiding basins whose sediments and volcanics, with interspersed unconformities, attest an unstable geosyncline.

Later evolution of the Pacific Border is most easily treated as northern and southern parts.

The Pacific Mountain System (Oregon and Northward) During early Cenozoic time, the subsiding geosyncline collected thousands of feet of rock, including deltaic deposits to the east, and marine clastics and volcanics to the west. In Miocene time, basalts of the Columbia Plateau spread westward, interfingering with

Fig. 14-32
*Basin and Range structure with sand dunes in foreground near Last Chance Range, Nevada.
Photo by John H. Maxson.*

sediments in the future site of the Coast Ranges.
The modern ranges emerged in the late Cenozoic. A late Miocene phase of deformation folded
the geosynclinal rocks into anticlines, trending northward through Oregon, and northwest to
west in northern Oregon and Washington. These
folds were then eroded to a low rolling surface
during the Pliocene.

The existing north-south grain of the region
appeared in late Pliocene or early Pleistocene
time. The earlier erosion surface was broadly
arched to form the Cascades and Coast Ranges,
with an intervening downwarp, the Puget Lowland. The Cascade erosion surface attained its
present elevation by the early Pleistocene.

Upon this surface, andesitic eruptions built
such towering strato volcanos as Mounts Baker,
Rainier, St. Helen, and Hood; as well as Mount
Mazama whose decapitation formed the scenic
caldera of Crater Lake (Figs. 14-33, 14-34). In
the Klamaths the Nevadan basement was broadly
upwarped in late Cenozoic time, fencing off the
northern downwarp from the interior valley in
California.

The Pacific Mountain System (California)
Broad-gauged reconstructions of the paleogeography and geologic evolution of California are—
to say the least—controversial. We start where
the story seems straightforward.

Fig. 14-33
*Mount Rainier, a dissected Cascade volcano with extensive active glaciers. Courtesy of the U.S.
National Park Service.*

The Sierra Nevada region has shed sediments into the subsiding Pacific Coast geosyncline since the Nevadan orogeny. The Nevadan orogeny was followed by a late Cretaceous mountain-building episode in the Sierras, when much of the Jurassic granite was digested by renewed intrusions into the mountain roots. During early Cenozoic time, the once lofty ranges were eroded to a low rolling upland exposing metamorphic pods and granitic masses formed, at depth, in the preceding orogenys.

In the later Cenozoic, the Sierra region was spasmodically upwarped, so that streams carved several generations of cyclic valleys into the earlier upland surface. However, the Sierras were not yet impressively high because floras

and faunas in the valley deposits indicate a relatively low-level environment. The Climactic uplift began in the Pliocene and continued through the Quaternary. In this phase the Sierras have risen as a great west-tilted fault block, now reaching 14,497 feet in the pinnacle of Mount Whitney (Fig. 14-35).

West of the Sierras, in the Great Valley region, a floor of Nevadan basement subsided unevenly during Cenozoic time. Local basins trapped deep-water sediments, notably during the Miocene and Pliocene. Late Tertiary sediments, which reflect shallower water, with time give way to Quaternary terrestrial deposits, in places 9000 feet thick. Instability of the region during deposition is shown by abundant uncon-

Fig. 14-34
Crater Lake showing Wizard Island, a cinder cone, with caldera rim in background. U.S. Forest Service photo by L. J. Prater.

formities, culminating in a mid-Pleistocene episode of folding, after which near-horizontal deposits lapped across the eroded edges of upturned strata. The evolution of the Great Valley is closely related to the adjacent Coast Ranges.

The problems of interpreting California's geologic history come to a head in the Coast Ranges. Unlike their counterparts in Oregon and Washington, which are made up largely of Cenozoic rocks, the California Coast Ranges expose considerable metamorphic and intrusive igneous rock. This basement includes two distinct assemblages. One is a crystalline group of highly metamorphosed schists, quartzites, gneisses,

and marbles intruded by granite bodies. Lithologically, the metamorphics resemble rocks in southern California, rather than those to the east across the Great Valley in the Sierras. From potassium–argon dating, granites near San Francisco are late Cretaceous—indicating an orogeny contemporaneous with the one producing much of the Sierran granite.

The other prominent basement group consists of moderately metamorphosed, although strong, deformed graywackes, shales, and cherts, along with interbedded basaltic flows—all of which are characteristic of the volcanic part of a geosyncline. Although largely unfossiliferous, hence

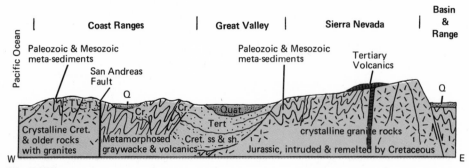

Fig. 14-35

Diagrammatic cross-section through California south of San Francisco Bay (based on Reed and Hollister, 1936; Hoots, Bear, and Kleinpell, 1954; Taliaferro, 1951; and Jenkins' California Geological Map, 1937).

difficult to date, this rock assemblage apparently includes Paleozoic and Mesozoic strata; so some at least are older than the crystalline basement group. Yet, younger granites nowhere intrude the graywacke-basalt group. Where adjacent, the two groups are separated by faults.

Sedimentary strata associated with the basement rocks may change markedly in thickness and facies in a few miles. The rocks in neighboring fault blocks may be markedly different indicating seemingly unrelated histories of uplift and subsidence, erosion and deposition. Structurally, the Coast Ranges are a jumble. Complex folds, normal and reverse faults abound. Most impressive is the strike-slip fault system dominated by the San Andreas Rift. This major crustal fracture slices 500 miles southeastward, from Tomales Bay north of San Francisco, through the Coast Ranges, and thence into the Gulf of California.

Until quite recently, most geologists assumed that the Coast Ranges evolved where they are today, and their deformation involved largely vertical movements. To some workers, the crystalline basement group represented the roots of pre-Jurassic land masses, extending into California as islands, or peninsulas, from the Pacific. Independent geosynclines between the land masses received sediments both from the western lands and the Sierra region to the east.

By another interpretation, the geosynclinal group of volcanics and graywackes was de-

posited on subsiding basement of the crystalline group in a continuous sea, west of the Nevadan orogenic belt. The local uplifts and basins, in this theory, did not originate until the late Cretaceous orogeny. Thereafter the volcanic geo-

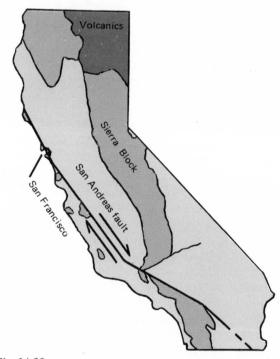

Fig. 14-36

Movement on San Andreas fault which carried splinters of Sierra block northward (based on Curtis, Evernden, and Lipson, 1958).

Fig. 14-37
Branch of San Andreas fault (looking northwest) near Indio, California. The low hills (lower left) are structurally different from the main hills (right of fault) and came from the south by horizontal fault movement.

synclinal rocks were stripped from the uplifts, exposing the crystalline basement group. In light of later evidence, all such interpretations have two flaws. The relative ages of the two basement groups are wrong, and the San Andreas and kindred faults are assumed late developments of relatively unimportant horizontal displacement.

Recent thinking emphasizes extensive slippage along the strike-slip faults. Some California geologists now suggest that during the late Cretaceous orogeny, the crystalline basement group actually originated in the southern part of the Nevadan belt, now extending through the Sierras. Then, 80 million years ago (still in the late Cretaceous), movement began on the San Andreas Rift, and basement rocks south of the present Sierra block gradually slid some 300 miles to the vicinity of San Francisco (Figs. 14-36, 14-37).[4]

Thus, the Coast Range crystalline rocks are splintered mountain roots jammed far north-

[4] If movement continues, Los Angeles may eventually come abreast of San Francisco.

westward into volcanic geosynclinal deposits. The suggestion—staggering at first thought—actually simplifies Californian paleogeography, for by it the late Mesozoic orogenies would have been restricted to a single north–south belt of the present Sierra axis which was then bordered by a single continuous geosyncline on the west.

Not all geologists believe in such a great horizontal displacement, but if the known rate of shift on the San Andreas fault in historic time, averaging 20 feet per century, is projected back 80 million years, a 300-mile displacement is quite possible. Most geologists would accept horizontal movement of at least 30 miles, since Miocene time, for the problem of the markedly different Tertiary rocks in now-adjacent fault blocks can be neatly solved by mentally sliding blocks back. The similar rock types and ancient shore lines (which make especially nice reference lines) can be matched across the strike-slip faults. As you might suspect, progressively older deposits do require increased amounts of "backsliding" for a match.

The complicated Cenozoic geology of coastal California seems to reflect the rising and subsiding, warping and breaking of blocks jostled by continuing movement along one of the world's great transcurrent fault zones. Cenozoic deformation had two peaks: one in the late Miocene when the present pattern of the Coast Ranges was established; the other at the end of Tertiary time when shifting seas drained into the Pacific leaving California emergent. Today the region, shaken by periodic earthquakes and marked by continued shifting of the ground, remains as it has been since the late Mesozoic—a restless orogenic belt where the North American continent is still actively evolving. Indeed, the Tertiary pattern, before California became emergent, may be still continuing in the islands, basins, and shallow banks of the sea floor off southern California today.

SUGGESTED READING

Clark, T. H., and Stearn, C. W., *The Geologic Evolution of North America*, New York, The Ronald Press, 1960.

King, P. B., *The Evolution of North America*, Princeton, N.J., Princeton University Press, 1959.

fifteen: The Pleistocene finale

While the basic continental structure has been several billion years in the making, the face of the land, as we know it today, was largely etched out in Quaternary time by weathering and mass wasting, streams, waves, wind, and the trademark of the Pleistocene, glacial ice.

The ice

During the Pleistocene, valley glaciers born in the highlands of Labrador grew into piedmont glaciers that expanded into continental ice sheets, overwhelming Canada and the United States north of the Ohio and Missouri Rivers (Fig. 15-1).

Continental Glaciers Movements of the ice that disappeared 10,000 years ago are reconstructed from the same sort of evidence that originally led to the concept of the Ice Age: striated bedrock, cobbles, and boulders trailed out from distinctive outcrops, great looping moraines, roche moutonée, drumlins, and other landforms. Careful mapping of the moraines has shown that the continental glaciers advanced along pre-existing lowlands as a series of broad lobes that eventually coalesced over most of the upper Mississippi valley (Fig. 15-2).

After Agassiz established the Ice Age concept, the next big advance in unraveling the Pleistocene was the discovery of multiple glaciation. The spread of the ice, it was discovered, was no single episode but, rather, four separate expansions separated by warm intervals of glacial retreat. The glacial maxima are called Nebras-kan, Kansan, Illinoian, and Wisconsin[1] from relic drifts in these type localities.

The surfaces of the much-eroded pre-Wisconsin glacial deposits lack morainic topography, and have well-integrated drainage systems. The latest stage, the Wisconsin, is the best known because its deposits are least weathered and eroded and form youthful moraines. Moreover the moraines and drift indicate that the Wisconsin stage was no single waxing and waning of the ice either, but included as many as seven alternations of cold and warm spells. Although the evidence is gone, the earlier glacial stages were doubtless just as complicated.

The interglacial intervals, recorded by deeply weathered zones on tills, are called Aftonian, Yarmouth, and Sangamon from type localities in the upper Mississippi Valley. Time since the last ice retreated is called post-Pleistocene or Recent by some geologists, although others consider it still part of the Pleistocene. Weathered zones on the pre-Wisconsin drifts reach depths of 10 feet and form compact clayey *B* soil horizons, called gumbotills. The long time required to produce gumbotills, along with incorporated pollen, peat, and other plant remains, as well as animal fossils, indicates that the interglacial intervals were both longer and, at times, much warmer than the time span since the Wisconsin. The lack of such deeply weathered zones on Wisconsin deposits seems to mean — in the long-range view — that the Recent could well be but the beginning of a new interglacial interval, and the ice might advance again.

[1] "Never Kick Indian Women" may help you remember them.

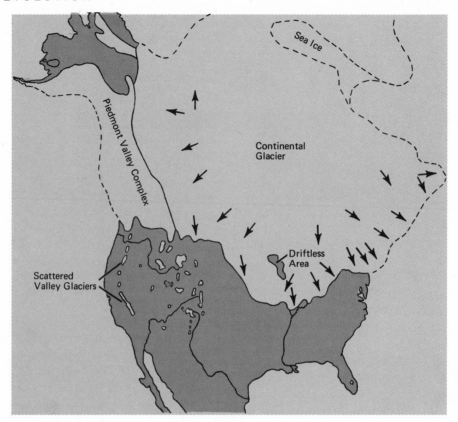

Fig. 15-1
Extent and types of glaciers in North America during maximum Pleistocene expansions of glacial ice (from Glacial Map of North America of the Geological Society of America, 1945).

Yet extensive as the great ice sheets were, not all of the higher latitudes were overwhelmed, for glaciers require adequate snowfall as well as intense cold. Thus, parts of Alaska and vast tracts of Siberia, regions of low precipitation, remained tundras—unglaciated, treeless arctic wastes where intense cold produced deep zones of permanently frozen ground. The Driftless Area of Wisconsin, an island of some 10,000 square miles surrounded by glaciers, also remained ice-free throughout most of the Pleistocene—but for a different reason. Ice lobes were channeled around this area.

Cordilleran Glaciation Alaska lacked a continental ice sheet, being occupied instead by ex-tensive piedmont glaciers, fed by a multitude of valley glaciers issuing from mountains and uplands, culminating in the great backbone of the Alaska Range (Fig. 15-3).

Most of the Cordillera through Canada and southward had more numerous and extensive valley glaciers by far than now exist. They were responsible for the cirques, horns, and U-shaped troughs creating a spectacularly rugged topography as far south as New Mexico in the Rockies, and the San Francisco Peaks in the Colorado Plateau of central Arizona. Some high mountains in the Basin and Range country of Nevada were glaciated. Valley glaciers in the Sierras carved out, among others, the spectacular trough of the Yosemite. The Olympic Range in the northern coastal region of Washington was strongly molded by ice, while the Cascades, which still bear hundreds of glaciers, provided ice for piedmont glaciers that merged in a thick sheet, filling the Puget Lowland.

Presumably the Cordilleran glaciers waxed and waned with the great continental ice caps, but correlation with Nebraskan, Kansan, and Illinoian stages of the interior lowland is difficult, because Wisconsin valley glaciers and strong erosion in the mountain regions have removed all but a few patches of earlier till. Continental and mountain sequences do interfinger from the Canadian–United States border northward, but they only show the relations of Wisconsin aged deposits.

Beyond the ice

Although glaciation was its most striking aspect, the imprint of Pleistocene climatic changes extends far beyond the glaciated regions.

Lakes The Pleistocene spawned myriad lakes, some still existent, and others now disappeared but recorded in lacustrine deposits, abandoned shorelines, and outlets (Fig. 15-4). Much of Canada, as well as Maine and Minnesota, are "lands of a thousand lakes" because uneven glacial scouring and deposition of hummocky moraines left many closed depressions.

Of the large lakes formed along the glacial margins, the Great Lakes remain as North America's largest existing freshwater bodies. Their basins were carved from pre-glacial stream val-

Fig. 15-2
Moraine topography in northeastern South Dakota. Photo by John S. Shelton.

Fig. 15-3
Alaska's Mount McKinley, highest mountain in North America at 20,269 feet, still carries relics of formerly more extensive Cordilleran glaciers. Courtesy of the Alaska Railroad.

leys by the continental ice sheets, and the lakes appeared as the Wisconsin ice front withdrew. The history of the Great Lakes makes a very complicated story of expansions and contractions, read from lake deposits, abandoned shorelines, and outlets. In essence, however, these lakes originally drained to the Mississippi through now-abandoned channels.[2] Lower escape routes emerged as the ice receded northward, first through the Mohawk and Hudson Valleys, then, as today, through the Saint Lawrence River (Figs. 15-5, 15-6, 15-7).

[2] Such as the former outlet now followed by Chicago's sewage canal.

The abandoned shores of the Great Lakes have been uplifted, indicating a rising domal uplift where the thickest ice once lay. Apparently the tremendous load of the Pleistocene glaciers depressed the earth's crust, while their wastage has allowed its gradual rebound. In a similar, and, perhaps, better documented case, involving recovery from the north European ice cap, tide gauge records coupled with fossil evidence on warped shorelines indicate a rebound, reaching a maximum of about three feet per century in the Baltic region, associated with a broad dome rising across Scandinavia.

Lake Agassiz, most widespread of North America's former Pleistocene lakes but never particu-

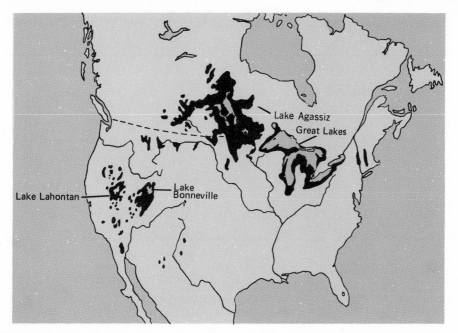

Fig. 15-4
Extent of Pleistocene North American lakes, now greatly reduced or gone (from the Geological Society of America Glacial Map, 1945).

larly deep, covered the flats of Manitoba and the Dakotas. Its shrunken relics include Lakes Winnipeg and Manitoba in Canada. Lake Agassiz also spilled into the Mississippi while the continental glacier dammed its northern margin, then drained off northward through a lower outlet into Hudson's Bay when the ice retreated.

The grabens of the Basin and Range country provided closed depressions that contained many Pleistocene lakes. Lake Bonneville in Utah, whose super-saline remnant is the Great Salt Lake, and Lake Lahontan, whose relics include Nevada's Pyramid Lake, were the largest. Such lakes, far removed from the continental glaciers, reflect either lower evaporation of cooler climates or increased precipitation accompanying glacial maxima. Lake Bonneville's complex history of deeper and shallower stages is recorded in lake deposits and abandoned shorelines reaching a thousand feet above the existing Great Salt Lake. Similar features indicate a comparable history for Lake Lahontan and other smaller lakes.

Streams That the Ohio and Missouri Rivers mark the approximate southern limit of continental glaciation is not coincidence. When the ice buried trunk streams of major drainage systems, north-flowing tributaries ponded along the glacial fronts. Eventually the marginal lakes overflowed to each other, cutting the channels of the Ohio and Missouri Rivers, which remained

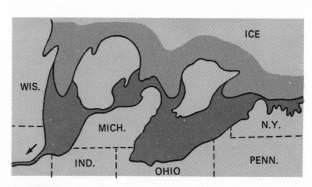

Fig. 15-5
Earlier episode in Great Lakes history when ice forced drainage into the Mississippi River.

361

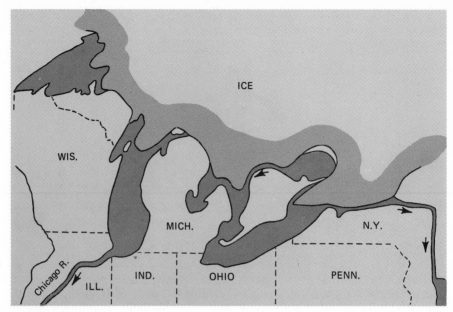

Fig. 15-6
Later episode when ice retreat expanded lakes and opened a new outlet through the Hudson Valley of New York.

the major tributaries of the Mississippi after the ice withdrew. Abandoned and drift-filled preglacial valleys clearly show that many present-day streams flowed to trunk streams north of the Ohio and Missouri. In New York, Pennsylvania, and Ohio, tributaries once drained to major streams that emptied into the sea either through the Saint Lawrence Valley, or westward through the former Teays River into the Mississippi. Likewise, many tributaries of the Missouri once flowed farther north to a pre-glacial trunk stream.

Stream regimens were upset during the Pleistocene causing the alternate back-filling and down-cutting responsible for extensive alluvial terraces. In the upper Mississippi Valley, and marginal to Cordilleran valley glaciers, streams beyond advancing glacial fronts were overloaded with debris, thereby aggrading their valleys with alluvium. Wasting glaciers, in turn, swelled streams with meltwater causing partial excavation of the fills. In the lower Mississippi Valley, however, geologists believe, instead, that

down-cutting accompanied glacial maxima. They reason that channel gradients steepened when sea level fell, thus giving streams greater cutting power, so they deepened their valleys. During the interglacial intervals of rising sea level, streams deposited in slack waters of drowning valleys to cause back-filling. Whatever the mechanism—perhaps each is correct in the regions for which it was proposed—thick alluvium and terraces are notable Pleistocene products.

Wind The work of wind has been especially prominent in the Quaternary. Loess deposits, wind-laid dust sometimes reworked in water, are widely distributed throughout the Mississippi Valley, for beyond the glacial margins, meltwater streams left broad flood plains of sand and silt. Clouds of dust, winnowed from these barren windswept flats, were carried away to settle in thickening deposits reaching several hundreds of feet deep in places.

Sand dunes were more widespread than today in various climatic phases of the Pleistocene.

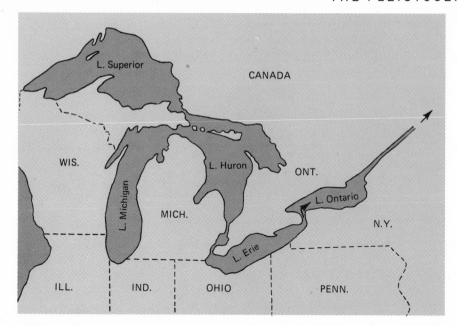

Fig. 15-7
Present Great Lakes with ice gone and drainage northeastward through the St. Lawrence River.

For example, the Sand Hills region of western Nebraska, some 24,000 square miles of now-stabilized grass-covered dunes, was a sea of shifting sand earlier in the Quaternary.

Deflation hollows were actively eroded during warm, dry interglacial times when the western plains and Cordillera were even more a desert than they are now. The blowouts range from the seven-mile-long Big Hollow of the Laramie Plains in southeastern Wyoming to many smaller depressions, some now occupied by permanent or ephemeral ponds.

Shorelines The earth's coastal regions are scarred by the world-wide fluctuations of Pleistocene sea levels. The oceans fell and rose, as water of the hydrologic cycle was alternately locked on land in glacial ice, then released during melting to swell the oceans.

Wave-cut terraces standing high and dry along many of the world's coasts bear marine fossils indicating warm interglacial oceans. So, it might seem that the maximum heights of Quaternary sea levels could be easily determined. Unfor-tunately, many uplifted shore lines—especially around the Pacific—have been warped and tilted by crustal movements after they were cut. Even in non-orogenic regions, the Gulf Coast, for example, inland terraces may warp down and disappear beneath later sediments, on approaching the shore. Some workers maintain that most coastal margins have been tectonically upwarped during the Quaternary, hence, sea level may well be near its maximum now. Yet, because the interglacial times were undoubtedly warmer than today, water released by the shrunken Greenland and Antarctic ice masses should have raised the ocean surface appreciably. The most likely estimate, from evidence in stable crustal regions, places sea level as at least 90 feet higher during past interglacial times.

At the glacial maxima, former sea floors were bared and streams drained to shores farther out on the continental margins. Thus, submerged stream valleys, drowned wave-cut terraces, and terrestrial deposits dredged from beneath the sea, have been used to estimate the low stages of Pleistocene sea levels. A eustatic fall of 500 feet, more or less, seems likely for the Illinoian stage, and 400 feet for the less-extensive Wisconsin glaciation.

Whether over or not, the Ice Age makes an appropriate finale to the geologic evolution of North America.

SUGGESTED READINGS

Dyson, James L., *The World of Ice*, New York, Alfred A. Knopf, 1962.

Flint, R. F., *Glacial Geology and The Pleistocene Epoch*, 2nd Edition, New York, John Wiley & Sons, 1957.

sixteen: Geology, present and future prospects

APPLIED GEOLOGY

The high standard of living in modern industrial society depends on good agricultural land, a variety of mineral resources, and trained people to efficiently exploit them. As a pure science, geology's goal is constructing and improving general concepts of the earth. In the applied science, these concepts are put to practical uses for the benefit of mankind, as in the development of mineral resources. Today at least three-quarters of all geologists work on such economic matters.

Industrial raw materials

Fuels The Industrial Revolution was built on coal. This burnable rock is largely the remains of woody plants that accumulated in swamps whose toxic waters of low oxygen content inhibited bacterial action and thus prevented decay, or rotting. After the swamp deposits were buried under later sediments, pressure and, in some cases, heat increased the ratio of elemental, or free, carbon by driving off water and volatile substances. The density and hardness of the coal also increased. Coals range from little-altered lignites whose woody character is apparent, through bituminous coals, to anthracite (hard coal) of glassy luster and the highest carbon content. World reserves of coal are tremendous—seven trillion tons by some estimates —so that generally only the thickest, most accessible, and best grades are being extensively

worked. The use of coal has steadily decreased in recent years, as oil and natural gas are more convenient to use and to handle. The coal industry employs few geologists, because it is highly automated and exploits long-established deposits.

With the tremendous and ever increasing consumption of oil—for heating, for gasoline, diesel, and jet engines, and for such industrial products as plastics and dyes—it is not surprising that over 40% of all geologists in the United States are in the petroleum industry. Although the origin of oil and gas is still not completely known, most probably originated in relatively stagnant basins on the sea floor from plant and animal residues in highly organic oozes. Conversion of these oozes to oil seems to require increased temperatures and pressures resulting from burial under later sediments.

Commercial "pools" of oil require special geologic conditions. These include: a source bed, often a dark shale; a reservoir bed, such as a permeable sandstone through which fluids can move; an impermeable cap rock to prevent escape of the oil; and some sort of structure to trap the oil. The first, and most obvious, traps to be investigated extensively were anticlines. Now the search is for less easily located traps which generally require geophysical and other special techniques. For example traps concealed by unconformities, and therefore not indicated by surface mapping, can be located by portable seismographs. Gravity surveys to detect light masses at depth are used in the Gulf Coast to

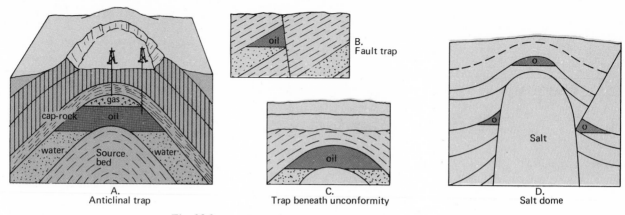

Fig. 16-1
Typical oil traps which have been commercially successful.

locate salt domes—great plugs of salt that rise from depth to intrude overlying sediments and thereby create a variety of traps. In general, the search for oil is limited to regions of thick sediments containing marine rocks.

Ores Uranium and other radioactive minerals occur in sedimentary, igneous, and metamorphic rocks. Although traditional energy sources are still cheaper, technological advances may soon make radioactive energy sources economically competitive. They would greatly benefit underdeveloped countries lacking coal, oil, or adequate water power.

From antiquity the higher civilizations have used metals. The bronze and iron ages are now replaced by the "age of steel" which consumes iron ore and many other metals at an extravagant rate. Copper, lead, tin, aluminum, manganese, zinc, silver, platinum, and gold are only a partial list of other metals now in great demand. Although metallic minerals occur in the three great groups of rocks, their concentration into ore bodies (metallic mineral accumulations which can be worked at a profit) is exceedingly rare. Improved technology has made lower grade mineral deposits into ore bodies as richer sources become depleted, but ores clearly present an economic problem. No mineral deposits are renewed: they are gone, once a mine is exhausted.

Despite geologic and technologic advances, the tremendous present-day consumption of metals could lead to a crisis for future generations.

Other Economic Minerals Sulfur, halite, potassium salts, gypsum, nitrates, and phosphates are among the many other geologic raw materials consumed in large amounts by modern industry. Agricultural use of chemical fertilizers, which are derived from geologic materials, has become increasingly important. In the face of the rapidly expanding world population, more efficient food production is essential.

Water and construction

Our most essential natural resource is fresh water. Even though water supplies are replenished by the hydrologic cycle, expanding cities, irrigation projects, and industries make the availability of fresh water a matter of universal interest. The problem is no longer restricted to desert and semi-arid regions, but it now concerns such humid regions as the densely populated eastern United States. An increasing number of geologists are applying their special talents to the better use of all our water resources, underground supplies as well as surface waters in lakes and streams.

Since civil engineering and geology clearly

overlap, an appropriate founder for modern geology was William Smith (canal engineer). Today, geology is applied increasingly in engineering projects. Preliminary investigations can lead to the cheapest and best sources for building stone, concrete aggregate, and other construction materials of geologic origin. And since all man-made structures rest on rock, preliminary geologic studies can greatly reduce the chance of collapsing dams, leaky reservoirs, highway failures, and settling and cracking of buildings; and it can help locate the safest places for man-made structures in active earthquake regions.

NEW FRONTIERS

Since events in World War II made it clear that science and technology are vital to the national interest, the government has given massive support to many fields, including oceanography and, most notably, the space program. In both these fields geology plays a significant part. As a result, geology today is in an exciting stage of new discoveries.

Submarine geology

The study of the oceans, which cover some 71% of the earth's surface, requires joint efforts by workers trained in many fields. Mathematics, physics, chemistry, and biology, as well as astronomy, geology, meteorology, and engineering technology are all involved. The roles of these interrelated fields in oceanography cannot be neatly separated; but we can say that submarine geology concentrates on the topography, unconsolidated sediments, solid rocks, and geologic structures beneath the oceans.

Economic Applications Although its purely scientific goal is a better understanding of the earth from evidence beneath the sea, submarine geology has considerable practical value. The Navy's marked interest and support clearly relates to military matters involving ships, submarines, and the associated sophisticated equipment and devices of modern warfare. Oceanographic research should, however, lead to better use of and new resources for the earth's increasing population. The oceans have always supplied much of mankind's food, and fish and other edible seafood are notably dependent on bottom conditions. The oceans also contain geologic raw materials.

Offshore drilling in the shallower waters off the Gulf Coast and Alaska is producing oil and gas, and more discoveries are anticipated. Much coal has been recovered by mining outward in rocks that dip under the sea from the British Isles. In Newfoundland, much iron ore is being mined, several miles out from shore underneath the sea floor. Gold and other valuable deposits found in modern and ancient beach and stream deposits along coastal areas strongly suggest that in the future similar economic minerals will be mined offshore in submerged beaches and bars. Manganese nodules on the deep floors of the Atlantic and Pacific Oceans range in size from microscopic to three-feet in diameter. In places they are abundant enough to be a potential source not only for manganese, which the United States lacks, but for copper, cobalt, and nickel also found in some of the nodules. The economic possibilities of the sea floor are hardly touched.

Instruments and Equipment Although oceanography might be said to date back to ancient seafaring people, submarine geology, a three-dimensional study involving the ocean bottoms, began with the British *Challenger* expedition of the 1870's. The expedition studied the Atlantic, Pacific, and Antarctic Oceans, making depth soundings with long lines and taking bottom samples; but the time required to make a single sounding limited observations to points several hundreds of miles apart, and did little to change the prevailing idea that the ocean floors were largely featureless. The diversity of the ocean bottom was not suspected until the 1920's, when the German ship *Meteor* made a voyage in the South Atlantic using an echo-sounder (fathom-eter). This device records depths by bouncing sound pulses off the ocean floor. For so long as depths were known only by reeling out weighted lines, our knowledge of the sea floor was limited to shallow waters, with very few points from the oceanic deeps.

Since World War II, modern echo-sounders which accurately and continuously record depths have revolutionized concepts of the earth's submarine topography. Now a variety of devices give information on the ocean floor and materials beneath. Although land-based seismographs probed the rocks of the crust and mantle beneath the ocean, a recently developed shipboard geophysical instrument continuously records not only the bottom depth but also the thickness of sediments beneath. Bottom samples are obtained by dredging; coring devices, lowered to the bottom, have penetrated as much as 75 feet of sediment under ideal conditions. Devices for recording variations in the earth's gravity, magnetic field, and heat flow from the bottom are among other geophysical instruments now used. Cameras, suitably protected and designed to trip a light near the bottom, provide many detailed pictures of the ocean floor. Direct observations are made by scuba divers to depths of about 200 feet; and bathyscaphs, such as the *Trieste*, can penetrate the deepest ocean trenches. Thus along with increased financial support, advances in submarine geology have depended on the development of sophisticated "hardware" and techniques.

The General Ocean Floor

Once thought largely flat, from lack of information, undersea topography is now known to be varied and complex. The submerged shelves marginal to the continental blocks give way to steeper continental slopes descending to the oceanic depths. The shelves and slopes are cut by submarine canyons, as large as any on land. At depth, the continental slopes grade into continental rises leading down to abyssal plains—the greatest flat expanses on the earth's rock crust. Yet the abyssal plains are broken by a variety of hills, conical mountains, and plateau-like platforms, as well as by deep narrow trenches and scarps. The most striking submarine feature is the global system of mid-oceanic ridges. Let us first consider the submerged continental flanks, then the deeper ocean basins.

Continental Terraces

Taken together the continental shelves, slopes, and rises form great submarine terraces whose sedimentary covers overlie sialic basement, or continental type rocks, contrasting with the simatic basement beneath the deeper ocean floors.

Continental shelves, forming the terrace surfaces, range in width from a few miles in parts of the Pacific Ocean to several hundred miles off northeastern North America. The outer limit of the shelves has been taken as the 100-fathom (600 foot) depth contour; but since the break from shelf to continental slope, which is the true boundary, varies considerably in depth from place to place, the 100-fathom figure is purely arbitrary. The continental shelves slope gently away from the shores, usually at less than one degree. Although broadly smooth, their surfaces have some relief. In the North Atlantic, for example, pronounced troughs and ridges occur off glaciated regions; farther south, partially filled river valleys and drowned off-shore bars and beaches reflect sea level shifts of more than 300 feet during the Pleistocene.

Although noticeably steeper than the shelves, the continental slopes rarely exceed five degrees (much less than most diagrams suggest) except where bounded by faults or coral reefs. The slopes extend downward several thousand fathoms. Some, descending into trenches parallel to their bases, reach six miles or more below sea level. Others, as off the Atlantic seaboard of North America merge into continental rises at depth.

The relatively smooth continental rises rarely have a local relief exceeding 10 fathoms (60 feet). However some rises are broken by submarine hills or seamounts, as off the coasts of Brazil and the Gulf of Alaska. The continental rises are generally considered to be embankments of deposits carried down by turbid currents to the bases of the continental slopes. Seismic profiles indicate that bedrock under the rises may be warped into troughs. Thus the slopes may be the surfaces on sediment-filled downwarps, which would represent a form of geosyncline.

Submarine Canyons Various types of sub-merged valleys cut the continental margins. Many are probably drowned stream valleys, glacial troughs, and fault valleys (grabens). Sub-marine landsliding and other mass movements probably produce some valley forms; other types may reflect erosive processes peculiar to the sea floor. However most interest has focused on the great submarine canyons which seem in a class by themselves.

Submarine canyons cross continental shelves and slopes, and extend as shallower valleys across continental rises to the abyssal depths. The canyons have winding courses and tribu-taries like normal stream valleys; their cross-profiles are V-shaped and their long-profiles slope continuously downward. Canyons cut dif-ferent materials including sediments, sedi-mentary rocks, and in some cases crystalline rocks, such as granite. Some canyons, although not directly aligned, seem associated with major streams on land, for example the Hudson Canyon off the Hudson River; but others are not related to present-day rivers. The size of some sub-marine canyons rivals such terrestrial gorges as the Grand Canyon of the Colorado River.

The origin of submarine canyons has pro-voked interest since the first report of one by J. D. Dana over a century ago. Imaginative but generally rejected hypotheses involve water "sloshing" back and forth on the continental shelves during Tsunamis (seismic sea waves) and submarine sapping of continental slopes by emerging artesian spring water. Because of their general form, some workers suggested that the canyons were carved on land by streams and, later, submerged. Stream-cutting might produce the upper parts of canyons, but since canyons reach depths exceeding 10,000 feet—far greater than Pleistocene lowering of sea level—sub-aerial erosion is a doubtful over-all mechanism.

Some workers believe that dense turbid flows of muddy water, called turbidity currents, eroded the canyons. But others object that although turbidity currents carry and deposit much mate-rial on the deep ocean floor, they cannot scour deep canyons—especially in crystalline rocks. Submarine "slumping" and mass movements, dense currents of cold water flowing along the sea floor, and various combinations of mecha-nisms have also been proposed. The origin of the canyons and many other submarine features are difficult problems because they may involve little-known oceanic processes, unlike the well-studied geologic agents on land. A long-time in-vestigator of submarine geology, F. P. Shepard, concludes that much more work is needed to answer the many questions about the origin of submarine canyons.

Origins of Continental Margins The develop-ment of the continent-girdling terraces consist-ing of shelves and slopes involves much theoriz-ing. Several kinds of shelf-slope forms are rec-ognized. Some represent large deltas forming over deeply subsiding areas. This is the case with the Mississippi River delta. On these the con-tinental slopes are very gentle, one degree or less. Some steep shelves are definitely bounded by fault scarps. Some of the steepest continental slopes (45° or more) have organic reefs of coral and algae that form buttresses holding back less consolidated sediments, as off the coast of Florida. Still another type of slope occurs along the Atlantic seaboard, where continental slopes are thinly veneered with sediments and, in places, expose geologic formations extending from land to the slope faces.

For many years the great terraces were at-tributed to a combination of cut-and-fill. The in-ner parts of continental shelves were consid-ered wave-cut surfaces on bedrock; the outer parts were thought to be wave-built extensions of eroded debris, deposited below the level of normal wave action. This concept is now re-jected for several reasons, the chief reason be-ing that the lower limit of normal wave action, once thought to be about 600 feet deep, is now considered to be no more than 60 feet deep. Another reason offered is that bedrock has been found in shelves and faces of the continental slope, off the eastern United States, where according to the concept only the youngest sediments should appear.

Most hypotheses under present consideration assume deformation of the earth's crust with a subsiding ocean floor adjacent to continental margins. The subsidence may involve either faulting or downwarping. The shelves of Australia and southern California are considered fault-controlled continental margins. The exposed bedrock in the continental slope of the eastern United States has been attributed to faulting, but the evidence is incomplete. Most workers consider this shelf the result of long-continued downwarping and filling with thick sediments to form a modern geosyncline. Whether downwarping along continental margins is caused by the load of sediments, or by tectonic (deep-seated) forces, or by both, is an old question.

Island Arcs and Trenches Island arcs and deep trenches are common around the rim of the Pacific, extending into other oceans as well. Such islands as the Aleutians, the Kuriles, the Mariannas, and Japan form arcs, typically convex toward the center of the Pacific. All are active volcanic regions built on elongate ridges rising from the ocean floor. The common presence of andesite in the volcanics of such islands leads many geologists to consider the arcs as parts of the continental crust, contrasting with the basaltic floors of the ocean basins. But at least some arcs are features of ocean basins. Although the Mariannas lie 1000 miles east of the Philippine Islands, they are separated from the Philippines by a basin with oceanic crust. And the Aleutians have basalt-floored basins on either side.

On their outer flanks, away from the continents, island arcs descend into narrow elongate trenches—some almost three times deeper than the broad ocean basins. The deepest known spot in the ocean bottom is about 35,700 feet (5950 fathoms) below sea level, in the Mariannas Trench; several trenches approach 35,000 feet in depth. Along the coasts of Chile and Peru, and along the coast of Central America from central Mexico almost to Panama, trenches border continental margins without intervening island arcs.

Island arcs are characterized by strong earthquakes, as well as volcanism. Significantly, the earthquakes originate at shallow depths (less than 35 miles) under the trenches, and at intermediate depths (35 to 150 miles) under island arcs. Under continental margins, they are deepest (up to 400 miles). This pattern suggests an active zone sloping from near surface in the trenches to greatest depths under the continents. Thus some workers suggest a major fault zone, wherein oceanic rocks are thrusting under the continental crust.

Abyssal Plains and Hills Taking the drowned continental margins as one major division of the earth beneath the sea, the true oceanic floor, underlain by basaltic crust, has two other major topographic divisions: the ocean basins, and a mid-ocean ridge system. The ocean basins contain abyssal plains and a variety of hills, mountains, and scarps.

Abyssal plains, known in the Atlantic, Indian, and north Pacific Oceans, have gradients of less than one foot vertical for one thousand feet horizontal. Some gradients are as low as 1:7000. They are the largest smooth surfaces on the earth's crust. The plains and adjacent rougher topography of abyssal hills lie as deep as 12,000 feet (2000 fathoms), and are the deepest broad regions of the ocean floor (exceeded only by the much deeper, but narrow, trenches along island arcs). Characteristically, the abyssal plains slope very gently away from bases of continental rises. Where continents lack rises and their slopes descend instead into trenches, abyssal plains are absent. Sediments on the plains include fine clays, which settle slowly into the depths, interbedded with sands, which contain shallow-water fossils. Bedding features indicate that they were carried down by turbidity currents.

Abyssal hills stand from a few tens of feet to several thousand feet above the ocean floor. Hills on the Atlantic's floor bound the abyssal plains in belts parallel to the Mid-Atlantic Ridge. On the Pacific floor, abyssal hills are far more widespread than in any other ocean. The origin of abyssal hills is speculative. Low dome-like forms in the equatorial Pacific may be laccoliths; others seem to be fault structures.

Several origins have been proposed for abyssal plains. That they originated as subaerial features is generally rejected because of the tremendous lowering of sea level required. That the plains are lava surfaces is yet another idea. However their extreme flatness would require exceedingly fluid lava to spread widely on the ocean floor—an unlikely occurrence, because water would quickly chill lava and domal eruption centers are missing on the plains. Some have suggested that the plains are very ancient remnants of ocean floor largely unaffected by deformation; however, seismic studies have since demonstrated hilly topography beneath sediments of the plains.

The most acceptable hypothesis, at present, explains abyssal plains as blankets of turbidity deposits burying older abyssal hills. Supporting the idea is the absence of plains near deep trenches and other barriers to the spread of turbidity-current deposits, as well as the merging of plains with continental slopes. The slopes are considered depositional features, and their presence would allow wide spreading of turbid currents cascading down continental slopes or emerging from submarine canyons.

Seamounts and Rises

Seamounts and Rises Positive features standing well above the ocean bottom are classed as seamounts and rises. The seamounts are individual peaks over 3000 feet (500 fathoms) above the adjacent floor. Widespread in ocean basins, seamounts also occur in trenches and along continental margins. Some are randomly distributed; however, many form generally linear groups. Since most seamounts have roughly conical shapes and expose volcanic rocks, they are probably submarine volcanos. Guyots, a special class of seamounts, are distinguished by flat tops from which sediments and fossils indicating shallow water have been dredged. They are generally considered volcanos that once emerged as islands, were truncated by wave action; then as the ocean floor subsided, sank to varying depths of as much as a mile below sea level.

Oceanic rises are broad features standing above the ocean floor that are not notable earthquake sites. The Bermuda Rise, an example in the North Atlantic, is topped by a volcanic pedestal reaching above sea level in the Bermuda Islands. The rise itself seems to be uplifted ocean bottom marked by a steep fault scarp on the east. The Hawaiian Islands are volcanic peaks standing on the elongate Hawaiian Rise, which is probably also volcanic.

Mid-Oceanic Ridges The third major division of the ocean floors includes the worldwide mid-oceanic ridge systems. Extending more than 30,000 miles from Iceland southward through the Atlantic into the Indian and Antarctic Oceans, thence into the Pacific, these ridges form the world's greatest continuous mountain system. In the Atlantic, where it has been most investigated, the ridge system reaches 1000 miles in width, occupying about one-third of the ocean floor; and stands over a mile and a half above the adjacent abyssal hills in places. This Mid-Atlantic Ridge is divisible into flank provinces, on both sides, marked by steps or benches rising toward the crest province in the center. Scarps separating steps of the flank province are attributed to faulting. The step surfaces are very uneven and hilly, except for a few smooth-floored valleys thought to have fills of deposits coming from higher parts of the ridge system.

The crest province of the Ridge, from 50 to 200 miles wide, has high, rugged, fractured plateaus on both sides that abruptly give way to rugged rift mountains forming the highest ridges. Splitting the mountains along their length is a most striking feature—a great central rift valley. The valley, 15 to 30 miles wide, is bounded by pronounced scarps of from 3000 to 9000 feet. Although almost entirely submarine, the ridge system emerges in scattered islands, such as the Azores, St. Helena, and St. Paul's Rocks; it also emerges to form Iceland, a large volcanic island with a central rift valley. More impressively, the system is thought by some to come ashore in east Africa. Here high plateaus are broken by central rift valleys containing such exceedingly deep lakes as Nyasa and Tanganyika. Because the east African rift valleys are grabens, and are generally considered to be caused by tension, the central rift valleys of mid-oceanic ridges probably are similar in origin.

Unlike the surrounding ocean bottom which is relatively free of earthquake centers, the ridge systems are active seismic as well as volcanic zones. Moreover, geophysical instruments indicate an exceptionally high heat flow from the earth's interior along the ridge axes, in contrast to the rest of the ocean floor, and to the continents.

The ridges, in turn, are sharply offset at right angles, or nearly so, by many remarkably straight *fracture zones*. These zones, which are marked by roughening and irregularities in the topography of the ocean floor, were first thought to be great strike-slip faults like the San Andreas Rift. Now it is thought that the ridge axes may be fixed in their positions while rocks during displacements always move out at right angles away from the ridge axes. Such fractures, which have recently been called transform faults, are of considerable theoretical importance, as we shall see.

THE DEVELOPMENT OF A NEW WORLD VIEW

In the late 1960's, investigations of the ocean floors led to an overall scheme that ties together many previously debated observations and ideas. To enthusiastic supporters, the theory of sea floor spreading caused a geologic revolution that requires an entirely new way of looking at the earth. But, as is often the case, in order to properly understand the revolutionary ideas, the older ones on which they are based must also be considered.

Gondwanaland The notion of a vast southern continent has persisted since antiquity. Ptolemy of Alexandria drew a world map in the second century B.C. showing the Indian Ocean surrounded to the south by *Terra Australis Incognita*, a vast land mass that joined eastern Africa to China. Although nobody had ever seen it, the land made a reasonable analogy with the Mediterranean and Caspian Seas that were well known then. Ptolemy probably got the idea from Hipparcus (a predecessor in the second century B.C.) who on noticing the tidal differences between the Atlantic and Indian Oceans theorized that they were separated by a great land barrier. Ptolemy's works disappeared with the fall of the Roman Empire. Their rediscovery in the mid-fifteenth century revived the legendary continent; but not until the late 1700's was the phantom apparently laid to rest when Captain James Cook, under sealed orders from the British Admiralty (to confirm or deny), found no such major continent short of the Antarctic. But perhaps Cook was 200,000,000 years late.

Geologists working in the southern hemisphere long favored some sort of super-continent in late Paleozoic to mid-Mesozoic time. Rocks in Africa and Madagascar, India, Australia, South America, and Antarctica are strikingly similar. Those at the bottom, usually lying on a Precambrian basement but sometimes lying on striated glaciated floors, are tillites (lithified glacial deposits) and varve-like claystones. Above them are terrestrial sandstones and shales containing coal seams. Still higher, the rocks are desert-type sandstones, either beneath or interbedded with great basaltic lava flows, and often intruded by basaltic dikes and sills. These total sequences are impressively thick, reaching 20,000 feet in India, as much as 35,000 feet in Africa, and not much less in Brazil. Strictly speaking, the Gondwana strata are in India (where the name was given); elsewhere strikingly similar rocks are called by such names as Karroo in Africa, Santa Catherina and Sao Benito in Brazil, and the Beacon Series in Antarctica. All such strata, which we shall call Gondwana rocks, indicate a general emergence of the continents. Being terrestrial, they were difficult to date because the standard rock column is based on marine fossils. Fortunately the Gondwana rocks interfinger with marine rocks in enough places to be correlated with the interval from the late Paleozoic to mid-Mesozoic (Devonian or Carboniferous to Jurassic).

The nature of Gondwana fossils has long intrigued paleontologists. The late Paleozoic vertebrate animals were apparently quite similar thoughout the whole world. Certainly the reptiles were remarkably similar on all the continental masses in middle and late Triassic rocks, where the fossil record is best. So, how did land-dwelling reptiles, such as cotylosaurs, mammal-like reptiles, thecodonts and dinosaurs, migrate from Africa to South America? The South Atlantic Ocean should have been an impassable barrier; moreover, until Cenozoic time the northern and southern continents in the old world were apparently separated by a major geosynclinal belt occupied by what is called the Tethys Sea. Of particular interest is a small, fish-eating, fossil reptile (called *Mesosaurus*), found in South America and South Africa but nowhere else. Though it lived in water, nobody believes it swam the Atlantic Ocean from one continent to the other.

Although the vertebrate faunas of Gondwana time were similar on all continents, the plant populations were not. A very distinctive assemblage of seed ferns, the *Glossopteris* flora, characterized the southern hemisphere, but was notably absent from the northern continents. *Glossopteris* was apparently adapted to the cool climates indicated by the glacial deposits in the southern hemisphere while tropical and semi-tropical coal swamps existed across North America, Europe, and Asia. If the continents and ocean basins had the same relations in Gondwana time as they do today, the spreading of *Glossopteris* plants across the South Atlantic and

Fig. 16-2
Glossopteris leaves from the Buckeye Range, Antarctica. Courtesy of Larry Lackey.

other ocean barriers would have seemed an insoluble problem to many geologists. Thus many believed that the distribution of both plants and land animals in Gondwana time demanded land connections where the present-day ocean basins exist.

Enter the controversial continent. Gondwanaland was first proposed as a continuous land across the southern hemisphere from South America on the west to Australia on the east. Then, sometime in the Mesozoic, two great fragments of the continent subsided to create the South Atlantic and Indian Ocean basins, leaving fragments standing as the present southern continents (Fig. 16-3).

The idea neatly solves the distribution of Paleozoic to mid-Mesozoic plants and animals in the southern hemisphere. They spread across Gondwanaland before it broke up. It also accounts for truncated continental structures, such as the Cape fold belt at the tip of South Africa; for down-faulted lavas beneath the Arabian Sea off the west coast of India; as well as for the observation that some ancient sediments, including glacial deposits, apparently came from lands that once existed off the present-day shores.

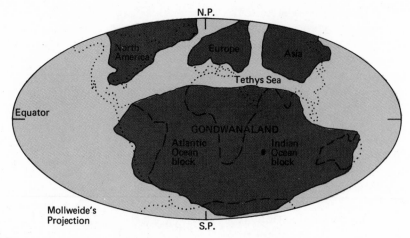

Fig. 16-3
Diagrammatic world map of the late Paleozoic showing the hypothetical Gondwanaland before the fragments subsided to create the South Atlantic and the Indian Oceans.

Despite this, the idea that vertical movements have sunk great continental blocks under the oceans has no advocates today. Theoretically, it was always hard to explain why great blocks that had long been parts of high-standing continents should ever founder—especially since sialic continental blocks are lighter than the denser sima beneath them. Most devastating was the eventual geophysical evidence that no granitic, continental-type rocks are in the floors of deep ocean basins.

Permanency of Continents and Ocean Basins
Until quite recently, one of the most venerated dictums of most American geologists was the permanency of continents and ocean basins. The concept, suggested by J. D. Dana in 1846, assumes that continents formed in the early molten stage of the earth when granitic material floated to the surface and "froze" into sialic continental masses upon denser underlying sima. The main postulate of the concept is that since Precambrian time the continental blocks and oceanic blocks of the earth's crust have always had the same relative positions and sizes. Orogeny and shifting seas have modified details of global geography on the high-standing continental blocks, but no major landmass has become deep

ocean floor, nor has oceanic floor risen to form a continental mass. The earth's major crustal blocks have not shifted vertically or horizontally since they originated.

There were several strong arguments for permanency. Because Precambrian rocks occur in Paleozoic and later fold belts, the Precambrian shields were extensive by earliest Paleozoic time and unquestionably floored large parts of the geosynclines involved in later orogenies. In North America, for example, Precambrian rocks crop out in the Blue Ridge Mountains far to the southeast of the Canadian shield; and far to the southwest in Grand Canyon and the mountains of the Basin and Range province. Moreover, Paleozoic and later belts of mountain building overlap each other. In Europe, rocks contorted in the Hercynian (late Paleozoic) orogeny formed the subsiding floor for the Tethyan geosyncline from which the Alpine-Himalayan mountain chain arose in Cenozoic time. Although it might seem strange at first thought, the extensive marine sedimentary rocks now seen on the continents are good evidence for permanency. Many of the sediments indicate deposition in shallow seas. The only uncontested deep-water deposits were clearly laid down in mobile geosynclinal belts rather than on uncontorted blocks of the deep ocean basins. Moreover, brown clays, characteristic of abyssal depths, are not found on continental blocks. Also, as previously mentioned, the oceanic depths have no sialic rocks that would indicate foundered continental blocks. Thus the case for permanency seemed strong, although the widespread Gondwana faunas and floras created an interesting problem.

Land Bridges These narrow causeways connecting continents were a compromise idea that maintained the permanence of continents and ocean basins while giving intercontinental connections for plant and animal migration. Professor Charles Schuchert of Yale was a leading exponent of early land bridges which later sank and disappeared. An analogy for the former land bridges is the Isthmus of Panama, an existing land bridge connecting North and South America. And, it is generally accepted that North America and Asia—now isolated—were connected across the Bering Straits as late as the end of Pleistocene time. Australia may have been accessible by land from Asia during intervals of Cenozoic time. Thus some students of the Gondwana problem proposed an elaborate system of hypothetical land bridges that provided migration routes between the southern continents and across the intervening deep ocean basins.

Today, purely hypothetical land bridges across the deep oceans are seriously doubted. George Simpson of Harvard, after study of the dispersal and evolution of isolated modern mammals and their Cenozoic forebears, strongly opposed land bridges except for the well-established routes known in later times. From the study of Mesozoic reptiles, Edwin Colbert of the American Museum of Natural History concluded that there is no evidence for land bridge connections in the Jurassic or Cretaceous, but for Triassic time he wasn't sure. Although bridges are much smaller than continental blocks, there are no known physical explanations for their sinking into the ocean depths, nor is there any evidence of them in the rocks and topography of the deep ocean floors. The established routes of past and present intercontinental migrations are all continental shelves like the Bering Straits where the water is now shallow, or zones of active mountain building like the Isthmus of Panama. But if subsidence of great continental blocks or of narrow land bridges seemed out of the question, there was another possible explanation for plant and animal distributions that also involved the supercontinent of Gondwanaland.

Continental Drift The jig-saw fit of continental outlines, especially of Africa and South America,

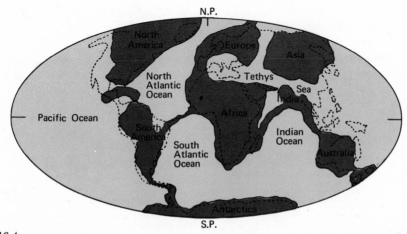

Fig. 16-4
Land bridges as a suggested solution to the late Paleozoic Gondwana problem. Based on Schuchert and others.

was noticed long ago. Perhaps Sir Francis Bacon can be considered the first driftist, for in 1620 he discussed the parallelism of the shores bounding the Atlantic Ocean. Antonio Snyder's map of 1858 showed the Americas, Eurasia, and Africa joined in a single super-continent in order to explain the similarity of coal-measure plants throughout the northern hemisphere. Although F. B. Taylor, an American, presented the idea in 1908, the concept of continental drift received little serious attention until the German meteorologist, Alfred Wegner, resurrected and began to aggressively promote it starting in 1910.

The driftists assumed that until Mesozoic time, the world had a single super-Pacific Ocean basin and either one or two super-continents. They put the existing continents together, like jig-saw pieces, in various possible arrangements. Some proposed a single original continent, called Pangea; others assumed two with Gondwanaland to the south, and Laurasia (North America–Eurasia) to the north with the Tethys as an intervening sea. After the break-up of the super-continents, sialic continental fragments were pictured as floating off over the sima, like icebergs in the sea, to produce the Atlantic Ocean basin as an ever-widening gap between the Americas and Europe-Africa. Later, the Indian Ocean appeared as Australia and Antarctica drifted apart. The Mid-Atlantic ridge, after its discovery, was taken to be the seam where the continent fragments were originally joined. Modern mountain chains were attributed to crumpling of the crust along advancing edges of drifting blocks as in the Cordilleran ranges of the Americas, and the rising island arcs off Asia. The great Alpine-Himalayan ranges were explained by the "bumping together" of Africa and India with Eurasia which crumpled the Tethyan geosyncline.

Aside from the jig-saw continental fit, the driftists assembled a vast amount of circumstantial evidence. They stressed the similarity of Gondwana rocks on all southern continents, and the similarity of Gondwana plants and animals as compared with diversification in later times. The biological problem was neatly solved if plants and animals never had to cross major ocean basins because they lived together on a single landmass before the break-up of Gondwanaland.

Moreover, if the southern continents are properly "slid back together" their broad structural elements show striking coincidences. The South American and African Precambrian shields fit neatly; and (with a bit of twisting) the Indian, Antarctic, and Australian shields can also be matched. Paleozoic folded mountain belts can be connected: the east-trending ranges through Buenos Aires in South America connect with the Cape folds of South Africa, and these in turn can be extended through the Antarctic to the Australian Cordillera. Alexander Du Toit, a South African, proposed that these ranges rose from a once-continuous geosyncline (the "Samfrau"). In the northern hemisphere, the Paleozoic mountain trends, including the Crystalline and Folded Appalachians in eastern North America, can be connected to those in northern Europe.

Great lava plateaus in South Africa (on the Drakensburg scarp) and some in southern Brazil —both of early Jurassic age—along with the extensive Deccan "traps" in India—of late Cretaceous and early Cenozoic age—could represent eruptions along fractures accompanying the

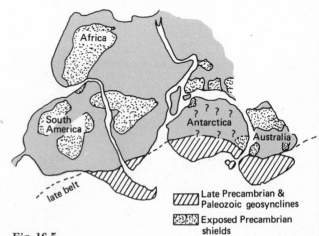

Fig. 16-5

Gondwanaland jig-saw puzzles. The African-South American Precambrian arrangement seems substantiated by recent studies (after Hurley). The late belt is mostly conjecture (based on Du Toit).

break-up of Gondwanaland. Also, the apparent off-shore source (from areas now occupied by oceans) of thick sedimentary sequences that lie on basement rocks in such places as Southwest Africa, Antarctica, and southeastern South America is easily explained if these continents were once parts of a continuous landmass. However, the strongest geologic evidence for drift was the distribution of the late Paleozoic glacial deposits found only in the southern hemisphere.

Today, Gondwana tillites are found mainly in tropic or near tropic regions. Assuming the doctrine of permanency, great ice caps must have covered the equatorial regions while mild climates prevailed in the higher latitudes during late Paleozoic time. Conceivably the continents were in their same relative positions and the terrestrial poles have migrated—thereby shifting the earth's broad climatic belts. Put the past poles where you like. If the continents had the same relative positions now as during late Paleozoic time (as permanency demands), the Gondwana tillites would have been so far apart that all the southern continents could not have had separate ice caps. Some must have been in tropical latitudes—unless, that is, the continents were clustered in a single Gondwanaland (Fig. 16-8).

Thus continental drift neatly solved the glacial problem, gave land connections for plant and animal migrations, connected shields and moun-

Fig. 16-7
Boulders in tillite (glacial deposit) of the late Paleozoic age from Australia. Courtesy of Rhodes W. Fairbridge.

tain trends, and avoided the foundering of continental blocks or land bridges. It satisfied the geophysical model of less dense sialic continents floating isostatically on the denser sima of the oceanic blocks. How could such an all-encompassing theory have been doubted?

Objections to Continental Drift The opposition to continental drift was not simply a matter of ingrained thinking and lack of imagination. In

Fig. 16-6
Glacially-striated pavement of the late Paleozoic age from Australia. Courtesy of Rhodes W. Fairbridge.

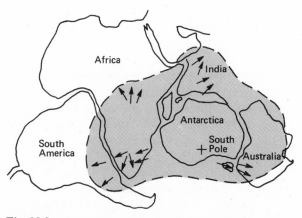

Fig. 16-8
Diagrammatic sketch of A. L. Du Toit's arrangement of the continents into Gondwanaland and a solution of the late Paleozoic glacial problem. Arrows show inferred directions of ice movement; dashed lines represent his inferred ice-cap boundary (after Du Toit).

379

the first place, the visual matching of continental outlines is not everywhere as perfect as between Africa and South America, and even here the lengths of the corresponding coasts do not match. In other places, a reasonable matching of margins requires much twisting about of the continents. And it was argued that even a perfect fit of margins did not, in itself, prove drift. Puddles in the low spots of an uneven brick sidewalk would not prove that the bricks had drifted apart; similarly the parallelism of shores might result from a global fracture system producing higher (continental) and lower (oceanic) blocks.

Moreover the matching of similar rock types and folded mountain belts could be explained by assuming the permanence of continents and ocean basins. Correspondences in themselves are not proof of drift, for Precambrian shields and later mountain belts have had comparable histories of geosynclinal deposition and orogenic folding, even where there is no possible connection. With suitable twistings, structural elements in the continents could be matched even if they had never been connected, and among "driftists" themselves, different arrangements of the continents in late Paleozoic time were proposed.

The striking similarity in Gondwana rocks could also be explained in terms of permanency. Today, similar rocks and soils are developing in such widely separated tropical rainforests as those of Africa and South America; modern glacial deposits are alike in Greenland and Antarctica (which are most obviously not connected), and deserts in different parts of the world are depositional sites of similar sand dunes. Thus it was logically argued that similar rocks reflect similar environments and hence are no proof of former connection.

Nor does the far-flung distribution of Gondwana plants and animals necessarily require a supercontinent (or even land bridges). Seeds of the *Glossopteris* flora could have blown great distances over water, and intervening islands could have provided way-stations in their dispersal; moreover, ocean currents can carry reproductive

structures of plants great distances before casting them upon the shore.

Evidence for the worldwide cosmopolitan fauna of land reptiles is not uniformly abundant in all Gondwana rocks — none have been found in Australia. And even granting a world-wide distribution, it was argued that the animals could have migrated across the northern hemisphere and then found routes to the south on an arrangement of the continents similar to the present. The Tethys Sea, a seeming barrier, was probably broken by late Paleozoic (Hercynian) mountain building in various places, which could have given routes across it for land animals.

The strongest opposition to drift always centered on mechanics. Wegner's idea of sialic continental rafts floating across denser sima was never acceptable because it was well established that both were a part of the earth's solid lithosphere. Even accepting such slippage, the driving forces were a mystery. Two were commonly invoked. The centrifugal force of the earth's rotation was said to cause the Gondwana continents to drift northward over the bulge of the equator. The tidal attraction of the sun and moon was proposed as dragging the continents westward at the same time. These forces exist, but theoretical calculations showed them grossly inadequate, by several million times.

Thus, in the conservative view of permanency of continents and ocean basins, neither the correspondences of continental outlines and structural trends nor the Gondwana rocks and fossils proved continental drift — but they certainly did not dispel the possibility either. The intriguing hypothesis of drift was defended by most geologists in the southern hemisphere and perhaps half of those in Europe, while Americans were generally opposed. Technical articles and symposia, pro and con, proliferated. Books included Wegner's *Origin of Continents and Ocean Basins* (1915), Alexander Du Toit's *Our Wandering Continents* (1927) in support of continental drift; and Walter Bucher's *Crust of the Earth* (1933) in opposition. Lester C. King, like Du Toit a South African, wrote a paper, the *Necessity for Conti-*

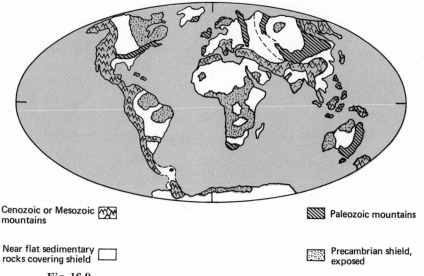

Cenozoic or Mesozoic mountains

Near flat sedimentary rocks covering shield

Paleozoic mountains

Precambrian shield, exposed

Fig. 16-9
Schematic map of the world's younger and older mountain chains.

nental Drift in 1952, but most Americans saw no such necessity then. In general, the game was stalemated until the 1960's.

New evidence for world patterns

Continental drift is again in the geologic lime-light. Geophysical techniques and the explosion in knowledge of the ocean floors produced the breakthrough. Although much of the case is from submarine geology, paleomagnetic discoveries on land since 1950 paved the way.

The earth behaves like a great dipole (bar) magnet whose lines of force align a compass needle with the north and south magnetic poles. What causes the earth's magnetic field is not surely known; perhaps its rotation affects the molten nickel-iron core to make the earth a giant dynamo. In any case, paleomagnetic studies assume that certain minerals are magnetized by the earth's existing magnetic field at the time the minerals are locked into rock. Both igneous and sedimentary rock can be used to determine the directions to the earth's magnetic poles when they were formed. In basaltic lava flows, which preserve the strongest relict magnetism,

magma first solidifies to rock which continues to cool until at a certain temperature (called the Curie point) the minerals become magnetized parallel to the earth's existing lines of force. In sedimentary rocks, the relict magnetism is far weaker (1/10,000th) than in basalts; however, magnetic minerals settling through water do become aligned with the earth's magnetic field before the rocks are consolidated. In both cases the magnetic minerals become minute compass needles showing their latitude (by the steepness of their dip) and the direction of magnetic north at the time they were incorporated in rock. Since the earth's magnetic field quite possibly results from the earth's rotation, it is generally assumed that the magnetic and geographic (rotational) poles have never been far apart.

Paleomagnetic studies, notably by P. M. S. Blackett and K. Runcorn of England, suggest that the earth's magnetic poles have wandered through geologic time—their past positions were quite different from those of the present day. Furthermore, measurements from rocks on different continents give different paths of polar wandering. That is, rocks of comparable age on a single continent give the same locations for ancient

381

poles; but, the different continents yield different pole locations for the same geologic times. The predicament of multiple north and south magnetic poles can be avoided if continental drift is assumed. By theoretically sliding the continents into different positions than they have today, the mineral compass needles on different landmasses can be re-oriented to point to single north and south poles in the past.

Not everyone accepted this paleomagnetic evidence because of the necessary assumption that magnetic and geographic poles have always been close and because the technique is difficult and may have flaws. Physicists were unimpressed for they argue the earth is a gigantic gyroscope that strongly resists any change in its rotational axis. But, perhaps the lithosphere slips as a unit over the stable gyroscopic interior. Thus one could accept or reject the paleomagnetic evidence; but if it is valid, the permanency of continents and ocean basins is denied.

Still later paleomagnetic work showed that the north and south magnetic poles seem to have periodically reversed themselves during geologic time. The cause of the reversals, which probably relates to the origin of the earth's magnetic fields, is not yet understood, but magnetic minerals in old lava flows are sometimes normal (like those of today), and in other samples indicate a north magnetic pole in almost the opposite direction. Allan Cox, while with the U.S. Geological Survey, and others constructed a time scale for geomagnetic reversals based on potassium-argon dating of a large number of lava flows having either normal or reversed polarity of magnetic minerals. This time scale covers only the last four million years—as older samples cannot be adequately dated because of increasing errors with time that are inherent in the potassium-argon dating method. The geomagnetic time scale (Fig. 16-10) contains longer intervals, called epochs, of dominantly normal or dominantly reversed geomagnetic fields (named after scientists who made important contributions to understanding earth magnetism). The longer intervals, in turn, contain shorter term reversals, called events (named from type localities). The scale had to be com-

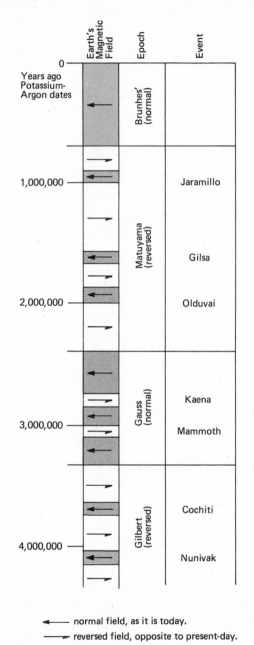

← normal field, as it is today.

→ reversed field, opposite to present-day.

Fig. 16-10
Geomagnetic time scale, based on Hoare, Condon, Cox and Dalrymple.

piled from widely separated localities because the ideal situation—a single great exposure containing all epochs, one above the other—has not been found. Aside from providing a dated stratigraphic succession for lava flows on land, the scale provided the key for dating volcanic rocks of the ocean floors.

By the early 1960's the global extent of the mid-oceanic ridge systems was becoming apparent; moreover, the ridges were revealed as seismically active zones with relatively high heat flow from the earth's interior. Studies of the ocean floors in general added two more significant observations: sediments on much of the floor were either absent or much thinner than anticipated if deposition had persisted, even at a very slow rate, since Precambrian time; and—remarkably—no sediments older than the Cretaceous had been found.[1] In the early 1960's, H. H. Hess, of Princeton, suggested that the apparent youth of the ocean floors might mean that the floors were moving out from the major oceanic ridges where rising currents in the earth's mantle brought up new material that was intruded in dike-like masses and then solidified to make new ocean bottom.

Sea-Floor Spreading The idea, presented tentatively, soon received support. Vine and Matthews of Cambridge, England, suggested a test. If consolidated ridge material was being forced outward by the intrusion of new material in the center, then the progressively older rocks on the ridge flanks should show paleomagnetic differences reflecting the normal or reversed magnetic field existing when the rocks solidified. The suggestion was soon confirmed when J. R. Heirtzler and others from Columbia University's Lamont Geological Observatory, using ship-borne magnetometers, discovered parallel bands of magnetic differences along the Mid-Atlantic Ridge, just south of Iceland. Similar discoveries in other ridge areas confirmed the banded patterns, which were assumed to represent vertically intruded igneous masses; and also showed that the bands correlated with the geomagnetic time scale (determined from horizontal lava flows on land).

Other new lines of evidence supported sea-floor spreading. Deep sea cores taken various

distances from the ridges show magnetic reversals in horizontal sediment layers. The closer the cores are taken to the ridge, the younger is the lowest sediment on basement rock—which confirms a spreading sea-floor, as sediment sequences should be progressively younger towards the ridges. A quite separate line of evidence involves the transform faults. Recent seismic studies show that earthquakes on the ocean bottom occur mainly along those parts of the transform faults between the offset ends of oceanic ridges, and that all earthquake foci are shallow. The shallow centers of origin suggest that rigid rock, whose slippage causes earthquakes, forms only a thin lithosphere in the ridge zones. The first movements of crustal blocks along the faults, which can be determined from seismic records, are just the opposite of the movement on strike-slip faults—that is, the rocks always move away from the ridge axes. Thus along the transform faults, the rocks slip in opposite direction along the fracture between the offset ridge ends; however, beyond the offset ends, rocks on both sides of the fracture would move in the same outward direction thereby minimizing any slippage that causes earthquakes. This situation is an expectable consequence of sea-floor spreading (Fig. 16-12).

The rates of sea-floor spreading can be calculated for the four million years of the dated geomagnetic time scale. In different areas the rates

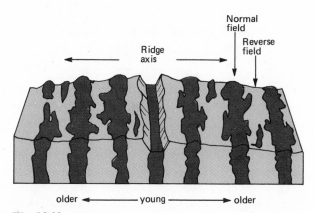

Fig. 16-11
Magnetic variations in oceanic ridges considered to be dike-like masses corresponding to the geomagnetic time scale.

---

[1] Jurassic sediments have recently been reported.

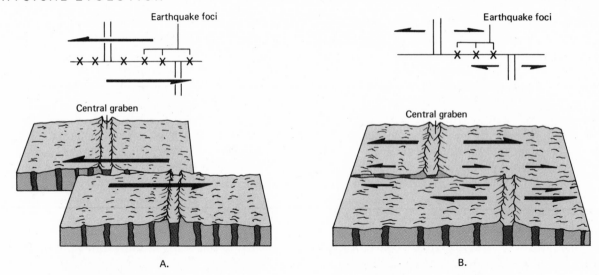

Fig. 16-12
Transform faults in mid-oceanic ridges. If the faults that were offsetting the mid-oceanic ridges were strike-dip faults, blocks would be moving in opposite directions, as shown in A. The preferred explanation, shown in B, is that the ridges are transform faults resulting from spreading from the ridge axes. Thus opposite movement (and earthquake foci) occur only between the offset ends.

range from about half an inch to about two inches a year. Though this might seem small by ordinary standards, it is very appreciable amount in geologic time—about equal to the rate of displacement on the San Andreas fault. An extension of the time scale far beyond the radiometrically dated interval has been proposed. By assuming that the spreading rate during earlier geologic times is the same as that of the last four million years (which is far from certain), a projected time scale has been established for over 170 field reversals that have been determined. The extended scale goes back over 70 million years. It fits rather well with Wegner's and Du Toit's earlier ideas on continental drift, wherein the break-up of Gondwanaland starting in late Paleozoic to mid-Mesozoic time produced the ever-widening south Atlantic Ocean basin and the movement of Australia away from Antarctica produced the Indian Ocean during the Cenozoic.

Thus the evidence seems good for spreading away from the mid-oceanic ridges. But if new crust is continually growing in the ridges, where does the oldest crust go? Calculations show that

shortening of the crust by crumpling in folded mountain ranges does not nearly balance new growth in the ridges. The suggestion that the earth is simply expanding was considered and soon rejected as an explanation. The key to the disposal of excess lithosphere seems to be in the region of the deep oceanic trenches—for instance, off the Chile-Peru coasts, and the Marianna Islands—where shallow to intermediate to deep earthquake foci slope away from ocean centers, down under the trenches. Here the deep foci long presented a problem because they are in the asthenosphere whose plastic rocks should lack the rigidity to generate seismic waves by slippage. The answer was suggested by Oliver and Isacks, of the Lamont Geologic Laboratory, from work in the Pacific near the Tonga Trench, south of Samoa. Their observations suggest that a slab of lithosphere descends deep into the mantle beneath the trench. Such solid material moving downward could cause the deep earthquake centers there, and probably the same occurs near other oceanic trenches as well. Though not proven, it is now assumed that the down-

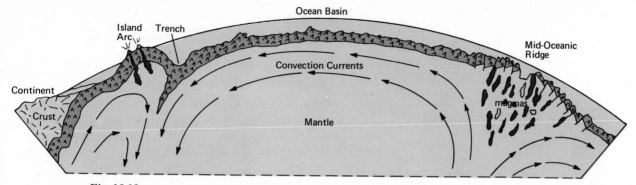

Fig. 16-13
A possible interpretation of the relation of mid-oceanic ridges to continental margins (after Holmes, Heezen, and others).

thrust lithosphere is reabsorbed in the plastic or partially molten asthenosphere. The belts of active volcanos, such as the "Circle of Fire" rimming the Pacific and branching into Indonesia, seem related to the deeply descending slabs of lithosphere. Sedimentary materials are possibly dragged downward, at such places as the west coast of South America, and become fused and mixed with basaltic materials to produce the andesitic magma that erupts in the world's great strato-volcanos.

Thus sea-floor spreading may involve a grand geologic cycle, wherein new lithosphere forms by injection of mantle material into the mid-oceanic ridges, is carried outward in solid slabs riding on the plastic asthenosphere, and finally descends under trenches to be reabsorbed in the plastic or partially molten mantle. Although it has not yet been well established, the driving mechanism for these global systems may be flat convection currents in the asthenosphere which rise under the ridges, spread out and drag along the bottoms of the slabs of lithosphere, and descend beneath the trenches (Fig. 16-13).

In what is being called *plate tectonics*, the American and Eurasian plates are visualized as slabs moving out from the Mid-Atlantic Ridge; the northern projection of the Antarctic plate and the Pacific plate move out from the East Pacific rise. Two plates meeting in oceanic regions create such features as the Tonga and Marianna

trenches and their associated island arcs. If an ocean-floor plate thrusts under the margin of a continent, as along the west coast of South America, marginal mountains, such as the Andes, may result parallel to offshore trenches. Where the Indian sub-continent thrusts under the Asian mass, two continent-bearing plates seem to come together to create the exceptionally high Himalayan mountains and the Plateau of Tibet. The Basin and Range province may be a unique location where the American plate has over-ridden the East Pacific Rise to create a broad zone of plate-faulted crust (Figs. 16-14, 16-15).

Sea-floor spreading is a most significant geologic idea because it ties together a mass of varied observations in a single broad conceptual scheme. It relates the rocks, plants, and vertebrate fossils of Gondwanaland; the earth's major topographic and structural elements: continents and ocean basins, modern mountain ranges, oceanic ridges and trenches; as well as the global patterns of volcanic and seismic activity. Thus the rapid geologic developments of the late 1960's, when sea-floor spreading with continental drift overturned the concept of permanency for continents and ocean basins, caused a true revolution in geologic thinking. This certainly does not mean that all past geology is wrong. Far from it. The new world view was built on a well-established and unchanged mass of geologic observation, technique, and theory, but from now on,

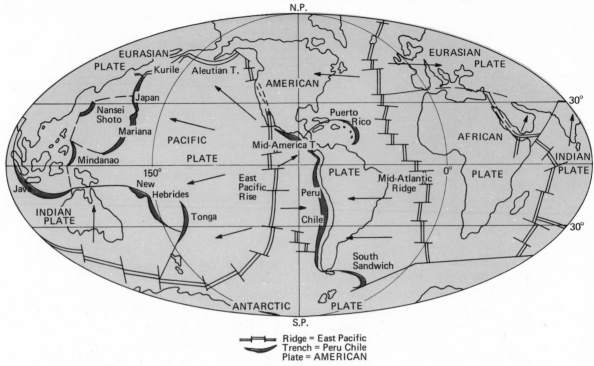

Fig. 16-14
Mollweide's map projection preserves areas, but distorts shapes on margins. Mid-oceanic ridges, deep trenches, and fault lines bordering major crustal blocks are indicated in the legend. After Heirtzler et al., J. Geophys. Res. 73, 2119–2136 (1968).

most geologists will see the details of world patterns from a new point of view. A more normal period of science has already begun when most geologists and geophysicists have joined the new "establishment" and will work towards applying, refining, and revising the scheme.

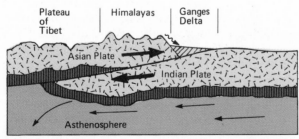

Fig. 16-15
Meeting of two continental plates to produce the exceptionally high Himalayas and the Tibet Plateau (after Argand, 1924).

Like any broad scientific concept, sea-floor spreading is not a dogma of divine revelation, but is human knowledge which is subject to testing, improvement, and change. Although the present case seems very convincing, new evidence and interpretations could eventually make sea-floor spreading as outmoded as theories of a shrinking earth and permanency of continents and ocean basins seem now.

There are many questions to be settled. Why was the breakup of super-continents delayed until late Paleozoic or early Mesozoic time? What happened in the earlier history of the earth? If mountains rise along the advancing edges of spreading blocks, how were the Paleozoic Appalachian Mountains created on the eastern edge of North America; what about Precambrian ranges whose roots are now preserved in the great shields? Why are the subsiding geosynclines under the Gulf Coast and Atlantic Coastal Plains not on the edge of a crustal block? The Peru-Chile trench contains undeformed sediments; why aren't these sediments contorted if spreading sea-floor is moving under and compressing the trench? Why do paleomagnetic studies indicate progressively younger ocean floor (not older as the spreading concept requires) approaching the Aleutian Trench?

We should not infer from the existence of these questions that sea-floor spreading is just another grand theory that will soon be replaced. The proposed mechanism of convection currents needs more testing, which may be forthcoming as geophysicists turn more attention to studies of the earth's upper and lower mantle in the next major phase of work.

Astrogeology

Before the space program, astrogeology (the study of planets and other solid bodies in the solar system) would have seemed little more than science fiction. Now space probes have sent back data and pictures of the earth's neighbors in space. Instrumented spacecraft have landed on the lunar surface, and in 1969 astronauts twice landed on the moon. Ultimately men may visit other planets, but the first step is the moon.

Lunar Characteristics The distance to the moon (actually from the earth's center to the moon's center) is about 239,000 miles, ranging from some 17,000 miles nearer to about 14,000 miles farther because the moon's orbit around the earth is elliptical. The lunar diameter of 2160 miles is about one-quarter of the earth's. Gravity on the moon's surface is about one-sixth as strong as on earth. Since the average lunar density of 3.3 (about 60% of the earth's 5.5) is comparable to the earth's basaltic crust, the moon seems to lack a dense central core.

Only one side of the moon is visible from the earth. Formerly all its surface may have been exposed to the earth when the moon spun faster; however, the moon now makes one rotation on its axis while making one orbital revolution around the earth. This peculiar coincidence—keeping the same face towards the earth—is attributed to a slowing of the moon's rotation by tidal friction from the earth's gravitational attraction. Thus features on the far side were unknown until Russian and American space ships sent back pictures from trips around the moon. Actually more than half, some 59%, of the lunar surface is seen from earth because the moon's axis is slightly inclined, making a bit more of each polar region visible as it moves through orbit; also the orbital velocity is not constant so a bit more of east and of the west sides are visible at different times.

The moon's surface is heated and lighted by the sun; moonlight is reflected sunlight (a small amount of sunlight reflected back from the earth also reaches the moon). Temperature changes on the moon's surface are extreme by earthly standards, and range through more than 400°F—from over 200°F above zero on the bright side to 240°F below (colder than dry ice) on the dark side. These extremes result because the powdery lunar surface permits little conduction and absorption of heat, and because the moon has no appreciable atmosphere to reflect, absorb, and distribute heat.

Several lines of evidence indicate the absence of a lunar atmosphere. The moon's strong shadows, clarity of surface forms, and lack of clouds are suggestive. Moreover stars disappear instantly behind the moon's edge without the fading or apparent shifting that an atmosphere would cause. Apparently, the moon's low gravity allows rapidly moving gas molecules to escape into space, in contrast to the earth, where a much higher escape velocity is needed to overcome the stronger gravitational attraction.

Because the moon has neither an atmosphere nor a hydrosphere, external geologic processes wearing down the lunar surface must be far more limited than those on earth. Streams, glaciers, wind, and waves—features of the earth's hydrologic cycle—along with most chemical weathering can be ruled out. Thus topographic forms on the moon must be far longer lasting

Fig. 16-16
Last quarter photograph of the moon showing the features mentioned in the text. Mount Wilson Observatory photograph.

than terrestrial landforms. Weathering and erosion of the lunar landscape probably result from marked temperature changes, gravitational flows and slides, and the impact of in-falling meteoroids (solid particles from sand size to great blocks of many tons). Unlike the earth where small meteoroids flash (forming meteorites) and are burned up by friction in the protective atmosphere, the impact of these particles may significantly modify the moon's unprotected surface. The special conditions on the moon are of considerable consequence to astronauts. On the lifeless, waterless, airless, and soundless, total desert which is the surface of the moon, they need protection from the extreme temperatures, destructive solar radiations of ultraviolet light, and bullet-like meteoroids.

Lunar Landforms Even to the unaided eyes of ancient observers, the lunar surface displayed two contrasting irregular divisions: darker areas

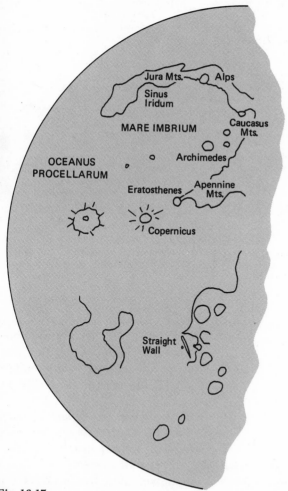

Fig. 16-17
Diagram showing the location of features in the preceding photograph.

(forming "the man in the moon") and lighter more reflective ones. Appreciation of the true diversity of its surface began when Galileo in 1610 turned his primitive telescope on the moon. He named the darker areas *maria* (Latin for seas), in the mistaken belief that they were large bodies of water; he saw mountains in the lighter areas, and the craters of the moon. Since then astronomers have studied and mapped the moon with telescopes in ever increasing detail. Now spacecraft have sent back thousandfold more detailed views of the lunar surface.

The maria, smoother plains contrasting with mountainous uplands, form almost half of the visible surface of the moon. Most of the 14 recorded maria are connected. *Mare Imbrium,* some 700 miles across and the largest individual "sea" is an offshoot of a large complex of maria called *Oceanus Procellarum.* The maria are considered to be filled depressions, but the nature of the fill (as we shall see) is debated. Although smooth compared to the mountainous uplands, maria are far from featureless. Besides prominent craters, a variety of lesser landforms are discernable in the maria (and also in the uplands). Rills in maria and uplands are trench-like features of uncertain depth, up to a mile wide and 150 miles long. They may be grabens (fault valleys), gouges left by flying debris chunks, or collapsed lava tubes. Linear scarps, such as the 30-mile long and 1000-foot high Straight Wall, are probably high-angle faults. Maria ridges are elongate welts, perhaps anticlinal flexures or erupted volcanics. Low irregular maria domes may be laccoliths or shield volcanos (Figs. 16-16, 16-17).

The highly cratered lunar mountains are irregular-shaped uplands—unlike the earth's linear chains of folded and faulted mountains. Individual ranges (named after terrestrial mountains) are represented by the Apennines, Caucasus, Alps, and Jura Mountains which form a partial rim rising abruptly from the north and east sides of Mare Imbrium. Heights of lunar mountains can be determined by trigonometry, using the length of their shadows and the calculated elevation of the sun above the horizon for

Fig. 16-18
High resolution oblique view of the crater Copernicus photographed by Lunar Orbiter II. The North wall (view is to the lunar north) is 10,000 ft. high; central peaks in the floor of the crater are 1000–3000 ft. high. The Carpathian Mountains are on the horizon. NASA photograph.

that part of the moon. Lunar peaks reach as much as 26,000 feet (comparable to the earth's largest mountains) above surrounding plains.

Craters as much as 400 miles wide form a third major topographic element scattered over the moon. Telescopic observation, which cannot resolve features with dimensions less than 1000 feet, reveal some 30,000 craters. Photos from spacecraft indicate the number of craters is tremendous, and they range down to small pits of an inch or so in diameter. The large craters are rimmed by ridges marked by sharp peaks, and having steep infacing slopes. Copernicus, as an example, is a crater with a 40-mile diam-

eter, and walls averaging 12,000 feet high. Its inner rim-surface is broken by concentric steps thought to be slump blocks. Such steps are common on craters over 12½ miles wide, but generally absent on smaller ones. Many craters have central peaks; Copernicus has a cluster of seven (Fig. 16-18).

Craters include two principal types. Primary craters, just discussed, may represent volcanic activity or meteoroid impact (their possible origins will be discussed). Secondary craters are smoother, shallower, and frequently elongate. They are interpreted as scars from chunks of debris ejected from primary craters. Secondary craters are concentrated around large primary craters, and frequently form clusters or strings. They extend farthest in rays radiating from some craters. Rays are bright streaks, best seen under direct light of the full moon. Because they disappear and cast no shadows under oblique sunlight, rays must have little if any relief. They may extend as much as 1500 miles from their source crater. Different craters have rays of differing brightness, and many craters have no visible rays. If ray material is altered with time, the rays may be clues to a crater's age.

Geologic Mapping of the Moon The U.S. Geological Survey's Astrogeology Branch, established in 1961, is mapping the geology of the moon. The first areas mapped contain possible landing sites for spacecraft. The maps are based on telescopic observation and interpretation of telescopic photos, now supplemented by detailed pictures sent back by space vehicles. To make such maps, a tentative geologic succession was established using the basic geologic principles for determining relative ages, namely superposition (the order of deposition of materials) and intersection (cross-cutting relations

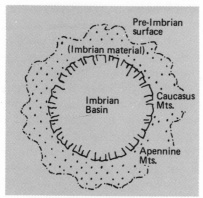

A. Imbrian Period, Apennine Epoch
    Creation of Imbrian basin and
    surrounding mountains.

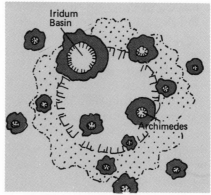

B. Imbrian Period, Archimedian Epoch
    Later craters form in and around
    Imbrian depression.

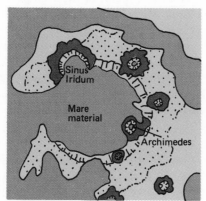

C. Late Archimedian Epoch
    Mare material floods region.

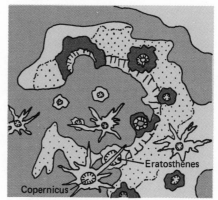

D. Post mare craters
    Older Eratosthenian Period craters
    now lack rays. The younger Copernican
    Period craters have rays which some-
    time cross the older craters.

Fig. 16-19
Schematic diagram of events in the Mare Imbrium vicinity, based on Shoemaker.

of features). The sequence of mappable units and corresponding time divisions largely reflects pre-maria, maria, and post-maria events with the Mare Imbrium region as the type locality (Fig. 16-19).

Relics of the oldest rocks represent the pre-Imbrian Period. Although once thought to form the entire surface of the moon, remnants of pre-Imbrian rocks are now thought to be in much cratered uplands to the south of Mare Imbrium. The Imbrian Period began when the large depression, now containing Mare Imbrium, was created along with associated rocks in such rimming ranges as the Apennines and Alps. This early event of the Imbrian Period (in the Apennian Epoch) was followed by a second epoch (the Archimedean) of Imbrian time when many craters and associated rocks formed on the larger Imbrian rim. Archimedes and the rim of the Sinus Iridum are representative craters. Maria material filled the floors of the Imbrian basin and associated craters at the end of Imbrian (later Archimedean) time.

Post-maria events produced craters and deposits on the maria surface (and in the highland regions also). The earliest interval of cratering, the Eratosthenian Period, produced craters which today lack ray systems, for example Eratosthenes, and are therefore considered relatively old features. The last cratering period, the Copernican, is characterized by craters with rays. Those of Copernicus extend across the older crater, Eratosthenes. This lunar geologic sequence is admittedly tentative, but it gives a preliminary framework for geologic mapping.

Correlation of the lunar geologic scale with that of the earth is difficult. However a possible approximation has been made by assuming that the rate of formation of large meteor craters on the moon is the same as on the earth. The rate on earth is based on study of long-stable regions, such as the central region of the United States. The rate has been projected back in time to account for the observed density of comparable craters in lunar maria. The method is loaded with uncertainties and debated assumptions, but it suggests that the oldest craters of Coper-

nican time are some two billion years old. If so, the face of the moon may be a little altered relic from well back in Precambrian time—a reasonable possibility on the lunar surface, which lacks the erosive workings of a hydrologic cycle.

Possible Origins of the Moon   Three sorts of speculative hypotheses have been proposed for the creation of the moon. In one view, the moon is a large mass of terrestrial material that was thrown out by centrifugal force, long ago when the earth spun much faster (the Pacific Ocean basin might be the scar from the event). This hypothesis explains the relatively low density of the moon as compared to the earth by assuming only crustal material and some mantle were expelled. However, theoretical calculations based on the energies involved do not support the concept (Fig. 16-20).

Perhaps the moon formed in the same way and time as the earth—from a separate clot of matter that grew by accretion in a cloud of gas and dust—and later went into orbit around the earth. By this second hypothesis, the moon should have about the same materials and density as the earth; however, the moon seems to lack a heavy central core.

In a third suggestion, the moon was once a separate planet orbiting around the sun. During a close approach of the two planetary orbits, the moon was captured and became a satellite revolving around the earth. This hypothesis accounts for the large size of the moon relative to the earth. Theoretical calculations indicate that such a capture is possible, but it requires very special conditions. Since the earth's origin is still debated, little wonder that the creation of the moon is mainly speculation.

Interpretations of Lunar Surfaces and Craters
Are the maria floored by deep pulverized debris or by flows of lava? Are the major lunar craters volcanic structures, meteoroid scars, or some combination of both? Conflicting interpretations of the major lunar features involve ideas about the thermal history of the moon; three differing concepts exist. The hot moon school, as-

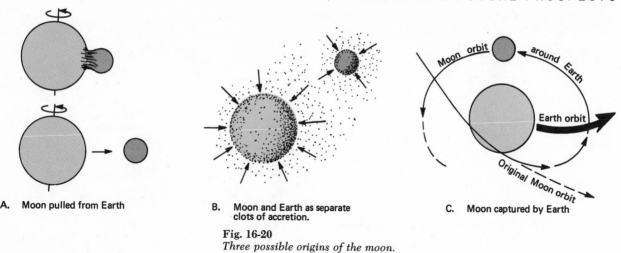

A. Moon pulled from Earth

B. Moon and Earth as separate clots of accretion.

C. Moon captured by Earth

Fig. 16-20
Three possible origins of the moon.

suming much igneous activity inside the moon, considers the maria as tremendous flows of lava and ash, and the craters as mainly volcanic structures. The cold moon school, which rejects major igneous activity, at least in the outer zones and on the surface of the moon, believes that meteoroids or other bodies striking the lunar surface formed the craters, and that the maria are filled largely with dust and fragments of debris. Some even predict ice layers beneath a pulverized blanket of insulating dust. The warm moon school, a compromise group, attributes large lunar craters to impact, but allows for volcanic eruptions and lava flows beneath a surface blanket of dust.

It might seem that recent Ranger, Luna, and Surveyor spacecraft would have sent back information settling many questions about the moon. They did demonstrate that maria surfaces have loose granular material with scattered rocks; and, most important, that the surface will support space vehicles and walking astronauts (some theorists had previously suggested that landing spacecraft would be deeply buried and lost in fine, thick dust). Hot moon advocates are pleased by the results. They admit the dust may be a pulverized blanket, or volcanic ash, but still believe there is lava a short distance beneath. The scattered rocks, seen in photos from the lunar surface, they consider

good evidence for volcanism. On the other hand, cold moon theorists see the loose granular surface material as exactly what they predicted. The scattered rocks, they consider lumps of material lithified by the impact of falling bodies. Such "instant rocks" have been found around craters made by rockets falling in the testing grounds of New Mexico, and have also been artificially produced. The warm moon school finds no reason to change their views from the spacecraft information.

Based on analogy with features on earth, both volcanic and impact hypotheses are still possible for the origin of large lunar craters. The craters are probably not ordinary volcanos, but they could be calderas. In the past the craters were compared to calderas resulting from quiet subsidence as in the shield volcanos of the Hawaiian Islands. Most lunar vulcanists, however, now look on the lunar craters as Krakatoa-type calderas, produced by internal collapse following violent eruptions of gas and ash from stratovolcanos. Some terrestrial calderas have central peaks such as the cinder cone of Wizard Island inside the Crater Lake caldera. Opponents of the caldera origin for lunar craters point out that terrestrial cinder cones are more often towards the edge than in the center of calderas. Moreover central peaks in lunar craters are usually craggy irregular forms rather than neat cones.

Fig. 16-21
Zuni Salt Lake, New Mexico. A terrestrial maar with central cinder cones. From Geology Illustrated *by John S. Shelton, W. H. Freeman & Co. Copyright © 1966.*

The lunar crater, Timnocharis, is occupied however by a dark-rimmed central cone with a small crater. Unlike large lunar craters, the floors of terrestrial calderas are usually higher than the terrain surrounding the relic volcanic cone.

More likely volcanic candidates for craters on the moon are *maars*. They are volcanos resulting from gas eruptions that eject ash and other pyroclastics with little if any associated lava. Slumping of the crater wall during eruptions, gives the maars a wide caldera-like depression surrounded by a pyroclastic rim having smooth outer slopes. Cinder cones form central hills in a few maars. The largest maars on earth, being about three miles across, are much smaller than the large lunar craters; however, on the moon more violent and deeper gas eruptions combined with lesser gravity there might create large maar craters. Because of their similar topography, maars and meteoroid craters on earth have often been confused. Their rock fragments and internal structures do differ, but such details cannot be determined for lunar craters by telescopic studies. Many workers would ac-

cept strings of relatively small, dark-haloed, primary craters as lunar maars, since those on earth are often aligned.

Perhaps most astrogeologists now favor the impact hypothesis for large craters on the moon. Although slower-falling chunks striking a surface at an angle leave elongate scars, meteoroids produce round craters and rims. Having a high velocity, meteoroids penetrate deeply into rock while generating explosive shock waves that both shatter a lens beneath the crater and blow fragments up and outward (Fig. 16-22).

Well-preserved impact craters on earth, such as Meteor Crater in Arizona, have wide central depressions with bordering rims, a few slump terraces on in-facing walls, and in some cases central mounds of jumbled blocks. These central piles have been attributed to rebound of rock depressed during impact, or to rapidly inflowing material from crater walls. Terrestrial meteoroid craters all lack rays, perhaps because the rays are rapidly obliterated by erosion. However craters from underground nuclear bomb tests—which some consider comparable to those

Fig. 16-22
Looking into Meteor Crater of Northern Arizona. The site of this huge impact crater is an area of study for U.S. Astronauts in a joint program of geological training of the astronauts by the U.S. Geological Survey and Manned Spacecraft Center, NASA, Houston, Texas. Photograph courtesy of U.S. Geological Survey.

of meteoroids—have ray systems. Impact craters differ from maars in one aspect useful for photo interpretation. Maar rims have smooth outer slopes, whereas impact craters have hummocky rim flanks, more like those of major craters on the moon.

Much present thinking favors a compromise between extremes of the hot and cold moon schools. Large craters are probably impact features, but volcanism is not eliminated. By one recent suggestion, the large terraced craters resulted from meteoroids that penetrated to a magmatic layer, thereby triggering eruptions of pelean-type clouds to create the ray systems. Flowage of underlying magma caused slumping of crater walls to form the characteristic concentric steps of larger craters. Whatever the origin

of major craters, the smaller dark-haloed chain craters seem volcanic; maria could well be lava plains under granular blankets. To date we have many interesting ideas about the surface of the moon; however, the hypotheses may soon be tested.

The Apollo Program Astronauts, including professional geologists, are being trained in terrestrial and lunar geology for the Apollo Program of manned landings on the moon. Training and field testing of geologic and geophysical equipment are conducted from Flagstaff, Arizona, located near Meteor Crater, and in a field of extinct volcanos and lava flows which are terrestrial sites resembling those on the moon. Teams of scientists in the Apollo geologic group are making plans so that explorations on the lunar surface will obtain the most significant information bearing on geologic questions about the moon. A ten-year program is proposed.

Early Apollo missions will stress engineering and technical problems of getting men to the moon, studying their reactions to the environment, and returning them safely back to earth. Brief geologic explorations on foot will emphasize specimen collecting and photographing to gather data on the surface structure and materials of lunar plains. More lunar orbiting flights are also planned to allow increasingly detailed mapping, with a ten-year goal of 1:120,000 scale maps for the whole surface of the moon.

Later when operational procedures have progressed, surface missions to study maria, highlands, and major craters are proposed. A lunar ground vehicle should be available to carry two astronauts and 600 pounds of geologic equipment over a five-mile radius of action. A rocket-propelled craft may be ready for low, rapid flights to distances of about ten miles, over terrain too rough for surface vehicles.

A still later stage of geologic exploration could involve lunar bases allowing prolonged stays to investigate lunar surface processes, make detailed studies of key areas for several months, and conduct drilling operations to depths of 100 feet. Also envisioned are laboratory surface vehicles with a 500-mile range for missions lasting as long as two months. Such vehicles would be equipped to quickly analyze many samples, and to make traverses to distant rendezvous for the construction of long geologic and geophysical profiles of the moon's crust.

CONCLUSION

Astrogeology fires the imagination, but there are other less dramatic yet important new geologic frontiers. A significant recent development is the rising use of mathematics and statistics in geology. For along with the rapidly increasing reliance on physics and chemistry, much geologic research is becoming quantitative. In the past, geology leaned strongly towards description, classification, and emphasis on cause-and-effect explanations. It has been a "descriptive" science having few concepts based on numerical measurements and stated in mathematical formulas. In contrast, physics has been an "exact" science since Galileo Galilei (1564–1642) introduced experiment and mathematics into the study of falling bodies by rolling balls down inclined planes (where time was more easily measured than in free fall). Chemistry did not become exact until the eighteenth century because it began by treating more complex matters like combustion, or burning, and the nature and behavior of gases.

The late arrival of quantitative geology, in the mid-twentieth century, reflects, in part at least, the complexity of the phenomena studied. In dealing with long past events, much critical evidence has been lost. Nor can we directly observe the earth's internal processes. Even to begin to understand such things as volcanism, mountain building, and erosional processes requires a tremendous amount of preliminary observation and description. Such phenomena involve many variables that can not be neatly sorted out and simplified for mathematical treatment.

Nevertheless, geologic features can be measured. In fact, a problem lies in choosing what is significant for understanding a wealth of measurable things. This requires intuition and experience in old-fashioned "classical" geology. The application of mathematical models, as well as statistical techniques for collecting and interpreting masses of numerical data, started quantitative geology. But, the major breakthrough is part of the instrumental revolution. The digital computer rapidly handles complex numerical geologic problems that would take a lifetime for an army of mathematicians to solve.

Yet along with the new developments, many rewarding studies remain in classical geology. Much of the directly accessible land surface of the globe still needs old-fashioned mapping and field work. And despite volumes of existing discussion in geologic literature, a host of questions, large and small, still need exploration. How are mountains formed? What causes climatic changes and Ice Ages? Have the continents drifted apart?

SUGGESTED READINGS

Submarine Geology

Barnett, Lincoln, and the *Life* Editorial Staff, "The Miracle of the Sea," in *The World We Live In*, New York, Time Inc., 1955.

Heezen, B. C., and Menard, H. W., "Topography of the Deep-Sea Floor," in *The Sea*, Vol. 3, New York, Interscience Publishers, 1963.

Shepard, F. P., *The Earth Beneath the Sea*, Baltimore, Md., Johns Hopkins Press, 1959.

Shepard, F. P., and Dill, R. F., *Submarine Canyons and Other Sea Valleys*, Chicago, Rand McNally & Co., 1966.

Trumbull, Lyman, Pepper, & Thomasson, *An Introduction to the Geology and Mineral Resources of the Continental Shelves of the Americas*, U.S. Geological Survey, Bulletin 1067, Washington, U.S. Government Printing Office, 1958.

The Development of a New World View

Heirtzler, J. R., "Sea-Floor Spreading," in *Scientific American*, Vol. 219, No. 6, pp. 60–70, 1968.

Vine, F. J., "Sea-Floor Spreading—New Evidence," in *Journal of Geological Education*, Vol. 17, No. 1, pp. 6–16, 1969.

Astrogeology

Anonymous, *Astrogeology*, U.S. Geological Survey pamphlet, Washington, U.S. Government Printing Office, 1967.

Baldwin, R. B., *The Face of the Moon*, Chicago, University of Chicago Press, 1949.

Eardley, A. J., *General College Geology*, New York, Harper & Row, 1965. See Chapter 23, "Astrogeology."

Hibbs, A. R., "The Surface of the Moon," in *Scientific American*, Vol. 216, No. 3, pp. 60–74, 1967.

Shoemaker, E. M., "The Geology of the Moon," in *Scientific American*, Vol. 211, No. 6, 1964.

epilogue: Friends of the post-recent

"*The world-wide, highly radioactive marker bed at this locality one foot thick, conformably overlays a beer-can conglomerate.*" Cartoon by Gunther Von Gotsche, from Wyoming Geological Association Newsletter.

appendix A: More about the fossil record

BIOLOGICAL INTRODUCTION

As tools in dating, correlation, and environmental studies, we have already discussed the importance of fossils, but more should be added, since an account of past life is a major theme of earth history.

Plants, animals, and the chemical cycle of life

Just as the physical world is unified by a great geochemical cycle, so is the world of life unified by chemistry. From a purely chemical point of view, life is part of a long-continued circulation of six main elements (C, H, O, N, P, S)[1] from the water, soil, and air, into complicated organic molecules, and back again. The most critical role in this great life cycle is played by plants. They freshen the air with oxygen and manufacture the food on which the animal kingdom depends; where the cycle is retarded, they may furnish coal and some of the volume of oil. Most important in this grand scheme of life is the remarkable process of photosynthesis, wherein the green cells of plants use solar energy to convert carbon dioxide gas and water into sugars and starches with the liberation of free oxygen.

Because of the abundant oxygen in its atmosphere, the earth is unique among planets of the solar system. If the present atmosphere is derived from volcanic exhalations—the presently favored scientific view—the free oxygen cannot be an original constituent, for this reactive element is absent from volcanic gases, being combined with hydrogen and carbon in H_2O and CO_2. Some oxygen might have resulted from the splitting of water vapor when the earth was still very hot, and some may be continuously formed by the solar radiation bombarding and breaking down water vapor in the outermost atmosphere. But the large proportion of oxygen is best attributed to photosynthesis, which began in geologically remote time with the appearance of the first primitive green plants.

In a sense, all animals are parasites, for they cannot make food from the earth's raw materials. A host of predators eat other animals, but toward the bottom of any food pyramid are vegetarians living off plants. The starches and sugars produced by photosynthesis are carbohydrates, energy producers essential for the active lives of animals. No less important, plants also manufacture proteins, the foods for growth and replacement of body tissues. Plants take nitrogen from compounds in soil and water and combine it with the carbon, hydrogen, and oxygen of carbohydrates to synthesize amino acids, the "building blocks" of protein. Then, by adding sulfur and phosphorus, they convert the amino acids into the extremely complex and varied molecules called proteins. These, mixed with considerable water, form protoplasm which makes up the cells of all living things.

Protoplasm is the essential stuff of life. Its constant physical and chemical changes, col-

[1] Carbon, hydrogen, oxygen, nitrogen, phosphorus, sulfur.

lectively called metabolism, enable it to build new protoplasm exactly like itself. It oxidizes organic foods to liberate the energy required for vital processes, producing waste materials of CO_2 and H_2O and, in the case of proteins, nitrogenous urea as well. On the death of an organism, decay bacteria break down its remains into the simpler substances from which it was constructed and into ammonia, the end-product of protein decomposition.

The simpler products of metabolism and decay return to the air, water, and soil, where they are recycled. Certain bacteria convert ammonia into nitrate compounds, fertilizers which can be assimilated and used again by plants. In special cases where bacterial decay is inhibited, coal may result from the partial breakdown of woody plant material, and oil from incomplete decomposition of simple plants and animals. When burned, the free carbon in coal and the hydrocarbons of oil are rapidly oxidized to CO_2 and other simple products, ending this interruption of the grand cycle. Perhaps the most striking aspect of the geochemical cycle, through geologic time, is the remarkable structural plasticity of protoplasm that has allowed the evolution of the myriad forms of plants and animals.

Organizing the record

If minerals seem difficult to comprehend because of their variety, the animal and plant kingdoms are an even greater challenge. As the living and fossil organisms so far described number over a million and a quarter, a system of grouping and naming is absolutely necessary to make any sense of them.

Classification The Swedish botanist, Carl Von Linne (1707–1778), better known by the Latinized name, Linnaeus, set up the system of biological classification which, with modifications, is in use today. Linnaeus did not invent taxonomy, the science of plant and animal classification, but in his *Systemus Naturae* published in 1758, he organized previous attempts into a gen-

erally workable system. The Linnaen classification, which is used by paleontologists, sorts living things into a hierarchy of progressively smaller groups.

All living things belong either to the plant kingdom or the animal kingdom,[2] each of which is subdivided into major branches called *phyla*. These are, in turn, subdivided into smaller groups called *classes*, the classes into *orders*, orders into *families*, families into *genera*, and genera into *species*, which represent the smallest groups and are composed of *individuals*. As an example, let us classify man according to this hierarchy: kingdom animal; phylum chordata (animals having backbones or cartilaginous columns); class mammalia (warm-blooded animals that suckle their young); order primate (who live in trees or walk on their hind legs, have five fingers and five toes with flat nails); family hominidae (tool makers); genus *homo* (human beings); species *sapiens* (including all living groups of men, to which you as an individual belong). Precise classification requires still further grouping by adding "sub-" or "super-" to certain of the original divisions. The Linnaen system is not a simple classification scheme, but nobody has proposed a more useful one.

The designation of species has given paleontologists considerable trouble, for they deal with extinct life forms. Biologists define a species to include animals that interbreed. This is fine for biologists, because they can examine the sexual preferences of their subjects; but almost by definition paleontologists cannot, and must define their species by structural similarities which may well reflect interbreeding but cannot be positively proven. Moreover, in dealing with countless generations, paleontologists must contend with gradually changing organisms, which makes it difficult to draw hard lines between ancestral and descendant species. Paleontologically, a species may be only a snapshot of changing life through time.

[2] Modern usage sometimes includes a third kingdom, the protista, unicellular organisms which are hard to classify as either plant or animal.

Nomenclature To name a plant or animal it is not necessary to list each group it belongs to in descending order of the Linnaen hierarchy; a dual system of nomenclature, also established by Linnaeus, suffices. It uses two names, one for the genus and one for the species, rather like the family name and given names used for people. But naming organisms is not as easy as you might think. For scientific purposes, modern languages will not do because they would bring the confusion of many tongues, and because there just are not enough common names to go around. Moreover, the same common name is often applied to quite different organisms in different places. A gopher, for instance, is a turtle in Florida, a ground squirrel in the High Plains, and a pocket gopher in the Rocky Mountains. So, names are made up using ancient Greek and Latin which are international, or once were, among educated people, and, being "dead" languages, their word meanings do not change with usage. Many such scientific names are quite descriptive, if one knows Greek and Latin; *"pachycephalus,"* for instance, means "thick head" to coin an uncomplimentary name; *Felis domestica* translates as cat, domestic, a species including all house cats; *Tyrannosaurus rex,* the "tyrant king" was the largest of the flesh-eating dinosaurs.

Originally, biological classification was strictly empirical, a descriptive "pigeonholing" of plants and animals by their similarities and differences. Animals with backbones, for instance, form a major group further divisible according to whether they have scales, feathers, hair, and various other structures. When the concept of evolution came in vogue and was reinforced by accumulated evidence from paleontology, the classification was seen to be genetic—organisms were related, the more complex being descendants of simpler ones. Classification had an integrated framework whose elegance is further evidence of evolution.

The Concept of Organic Evolution As the physical world has gradually changed through geologic time, so has the world of life, for converging lines of evidence clearly indicate that more-advanced plants and animals developed from simpler ancestors. This is the doctrine of organic evolution which, like physical Uniformitarianism, has triumphed over catastrophic explanations. Baron Cuvier, for instance, who was one of the first to recognize faunal succession, was a whole-hearted Catastrophist, convinced that differing populations were specially created in their final form, and later exterminated wholesale, to be eventually replaced by newly created and different forms. Today, no competent scientists dealing with life and its history doubt that organic evolution has occurred; the uncertainties now revolve around its causes.

Biological evidence of evolution

Several lines of evidence for evolution are biological, being based on the study of living plants and animals.

Experimentation Man has experimentally accelerated changes in certain groups by selective breeding. All dogs from Chihuahua to Saint Bernard have been produced from wolf-like forebears. The highly productive types of hybrid corn result from selective breeding. Unfortunately, so do bacteria immune to antibiotic drugs. The disease germs are an expanded population descended from a few ancestors who managed to survive the application of the drugs, and, unlike the other examples, are a case of unplanned experimentation. However, despite their seeming differences, all dogs belong to a single species, or kind, of animal *Canus familiaris,* because they can all interbreed. Moreover, general experimentation has not produced a new genus. So such cases, although suggestive, are not in themselves proof of evolution.

Comparative Anatomy The anatomy of living forms is best explained by evolution. For example, the skeletal plan of all legged vertebrates

401

including such diverse animals as lizards, dogs, monkeys, and men can be matched bone for bone. In examining the front limbs, the flipper of a seal and the wing of a bat, although used for quite different purposes, have corresponding bones which can also be matched in the arm of a man or the front legs of a crocodile. Each has a single upper bone (called the humerus), two bones below the elbow (the radius and ulna), a cluster of wrist bones (carpals), and groups of finger or toe bones (phalanges). The bones do differ in shape and size, but this reflects their special uses. The soft anatomy, including muscles, nerves, the circulatory systems, and internal organs, are also remarkably similar. Moreover, structural resemblances can be demonstrated in groups of invertebrates and plants. Such anatomical similarities are most easily explained if groups of animals and plants are related, rather than products of special creation.

The biological case is further strengthened by *vestigial structures*. The appendix in man has no function although in other animals, rabbits for instance, it is a functional part of the digestive system. Pelvic girdles in some snakes, wings of ostriches, and splint bones of horses are all useless structures corresponding to functional parts of other creatures. All such remnants suggest a degeneration of features once useful in some ancestral form, hence, evolution.

Embryology   "Ontogeny recapitulates phylogeny" is an impressive statement attributed to the German zoologist, Haeckel, which is known as the Biogenetic Law. It means that as an individual animal develops from a fertilized single cell through the early stages before acquiring its adult form (this individual history being ontogeny), the animal retraces the history of its entire race (phylogeny). In man, for example, human embryos pass through stages when they have non-functional gills (suggesting an aquatic life) and tails, and in a late prenatal stage are covered with hair which is lost before birth. Support for the parallelism of individual and racial development is given in the paleontological record of many invertebrate stocks where juvenile forms show stages like the adult forms of earlier geo-

logic periods. Admittedly, living forms do not follow the sequence perfectly because many phylogenetic stages may be omitted, the sequence may be partly juggled, and sometimes new features appear that do not characterize an adult ancestor.[3] Thus, the biogenetic "law" is really not a law. In general, however, animals which are thought to be closely related from other lines of evidence have similar embryonic development; differentiation and specialization come about at maturity. Thus the similarity of earlier stages strongly suggests a common descent.

Biochemical Evidence   Human blood yields little precipitate when mixed with the blood serum of a reptile, somewhat more with that of a monkey, and large amounts when mixed with serum from anthropoid apes. In short, the closer the assumed relationship of animals, the more similar their blood. Any one of these "facts of life" is hardly proof, yet they do give converging lines of evidence. This biological case for organic evolution is strong because it deals with the complete spectrum of living organisms whose whole anatomy, both hard and soft, can be studied in great detail, and which can be manipulated, or experimented with, to some extent. Moreover, the work of Alfred R. Wallace, and especially of Charles Darwin, that established the concept was largely based on living forms. But biology treats only the end products, plants and animals as they now exist, so its case rests entirely on circumstantial evidence.

PALEONTOLOGY

Paleontologists

For the record of life through the ages, we are indebted to paleontologists — hybrids, part geologist and part biologist. In defining their work, some purists talk of paleobiology which includes *paleobotany*, the study of fossil plants, and *paleozoology*, the study of fossil animals. Commonly,

[3] The umbilical cord is a most obvious example.

however, those who deal with animals call themselves paleontologists: *invertebrate paleontologists* deal with spineless creatures, such as worms, sponges, clams, and crabs; *vertebrate paleontologists* study animals with a spinal cord; *micro-paleontologists* squint through a microscope at tiny non-cellular organisms or minute invertebrates. Whatever the label, they must be well grounded in biology, for in paleontology the present is as much the key to the past as in other geologic fields.

Since fossils are defined as evidence of past life, the question arises, how far past? The long-extinct dinosaurs are clearly fossils; the remains interred in the local cemetery are not. "If it still smells take it to a zoologist, if not to a paleontologist" is an oversimplification. The beginning of written history is used by many paleontologists as a convenient dividing line between present life, treated by biologists, and "prehistoric" life, or fossils. But some would quibble, so perhaps we can only say that fossils are those past remains that paleontologists and paleobotanists study. In any case, without fossils, and paleontologists too, there would be no satisfactory history of the earth.

The uses of paleontology

Beside being *time pieces* and *environmental clues*, fossils are—by definition—signs of past life; so paleontologists with a more biological bent use them to reconstruct the particular plants and animals they represent, and study them as communities of individuals interacting with each other, and, perhaps most important, use them to gain some insight into organic evolution.

Reconstructing Extinct Organisms Restorations of animals are largely based on hard parts. External skeletons, or shells, are often found intact in the case of clams and other small invertebrates living in marine environments where quick burial and preservation are common. Vertebrate skeletons, however, are usually found as dismembered pieces, for unless those on land were mired in a swamp, overwhelmed by an

ash fall, or caught in some other comparable situation, their burial takes time, leaving them prey for scavengers. Yet, from a knowledge of the skeletal anatomy of modern animals, skillful piecing together of fragments, and those few lucky finds of complete skeletons, paleontologists have a good idea of the boney structure of most fossil vertebrates.

Clothing skeletons with muscles, fat, hair, and skin, or filling in the fleshy anatomy of invertebrates requires, at best, a certain amount of guesswork, for corruptible flesh is rarely preserved, and largely known only in such late fossil forms as the Pleistocene mammoths frozen in the Arctic tundras. Mummified remains are even more rare, although in Wyoming two dinosaurs were dried out before fossilization, thereby preserving details of their hides. Such things as the color of extinct animals, vertebrate or invertebrate, may never be surely known. For instance, dinosaurs may have been either gaily colored or somber; the modern reptiles, to which they may be compared, are found with both types of coloration.

But bone and meat are functionally related, so museum mounts, pictures, and the like, showing the living shape of extinct animals are not pure guesswork. Based on the anatomy of living animals and the mechanical workings of their various parts, musculature can be inferred from the size and shape of bones, and the scars where muscles were attached. Fatty structures, however, are less predictable. Whether fossil camels had humps is as impossible to determine from skeletons as whether a man had a paunch or a woman was curvaceous. Yet, reconstructions do represent the admirable urge of paleontologists to present their scraps of stone as living things, and, overall, most reconstructions are not concoctions of unbridled imagination. For instance, lobe-finned fish, a group from which amphibians probably arose, were thought to have been extinct since Cretaceous time. Since 1938, however, representatives of the lobe-fins have been taken from deep waters off Africa. They are remarkably similar to reconstructions of a kind of Cretaceous lobe-fin previously known only from reconstructions based on fossils.

Environments and Ecology Once fossils are visualized as living plants and animals, they allow the reconstruction of past environments. Any animal, including fossil forms, reflects the sum total of complexly interwoven physical and biological elements of the worlds in which they lived. The basic elements of environments, past and present, are heat, light, and the surrounding medium. So, to prosper, organisms must be adjusted to temperature, pressure, and movements of their native air or water—to deep or shallow, muddy or clear water in oceans, streams, and ponds; to humid temperate climates, tundras, rainforests, or deserts—in short, to the many elements of their surroundings. In an earlier section we mentioned how different forms that reflect different conditions have caused problems in correlation, as well as helping in determining environments of depositions.

Many paleontologists today are much interested in ecology—the study of organisms in relation to their biological communities and to their physical surroundings, so that they can survive, grow, and reproduce their kind. It is the study of total environment or, put another way, "the balance of nature." For instance, in a modern Rocky Mountain population, deer are browsers on leaves and twigs and do not really prosper on hay, and mountain lions prefer a diet of venison. Squirrels live on nuts and seeds and are, in turn, preyed on by agile martens who are no threat to deer; and so it goes. Each animal has a somewhat different role or ecological niche to fill, and should two groups with similar demands come together, one of them must change its habits, depart, or die out. These relations are not completely understood in living populations, so the study of paleoecology based on fossils is even more challenging.

Evidence of Evolution The proof of evolution has come from the fossil record which yields the only direct, that is, observable, evidence of gradually changing forms of plants and animals. Faunal succession, seen in rocks stacked one on the other, adds the needed dimension, unavailable to biologists—the geological dimension of time. There are certain drawbacks to working with fossils. As previously mentioned, the reconstruction of individuals as they were in life is often difficult and tentative in varying degrees. More important, the fossil record is definitely biased towards certain groups, so that very rarely is anything like a complete population represented as it must have been in life. Marine invertebrates having resistant hard parts, such as clams, coral, and the like, are preserved out of all proportion to their relative importance in the original living population, because they had hard parts and lived in an environment where rapid burial was common. Yet, there is no doubt that even in the seas multitudes of delicately armored, and soft-bodied shell-less creatures lived with them. The Burgess Shale of Cambrian age in the Canadian Rockies has a locality where, because of unique conditions, a multitude of soft-bodied invertebrates are preserved. All other Cambrian fossil localities would leave the erroneous impression that the early Paleozoic seas were populated almost entirely by hard-shelled forms. On land, the chances of preservation, in general, are poor because of the dominance of erosion, but a few places such as the Cenozoic Florissant Lake beds of Colorado do give rare, but significant, glimpses of the true diversity of past floras and faunas.

The genealogical record of the commonly preserved organisms is not as complete as we would like it. Because of unconformities, changes in conditions suitable for preservation, and migration of populations, there are gaps in the vertical record of changing faunas, through time—recall that the master geologic rock column had to be pieced together from many different localities. However, despite the admitted imperfections of the fossil record, hundreds of thousands of fossils have been collected and studied, and, even if they represent a miniscule fraction of former life, they quite adequately demonstrate certain basic facts. Life began in the remote past as simple organisms and has been continuous, and more complex forms have evolved from simpler ones, which is the essence of the geological account of life through the ages.

appendix B: Elementary aspects of maps

Since maps are an essential geologic tool, their general characteristics and features should be understood. A map is a two-dimensional diagram of an area of the earth's surface, and is usually to an exact scale. That is, they are drawings on flat paper of the ground and associated features, and they usually show things as a small fraction of their true size.

Maps give two general types of information: *planimetric information,* which gives the place or location of things, and *topographic information,* which shows relief, or landscape features. Planimetric information includes such things as the location of roads, cities, and towns (as on a highway map), land ownership, the location of rivers, lake and sea shores, and the location of rock types or units (on geologic maps). Topographic information indicates slopes, the unevenness of the ground associated with mountains and valleys, plains, and other relief features.

Map orientation and declination

With a few exceptions, maps are constructed so that the top of the map is north, the bottom south, the right side east, and the left side west. To read a map in the field, it is best to orient the map with the ground. To do this, turn the top of the map towards north on the ground; then points on the map will correspond in direction to points on the ground surface.

Declination is the difference between true north (the direction to the North Geographic Pole) and magnetic north (the direction which a compass needle points). It is given in degrees of angular measure, and shown by a V-shaped symbol in which a T or star indicates True North, and a half arrow sometimes with an MN shows Magnetic North. (Some declination symbols show still another north, marked by a Y or GN, which is Grid North of the military grid system.)

True North of the Geographic Grid (the system of latitude and longitude) coincides with the earth's axis of rotation, but the earth's magnetic poles do not coincide with the axis of rotation. The Magnetic North Pole is in the Arctic Islands of Canada; and to complicate matters further, the magnetic pole slowly migrates with time, thus changing declinations. The change is slight, however, for recently made maps, and charts and tables are available to determine necessary corrections.

One should know the declination in an area for the following reasons: declinations are different on different maps; most directions in the field are taken with magnetic compasses (some compasses can be adjusted to read true directions, but some cannot); and maps are constructed in reference to true directions (not magnetic).

Map scales

The scale of a map is the ratio between the distance separating two points as measured on the map, and the actual distance separating the same two points on the ground. For instance, on a map the distance between the centers of city A and city B, as measured with a ruler, might be one inch (map distance); but the actual distance between the two cities is 50 miles (ground distance). The general scale relation can be given as a simple formula:

$$\text{map scale} = \frac{\text{map distance}}{\text{ground distance}}.$$

Map scale can be presented in three different ways; however, all give the ratio of map to ground distance. The *Fractional Scale* (sometimes called the R.F., meaning representative fraction) is the most important and widely used. For example, $\frac{1}{10,000}$ (sometimes written as $1:10,000$) is a fractional scale indicating that one unit measured on the map is equal to 10,000 of the same units on the ground. No particular unit of measure is implied or required for use with such a scale. Thus, any unit can be substituted into the scale. As examples, $1:10,000$ can be taken as one inch (on the map) equals 10,000 inches (on the ground), or one foot (map) equals 10,000 feet (ground), or

one centimeter equals 10,000 centimeters. So long as the same unit of measure is assumed for the top and bottom of the fraction, any units may be used. Thus, this is a truly international scale wherever arabic numerals are used.

The *Word Scale* makes it easier to visualize scale relations. In it, the map distance is stated as some convenient small unit, and the ground distance is given in a common larger unit. Examples would be: "one inch equals two miles," or "one centimeter equals one kilometer," or "1″ = 1000 ft." Although convenient, such scales are not international since you could read them only if you knew the language and units of measure used.

The *Graphical Scale* is most useful for measuring distances on maps. In these scales an actual line is drawn on the map (usually at the bottom) and divided into segments which are labelled with corresponding ground distances. These scales are constructed to any convenient ground units; but, where more than one certain unit is desired, a separate scale must be drawn for each.

The United States Land Survey

The United States Land Survey system, invented by Thomas Jefferson, was adopted by Congress in 1785 for the survey of the Northwest Territories. It is now used for location and land designation in the United States, except for the original thirteen colonies, some other eastern states, and Texas.

The system is based on squares, six miles on a side, which are called Congressional Townships. These townships are located in reference to the intersection of a true north–south line, or Principal Meridian (Fig. B-1a), and a true east–west line, a geographic parallel called a Base Line. Some 32 different systems of townships are controlled by intersecting Principal Meridians and Base Lines which are given either numbers or names.

Land in the first east–west row of townships north of a given Base Line is designated as being in Township One North (T.1N.); land in the second row is designated as being in T.2N., etc.

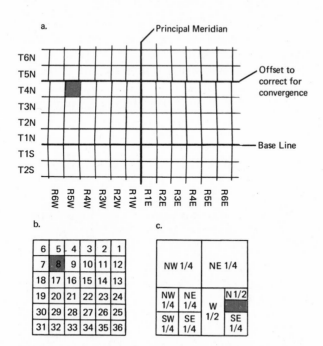

U.S. Land Survey Diagrams

Fig. B-1
U.S. Land Survey diagrams: (a) Division into townships. (b) Divisions within a township. (c) Divisions within a section.

South of the Base Line, land is designated as T.1S., T.2S., etc. The north–south columns of townships are designated as Ranges. Range One West (R.1W.), and Range One East (R.1E.) lie on their respective sides of a Principal Meridian. R.2E. and R.2W. are the next columns out from the Principal Meridian, R.3W. and R.3E. next beyond, and so on, to the limits of the area controlled by a particular Meridian and Base Line. Thus, the Congressional Township in the accompanying illustration would be designated as T.4N., R.5W.

Since the townships are bounded on east and west by true north–south lines, or geographic meridians, the townships would become markedly narrower progressively farther away from the base line because meridians converge towards the Poles. Thus a correction is made by setting back the townships to a six-mile width at the north side of each four sets of townships (i.e., at T.4N., T.8N., T.12N., etc.).

Each township is divided into 36-mile squares, called Sections. The sections are numbered as shown in Fig. B-1b. Thus, land shown by the shaded square would be designated as S 8 T.4N., R.5W.

The sections are divided according to aliquot parts; for example, into the northeast, southeast, northwest, and southwest quarters; or northern and southern, and eastern and western halves. In turn, a unit such as a quarter-section can be further divided into parts using the same system (Fig. B-1c), and these smaller parts can be further subdivided by the same method. Thus, in the accompanying diagram the area described (the shaded rectangle) is the S½ NE¼ SE¼ sec. 8 T.4N., R.5W. of the 6th Principal Meridian. The smaller land designations of the U.S. Land Survey may seem complicated, but always remember that land designations start with the smallest unit and progress to the larger ones.

Introduction to topographic maps

Four main methods are used to represent relief, or topography, on maps, and some maps combine several methods. In the method of *altitude tints*, different colors are used for specified ranges of elevations. For instance, green might represent elevations from zero feet (sea level) to 1000 feet above sea level; yellow might indicate elevations from 1000 to 2000 feet; brown, 2000 to 3000 feet; red over 3000 feet (Fig. B-2). However, check each map used, for the colors for various ranges of elevations are not always the same. This system of altitude tints is commonly used on small-scale maps (which cover large areas), air navigation maps, and some large-scale (small area) foreign maps.

The method of *hachures* makes use of many short lines, each aligned with the direction of steepest slope. Although complicated methods of hachuring were constructed for use on detailed maps of small areas in the past, simple hachures are used today mostly for small-scale maps requiring no great detail.

Relief is also shown by *shading*—most commonly assuming a northwest source of illumination (representing the sun's position), so that east-to-south slopes are shown by shadows and west-to-north slopes appear illuminated. Shaded relief maps give a strong visual impression of topography, resembling the ground as it would be seen from an airplane. Although shading is sometimes used alone as on maps issued by some airlines, it is often combined with other methods.

Although each of the methods just described for showing relief serves certain purposes, the most precise information as to elevations is provided by the system of *contour lines*. A contour is a line on a map connecting points of equal elevation. On any particular map, the contour lines have a constant vertical spacing called the contour interval (a few maps use two different intervals). To help visualize contours, consider that a river has been dammed and the water rises in the resulting lake. If air photos are taken at each five-foot vertical rise of the lake surface, the shorelines represent contours having a five-foot contour interval (Fig. B-3). Where slopes around the lake are gentle, these successive "contours" will be widely spaced because the water has spread far *laterally* during its rise. If slopes are steep, the "contours," or lake shores, will be

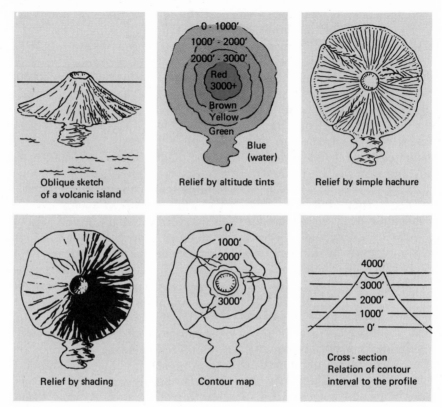

Fig. B-2
Methods of showing relief maps. The same volcanic island is illustrated by various methods.

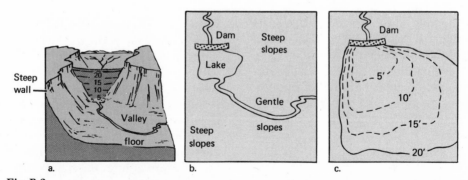

Fig. B-3
(a) Oblique view of a lake starting to fill behind a dam. (b) Map view showing the lake shore after a 5-foot vertical rise in water level. (c) Lake shore shown at successive rises in water level. The dotted lines approximate contours.

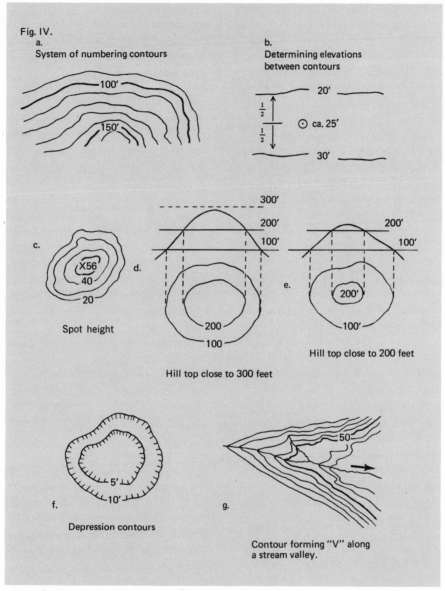

Fig. IV.

a. System of numbering contours

b. Determining elevations between contours

c. Spot height

d. Hill top close to 300 feet

e. Hill top close to 200 feet

f. Depression contours

g. Contour forming "V" along a stream valley.

Fig. B-4
Contours as they are indicated and read on maps of the U.S. Geological Survey.

closer together, since the water is restricted as the lake deepens. The same idea applies to the reading of contour maps; closely spaced contour lines mean steeper slopes, and widely spaced ones indicate gentler slopes.

The contour interval selected for a particular map depends on the scale of the map and the relief of the area represented. Small-scale maps (covering large areas) usually require large contour intervals of 50, 100, 200 feet, or more. On the other hand, maps of smaller areas (large scale) tend to have intervals of 25 feet or less.

Relief also determines the C.I. (contour interval) used. Mountainous regions (high relief) require large contour intervals so that the lines will not merge into a solid and unreadable mass. Near-flat areas (low relief) require small contour intervals to bring out topographic detail. Some maps of very flat areas use contour intervals as small as one foot.

On the commonly used maps of the U.S. Geological Survey, the contours (shown as brown lines) require close observation because they are often closely spaced (Fig. B-4). Because of this, not every contour is labelled as to elevation. By convention, every fifth contour is made heavier than the others and labelled. To get the elevation of an unlabelled contour, find the nearest labelled one and—using the contour interval—count and calculate the elevation of unmarked line. If a point lies between contours, its elevation can be approximated. If the point is between a 20-foot and 30-foot contour, one can safely say its elevation is more than 20 feet and less than 30 feet. However, assuming the ground slope is constant between the contours, a closer approximation is possible. If the point is half-way between the contours horizontally on the map, you can assume it is also half-way vertically, and therefore has an elevation of 25 feet. A point one-quarter of the distance from a 50-foot contour towards a 60-foot contour could be assumed to have an elevation of about 52.5 feet, and so on.

Hills are special problems. Some do have their tops marked by spot heights (brown ×'s) giving the elevation. In other cases, the elevation can be safely stated as higher than the last contour shown on the hill and lower than the next not appearing. Thus, the summit of a hill might be described as more than 100 feet, but less than 120 feet. However, a closer approximation is possible assuming the hill is smoothly rounded. Where the diameter of the last closed contour is wide, you can assume the highest point is near the next highest contour that does not show. If the hill were a flat-topped mesa, you could be wrong; but usually, by studying several hilltops on the map the probability of mesas can be determined. On the other hand, if the last closed contour has a small diameter—compared to the general contour spacing—one can assume that the height is close to the last closed contour.

Because most landscapes are cut by stream valleys, large and small, contours commonly have V-shaped deflections where they cross a drainage line. A simple but useful rule for reading or sketching contour lines is that the point of the V is directed upstream and the widening of the V is downstream.

Special contours show closed depressions such as volcanic craters or hollows containing lakes. Such depression contours are marked by hachures pointing towards the center of the depression. These contours are read in the same way as regular contours in terms of contour interval and elevations.

This discussion points out what contours are. However, the real art of reading contour maps is the ability to interpret geologic landforms, structures, and rock types indicated by the contour patterns. This demands some training and the ability to visualize the earth's surface in three dimensions from squiggly brown lines on a flat piece of paper.

GLOSSARY

This glossary contains the "less ordinary" geologic terms, some common ones that are usually misused, and some nontechnical words that may be troublesome to the average student. It is designed to help the reader of this particular book; it is no substitute for a standard English Dictionary, or the more specialized and extensive *Dictionary of Geologic Terms* or the *Glossary of Geology and Related Sciences* published by the American Geological Institute.

Abrasion As applied to wind action, the natural sand blasting of rock surfaces by wind-blown material.

Absolute dating Dating of a geologic feature or event in years.

Abyssal Related to the deepest parts of the ocean.

Acraniata A chordate animal with no definite head, brain, or paired appendages.

Adaptive Showing favorable adjustment to a situation or surroundings.

Adventitious Formed in odd places or without any particular order.

Agate A very finely crystalline kind of quartz containing colored layers.

Agglomerate A volcanic rock composed of coarse, often angular, fragments.

Aggrade To build up or raise a stream channel or land surface by deposition.

Algae A large group of non-vascular plants that have chlorophyl, but lack roots, stems, or leaves.

Alluvial fan A fan-shaped landform developed where a stream deposits material when flowing into an area of lesser slopes, as, for example, a mountain stream emerging into a flat floored major valley.

Alluvium Clastic deposits laid down by the action of modern streams.

Amino acids The building blocks of protein.

Ammonoid An extinct shelled cephalopod having folded or wrinkled cross-partitions in its shell.

Amoeba A very simple, very small, one-celled animal.

Amphibian A vertebrate animal which has gills in the immature swimming stage, can travel on land but (with a few exceptions) must breed in water.

Analogy A similarity of function or properties without necessarily being identical. Or, reasoning by comparing something to something better known.

Andesite A fine-grained volcanic rock lacking quartz, and composed mainly of feldspar (plagioclase) and dark iron-magnesian silicates. Named after Andes Mountains whose volcanos contain this rock.

Angiosperm Flowering plant. The dominant vegetation of the present day. Seeds are covered. Many trees, shrubs, vegetables and flowers are examples.

Antecedent (stream) Refers to a stream that maintains its previous course when mountains or hills are uplifted across it.

Anthracite "Hard" coal. It is black with a glassy luster, and has a high percentage of fixed carbon.

Anthropoid Of a group of higher primates including man, apes and monkeys.

Anthropomorphism To ascribe human attributes to other natural things.

Antibiotic Harmful to or destroying bacteria.

Anticline A fold in which the center moved upward relative to the sides when it formed. It is, or was, convex upward.

Aphanitic Refers to textures of fine-grained igneous rocks which have crystals too small to be readily visible without magnification.

Aquifer A rock layer or zone from which water can be obtained.

Archaic Belonging to an earlier time.

Archipelago A chain or group of islands.

Arête Sharp, knife-like ridges between glaciated valleys.

Arkose A sandstone containing abundant grains of feldspar as well as quartz.

Artesian spring A place where water is rising from depth under pressure.

Artiodactyl A hoofed mammal having an even number of useful toes such as the pig and cow.

Arthropod An invertebrate animal having jointed legs and a segmented shell of chitin. Insects, spiders, and crabs are examples.

Ash (volcanic) Fine, dust-sized solid material erupted by volcanos.

Astrogeology The study of planets and other solid bodies in the solar system.

Aves The birds.

Badland A region almost totally lacking vegetation

and eroded into a rough miniature mountain country of intricately dissected gulleys, ridges, and pinnacles.

Bar A ridge, usually of sand or gravel, in a sea, lake or stream. Bars may be submerged or rise above the water.

Barrier beach A long sand ridge rising above the sea which is separated from the shore by a lagoon.

Basalt A dark-colored, fine-grained, igneous rock containing dark feldspars and ferromagnesian minerals. The most abundant type of volcanic rock worldwide.

Batholith A very large intrusive body of granite or granitic rocks. They are exposed at the ground surface only after long erosion.

Bathyscaphe A specially designed submarine for very deep diving.

Beach A sand, pebble, or cobble covered slope along the water's edge.

Bed load Stream-carried material that remains in contact with or bounces along the bottom of the stream channel.

Bedrock Solid rock either exposed at the earth's surface or covered by unconsolidated materials.

Belemnoid An extinct cephalopod commonly leaving its cigar-shaped internal skeleton as a fossil.

Biased Slanted. Showing partiality or preference.

Bituminous (coal) "Soft" coal. It is black, has a blocky fracture, and gives off volatile matter on burning.

Bivalve An animal having two shells, such as a clam.

Bomb (volcanic) Large fragments blown out of a volcano as solid or plastic masses.

Brachiopod A marine animal having two unequal shells, commonly attached to the sea bottom by a fleshy stalk.

Breakers Collapsing waves that have moved into shallow water near shore.

Bryophyte A group of non-vascular plants that may have stems and leaves, but lack true roots.

Bryozoans Small colonial animals living mainly in the sea. Called "moss animals," they build lace-like, twig-like, or mounded colonies.

Calcite The mineral composed of calcium carbonate $(CaCO_3)$.

Caldera A large depression commonly steep-sided and several times as wide as it is deep found in volcanic areas, often in the center of a volcano.

Canine Of or related to a dog. Also a stabbing tooth in mammals.

Capacity (of streams) The ability of a stream to transport in terms of the total amount of debris it can carry past a given point in a given unit of time.

Carapace A boney or chitinous shell covering an animal's back.

Carbohydrate An organic compound containing carbon, hydrogen and oxygen—such as sugar or starch.

Carbonaceous Coaly or containing carbon.

Carbonation As a form of chemical weathering, refers to reactions involving carbon dioxide and water that create soluble carbonates.

Cartilaginous Composed of gristle, or tough elastic animal substance.

Catastrophism The concept that widespread, or world-wide, often violent events of far greater magnitude than can be observed at the present time have created rocks and topography of the earth and suddenly exterminated large groups of living things at various times.

Cave A natural cavity, large enough to be entered by man, that extends back into total darkness.

Cephalopod The most advanced group of molluscs. They swim by expelling a water jet. The squid, octopus, and shelled nautilus are examples.

Cetacea Mammals leading a fish-like existence such as the whale.

Chert A very dense sedimentary rock composed largely of very finely crystalline silica.

Chitinous Having an organic composition like fingernails.

Chlorophyl The green substance in plants that is responsible for photosynthesis.

Chordate An animal with a backbone or stiffening internal flexible rod.

Chronology The measuring of time or ordering of events.

Cinders (volcanic) Rough sand to pebble-sized materials erupted by volcanos.

Cirque The rounded, armchair-like head of a glacial valley.

Clastic Composed of fragments of older rocks or solid organic material.

Clay May refer to certain specific very finely crystalline *minerals*, or to materials consisting of solid particles of the finest *size*, or to materials that are plastic and *moldable* when wet.

Claystone A consolidated sedimentary rock consisting largely of clay particles.

Cleavage (mineral) A tendency to split more readily in certain parallel directions than in others.

Coagulate To form a clot or jelly-like mass.

Coal A combustible black (sometimes brown) rock formed by the alteration of plants, mainly woody, so that the carbon content is increased.

Coast A zone of indefinite width from the waters edge inland to a major topographic change.

Coelenterata A group (phylum) of simple animals having a two-layered body and a simple digestive track with a single opening which may be surrounded by tentacles. Jelly fish are an example.

Colloidal suspension (in waters) Refers to very fine particles of clay size held up in water by the continuous movement and jostling of water molecules.

Colonial Refers to a group of similar animals living in such close connection that the individuals are not readily recognizable from the mass of the resulting structure.

Competence (of streams) The ability of a stream to transport in terms of the largest sized particles or boulders it can move.

Concretions Nodular masses which are more resistant than the sedimentary beds containing them.

Conduction The transfer of heat (or sound or electricity) through material without movements of masses of the material.

Condylarth Primitive hoofed mammals.

Conglomerate A sedimentary rock composed mainly of rounded fragments larger than sand. It is composed of pebbles, cobbles, or larger fragments.

Convection The transfer of heat through a liquid or gas by movements of masses of the material.

Correlation To determine that rocks in different places are of equivalent age. Or that events in separate areas occurred at the same time.

Corrosion (of streams) Stream erosion accomplished by solution of rocks.

Coral A marine organism that lives attached to the bottom as a solitary individual or together in colonies. Their calcareous external skeletons may form large limestone masses, or reefs. They are coelenterates.

Cordillera A mass of mountain ranges, valleys and plains which has an overall elongation or trend. More specifically the north-trending mountainous region of North America extending from the edge of the Great Plains to the Pacific Ocean.

Cosmic Belonging to the universe.

Cosmic ray Intense, penetrating radiations coming from outer space.

Cosmogony A branch of astronomy dealing with hypotheses for the origin of the Universe.

Cotylosaur An extinct ancestoral reptile.

Crinoid A marine invertebrate animal attached to the sea floor by a flexible jointed stalk, and having a head or cup with many radiating arms. A "sea lily."

Cross-laminations Sloping layers lying at a distinct angle to the larger layers which contain them (cross-bedding).

Crossopterygian A fish with lungs and fins with stalks of bone surrounded by flesh.

Crystal A solid bounded by smooth faces whose arrangement results from an orderly and repeated internal arrangement of atoms.

Crystalline Having a definite and repeated arrangement of atoms (ions).

Crystalline rocks Commonly used loosely to refer to igneous and metamorphic rocks (not sedimentary). More exactly, the term applies to any rock having easily discernable crystals.

Cycad A tree with a stubby trunk and palm-like fronds. A gymnosperm plant.

Daughter product Element produced from another element during radioactive decay.

Deduction Reasoning from a general principle to particular conclusions or consequences.

Deflation The blowing away of material by wind action.

Deformation Change in original shape or volume.

Delta A low plain underlain by deposits laid down where a stream flows into an ocean, lake or other standing body of water.

Dendritic Refers to a stream pattern that is generally tree-like in its branchings.

Density Mass per unit volume.

Deposition (geologic) The settling out of particles or precipitation of materials in solution to form a rock or potential rock.

Desert A region of sparse vegetation that usually does not support much life.

Desilication Includes various chemical weathering reactions that remove silica from rocks and soil.

Dew point The temperature at which an air mass is saturated with water vapor.

Diamond Composed of pure carbon and is the hardest mineral known.

Diatom A single-celled microscopic plant that lives in water and secretes a siliceous skeleton.

Differentiate To separate into unlike parts.

Dike A flat, tabular igneous intrusion that cuts across older structures.

Dip The inclination of a rock layer or surface measured from the horizontal. It is at right angles to the strike.

Discharge (stream) The amount of water flowing through a cross-section of a stream in a given unit of time.

Disconformity An unconformity wherein the older and younger beds are parallel.

Dramatis personae The cast of characters in a play.

Drift (glacial) A general term for any deposits associated with glaciation. They could be laid down by ice, melt-water streams, or in glacial lakes.

Dune A mound, ridge, or hill piled up by wind. Usually dunes consist of sand, but silt and clay dunes also exist.

Dunite A crystalline rock largely composed of the mineral olivine. A variety of periodotite.

Echinoderms A group (phylum) of animals having a five-fold, radial symmetry. An example is the star fish.

Echinoid A free-moving, marine, invertebrate animal having a five-rayed symmetry. They belong to the phylum Echinodermata. Sea urchins are an example.

Eclogite A granular rock largely composed of garnet and pyroxene.

Ecology The study of organisms and how they relate to their environment.

Edentate A mammal that lacks teeth or has simple teeth without enamel.

Effluent Flowing out of. May refer to a stream receiving some water from ground water.

Elasticity The property applied to bodies which return to their original form after a distorting force is removed.

Embryology The science dealing with the development of plants and animals after fertilization but before they develop their typical form.

Empirical Based on observation with little or no interpretation.

Enigma Something puzzling.

Environment All the conditions in a place which influence communities of life.

Epeirogeny Broad movements of the earth's crust. May cause major uplift and downwarping, but the rocks involved are not intensely folded.

Epicenter The apparent point of maximum intensity of an earthquake at the surface of the ground.

Epoch A unit of geologic time. A subdivision of a geologic period.

Era A major division of geologic time. Generally five eras are recognized (see a geologic time scale).

Erosion The progressive removal, or carving away, of rock and other earth materials by geologic processes acting on or near the earth's surface.

Erratic A glacial-transported boulder of different rock type than the rock on which it rests.

Escape velocity The velocity a particle or object must reach to escape from the gravitational attraction of the earth (or other massive body).

Esker A long sinuous ridge of stratified meltwater material laid down in streams flowing beneath a glacier.

Estuary The lower part of streams or drainage channels which are affected by the rise and fall of tide from the adjacent sea.

Eurypterid An extinct arthropod with poison glands but no antennae.

Eustatic change A world-wide change in sea level.

Evaporite A rock made of minerals whose deposition resulted from complete, or extensive, evaporation of water in which they were dissolved.

Evolution Progressive change, often to more complex forms.

Exhumed Re-exposed by the removal of rock material.

Exoskeleton A shell, or hard protective outer cover of an invertebrate animal.

Extrusive (igneous) Molten rock material that rises and pours or is ejected onto the earth's surface.

Facies Differences from place to place in a rock unit laid down at the same time. (The meaning of the term is complicated by several different interpretations.)

Fathom Six feet. A nautical unit for depth measurement.

Fault A fracture along which rock masses have been offset.

Fauna A group of animals that lived together in a place or time.

Fern Plants with large feathery leaves on whose backs reproductive spores are produced. They are the more primitive, dominant group of living plants (Pteropsida).

Ferromagnesian (minerals) Generally dark minerals containing much iron and magnesium as well as silicon and oxygen.

Filamentous Thread-like.

Finite (dating) Measured in years.

Fiord A narrow, steep-walled, glacial trough flooded by the sea.

Fissure A long narrow fracture, or crack in rocks.

Flocculation The process of aggregating, coming together, in fine clots. Applies to the settling of clay particles in water.

Flora A group of plants that lived together in a place or time.

Fluid A liquid or gas. Something that readily changes shape and flows.

Focus (Plural: Foci) The true center of an earthquake. The place of maximum intensity at depth.

Foliation A tendency of metamorphic rocks to part along parallel planes or contorted surfaces.

Foraminifera One-celled animals living mainly in salt water that secrete calcite or cement foreign grains together to form a protective cover.

Formation Rock masses forming a unit convenient for description and mapping.

Fossil Any evidence of ancient life preserved in rock by natural causes.

Fungi A group of non-vascular plants lacking roots, stems, or leaves. They lack chlorophyl and feed on organic matter.

Fusion Melting things together.

Gametophyte A plant which bears male and female elements which produce a non-sexual spore-producing plant.

Gastropod A snail.

Geanticline A complex mountainous belt of folded and faulted rocks from which sediments for a geosyncline are derived.

Genealogy A history of the descent of a person or family from their various ancestors.

Genetic Relating to origin.

Genus (Plural: Genera) A group of related animals. A group of species.

Geochemistry The science dealing with the abundances and distribution of chemical elements in the earth's crust, hydrosphere (water), and atmosphere.

Geochronology The study of time in relation to the history of the earth.

Geology The science which deals largely with the

composition, structure and topography of the solid earth; the internal and external forces acting on it; its history of physical change and past life.

Geometric Having to do with space relations.

Geophysics The science which applies the theory, methods, and techniques of experimental physics to the study of the earth including the hydrosphere (waters) and atmosphere.

Geosyncline A large, generally linear downwarp filled with sedimentary and, in some cases, extrusive igneous rocks.

Geyser A hot spring that periodically erupts water and steam into the air.

Glacier A large natural mass of ice, derived from snow, that originates on land and shows evidence of flowage.

Graben A structural valley representing a down-dropped block between normal faults.

Graphite A very soft, black to grey mineral composed of pure carbon.

Graptolite An extinct group of marine invertebrates whose relation to other major groups is not surely known. Usually preserved in dark shales as small branches having many small cups.

Gravity The force of attraction between masses in the Universe. (Most commonly related to the mass of the earth).

Graywacke A sandstone containing angular quartz and feldspar fragments and some rock fragments with clay-sized filling in between the sand-sized grains. A generally tough dark-colored rock.

Ground water Water underground in the zone where rocks are saturated.

Guyot A submarine mountain having a conical, volcanic shape but with a flat, truncated top.

Gymnosperm Plants reproducing by seeds which are usually exposed and held in cones. Pine and fir trees are examples.

Halite The mineral composed of sodium chloride. Rock salt.

Half-life The time required for half the atoms of a radioactive element to break down into different products.

Headland Generally, a bold projection of land into an ocean, sea, or lake.

Hematite A common iron oxide mineral.

Heterogeneous Containing a mixture of different things.

Hiatus A "gap" in the rock record resulting from erosion or non-deposition.

Hierarchy People or things arranged in a graded system of higher to lower ranks.

Hornfels A tough, unfoliated, metamorphic rock resulting from contact metamorphism of fine-grained rocks.

Horst A mountain uplifted between normal faults.

Hybrid The offspring of two different types of plants or animals.

Hydration The chemical combination of water with a compound to form a new compound.

Hydrosphere All the water on the earth's rock crust including the oceans, lakes, swamps, streams, glaciers and similar features.

Hypothesis A tentative explanation that needs more testing for certain observations or facts. A possible theory.

Igneous (rock) Rocks formed by solidification of once melted material, or magma.

Incisor A front or nipping tooth.

Induction Reasoning from particular facts or observations to a general conclusion.

Infiltration In relation to ground water, refers to the movement of water from the surface into the ground.

Insectivore A mammal that lives on insects and worms.

Intensity (of earthquake) The strength of an earthquake measured by readily observable features such as the effects on manmade structures. It differs from magnitude, which is earthquake strength measured by instruments.

Intrusive (igneous) Penetrating into older rocks as a molten mass and later solidified at depth without reaching the earth's surface.

Invertebrate An animal without a backbone.

Isostasy The concept that large lighter masses of the earth's crust are floating on denser material beneath.

Joint A fracture which has not offset rock on either side. (If slippage has occurred, a fracture is called a fault.)

°K (Kelvin) A temperature scale like the Centigrade except that zero is −273°C.

Karst Regions in limestone, or similar rocks, that have a topography marked by sink holes, disappearing streams, and other features resulting from extensive solution of the rock.

Kettle A depression in glacial drift left where a block of ice has melted.

Kinetic Resulting from motion.

Labyrinthodont An extinct amphibian with an infolded pattern of tooth enamel like that of a lobe-finned fish.

Laccolith A lens shaped, igneous intrusion that bows up surrounding sediments.

Lagoon A protected body of water between reefs, barrier beaches, or islands and the shore.

Larva The early form of an animal when it does not resemble the parent.

Laterite A red soil in humid tropical regions. It contains much oxidized iron and aluminum and is leached of silica.

Lava The molten rock material flowing onto the earth's surface from volcanic action. Also, the same material after it becomes rock.

Leach To remove a soluble substance by downward filtering water.

Lignite A brown to brownish black coal that still retains texture of the original wood.

Limb (of fold) One side, or flank, of a fold.

Limestone A sedimentary rock composed mainly of calcium carbonate, the mineral calcite.

Lithification The conversion of loose sediments into consolidated rock.

Lithologic Relating to the overall physical characteristics of a rock unit or specimens. Usually refers to features that can be directly observed or at the most by using a magnifying glass.

Lithosphere The outer solid or rock part of the earth. Essentially the earth's crust and uppermost solid mantle.

Load (of streams) The sediment and other materials carried along by a stream.

Loess Deposits of wind-blown dust which are largely silt size and generally tan to buff in color. (Sometimes reworked by streams.)

Luster The appearance of a material in reflected light.

L-wave The slowest moving earthquake waves that follow the earth's surface.

Lycopsida Spore-bearing plants with solid stem. d minute spirally arranged leaves.

Maar A volcanic explosion crater not associated with lava.

Magma Molten parent material of igneous rocks.

Mammoth A large, extinct, hairy elephant that lived in northerly climatic zones.

Manganese A metallic element used in steel making.

Mantle (of earth) A major zone of the earth between the crust and core. Thought to consist of dense rocks containing mostly iron-rich silicate minerals.

Maria Darker areas on the moon's surface originally thought to be seas.

Marine Related to the sea.

Marsupial A mammal whose young are born in a very immature stage and cared for in the mother's pouch.

Mastodon An extinct relative of the elephant.

Meander A bend or large arc in a river.

Metabolism The chemical and physical processes in a living organism involving the making and breakdown of protoplasm.

Metamorphic (rock) Rocks so changed by heat and pressure that their original characteristics are lost.

Meteorite A particle or mass from outer space forming an incandescent streak as it is burned by friction on entering the earth's atmosphere.

Meteoroid A solid particle from outer space ranging from sand-size to great blocks.

Microseisms Almost continuous weak tremors in the earth from winds, storms, and other causes not related to earthquakes.

Mineral A naturally occurring solid having a definite repeated internal structure and a characteristic chemical composition. It is crystalline.

Miscegenation Interbreeding between different races.

Mohole A project to drill through the earth's crust into the mantle. Temporarily, at least, it's cancelled.

Molar A cheek tooth for grinding or shearing.

Mollusc A numerous and varied group (Phylum) of invertebrate animals having well developed circulatory, digestive, and sensory systems. Clams, snails, and squids are examples.

Monadnock An isolated hill or low mountain standing above a much eroded, low rolling plain (or peneplain).

Monocline A flexure causing a local steepening in strata between generally horizontal rocks at its top and bottom.

Monotreme An egg-laying mammal.

Moraine Refers to certain landforms composed of glacial till.

Mountains Generally, any high rugged topography. Geologically, rugged regions of volcanic or markedly deformed rocks.

Nappe Large rock mass that has moved some distance either by low-angle faulting, recumbent folding, or both.

Nautiloid A shelled cephalopod having simple saucer-shaped cross-partitions in its shell.

Nitrate A compound containing nitrogen and oxygen (NO_3).

Nebula A large luminous cloud of gas and dust in space.

Névé Granular ice derived from snow (also called firn).

Noble gas Gases such as neon and argon whose atoms do not tend to combine into compounds.

Nova A star which suddenly increases greatly in brightness, then fades. A bursting star.

Nucleus A central unit around which other matter is gathered. The central part of an atom. Or a directive body found in some cells.

Orbit The path of a body moving around another body.

Ore An accumulation of minerals or rock from which a metal can be extracted at an economic profit.

Organic Related to life. Or, compound of carbon.

Ornithiscian Refers to a dinosaur group whose pelvic or hip structure was like that of birds.

Orogeny Mountain building associated with folding and faulting.

Ostracoderm A primitive jawless fish with a head armored by bone.

Outcrop An exposure of bedrock at the ground surface.

Oxidation The combination of a substance with oxygen. Also, the loss of electrons from an atom, or ion.

Paleogeography The physical geographic features of a region at some given time in the geologic past.

Paleontology The science that deals with past life based on the study of fossils.

Pediment A generally gravel-covered surface sloping away from the base of a mountain front. It is cut fairly evenly across rocks, although some rocks may be hard and others poorly consolidated.

Pelecypod A clam.

Peneplain A low rolling surface of broad extent near sea level which results from prolonged erosion of formerly elevated land.

Peridotite A coarse-grained igneous rock containing olivine and sometimes other ferromagnesian minerals. It has no quartz and little, if any, feldspar.

Period (geologic) A fundamental unit of geological time which has worldwide application.

Perissodactyl A hoofed mammal having an odd number of useful toes. The horse and rhinoceros are examples.

Permeability In relation to ground water, permeability refers to the ability of rocks or rock material to transmit water or other fluids.

Phosphate A compound containing phosphorous and oxygen (PO_4^{-3}).

Photosynthesis The making of carbohydrates from water and carbon dioxide using the energy of sunlight.

Phylum A major division of the plant or animal kingdoms.

Pisces The fish.

Placental Refers to mammals whose young are born in a relatively mature state.

Placoderm A primitive fish with jaws. Some had bone armor.

Planet A large non-luminous body moving in orbit around a star.

Plankton Floating or drifting life in the sea.

Plant A form of life having no central nervous system, no means of locomotion, that can make use of simple food materials from soil, water, air, or other organisms.

Plastic Having some characteristics of solids and some of liquids.

Plateau Generally, any extensive flat-topped highland. Geologically, a highland underlain by near horizontal rock layers which may be flat-topped or highly dissected.

Pleistocene See the geologic time scale. A time division corresponding to the latest major glaciation of the earth. The term also refers to deposits of that time.

Plunge (of a fold) The dip of a fold axis.

Plutonic (rocks) Refers to rocks formed at considerable depths beneath the earth's surface. Includes some igneous and some metamorphic rocks.

Pollen Minute grains carrying the male elements for fertilization in seed plants.

Polymorphic change A change of one mineral to another without leaving the solid state.

Porphyritic (texture) Refers to igneous rocks in which larger crystals are surrounded by finer grained or glassy material.

Porifera A group (Phylum) of multi-celled, simple animals having no separate organs or special tissues. The sponges.

Porosity Refers to the total void, or pore, space in a rock or rock material.

Precipitation Chemically, the separation of substances from solution. Also, the falling of rain or snow from the atmosphere.

Predator One who preys on others.

Preempt To be established beforehand.

Primate A mammal with five digits bearing flat nails on feet, or hands adapted for grasping. Man and monkeys are primates.

Primordial First, or original.

Proboscidian A mammal whose nose and upper lip form a trunk, i.e. the elephant.

Progenitor An ancestor or parent.

Protoplasm The semi-liquid, somewhat granular, material of an animal or plant cell.

Prototype A primitive form.

Protozoa The single-celled animals.

Psilopsida Extinct group of the most primitive vascular plants.

Pteropsida The most numerous group of living vascular plants. Includes ferns, gymnosperms and angiosperms.

Pumice A very light weight and light colored volcanic rock resulting from solidification of a very frothy lava. Being non-crystalline it is structurally a glass.

Pyroclastic (rocks) Rocks composed of volcanic particles and fragments.

Quadruped A four-footed animal.

Quantitative Relating to amounts which can be stated in numbers.

Radiation (of plants or animals) The spreading of organisms into new environments.

Radioactive Refers to elements that break down into other elements by giving off particles from their nuclei.

Radiolaria A group of marine, one-celled animals having complicated siliceous skeletons.

Radiometric Related to the measurement of the breakdown of radioactive elements.

Radium A radioactive element obtained mainly from uranium ores.

Radula A rasp-like tongue, characteristic of certain invertebrates (molluscs).

Redbed A general name for red sedimentary rocks which are most commonly sandstones or shales.

Regolith The same as waste-mantle.

Rejuvenation (of stream) When a stream comes to have increased energy so that it starts deepening its valley. Climatic change or uplift of a region might cause this.

Reptile A cold-blooded, air breathing vertebrate with a scaley or platy skin. Most lay eggs with shells although in a few the young are born alive.

Reverse fault A fault whose hanging wall has moved up relative to the footwall.

Rift (valley) A valley formed by sinking of a strip between two faults. Usually a graben.

Rill The smallest type of distinct stream. A small trickle of water or its dry channel.

Rills (on the moon) Trench-like features of uncertain depth, but up to a mile wide and 150 miles long.

Ripple marks Small ridges and troughs in unconsolidated materials, such as sand, caused by moving water or air.

Rock Natural aggregate or mass of mineral matter forming an appreciable part of the earth's crust.

Rodent A mammal whose teeth continue to grow through life and are designed for gnawing. Rats and squirrels are examples.

Ruminant A hoofed animal that stores food in a complex stomach, then returns the food to the mouth for more chewing before final swallowing and digestion.

Saltation A hopping or skipping motion of particles carried along by wind or streams. The particles periodically drop to the ground or channel bottom, bounce, and become suspended until they again drop.

Sarcodina A group of one-celled animals that extrude movable parts for locomotion.

Saurischian Refers to a dinosaur group whose pelvic or hip structure was like most other reptiles.

Savanna A grass-land with sparse clumps of trees and having marked wet and dry seasons.

Scarp A steep slope, or cliff-like form.

Schist A medium- to coarse-grained metamorphic rock that is mainly composed of flat tabular minerals.

Scoria Dark-colored volcanic lava having basaltic composition and glassy texture.

Scorpion A small land-dwelling arthropod, looking somewhat like a miniature lobster and having a jointed tail with poisonous stinger.

Sedentary Not given to much movement. Fixed in place.

Seed A plants' many-celled reproductive structure having an embryo plant with a food supply and protective cover.

Sedimentary (rock) Rocks formed from materials once carried in water or air that have since settled, been precipitated, or even secreted by plants and animals to form layers on the earth's crust. Or, rock formed by deposition at the earth's surface of material derived from older rocks.

Seismic Related to earthquakes or other earth vibrations.

Seismograph An instrument for recording earthquake waves and other vibrations in the earth.

Seismology The science dealing with earthquakes and earth vibrations.

Septum An internal partition.

Series A time-rock unit corresponding to an epoch.

Shark A fish with a cartilaginous skeleton.

Shelf The zone of shallow sea marginal to a continent.

Shield Broad rolling lowlands eroded on largely crystalline rocks forming the core of a continent.

Shrew A small, active, mouse-like, insectivore.

Sial The granitic zone of the earth's crust. The term is derived from silicon and aluminum which are abundant in its rocks.

Silica The compound silicon dioxide (SiO_2).

Silicate Compounds containing silicon and oxygen in a crystalline structure based on the silicon tetrahedron.

Siltstone A consolidated sedimentary rock consisting of fragments between sand and clay in size.

Sill A flat tabular igneous intrusion that parallels older structures.

Sima The basaltic lower part of the earth's crust whose rocks contain silicate minerals rich in iron and magnesium.

Sink A closed depression in the ground resulting from solution or collapse in limestone areas.

Siphuncle An internal calcareous tube in a shelled cephalopod.

Slate A very fine-grained metamorphic rock which tends to split into smooth flat chips and slabs.

Slump A type of mass movement in which a block of material moves as a unit down and out on a curved plane of slippage.

Soil Unconsolidated earth material characterized by horizons roughly parallel to the ground which are produced by organic and inorganic processes. In civil engineering, any unconsolidated earth material is termed soil.

Sounding (nautical) To determine the depth of a water body.

Species A group of plants or animals of very similar structure and relationship. Living species interbreed and produce fertile offspring.

Spectroscope An optical instrument for separating light into different wave lengths for study.

Speculative Related to theorizing from very little evidence.

Sphenopsida Plants with spore-bearing cones, hollow-jointed stems, and small leaves at the joints.

Spit (coastal) A small land projection into the sea. Many are sandy extensions of a beach into open water.

Spore An asexual, usually single-celled, reproductive structure of plants.

Sporophyte A non-sexual plant which produces spores that develop into sexual plants.

Spring A natural place where water seeps out of the ground for extended periods.

Stack A steep-sided pinnacle isolated by wave attack from a cliff of which it was once a part.

Stalactite An icicle-like projection of limestone projecting down from the ceiling in a cave.

Stalagmite A mound or projection of limestone projecting up from the floor of a cave.

Starch A carbohydrate food substance.

Stratification A layered or bedded structure formed during the deposition of sedimentary rocks.

Stream A mixture of water and rock waste flowing in a definite linear channel.

Striation A fine linear groove or ridge.

Strike The compass direction of an imaginary horizontal line on a sloping surface or rock layer.

Subaerial On land (as opposed to being under water).

Subsidence A mass movement, a dominantly vertical settling of material resulting from loss of mass at depth.

Subterranean Underground.

Superposition (of rocks) The laying down of rock layers in order, one on top of the other. It implies that the older layers are beneath younger layers.

S-wave The secondary seismic wave. It passes through the body of the earth and gives a shaking or up-and-down motion to particles in its path.

Syncline A fold in which the center moved down relative to the sides when it formed. It is, or was, concave downward.

System A time-rock unit corresponding to a geologic period.

Talc A very soft mineral with a greasy "feel." A magnesian silicate found in metamorphic rocks.

Taxonomic Pertaining to the systematic classification of plants and animals.

Taxonomist A scientist who specializes in the classification of plants or animals.

Technology The application of science to practical or economic uses.

Tectogene A large, deeply downbuckled pod of sediments and volcanic rocks.

Tectonic Related to structures in the earth's crust caused by deformation (not of volcanic origin).

Tentacle A fleshy arm-like projection from an invertebrate animal.

Terrace A step-like landform having a flat or gently sloping surface that is bounded on one side by a more steeply rising surface and on the other by a descending one.

Test (of animal) A hard cover or supporting structure of invertebrate animals.

Tetrapod A vertebrate animal with four limbs. Amphibians, reptiles, birds, and mammals are tetrapods.

Thallophyta A group of non-vascular plants lacking roots, stems, or leaves.

Thallus A plant body consisting of a mass of tissue with little differentiation into organs typical of higher plants.

Thecodont An extinct reptile that was ancestral to crocodiles, birds, and the extinct flying reptiles.

Theory An explanation of relationships between certain observed phenomena that has withstood considerable testing.

Therapsid An extinct reptile group with some mammal-like structures.

Till Deposits laid down by the direct action of glacial ice. Usually a poorly sorted mixture of particles from clay to boulders in size.

Trace (of fault) The line made by the intersection of a fault plane with the ground surface.

Traction Refers to a method of stream transport where the load carried is in constant contact with the channel bottom. Movement is by rolling, skidding, etc.

Transmutation The change of one chemical element into another.

Trellis Referring to a stream pattern, it describes one with several long parallel trunk streams that are joined at right angles by short tributary streams.

Trilobite An extinct arthropod whose shell was divided into three longitudinal regions.

Tuff Volcanic ash consolidated into rock.

Tundra Tree-less arctic areas.

Turbid Cloudy, filled with stirred-up fine sediments.

Ultra-violet (light) Extremely short wave lengths of light.

Unconformity A buried erosion surface with older rocks beneath and markedly younger rocks above.

Uniformitarianism The general geologic rule that "the present is the key to the past," or that the processes operating today have acted the same throughout geologic time.

Ungulate A hoofed mammal, such as a horse.

Unloading (in weathering) A weathering process in which rock breaks into slabs roughly parallel to the ground because of a slight expansion in rock after a thick mass of overlying material is eroded away.

Uranium A heavy radioactive metallic element found only in compounds.

Urea A very soluble crystalline solid found in the urine of mammals. Also produced synthetically for use in making plastics and other products.

Varve A thin sedimentary layer that represents one year of deposition. It may consist of a summer and a winter lamination.

Vascular Plants or animals having a system of vessels and ducts for distributing dissolved foods and nutrients.

Ventifacts Pebbles or cobbles with flat faces often intersecting as sharp ridges that have been modified by wind-blown sand.

Vertebrate Animal with an internal, jointed spinal

column of cartilage or bone, a skull, and paired appendages.

Vesicles Small cavities as found in some volcanic rocks.

Vestigial A small or useless organ or limb that was functional in ancestral animals.

Virus A substance that contains the chemical elements of protoplasm and acts as a living disease-producing organism in plants or animals but when isolated forms a crystalline structure like a mineral. It seems to link the mineral and life kingdoms.

Viscous Fluid but resisting flow. Does not change form quickly as more perfect fluids do.

Volatile Easily vaporized.

Volcanism (vulcanism) The processes creating volcanic rocks, volcanos, and related eruptive features.

Volcano A mountain resulting from the ejection, or eruption, of molten rock material and fragments from a vent extending into the earth.

Water table The top of the zone in which rocks are saturated with ground water.

Water witch A person who claims to locate water underground using forked sticks, rings suspended from threads, and other divining instruments.

Waste-mantle The unconsolidated rock materials that may cover solid bedrock (regolith).

Weathering The physical and mechanical breakdown of rock in place at or near the earth's surface because of exposure to the atmosphere.

Well A man-made excavation to obtain underground water.

Wind gap A notch through a ridge that is no longer occupied by the steam that caused it.

Yardangs Sharp crested ridges separated by troughs resulting from wind erosion in soft rocks.

Index

Photograph acknowledgments

Chapter opening

1   Apollo 8 earth view. Courtesy of NASA.

2   Gypsum crystal with sand grains from Oklahoma. Courtesy Southwest Scientific Supply House, Scottsdale, Arizona.

3   Microphotograph of a tuff. Courtesy of Robert S. Houston, University of Wyoming.

4   The Bridge on Bridge Mountain, Zion National Park, Utah. National Park Service photo by E. T. Scoyen.

5   Crescent-shaped sand dunes in Saudi Arabia. Courtesy of Arabian American Oil Company.

6   Drumlins in barrens of the Canadian Shield. R.C.A.F. photo courtesy of Canadian Department of Mines and Technical Surveys.

7   California earthquake. U.S. Information Agency photo, National Archives.

8   Church tower of San Juan village, standing in 20 feet of lava. Photo by Tad Nichols.

9   Syncline and West Henrietta fault, SW Tyrone Quadrangle, Pennsylvania. Courtesy of John S. Shelton.

10   Cross-bedding in Sand Creek, Wyoming. Courtesy of the author.

11   Hand specimen of fossiliferous limestone. Photo by Tad Nichols.

12   Cretaceous stemless Crinoids (Uintacrinus). Photo courtesy of Chicago Natural History Museum.

13   Canadian Shield, R.C.A.F. photo courtesy of Canadian Department of Mines and Technical Surveys

14   Red Rocks Amphitheatre, Denver, Colorado. Courtesy of U.S. Forest Service.

15   Mammoth Glacier. Courtesy of the University of Washington.

16   Astronaut Edwin E. Aldrin, Jr., walking on moon during Apollo 11 flight. Courtesy of NASA.